Ian Rutledge is an economist and histo
of Cambridge where he received his Ph
is Research Director and co-founder
Information Services. He has taught a
Sheffield and for the Workers' Educational .... His other publications
include *Addicted to Oil: America's Relentless Drive for Energy Security*. He lives
in Chesterfield, Derbyshire.

'A well-crafted and lively account ... While offering abundant detail on
military operations, lines of communications and warfare tactics, *Enemy on
the Euphrates* also makes for a very lively and human-centred read of imperial
history. Populated by a remarkable crowd of spies, diplomats, soldiers,
clerics and tribal leaders, Rutledge's account displays a novelist's taste for
intrigue, espionage, gunboat diplomacy, personal hardship and murder.'
BBC History Magazine

'An excellently produced book that admirably succeeds in illuminating an
important episode in British imperial history' *History Today*

'Rutledge does an excellent job of conveying the logistical difficulties
confronting any military leadership, let alone one operating thousands of
miles from home and in physically challenging and hostile enemy territory ...
deserving of a wide readership' *Middle East Journal*

'As the legions of ISIS set up their proto-Caliphate in Iraq, the word 'prescience'
comes forcibly to mind' *The Oldie*

'*Enemy on the Euphrates* is that rare treasure that combines a fascinating
account of important historical events with penetrating geopolitical analysis.
Anyone seeking an understanding of the role of oil in shaping modern Middle
Eastern history will want to read this book.'
Michael Klare, author of *The Race for What's Left: The Global Scramble for the
World's Last Resources*

'A lively and well-researched account of the events leading up to the Iraqi 'revolution' of 1920, using a number of hitherto unused British and Arabic sources.
The leading Arab and British personalities are well-drawn, and the narrow
moral universe of the British administrators is especially well portrayed.'
Peter Sluglett, author of *Britain in Iraq: Contriving King and Country*

ENEMY
ON THE
EUPHRATES

The Battle for Iraq, 1914–1921

IAN RUTLEDGE

SAQI

First published 2014 by Saqi Books

This paperback edition published 2015

Copyright © Ian Rutledge 2014

ISBN 978 0 86356 170 2
eISBN 978 0 86356 767 4

Cover image: British troops marching through Mesopotamia during
World War I, circa 1916 (Photo by FPG/Hulton Archive/Getty Images)

A full CIP record for this book is available from the British Library.

Printed and bound by CPI Group (UK) Ltd, Croydon, CR0 4YY

SAQI
26 Westbourne Grove
London W2 5RH

www.saqibooks.co.uk

For Diana, as always.

And for my beloved children,
Joanna, Daniel, Zoe and Emilie

What we want is some kind of modicum of Arab institutions which we can safely leave while pulling the strings ourselves, something which won't cost very much ... but in which our influence and political and economic interests will be secure.

Sir Arthur Hirtzel, February 1920

Whereas most westerners have no knowledge of the 1920 uprising, generations of Iraqi schoolchildren have grown up learning how nationalist heroes stood up against foreign armies and imperialism in towns like Falluja, Baquba and Najaf – the Iraqi equivalents of Lexington and Concord.

Eugene Rogan, *The Arabs: A History*

Contents

List of Illustrations

List of Maps

Note on Arabic Transliteration

This has been kept as simple as possible. The symbol ' has been used for the letter 'ayn and ' for the glottal stop hamza. The feminine ending *taa marbuta* has simply been rendered as a final a (not 'ah' or 'at'). No subscript or superscript marks have been used. When an Arabic word or name which has entered the English lexicon appears, its customary English spelling has been retained (e.g. sheikh, not *shaykh*).

Glossary

agha   Turkish title equivalent to Arabic 'sheikh'.

al-'Ahd   The Pledge. Secret organisation of Ottoman army officers opposed to Turkish domination, formed shortly before outbreak of the First World War.

al-'Ahd al-'Iraqi Branch of al-'Ahd formed after the end of the First World War and dedicated to some form of Independence in Iraq; generally more moderate than Haras al-Istiqlal and willing to seek accommodation with British interests.

ayalet   Name for a region of the Ottoman Empire. The system of ayalets was abolished in 1864 and replaced by a greater number of smaller vilayets. The term was resurrected in Mark Sykes's proposals for the De Bunsen Committee in 1915.

bellum   Small, double-bowed, flat-bottomed Iraqi river vessel with a draught of less than eighteen inches, paddled, or powered by punt-pole; similar to but usually larger than the mashuf.

bey   Ottoman (Turkish) honorific title, in its military usage meaning a high-ranking officer, but subordinate to a pasha.

budoo   British Army slang for Bedouin. Generally, a term of abuse for all Iraqi tribal Arabs.

caliph   Successor to the leadership of the Islamic community. (*See also* Shi'i and Sunni.)

Dar al-Hujja	Conference hall of the Grand Mujtahid in Karbela'. Literally, 'House of Religious Debate'.
division (1)	Administrative region in British-occupied Iraq of which there were sixteen in 1920.
division (2)	Unit of the British Army usually comprising three brigades and commanded by a major general.
fatwa	In shari'a law, a decision made by a qualified person e.g. a mujtahid; it may constitute a legal precedent.
faylaq	A corps in the Ottoman army.
Haras al-Istiqlal	The Independence Guards – a nationalist organisation based in Baghdad.
havildar	Rank assigned to Indian soldiers in the British Imperial Indian Army, equivalent to sergeant.
Hejaz	The western part of the present-day state of Saudi Arabia, bordering the Red Sea.
heliograph	A means of military communication using a wireless solar telegraph that signals by flashes of sunlight (generally using Morse code) reflected by a mirror.
Istanbul	Capital of the Ottoman Empire on the European side of the Bosphorus. In 1920 the British still referred to it by its Christian name – Constantinople.
Jam'iyyat 'Arabiyya al-Fatat	The Young Arab Society – a secret organisation for the promotion of Arab interests within the Ottoman Empire, established before the First World War. Some of its members desired an independent Arab state.
Jam'iyyat 'Iraqiyya al-'Arabiyya	A nationalist organisation based in the mid-Euphrates region which favoured an alliance with Mustafa Kemal and the Bolsheviks.
Jam'iyyat Nahda al-Islamiyya	The Islamic Renaissance Movement – a small, secret organisation formed in Najaf in 1918, dedicated to the expulsion of the British from Iraq.

Jam'iyyat Takhlis al-Sharq al-Islami	Organisation for the Liberation of the Muslim East. Bolshevik Organisation set up under the aegis of the Eastern Department of Narkomindel (People's Commissariat for Foreign Affairs) whose function was to encourage the resistance of the Muslim peoples against European domination.
jemadar	Rank assigned to Indian soldiers in the British Imperial Indian Army, equivalent to second lieutenant.
jihad	A war or campaign in defence of Islam.
khan	Guest house for Muslim pilgrims or other travellers.
Khedivate	An autonomous tributary state of the Ottoman Empire. The British retained the name after they had effectively taken control of Egypt in 1882.
kufiyya	Typical headdress of tribal Arabs.
levies	British-officered Arab or Kurdish auxiliary troops.
madhbata	In this context, a set of demands or petition.
madrasa	An Islamic school, either religious or secular.
mahalla	A city quarter or district. Each of Najaf's mahallas had its own headman and legal code.
mahayla	Iraqi river boat with lateen sail, between fifty and eighty feet in length and with a draught of between three and four feet; also known as a safina.
mandate	The right of control over a defeated enemy territory but with the assumption that the mandatory power will prepare it for eventual independence. In practice, a mandated territory was little more than a protectorate.
mashuf	Very small canoe-like Iraqi river vessel typical of the marsh lands, similar to but usually smaller than the bellum.
maulud	Celebration of the birth of the Prophet Muhammad.
memsahib	'Respectable lady'; term used by Indians to denote European wives.
mirza	Honorific title of Persian origin, literally 'prince' but, more generally, 'sir'.

monitor	A shallow-draught warship with heavy guns for coastal bombardment.
mujahid(in)	Person(s) fighting on behalf of Islam.
mujtahid(in)	Senior Shi'i cleric(s), qualified to make independent decisions based on Islamic jurisprudence and theology.
mukarrama	Meaning 'venerated', 'revered', an epithet customarily used for the holy city of Mecca.
mulazim	Second lieutenant in the Ottoman army.
mulazim awwal	First lieutenant in the Ottoman army.
mutasarrif	Senior Ottoman official, usually translated as 'governor'.
mutasarriflik	Administrative region of Ottoman Empire which (unlike the vilayet) was directly under control of Ottoman Ministry of the Interior. (Also known as a sanjak.)
Noperforce	North Persia Force – the contingent of British troops stationed in North Persia to defend the Persian Government against Bolshevik and nationalist forces.
pasha	Ottoman (Turkish) honorific military title meaning 'general'.
qadi	Muslim judge administering shari'a law.
qahwaji	A tribal sheikh's coffee maker, but also, often, his advisor and assistant
qishla	Turkish word for fort.
Qur'an	Islam's holy book.
risaldar	Indian cavalry officer in British Imperial Indian Army equivalent to captain
safina	*See* mahayla.
sanjak	*See* mutasarriflik.
sayyid (pl. sada)	Lineal descendant of the Prophet Muhammad through his grandson Husayn ibn 'Ali (Shi'i usage). The authenticity of such claims may be questionable. *See also* sharif.

Sayyid al-Shuhada' 'The Prince of Martyrs', one of the Shi'i titles for the Imam Husayn (*see* sayyid).

Senussi   A Muslim political and religious order in Libya and the Sudan. Fought against the Italian occupation in 1911 and against the British between 1915 and 1917.

sepoy   Indian infantryman in British Imperial Indian Army.

serai   Turkish word for palace. In this context meaning local administrative headquarters of the government.

shabana   Arab police in British service.

shamal   The prevalent north wind in Iraq which brings hot dry air in the summer and cool moist air during the winter.

shari'a (law)   Islamic jurisprudence, of which there are four Sunni schools and three Shi'i schools.

Sharif (of Mecca)   Senior Ottoman official responsible for the holy cities of Mecca and Medina; appointed directly by the Ottoman sultan from among high noble (sharif) families.

sharif (pl. ashraf)   Lineal descendant of the Prophet Muhammad through his grandson Hasan ibn 'Ali (Sunni usage). The authenticity of such claims may be questionable. *See also* sayyid.

Shi'i   The minority and second largest sect of Islam. Also the name for an adherent of the Shi'i sect of Islam. Shi'i Muslims believe that God (through his Prophet Muhammad) chose Muhammad's closest living male relative, his cousin and son-in-law, 'Ali ibn 'Abu Talib, to be his rightful successor and subsequently through the family line of 'Ali's son, Husayn.

sirdab   An undergound living room whose cooler atmosphere provides relief from excessive summer heat.

sowar   Indian cavalryman in the British Imperial Indian Army.

Sunni	The majority and largest sect of Islam. Also the name for an adherent of the Sunni sect of Islam. Sunni Muslims believe that Muhammad decreed that his rightful successor was to be chosen from among the Prophet's companions (regardless of family relationship). Although Sunnis recognise 'Ali as one of the four 'rightfully guided' caliphs, he is the fourth one, rather than the first (as in Shi'i Islam).
'ulema'	Generic term for Islamic clergy whether Sunni or Shi'i.
vali	Ottoman governor of a vilayet.
vilayet	Administrative region of Ottoman Empire, ruled by a vali; originally derived from Arabic *wilaya*. In the case of Iraq, there were three vilayets: Basra, Baghdad and Mosul.
Wahhabi	Puritanical sect of Sunni Islam founded by Muhammad ibn 'Abd al-Wahhab in the eighteenth century and revived under the aegis of the Emir 'Abd al-'Aziz ibn Sa'ud in the early twentieth century; fiercely anti-Shi'i.

Abbreviations

ADC
: Aide-de-camp; military officer acting as personal assistant to one of higher rank.

APO
: Assistant political officer: junior administrative official of the British Empire, usually a military officer with the rank of lieutenant or captain.

AT (wagons)
: Animal transport wagons pulled by mules, used extensively in the Indian Army.

AT (Wilson)
: Affectionate nickname for Arnold Talbot Wilson used by his staff.

CIE
: Commander of the Most Eminent Order of the Indian Empire: military decoration of the Imperial Indian Empire.

CMG
: Commander of the Order of St Michael and St George: an order of chivalry awarded by the monarch for some distinguished service (military or civilian) to Britain or the British Empire.

CUP
: Committee of Union and Progress. Political organisation which overthrew the despotic Ottoman government of Sultan Abdul Hamid in 1908. Initially democratic in orientation, by 1913 the CUP had become a virtual dictatorship of its three leading members: Enver Pasha, Djemal Pasha and Talat Pasha.

DSO
: Distinguished Service Order: military decoration in the British Army.

GHQ
: General headquarters (of the British Army on campaign).

GOC(-in-chief)	General officer commanding (of a particular city, region, etc.). The GOC-in-chief, typically a general or lieutenant general, is the highest ranking British officer in a particular theatre of war.
LAMB	Light armoured motor battery: a squadron of four armoured cars.
MC	Military Cross: military decoration in the British Army.
NCO	Non-commissioned officer, e.g. sergeant or corporal.
PIPCO	Petroleum Imperial Policy Committee.
PO	Political officer: administrative official of the British Empire, usually a military officer with the rank of major or lieutenant colonel.
Rs	Rupees: Indian currency.
RUMCOL	Rumaytha relief column.
SAMCOL	Samawa relief column.
TPC	Turkish Petroleum Company.

Preface

Between July 1920 and February 1921, in the territory then known to the British as Mesopotamia – the modern state of Iraq – an Arab uprising occurred which came perilously close to inflicting a shattering defeat upon the British Empire. The story of this uprising is one which once engaged the closest of attention among the British public but over many decades slipped back into the mists of exclusively academic history, almost completely erased from the collective memory.[1] And so it would have remained had it not been for the ill-fated US invasion of Iraq in 2003. Once the 'insurgency' against the subsequent occupation had begun, it wasn't long before a much older, forgotten insurgency in Iraq came to light with journalists, historians and even functionaries of the US occupation drawing lessons and making comparisons – some appropriate, some less so – with that much earlier event.[2] At the same time some of those fighting the Americans and their allies in Iraq began to portray their own violent resistance to foreign intervention by referencing that armed struggle in which some of their grandparents might have participated.[3]

To the vast majority of European and American historians of the twentieth-century Middle East, the 'Arab Revolt' has usually meant 'Lawrence of Arabia' and the pro-British rebellion of the Sharif of Mecca and his sons against the Turks during the First World War. However, in reality, this pro-British 'Arab Revolt' was a fairly puny affair involving only a fraction of the Arab combatants taking part in the *anti*-British revolt which took place in Iraq a mere eighteen months after the end of the war.

Indeed, measured in enemy combatant numbers, the 1920 insurrection in Iraq was the most serious armed uprising against British rule in the twentieth century. At the height of the rebellion the British estimated that around 131,000 Arabs were in arms against them. Estimates by Iraqi historians are considerably greater – in one account around 567,000.[4] By way of comparison, the British faced perhaps a maximum of 120,000 rebel fighters in the Kenyan 'Mau Mau' rebellion of 1952–6,[5] 15,000 rebel combatants during the Irish war of independence 1919–21, around 10,000 'regular' Arab fighters during the Palestine insurrection of 1936–9, a similar number of jihadis in the second 'Mad Mullah' rebellion in Somalia in 1907–20, 8,000 guerrillas of the Communist Malayan Races Liberation Army supported by around 30–40,000 civilian support and supply forces during the Malayan 'Emergency' of 1948–60, and a mere 300–500 Greek EOKA fighters during the Cyprus emergency of the 1950s. As for Lawrence's pro-British Arab Revolt in 1916–18, the maximum number of Bedouin mobilised never exceeded 27,000, supported by around 12,000 deserters from the Ottoman army; and of the Bedouin, only a small minority actually took part in combat operations.[6]

Moreover, unlike Lawrence's 'Arab Revolt', the insurrection of 1920 was no affair of sporadic guerrilla fighting. It was a war: one in which a huge peasant army led by Shi'i clerics, Baghdad notables, disaffected sheikhs and former Ottoman army officers and NCOs surrounded and besieged British garrisons with sandbagged entrenchments and bombarded them with captured artillery; where British columns and armoured trains were ambushed and destroyed; where well-armed British gunboats were burned or captured; a war in which the insurgents established their own system of government and administration in the 'liberated zones' centred on the two 'holy' cities of Najaf and Karbela': a war which, at one stage, Britain came very close to losing and which was won only with the help of a massive infusion of Indian troops and, especially towards the end of the campaign, the widespread use of aircraft.

In addition to tracing the course of this great anti-colonial revolt, we also consider why it occurred and, in particular, why the epicentre of the uprising against the British was on the second of the two great Mesopotamian rivers – the Euphrates. Political events in Baghdad also made an important contribution to the revolt and, at its height, some of the tribes to the west and north-east of the capital also joined the uprising; nevertheless, it was on the middle reaches of the Euphrates and in the two 'holy' cities of Najaf and Karbala' that the British faced the most violent and sustained opposition. Conversely, large areas bordering the River Tigris remained largely unaffected by the events of 1920–21.

What was it, therefore, about the mid-Euphrates region which made its more than half a million inhabitants so bitterly opposed to the continuing British occupation of Iraq after the Great War had ended? To answer this question we need to explore the region's social, religious and political characteristics and the specific experiences of its sheikhs, tribesmen and Muslim clergy during both the war and its immediate aftermath.[7]

During the early stages of the First World War in the Middle East, this densely populated and predominantly Shi'i part of Iraq became the major recruiting ground for the Ottoman jihad against the British invasion, a campaign in which – for a time – the Arab tribes threw their considerable weight behind the military operations of their Turkish overlords. However, after the defeat of the jihad in April 1915, the mid-Euphrates region enjoyed a two-year respite of almost complete freedom from both British and Turkish control and its inhabitants experienced an unprecedented period of anarchic independence. As a consequence, the imposition of British rule at the end of the Great War – in spite of wartime promises of 'complete liberation' – was felt to be particularly onerous among the region's landlords and peasants alike. The manner in which this resentment grew and gradually came to express itself in armed resistance therefore forms a central part of our story. And, perhaps not surprisingly, it was from the ranks of the 1914–15 mujahidin that some of the foremost tribal leaders of the 1920 uprising emerged.

Finally, in discussing the causes of the 1920 uprising, some serious consideration must also be given to the reasons why – two years after the defeat of the Ottoman armies – Britain was still occupying Iraq and appeared to have every intention of remaining in de facto control for many years to come. This was in spite of the fact that in 1920 public opinion in Britain itself was strongly opposed to any continuing involvement in the Middle East generally and in Iraq in particular.

Although the men who ran Britain's great empire quarrelled bitterly about exactly *how* Iraq should be held in the imperial grasp, they were generally agreed about *why*. When Britain, France and Russia went to war with Germany and Austro-Hungary in August 1914, these Great Powers did not have any plans to permanently dismember and retain each other's territory (with the exception of France's desire to recover Alsace-Lorraine – lost to the Germans in the Franco-Prussian War of 1870–71). But when the Ottoman Empire entered the war as an ally of Germany at the end of October 1914, the Allies had no such reservations about carving up that vast and venerable empire. After all, in the conventional European imperialist mindset, the Ottomans – Turks, Arabs, and Kurds – were 'Orientals' with a long history of lassitude, improvidence, corruption and cruelty and could not be allowed to continue to govern themselves in such an irresponsible manner. So, by early 1915, Russia had made it clear that, when the Ottomans were defeated, it expected to receive their capital, Istanbul, along with the Turkish Straits and two islands in the northern Aegean. France and Britain were therefore invited to identify which parts of the Ottoman Empire *they* would like to acquire.

The response of the British government was rather more subtle. It wasn't so much *territory* Britain required (although that might eventually be necessary) but economic opportunities and access to natural resources. Perhaps these could be obtained without the actual partitioning of the Ottoman Empire? – at least that was the initial view of the government committee established to consider the matter in April 1915. And of all those tempting economic prospects which that committee considered, there was one to which its deliberations devoted more attention than any other – oil: specifically, the potentially huge oil resources which were believed to exist in the Ottoman vilayets of Baghdad and Mosul. In short, Britain's presence in Iraq, which was initially prompted by threats to its nascent oil industry at the head of the Arabian Gulf, might need to be perpetuated for a number of years until suitable arrangements had been made for those, as yet unexplored, oil reserves to fall into the hands of British-controlled companies.

For a time – during the middle years of the Great War – this imperial quest for oil slackened somewhat as other, conflicting, objectives came to the fore, in particular the complexities of satisfying the territorial demands not only of Britain's existing ally, France, but also those of a new ally, the Sharif of Mecca. However, by 1917 it had become clear to all that the nature of war had fundamentally changed: henceforth wars would be increasingly mechanised and oil-fuelled. Indeed, as the secretary to the Committee for Imperial Defence put it, 'oil in the next war will occupy the place of coal in the present.' Therefore, obtaining 'possession of all the oil-bearing regions in Mesopotamia and Southern Persia' would be 'a first class British war aim'.

So, by early 1918 the War Office was conducting detailed geological surveys of Iraq's petroleum resources in those parts of Iraq already under British occupation and, as hostilities came to an end in November of that year, the British government ensured that the frontiers of their new 'friendly native state' would encompass all those parts of 'Mesopotamia' which were believed to contain oil.

None of this is to claim that oil was the *only* motivating force behind British military and diplomatic policy towards Iraq as the First World War drew to a close: establishing a secure air route to India, countering the new 'threat' of Bolshevism and simply maintaining imperial prestige were also factors requiring some form of control over Iraq for the foreseeable future. Nevertheless, as our story will demonstrate, the 'imperial quest for oil' runs like a sinuous black thread through this particular piece of historical tapestry during the years 1914 to 1921, and beyond.

The Principal Actors

The British

GERTRUDE LOWTHIAN BELL
Arabist, explorer, travel writer. In 1920, oriental secretary in Baghdad. Originally an ally of Wilson but later turned against him. Friend of Lawrence.

WINSTON CHURCHILL
First Lord of the Admiralty, responsible for the part-nationalisation of the Anglo-Persian Oil Company in 1913. Resigned from the Liberal government after the failure of the Gallipoli campaign in 1915. In 1920, minister of war in the coalition government, where he was responsible for dealing with the revolution in Iraq.

SIR PERCY COX
Chief political officer in Iraq during the Great War. High commissioner for Iraq after his return to Baghdad in October 1920.

LIEUTENANT GENERAL AYLMER HALDANE
Commander-in-chief of British forces in occupied Iraq, 1920–21.

LIEUTENANT COLONEL MAURICE HANKEY
Secretary to successive War Cabinets. Friend and political ally of Sir Mark Sykes. Member of the De Bunsen Committee which established Britain's economic objectives in the war against the Ottoman Empire.

COLONEL T. E. LAWRENCE
Self-aggrandising hero of the Arab Revolt against the Turks in the Hejaz in 1916–18. Between 1918 and July 1920 close confidant of Emir Faysal,

ruling a semi-independent Arab government in Syria. By 1920 a fierce critic of Arnold Wilson's administration in Iraq.

LIEUTENANT COLONEL GERARD LEACHMAN
Senior political officer responsible for the Dulaym Division in occupied Iraq.

MAJOR GENERAL GEORGE A. J. LESLIE
Second in command in Iraq at the time of the uprising. Commander of the Anglo-Indian troops in the key, mid-Euphrates region until his dismissal by Haldane in November 1920.

JOHN LYLE MACKAY, LORD INCHCAPE
Self-made businessman with strong government contacts and ambitions to control shipping on the Tigris and Euphrates. One of the two government-appointed directors on the board of the Anglo-Persian Oil Company.

SIR MARK SYKES
Catholic Tory landowner and amateur orientalist. Together with Hankey, a member of the De Bunsen Committee. In 1918, author of the Baghdad Declaration and the Anglo-French Declaration, both offering self-rule in Iraq.

LIEUTENANT COLONEL ARNOLD T. WILSON
Indian Army political officer and acting civil commissioner (head of the occupation administration) in Iraq until October 1920. Later, managing director of the Anglo-Persian Oil Company.

The Arabs

EMIR ʿABDALLAH
Second son of Emir Husayn al-Hashimi, Sharif of Mecca. In early 1920 he was the favoured candidate of the nationalists to lead an independent Iraq.

JAʿFAR AL-ʿASKARI
Iraqi-born Ottoman army officer and member of the secret anti-Turkish organisation al-ʿAhd who deserted to the British during the

war. Returned to Iraq towards the end of the 1920 revolution to become defence minister in a puppet government controlled by Britain. Brother-in-law of Nuri al-Sa'id.

'ALI AL-BAZIRGAN
Former Ottoman official and leading member of the nationalist Haras al-Istiqlal. One of the founders of the Ahliyya public school in Baghdad whose teachers and alumni agitated against the British occupation.

LIEUTENANT MUHAMMAD SHARIF AL-FARUQI
Junior officer from Mosul in the Ottoman army and member of al-'Ahd, the secret society of (mainly Iraqi) Arab officers opposed to the Turkish dictatorship. Defected to the British during the war. Returned to Iraq towards the end of the 1920 uprising.

EMIR FAYSAL
Third son of Husayn, Sharif of Mecca. Protégé of Lawrence during and after the Arab Revolt against the Turks. Emir of semi-independent Arab state of Syria (1918–20). In 1921, placed on the throne of Iraq in a move engineered by Churchill, Bell and Lawrence.

EMIR HUSAYN AL-HASHIMI
Sharif of Mecca and, later, King of the Hejaz. In late 1920 his short-lived kingdom provided sanctuary for some of the leaders of the Iraqi insurrection, including Ja'far Abu al-Timman, Yusuf Suwaydi and Sayyid Muhsin Abu Tabikh, but avoided providing any material aid to the uprising for fear of losing British political support.

SHEIKH AL-SHARI'A AL-ISBAHANI
Senior mujtahid of Persian origin based at Najaf who took over leadership of the uprising after the death of Mirza Muhammad Taqi al-Shirazi.

MIRZA MUHAMMAD RIDHA
Son of the Grand Mujtahid Mirza Muhammad Taqi al-Shirazi. President of Jam'iyyat 'Iraqiyya al-'Arabiyya which stood for Iraqi collaboration with the Turkish nationalist leader Mustafa Kemal and the Bolsheviks. Exiled to Persia by the British in 1920 before the outbreak of the insurrection.

NURI AL-SA'ID
Iraqi-born junior Ottoman army officer and member of the secret anti-

Turkish organisation al-'Ahd who deserted to the British during the war. Returned to Iraq towards the end of the 1920 insurrection after offering his services to the British in crushing the uprising. Brother-in-law of Ja'far al-'Askari.

SAYYID MUHAMMAD AL-SADR
Son of the Kadhimayn mujtahid Sayyid Hasan al-Sadr. Along with 'Ali al-Bazirgan, one of the founders of the Ahliyya public school in Baghdad, a hotbed of nationalist agitation. Leading member of the nationalist Haras al-Istiqlal and insurgent commander during the insurrection.

MIRZA MUHAMMAD TAQI AL-SHIRAZI
Shi'i Grand Mujtahid of Persian origin and spiritual leader of the 1920 uprising. Died in August 1920 in Karbela' at the height of the rebellion.

YUSUF AL-SUWAYDI
Elderly Baghdad Sunni notable and leading member of the nationalist Haras al-Istiqlal.

SAYYID MUHSIN ABU TABIKH
Wealthy landowning sayyid and veteran of the jihad against the British invasion in 1914–15. One of the principal leaders of the uprising in the mid-Euphrates region, he was appointed mutasarrif, to govern insurgent-controlled territory.

JA'FAR ABU AL-TIMMAN
Baghdad Shi'i merchant and one of the most important leaders of the nationalist organisation Haras al-Istiqlal. Campaigned for the Shi'i and Sunni Muslims to unite against the British occupation.

PART ONE

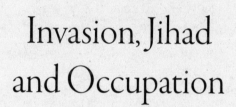

Invasion, Jihad
and Occupation

THE OTTOMAN EMPIRE C.1900, SHOWING THE PREDOMINANTLY

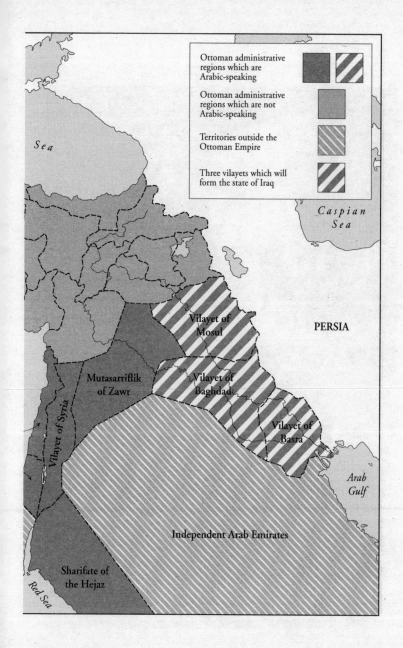

ARABIC-SPEAKING VILAYETS AND OTHER ADMINISTRATIVE REGIONS

Sir Mark Sykes, May 1913

Indications of Oil

One morning sometime in October 1905 – we don't know precisely when or where – the twenty-six-year-old Sir Mark Sykes, 'honorary attaché' at the British embassy in Istanbul, capital of the Ottoman Empire, made contact with an employee of a German engineering company surveying the territory of northern Iraq for the planned Berlin to Baghdad Railway. Perhaps they met in one of those ubiquitous Istanbul coffee houses, sipping that dark viscous liquid flavoured with cardamom, chatting and smoking just like any pair of European merchants doing a little business. We do know, however, that at some stage in the proceedings, the German gentleman passed a small package to Sykes which he quickly slipped inside his jacket pocket and in return – so we might reasonably surmise – an equally small package containing a sum of money was passed to the German engineer. Back at the embassy, Sir Mark unwrapped the package and checked the contents of the small notebook which it contained. Satisfied that the material he had been promised was actually there, he telephoned the British ambassador, Sir Nicholas R. O'Conor, to arrange an appointment with him at the ambassador's earliest convenience.

Sir Mark Sykes was no ordinary junior embassy official. He was the only son of Sir Tatton Sykes, an extremely wealthy landowning grandee with estates in the East Riding of Yorkshire. Over the previous ten years he had travelled widely in the territories of the Ottoman Empire and had gained the reputation of being an expert on 'the East'. Over the next ten years he would become, successively, the Conservative Member for the parliamentary constituency of Hull Central, the commander of the

Yorkshire Territorial Army Battalion and the personal representative of the war minister, Lord Herbert Horatio Kitchener of Khartoum, in all matters pertaining to British strategic and commercial interests in the Middle East. By 1916 he would be the government advisor whose opinions, ideals and prejudices were the most influential factor shaping the British Empire's war aims in the struggle against the Ottoman Empire.

Sykes's chief, O'Conor, a tall, languid Irish landowner and Britain's ambassador in Istanbul (which the British persisted in calling Constantinople) since 1898, was rather fond of his earnest young attaché, a fellow Catholic, who seemed happy to relieve him of some of the more tedious diplomatic work. Moreover, in those years before the First World War, O'Conor and Sykes shared a certain affection for the old Ottoman Empire. This once-great multiethnic and multireligious super-state, with a population of 21 million (a third of whom were Arabs) distributed over thirty-three vilayets and stretching from the Balkans to the frontier with Persia, had long since become critically weakened by a combination of war, rebellion, debt and the economic penetration of European capitalism. It was debt in particular that was the Achilles heel of the Ottoman state. Failure to repay immense loans from European banks had resulted in the creation of a European-controlled Ottoman Public Debt Administration which syphoned off the empire's taxes and customs duties. Britain was part of that organisation, but since the 1850s had also seen the Ottomans as a useful bulwark against tsarist Russia's attempts to expand south and gain access to the Mediterranean. So in 1905, this affection for Sultan Abdul Hamid II's ramshackle empire on the part of O'Conor and Sykes was also a reflection of Britain's long-standing foreign policy.

When Sykes made his telephone call to Sir Nicholas, the ambassador was ensconced aboard his yacht anchored in the Golden Horn, his preferred place of residence. However, in due course he received Sykes's message and shortly afterwards asked the attaché to join him for dinner. After the meal Sykes was invited to outline the contents of the small notebook he had obtained from the German engineer and which he had meanwhile written up as a detailed memorandum. The ambassador was impressed and the following day, 15 October 1905, he dispatched Sykes's document to the Foreign Office, with a covering note of his own and marked 'SECRET'.[1]

Ten days later, Mr Richard P. Maxwell, senior clerk in the Commercial Department of the Foreign Office, selected a dossier from the pile upon his desk and read the following:

SECRET. From H.M. Ambassador in Constantinople. 'Report on the Petroliferous Districts of the Vilayets of Baghdad, Mosul and Bitlis; prepared by Sir Mark Sykes, Hon. Attaché.

The following accounts of the various Petroleum springs and asphalt deposits have been compiled from a report made to the Imperial Ottoman Government by an Engineer dispatched to the above mentioned Vilayets in 1901. The large map shows the distribution of the springs and deposits, the red Roman Numerals corresponding with the numbers scheduled in the following order. Where obtainable a large scale sketch has been appended to the verbal description showing the nature of the locality described.[2]

Maxwell ploughed on,

No. I, Bohtan. 30 Kilometres up the Bohtan river ... No. II Sairt ... No. III Zakho ... No. VI Baba Gurgur ... The Petroleum Springs of Baba Gurgur are among the richest and most workable in the Vilayet of Mosul. They are situated in the vicinity of Kirkuk, being about 6 miles from the town at the foot of the Shuan Hills. They cover an area of about half a hectare and owing to the great heat are constantly burning, the petroleum in this zone seems limited to an area of 25 hectares, but still the deposits [are] of great promise.[3]

There followed descriptions of a further nine petroleum deposits, at the end of which the author had made the suggestion that they 'could be worked by means of pipelines leading from the springs to the sea'.

However, in a rather complacent letter to the ambassador of 25 October also classified 'SECRET', Maxwell merely commented that printing the report with or without the maps ... 'was hardly worthwhile, although it might be shown to D'Arcy if he would call to see it'. (William Knox D'Arcy's company was currently exploring for oil in southern Persia.) Finally, the Foreign Office official added that Sykes 'might be thanked for the trouble he has taken'.[4]

In Istanbul Sir Nicholas must have read the reply with some irritation. This was not the first occasion on which the embassy had informed the Foreign Office about the existence of potentially rich oil deposits in northern Iraq. A year earlier, with rumours circulating that the sultan had recently awarded an oil concession to the German company planning to build the railway to Baghdad, he had sent the foreign secretary, the Marques of Lansdowne, a map of the oil-bearing districts obtained by the embassy secretary, also from German sources.

On that occasion the foreign secretary had instructed O'Conor to pass the map on to the representative of the British D'Arcy Group who were showing interest in obtaining their own oil concession in Iraq. O'Conor had suggested to D'Arcy's agent that the embassy might intervene with the sultan's ministers using its diplomatic influence to expedite a favourable response. But D'Arcy's representative had declined the offer, replying that diplomatic intervention might actually complicate his current negotiations with those same ministers. It had been a serious miscalculation: negotiations had subsequently broken down. And now the Foreign Office seemed to be losing interest in the matter altogether in spite of the fact that Sykes's report had provided precise details of the different oil deposits which confirmed the veracity of that original map O'Conor had sent to London. There was no doubt about it: in the matter of oil concessions the Germans were stealing a march on Britain.

Sykes must also have been frustrated by the Foreign Office's rebuff to his intelligence-gathering efforts. But then, he knew there were those in Whitehall who regarded him as just an amateur, a 'gentleman' interloper among seasoned professionals. Indeed, in reality, his claim to expertise on matters pertaining to 'the East' was somewhat flimsy. Although Sykes had usually travelled on horseback on the eastern journeys of his youth, these had not been dangerous adventures of discovery like those of the great Victorian explorers of the Middle East, men like Sir Richard Burton, Charles Doughty or William Palgrave. He had usually been accompanied by a retinue of Turkish soldiery, guides and servants and was offered considerable hospitality at the various staging posts along his route. Between journeys Sykes had begun to study Arabic in a desultory way, tutored for a time by one of Britain's foremost experts on both Persian and Arabic, Professor E. G. Browne of Cambridge University; but Sykes never mastered the Arabic script and what little he learned was transliterated into the Roman alphabet.[5]

Although well received at the time, Sykes's scholarly accomplishments in this area were rather meagre. They were confined to a travel book, *Through Five Turkish Provinces*, published in 1900, and another in 1904 entitled *Dar-ul-Islam: A Record of a Journey through Ten of the Asiatic Provinces of Turkey*. Sykes's writing had a keen eye for the picaresque and exotic with flashes of real humour; but it also displayed a darker side where Sykes gave voice to his prejudices against Jews, Armenians and urban Arabs. The latter were denigrated as 'cowardly' as well as being 'insolent and despicable' and 'vicious as far as their feeble bodies will admit'.[6] Turks and Kurds, on the other hand, who from time to time massacred their wretched Armenian neighbours, Sykes regarded as 'good, rugged fighters'. Nevertheless, in the company of his friends he was not averse to posing as an experienced orientalist, smoking a hubble-bubble and sitting cross-legged on the floor.

So, when Ambassador O'Conor informed Sykes of the Foreign Office's unenthusiastic response to the intelligence on potential Iraqi oil resources which he had gathered, Sykes must have been equally irritated; but he probably shrugged off the slight, his imagination already moving on to new enthusiasms – more horseback journeys to distant locations; more friendly encounters with cheerful bandoliered cut-throats; more amusing after-dinner anecdotes for his rich friends.

Nevertheless, ten years later, with the strategic importance of oil better understood, Sykes's attention would be drawn once again to the petroleum potential of Iraq, and by then, he himself would be occupying a far more influential position in the machinery of state. On the other hand he was never to see the day – 14 October 1927 – when the top of the number 1 well at Baba Gurgur, that 'richest and most workable' deposit cited in his report, blew out and the first major discovery of oil in Iraq was made.

Lieutenant Wilson's First Mission

One hundred and twenty miles inland and north-west from the head of the Arabian Gulf, and fifty miles upstream of the port of Basra, the great Mesopotamian rivers Tigris and Euphrates merge to form a broad navigable waterway known as the Shatt al-'Arab. This immensely wide waterway then flows on, in a south-easterly direction, before emptying its coffee-coloured contents into the blue-green Gulf. Along its southern half the Shatt al-'Arab forms the boundary between the Arab lands and the ancient civilisation of Persia. About halfway between Basra and the sea, on the Persian side, the Shatt al-'Arab is joined by the River Karun which rises in Persia's Bakhtiari mountains, thence curving southward through a broad alluvial plain before adding its turbid, reddish stream to those of the Tigris and Euphrates. Adjacent to the mouth of the Karun lies the tip of the forty-mile-long island of Abadan, separated only by a narrow waterway from the Persian mainland. In the early 1900s it was an almost featureless area of mud flats and a few date-palm gardens, occasionally subject to inundation, whose future economic and strategic importance could never have been remotely imagined by the Arab and Persian tribesmen who occasionally traversed its dreary landscape.

About one hundred miles up the Karun lies the once small town of Ahwaz, capital of the Persian province of Arabistan (now Khuzistan), where the British maintained a strong consular presence in the years before the First World War under the watchful eye of the imperial government in India. It was to Ahwaz that Lieutenant Arnold T. Wilson of the 32nd Sikh Pioneers was ordered on 29 November 1907, accompanied by twenty

Indian troopers of the 18th Bengal Lancers, ostensibly to reinforce the guard of the Ahwaz consulate but in practice to protect the employees of the British Concession Syndicate drilling for oil in the foothills of the Zagros mountains, seventy miles to the north-east.

Lieutenant Wilson was just twenty-three years old, one of seven children of a twice-married Rochdale clergyman. Educated at Clifton College and the Royal Military Academy at Sandhurst, he was a rather gauche and lonely young man who spent much of his leisure time avidly reading British imperial history. His greatly admired older half-brother, Edward, who had gone to South Africa to work for the British South Africa Company under the celebrated empire-builder Cecil Rhodes, was a formative influence on his political education and by his late teens Arnold had become a fervent imperialist. At Sandhurst he excelled in every field and at the end of his first year passed out First and was awarded the Kings Medal and Sword for General Proficiency and Military Engineering. Something of a prig, he didn't make friends easily and could sometimes be unfeeling in his treatment of those he considered less able than himself. A competent horseman, he had little patience for a skittish or recalcitrant mount. One particular horse he describes to his parents as a 'brute' which 'needed rough handling and a firm hand, which is more in my line than gentle handling'.[1] It was a description of his attitude to rebellious independence which would later manifest itself on a grander scale.

In 1903 Wilson had been commissioned with the 2nd Battalion of the Wiltshire Regiment and posted to Rawalpindi, a garrison town in Britain's vast Indian Empire. However, he soon found life in a peace-time British regiment boring and chafed at what he considered his underemployment – something which did not seem to bother many of his fellow junior officers. An intelligent and ambitious individual, Wilson began to feel increasingly frustrated by the lack of opportunities to exhibit the knowledge and skills with which Sandhurst had furnished him and in December 1904 he transferred to an Indian regiment, the 32nd Sikh Pioneers, where opportunities for both promotion and adventure seemed more promising.

Wilson also began to take an interest in army sanitation. Indeed, matters of health, general orderliness and 'clean-living' became something of an obsession with him. Wilson's prescription for maintaining his own robust good health was a cold bath taken at sunrise. At the same time, his hitherto conventional Christianity was evolving into a more earnest dedication to Bible-reading. The hymn 'Onward Christian Soldiers' came to mean something intensely personal for this fourteen-stone, physically strong, self-confident and intensely patriotic young man. He remained, however, something of a loner. He had none of the social graces or accomplishments: he did not dance or play tennis, golf or bridge. He disliked games, although he forced himself to acquire some proficiency at football and hockey. He had little opportunity to be in the company of women and remained intensely shy of them.

By 1907 Wilson had become interested in the political life of the Indian Empire and wrote a number of articles for various Anglo-Indian journals. He began to see his future as an officer of the Indian Political Service which administered almost every aspect of daily life throughout the subcontinent's sprawling land mass. In September 1907 he presented himself to the Foreign Department of the government of India at Simla, where he was offered the first step on the ladder towards becoming a 'Political' – a six-month posting with the Intelligence Branch of the chief of staff. Only twenty-four hours after his appointment to 'I' Branch was confirmed, Wilson received an urgent telegram advising him that he was to be sent to south-west Persia on 'special duties'.

Persia was then in a state of political flux. The territories of this nominally sovereign state owed allegiance to a central government in Tehran ruled by the weak and corrupt Muzaffar ed-Din Shah of the Qajar dynasty, whose predecessor, Nasr ed-Din Shah, had compelled his reluctant harem to dress as Parisian ballet girls as part of a somewhat misconceived modernisation drive.[2] Modernisation of a very different kind had arrived in 1901 when William Knox D'Arcy, an English millionaire who had made his fortune in Australian gold mines, acquired a concession from Muzaffar ed-Din Shah to search for oil in return for a down payment of £20,000, a further £20,000 in shares and 16 per cent of the net profits of any company formed to work the concession. The contract area covered half a million square miles and would last for sixty years.[3]

Thereafter, reaction to the shah's propensity for granting concessions to Europeans in return for payments which were squandered on royal extravagance led to demands for a curb on the shah's powers and the establishment of the rule of law. In 1906, Muzaffar ed-Din was compelled to accept the setting-up of a constitutional council, the Majlis, by a revolution led by merchants, artisans and mullahs. But after his death the following year and a counter-revolution by his son Muhammad Ali Shah in 1908, the country became mired in civil war. Meanwhile, in 1907, an agreement between Britain and Russia carved Persia up into spheres of influence – for the Russians, the north including the capital, and for the British, the south, with a so-called 'neutral zone' in between. In practice, however, the southern parts of the neutral area, believed to contain valuable oil resources, became increasingly under the influence of the British zonal headquarters at Bushire on the Arabian Gulf.

This was the political and social environment into which Lieutenant Wilson and his men headed on New Year's Day 1908. Leaving Ahwaz, he and his men rode to Mamatayn, a few miles north of the town of Ram Hormuz and one of the two places where the Concession Syndicate's Canadian drillers and their Persian labourers were hammering through layers of rock with simple percussion rigs in search of the so-far elusive oil.

One can imagine the enthusiasm of this dedicated young soldier of the empire as he embarked on this, his first real independent mission in a land barely touched by European civilisation and largely under the control of the Bakhtiari khans, chieftains of a fiercely independent nomadic people who scorned any allegiance to Tehran. As he and his cavalry troopers rode through sweltering desert, fertile river basins and towering gorges cut through gypsum and limestone cliffs, the young lieutenant was elated by the scenery and wildlife, the unfamiliar trees and flowers and the frequent encounters with remnants of ancient civilisations. In his diary for March 1908 he notes, in particular, the 'great beds of wild narcissus' carpeting the hills and valleys. 'My men, like Persians', he records, 'bend low to their stirrups to smell them as they ride slowly through,' adding, 'I can remember no time when my mind, and eyes and ears enjoyed during all my waking hours such a feast of beautiful and interesting things.'[4]

Arriving at Mamatayn, one of the two places where the Concession Syndicate is drilling, in a narrow gorge smelling of hydrogen sulphide with sheer cliffs of gypsum overlaid with gravel, Wilson is welcomed into the camp by G. B. Reynolds, the manager of the company's operations and a self-trained geologist who has previously been in the service of the Indian Public Works Department. The two men quickly become friends. Reynolds is the older man at fifty, but very active in body and mind. Like Wilson, he is accustomed to long journeys on horseback or mule; a successful autocrat in his dealing with both his Canadian roughnecks and the local Bakhtiaris – 'a solid British oak', as Wilson would later describe him.

In the following months Wilson and his men patrol the rugged mountainous regions surrounding the oil company's field of operations. The local Bakhtiari khans, whom he describes as 'looking like stage assassins with Martini-Henry rifles and fifty or more cartridges and a knife or two', are being paid £2,000 a year for 'safeguarding' the oil company's property and plant. Wilson quickly recognises that this is little more than protection money. Nevertheless, he soon comes to like them and to envy their hardiness.

One spring evening, while the Canadians, mistrustful of 'dirty native food', consume their canned European provisions and drink whisky to excess, Wilson and Reynolds share a meal of fresh local food: soup made from the bones of an old cow his cavalrymen have killed and eaten, chicken – boiled first and then grilled – stuffed with raisins, pistachio nuts and almonds and afterwards, dried figs, apricots, cherries and plums.

Afterwards, Reynolds explains his predicament. Hundreds of thousands of pounds have already been spent and there is still no discovery of oil. Reynolds is worried that the oil company's shareholders are losing patience. One final possibility remains: to move the drilling operations to Maidan-i-Naftun, a location whose name, 'the plain of oil', certainly sounds promising. Moreover, an ancient temple nearby is supposedly of fire-worshipping Zoroastrian origin, giving further credence to the notion that there are petroleum resources somewhere in the vicinity. Reynolds therefore tells Wilson that he is going to move all the equipment there – it will be their last chance.

So by April 1908, with the temperature already reaching 115°F and the nomadic Bakhtiari tribesmen departing for their summer pastures high in the Zagros mountains, Reynolds and his drilling team are at Maidan-i-Naftun, grimly persevering with two new wells. Then Reynolds receives the telegram from the Concession Syndicate which he has been dreading. He should continue drilling down to 1,600 feet and then, if no oil is found, abandon the operations and transport his equipment back to Ahwaz and thence down the Karun river to Muhammara.

On hearing this Wilson is enraged. He immediately writes to his direct superior in the Indian Political Service, Major Percy Cox, warning that if the British pull out, their place will soon be taken by the Germans or by one of Rockefeller's companies. 'Cannot government be moved to prevent these fainthearted merchants masquerading in top hats as pioneers of Empire, from losing what may be a great asset?' he writes despairingly to Cox. Meanwhile, Reynolds decides to continue drilling for a little longer, convincing himself that it is possible that there has been error is the coding of the telegram and that it would be unsafe to follow its instructions until he receives further written confirmation. With luck this should give him about one more month.

Tuesday 26 May, 1908: it is an exceptionally hot night and Wilson is sleeping outside his tent. Just after 4.00 a.m. he is awakened by a great rumbling noise and shouts of jubilation from the Persian oilfield labourers. He runs towards the sound of the commotion and witnesses an amazing sight: the long-awaited breakthrough. A huge column of oil is spouting from the primitive percussion drilling rig, fifty feet above the top of the rig, tumbling down over the delighted drillers and labourers and almost smothering them with the accompanying gas. The Concession Syndicate – later to become the Anglo-Persian Oil

Company; and later still, British Petroleum – has struck oil at a depth of 1,200 feet. The first commercially exploitable oilfield in the Middle East has been discovered.

Wilson quickly swallows some yoghurt and flat bread, mounts his stallion and gallops to the Persian telegraph office, thirty miles away at Shushtar, to inform his superiors at Bushire on the Gulf coast of the important news. But when he arrives he realises that he doesn't have the current secret telegraph code book with him. Instead he gets out the Bible which he always carries with him and consults the Old Testament. Having found the verses he is looking for, he wires to Bushire the following: 'See Psalm 104 verse 15, third sentence and Psalm 114, verse 8, second sentence.' When the officers of the Indian Political Service at Bushire check the message against their own Bible, they read 'That he may bring forth … oil to make his face shine' and 'Who turned the flint-stone into a springing well'. They know instantly what Wilson is referring to and the information is immediately sent off to the Concession Syndicate's offices in Glasgow, the Foreign Office and the Admiralty.[5]

The Admiralty were delighted. Since 1904, when Admiral John 'Jackie' Fisher had become First Sea Lord, it had been encouraging and supporting D'Arcy's oil-exploration activities. Fisher had set up a special committee to study the question of converting the Royal Navy's warships from coal to oil and he used his considerable influence to encourage the Scottish directors of what was then Britain's only oil company – Burmah Oil – to refinance D'Arcy's struggling Persian enterprise when its expensive drilling operations were failing to find reserves. The Concession Syndicate Ltd, which acquired D'Arcy's original company, First Exploitation Ltd, in May 1905, was the outcome of those endeavours. Following the successful discovery at Maidan-i-Naftun, a new company with a capital of £2 million – the Anglo-Persian Oil Company – was established in April 1909 and Fisher was now able to push forward with his plans to revolutionise the British navy in the knowledge that in years to come the country would have control of a major oilfield in a region effectively under British rule and with good communications with its Indian Empire.

By 1912, a 138-mile, eight-inch-diameter pipeline had been laid from Maidan-i-Naftun – now renamed Masjid-i-Sulayman after the nearby ancient fire temple – to an oil-receiving terminal and refinery at Abadan island. Meanwhile, Wilson had become de facto advisor to the Anglo-Persian Oil Company, personally undertaking land and property acquisitions on its behalf, and in May 1909 he accompanied his immediate superior, Major Percy Cox, to begin negotiating the agreement for the lease of part of Abadan island with Sheikh Khaz'al of Muhammara, the wily Arab potentate whose domain lay on the neighbouring Persian mainland and who, although nominally a vassal of the shah, was, in reality, an independent ruler.

Although the negotiations were protracted, Sheikh Khaz'al was eventually given assurances of continuing British protection while he himself relented on certain contractual demands, and the agreement to lease part of Abadan was signed. Afterwards Cox, who by now had formed a very high opinion of Wilson's work, appointed him as his assistant and he was instructed to carry out detailed topographical investigations of the whole area surrounding Anglo-Persian's field of operations in case disturbances among the local tribes should require military intervention. A few years later Wilson was to tell his parents, 'Whatever happens to all the other matters I have dealt with in this part of the world I shall, I am sure, always be proud of having helped to start the Oil Company on sound lines.'[6]

However, difficulties at Anglo-Persian's operations continued. On its first test, in July 1912, the refinery broke down. When it was finally in operation it became clear that the quality of its products was poor: the kerosene extracted for lighting – still a major market for the crude oil – had a dirty yellow tinge and quickly filmed-up the oil lamps in which it was used. And lurking in the background, the huge Royal Dutch/Shell Company, with whom Anglo-Persian had a contract for the marketing of its products, was beginning to deploy its formidable financial power towards a possible takeover of its smaller partner – or at least that was what the directors of Anglo-Persian feared.

By the autumn of 1912, with problems such as these still mounting, the Anglo-Persian Oil Company was fast running out of capital; but millions

Churchill as First Lord of the Admiralty, 1912

more were needed for development of the company's oilfields. Charles Greenway, Anglo-Persian's first managing director, a monocle- and spats-sporting gentleman who in spite of his 'Champagne Charlie' image had a sound experience of the oil business, now began pressing the government for a subsidy. But although the initial response from government was encouraging, by the following year no practical outcome had been achieved, although Winston Churchill, First Lord of the Admiralty, had made it clear that he was sympathetic towards the company's plight.

The navy was now building more oil-fired warships but the great battleships of the fleet remained coal-fired. Admiral Fisher, now in retirement, continued to campaign for these super weapons of the day to be fuelled by oil. This would increase their speed from an average twenty knots to a world-beating twenty-five. But with Anglo-Persian once again struggling to survive, where were the future secure supplies of oil to come from? Not from a monopoly controlled by Royal Dutch/Shell, argued Anglo-Persian and its supporters in the Admiralty who questioned the 'Britishness' of a company which was only 40 per cent British-owned and whose two managing directors were respectively Dutch and Jewish. So the solution *had* to be Anglo-Persian, but how were its chronic financial problems to be solved?

Churchill responded with a proposal of breathtaking originality. On 17 June 1914 he introduced a Bill in the House of Commons to partially nationalise Anglo-Persian. The Bill contained two principal elements: firstly, the government would invest £2.2 million in the company in return for 51 per cent of its equity, and secondly, the government would place two directors on the Anglo-Persian board. Despite strong criticism both within Parliament and outside it, the Bill was eventually passed by an overwhelming majority, 254 to 18: the British government was now a direct participant in the international oil business. But the new Anglo-Persian remained a far cry from any kind of experiment in state socialism.[7]

Since only two government nominees would be on the board of directors, the company remained in all relevant respects a private one. And who were these government directors? One was Admiral Sir Edmond Slade, representing the interests of the Admiralty; the other was James Lyle Mackay, Lord Inchcape, chairman of the Peninsular & Oriental Steam Navigation Company, vice-president of the Suez Canal Company and a director of Hong Kong & Shanghai Bank, a self-made predatory capitalist in the classic mould: in matters of economic policy a devout believer in the superiority of market forces over state intervention – except, that is, in cases where such intervention served his own extensive business interests.[8] In spite of his role in Anglo-Persian as a government appointee, there was nothing to prevent Lord Inchcape from owning shares in the company and his private interest in the oil business would later encompass investments in an Anglo-French consortium, the Middle East Development Company, which had plans for oil exploration in Syria and Arabia.[9] But Inchcape had another motive for his involvement in Anglo-Persian and its subsidiaries. As the leading shipowner of the day, the availability of cheap oil supplies to fuel his own fleet was extremely important to him and he would later use his position on the board of Anglo-Persian to lobby to reduce the price of oil for his P&O liners and merchant ships.[10]

There was, however, a further implication of Churchill's Act. Britain had now committed itself to a strategic involvement in a region on the frontiers of the Ottoman Empire and within a few hours' march of Ottoman troops based at the Iraqi city of Basra.

And this was not the only point at which British oil interests touched upon the Ottoman Empire's Iraqi territories. As Sykes had already discovered, in 1905 German engineers working on the Berlin-to-Baghdad railway project acquired geological data indicating that northern Iraq could be a richly petroliferous area and, as Ambassador O'Conor had feared, they had subsequently passed this information to representatives of the Deutsche Bank in Berlin. They, in turn, sought a concession from the Ottoman government to begin drilling operations in the area of Mosul. However, in 1912, Deutsche Bank transferred its claims for a concession to the Turkish Petroleum Company (TPC), whose capital was distributed between Royal Dutch/Shell, the Deutsche Bank, and an entity named the 'Turkish National Bank'. Shell and Deutsche Bank each held 25 per cent of the company's capital with the remaining 50 per cent in the hands of the Turkish bank. However, in spite of its name, half of the latter's equity was actually owned by British financial interests.

Meanwhile, an envious Anglo-Persian Oil Company looked on with deep chagrin at the success of its rival, Shell, which had now seemingly gained a foothold in what could turn out to be another major petroliferous area, and to further complicate matters the British ambassador in Istanbul reported that the Turks themselves had plans to set up an oil company to work the oil, not only around Mosul but also in the vilayets of Baghdad and Basra, prompting the British foreign secretary, Sir Edward Grey, to send a sharp protest note to the Ottoman government in July 1913 followed by a further ultimatum on 12 March 1914.[11] The British government informed the Turks that it would not agree to the economic concessions they were currently requesting – primarily an increase in Ottoman import tariffs – unless they, in turn, agreed that the TPC should amalgamate with Anglo-Persian. So on 19 March 1914, in a deal orchestrated by the Foreign Office, the TPC was restructured whereby a subsidiary of Anglo-Persian, the D'Arcy Exploration Company Ltd, acquired 50 per cent of TPC, leaving the Deutsche Bank and Shell with 25 per cent each.[12] Three months later the British and German ambassadors in Istanbul were informed that an application by the TPC for an oil concession comprising the vilayets of Mosul and Baghdad would be granted, but that ratification and written confirmation would have to wait until certain stipulations were made as to the extent of Ottoman government participation in the new company's profits and the size of the royalty to be paid.

It was never to be. On 28 June 1914, a Serbian extremist assassinated the Austrian Duke Franz Ferdinand in Sarajevo and a month later (28 July) the Austro-Hungarian Empire declared war on Serbia. Thereafter, a fatal interlocking network of international treaties dragged all the major powers into war. At midnight on 30 July, the tsar ordered total mobilisation of the Russian armed forces in support of Serbia. In response, on 1 August, Austria's ally Germany also began mobilisation and the following day signed a secret alliance pact with the Ottoman Empire. On 3 August, Germany declared war on Russia's ally France and invaded Belgium. This in turn triggered Britain's declaration of war against Germany the following day. Finally, after completing its mobilisation, on 31 October the Ottoman Empire joined Germany and Austria in their war against the Allies.[13] And now, the British oil interests at Abadan and in south-west Persia had suddenly become uncomfortably close to enemy soil.

'Protect the oil refineries'

Many years after the end of the First World War, Lieutenant Wilson – by then, Lieutenant Colonel Sir Arnold Wilson MP – reflected on the events which had tumbled Britain into a major war in the Middle East at the beginning of November 1914. When 'the little war cloud first arose in the West, no bigger than a man's hand', he mused, 'it occurred to no one in Turkish Arabia that it would overshadow them within a few months bringing terror and doom to pygmy man.'[1] Neither could he, nor anyone else, ever have imagined that within six years nearly 30,000 British and Indian soldiers and an equal number of Turks and Arabs would perish – as Wilson put it – 'in the flower of their youth in the country of the two rivers and the rocky wastes of Kurdistan'.

Unlike the other major powers bound by those toxic international treaties, there was nothing inevitable about the outbreak of hostilities between the two empires – Ottoman and British. Although the latter's long-standing diplomatic support for the former was beginning to weaken somewhat,[2] the British government had shown little concern when a revolutionary organisation, the Committee of Union and Progress (CUP), overthrew the government of the paranoid and despotic Sultan Abdul Hamid II in 1908, and had maintained a studied neutrality in the 1912 Balkan War which had driven Turkey from most of its European possessions. True, by 1914 there was a powerful pro-German faction within the Ottoman government, notably in the person of its virtual dictator, the dapper, thirty-three-year-old Enver Pasha; but there were also elements within the ruling CUP which had no wish for an armed struggle against the British Empire. Nevertheless, once hostilities had commenced in Europe in August 1914, a long, smouldering fuse of war began to slowly burn its way towards the British possessions and dependencies at the head of the Gulf.

Difficult though it is to say precisely how that fuse was lit, Winston Churchill, First Lord of the Admiralty, was probably one of the incendiarists. Britain had been building two Dreadnought class battleships for Turkey on the Tyne, the *Sultan Osman* and the *Reshadieh*. The ships had cost Turkey £7.5 million, a huge sum of money for a bankrupt nation, and the cash had been raised by public subscription in the hope that the new warships would enable the Ottoman Empire to recover islands in the Aegean and Dodecanese which had been lost to Italy and Greece in the wars of 1911 and 1912. The *Sultan Osman* had been completed and Turkish crews had arrived to man both vessels, but the ships were awaiting the construction of a larger dock sufficient to hold them at Istanbul. On 28 July, the day on which Austria declared war on Serbia, Churchill proposed that both ships should be requisitioned for the Royal Navy and on 31 July the cabinet approved their seizure.

These events enraged Turkish public opinion and Churchill's action played into the hands of the Germanophile Enver Pasha, who had been secretly negotiating with Berlin for an Ottoman–German pact behind the backs of his colleagues in the CUP. Consequently, on 2 August 1914, Germany and the Ottoman Empire signed an alliance, although the Turks decided to make no formal declaration of war against the Allies until their mobilisation was completed. Meanwhile, two German warships, the 23,000-ton battlecruiser *Goeben* and the light cruiser *Breslau*, had been ordered to the western Mediterranean with a view to attacking ships ferrying troops to France from its North African colonies. On 3 August they were secretly dispatched to Istanbul, from where they were allowed to pass through the Dardanelles into the Black Sea. On 27 October the two ships, accompanied by Ottoman vessels, began to bombard the Russian ports of Odessa, Sevastopol and Feodosia. Three days later, Britain, France and Russia withdrew their ambassadors from Istanbul and on 31 October the Ottoman Empire declared war on the Allies.[3]

While these events were unfolding and relations between London and Istanbul were beginning to deteriorate, anxiety began to grow over the security of Britain's oil operations at Abadan island and its Persian hinterland.[4] At that time the oilfield at Masjid-i-Sulayman and the Abadan refinery were producing only around 8,000 barrels per day, a very modest production level by world standards,[5] but there were expectations of substantial future increases and the Royal Navy needed every barrel it could get its hands on. Admiral Slade, one of the government's two representatives on the board of Anglo-Persian, wrote a memorandum to this effect urging the dispatch of troops to defend the oil installations. But initially, Churchill thought there were simply not enough troops available. In a minute attached to Slade's memorandum he therefore concluded – no doubt ruefully, given his previous support for Anglo-Persian – that 'we shall have to buy our oil from elsewhere.'

However, throughout September and October 1914 consultations between London and the government of India continued as to how best to protect the nascent British-owned oil industry should hostilities with the Ottoman Empire commence. Although the government of India was reluctant to do anything which might ignite Muslim passions – and there were already reports of strong anti-British sentiments among the population in Baghdad and Basra[6] – feelings in favour of a landing in southern Iraq grew in strength, fortified by the view that Britain must do all it could to protect its client sheikhdoms at Kuwait and Muhammara, especially since it was Sheikh Khaz'al of Muhammara who was the British oil industry's 'landlord' at Abadan. On 2 October the crucial decision was made. A brigade-strength expeditionary force of Anglo-Indian troops in five transport ships supported by the old battleship HMS *Ocean* would put to sea on 16 October with orders to make what was described as a 'demonstration'.[7]

Meanwhile, on 29 September, the Royal Navy sloop HMS *Espiègle*, mounting six 4-inch guns and four 3-pounders, was ordered to enter the Shatt al-'Arab, followed by the armed merchantman *Dalhousie*, while another sloop, the *Odin*, stayed to patrol the mouth of the estuary. *Espiègle* then sailed up the Shatt al-'Arab and anchored off the Sheikh of

Muhammara's capital at the mouth of the Karun. Whatever was intended by this exercise in gunboat diplomacy, its impact only exacerbated the growing tensions between Britain and the Turks. The governor of Basra, Subhi Bey, demanded the ship's departure by 21 October, threatening to blockade it if it didn't withdraw by that date. So *Espiégle* dropped back to Abadan; but it did so under heavy small-arms fire from the Ottoman side of the river.

At the same time, the small expeditionary force of one British battalion and three Indian battalions with two 10-pounder mountain batteries, from Sir Arthur Barrett's 6th (Poona) Division, which had put to sea on 16 October for the purpose of making the 'demonstration', sailed for the Shatt al-'Arab with the following orders:

1) Protect the oil refineries, tanks and pipelines.
2) Cover the landing of reinforcements.
3) Assure local Arabs of our support against Turkey.[8]

The landing force was commanded by Brigadier General W. S. Delamain of the Indian Army and accompanying him as chief political officer was Arnold Wilson's superior, Sir Percy Cox. The brigade arrived at the sandbar which obstructs the mouth of the estuary on 3 November and, after sweeping for mines, sailed up to Abadan. Meanwhile the sloop *Odin* bombarded the Turkish fort on the Fao peninsula which was later stormed and occupied by Royal Marines from the battleship *Ocean*. After making a difficult landing without barges or landing stages, the Anglo-Indian force deployed at a small Arab village called Saniyya on the right bank of the Shatt where, on 11 November, it was briefly and ineffectually attacked by around 400 Ottoman troops. A few days later, the remainder of the 6th Division under Lieutenant General Sir Arthur Barrett arrived to reinforce Delamain's men and on 19 November, in a driving rainstorm, General Barrett ordered his men forward through a sea of mud to attack the old Turkish fort of Zayn, where the Ottoman troops had concentrated. With the support of a battery of royal field artillery the 4,000 Turkish and 1,000 Arab defenders were overwhelmed and fled back towards Basra. However, two Indian battalions were quickly loaded onto the sloops *Espiégle* and *Odin*, which steamed rapidly up to Basra, arriving unopposed at the port before the retreating Turkish troops on 21 November. Barrett's force then pursued the Turks to Qurna, at the junction of the Tigris and Euphrates, which was captured on 9 December after some heavy fighting.

During this first, successful phase of the invasion the British forces suffered one small but significant loss. In an inconclusive skirmish on 17 November, Sir Percy Cox's assistant political officer (APO), Captain R. L. Birdwood, was killed. At the time Lieutenant Arnold Wilson was in London, having just completed an arduous journey along the Turko-Persian frontier as part of an expedition to delineate the border between the two territories which had been a bone of contention for many years. News of the outbreak of hostilities between Russia and the Ottoman Empire reached him as he and his companions crossed the Ottoman-Russian border on 29 October and he straightway made for Archangel, from where he took ship to England. He was expecting to be sent to the front in France but suddenly received orders to set off immediately for Basra, where he was to replace Birdwood as Cox's APO. He arrived there on 28 December 1914. An obscure British junior officer had been killed in action. A barely less obscure British junior officer had replaced him. But within a few years this seemingly unremarkable event was to have major repercussions.

Arab Mobilisation on the Euphrates

At the outbreak of war, the great Victorian military hero Lord Herbert Horatio Kitchener of Khartoum gave up his post as consul general in Egypt to become war minister, to the delight of the British public. The tall, square-headed, sixty-three-year-old viscount, whose Maxim guns had wiped out thousands of spear-carrying Sudanese at the battle of Omdurman in 1898, was the object of almost hysterical adulation by the British public. This porcelain-collecting lifelong bachelor, with a penchant for interior decorating, was convinced that with millions of Muslim subjects within her Indian Empire, Britain faced both dangers and opportunities in a war against an Ottoman enemy which was now urging a jihad against the Allies – a holy war sanctioned by the fact that the CUP's new puppet sultan, Mehmet V, was also the caliph, Islam's supreme leader and nominally the ultimate successor of the Prophet Muhammad. The threat of Turkish subversion spreading throughout the British Empire's 70 million Muslim subjects in India and millions more in Egypt and the Sudan – where Kitchener had first-hand experience of militant Islam in his war against the followers of the Mahdi – was, he believed, a very real one.

Kitchener lived at a time when fear of a mysterious religious uprising in 'the East' was already capturing the popular imagination. Among those who warned of such a threat was John Buchan, wartime director of information and writer of espionage novels. In his 1916 thriller *Greenmantle*, Sir Walter, a Foreign Office official, asks secret agent Richard Hannay to call on him.

'There is a dry wind blowing through the East, and the parched grasses wait the spark. And the wind is blowing towards the Indian border. Whence comes that wind, think you?'

Sir Walter had lowered his voice and was speaking very slow and distinct. I could hear the rain dripping from the eaves of the window, and far off the hoot of the taxis in Whitehall.

'Have you an explanation, Hannay?' he asked again.

'It looks as though Islam had a bigger hand in the thing than we thought,' I said. 'I fancy religion is the only thing to knit up such a scattered empire.'

'You are right,' he said. 'You must be right ... there is a Jihad preparing ... the question is how? ... Supposing there is some Ark of the Covenant which will madden the remotest Moslem peasant with dreams of Paradise? What then, my friend?'

'Then there will be Hell let loose in those parts pretty soon.'[1]

Muslim peasants dreaming of Paradise; preparations for a jihad; the threat to the Indian border – these were all very real in the minds of Britain's rulers at this time, especially among those whose experience had been formed largely through imperial service. But Kitchener believed that possibilities of countering the call to jihad were also present. Given the increasingly pan-Turkish nationalism and small but noticeable displays of secularism apparent among the new rulers in Istanbul, there was also the opportunity to sow disaffection among the Muslim notables in some of the peripheral Ottoman territories – in particular the Arab lands.

Some such disaffection already existed and it was beginning to coalesce with ideas of a cultural and political 'Arab Awakening' emanating from small groups of intellectuals in Syria and the region which would later become Lebanon.[2] Although, as yet, falling a long way short of a demand for independence, it was nevertheless an embryo movement for some kind of self-determination and was beginning to reach out, not just to highly educated urban notables, but even to some of the sheikhs and landowners of distant rural backwaters like the mid-Euphrates region of Iraq.[3] If Britain could play upon the anxieties of local Arab rulers with vague promises of support for some kind of devolution under the protective shield of the

Lord Kitchener, War Minister 1914–1916

British Empire, it might counteract the emotional appeal of the Turkish call to jihad. As Sir Mark Sykes – recently adopted as Kitchener's protégé – had argued in Parliament in the spring of 1914, 'There are native states which exist in the provinces of the Ottoman Empire at the present moment which could be made into independent states. If the worse came to worst, there are Armenians, Arabs and Kurds who only wish to be left in peace to develop the country.'[4]

However, there was a critical weakness in this political strategy of Kitchener and Sykes, because one of the reasons for disaffection with the new authorities in Istanbul among many of the notables in these potentially friendly 'native states' was a growing belief that the Ottoman revolution of 1908 had proved singularly unable to roll back the swelling tide of European economic penetration threatening the traditional fields of activity which were the prerogative of those same notables. Indeed, if anything, the new rulers in Istanbul seemed to be facilitating this invasion of foreign capitalism. In some of the empire's Arab provinces fears grew that they were in danger of exchanging a subordinate position within a Muslim empire for an equally subordinate position within a Christian one; and the Arabs of Iraq, in particular, began to cast anxious glances towards that great outpost of European imperialism on their eastern flank – Britain's Indian Empire.

In fact, only a few years before Kitchener and Sykes had begun to speculate about the possibilities of fomenting pro-British subversion in the Ottoman Empire's Arab lands, an explosion of anti-British feeling had erupted in Baghdad in what became known as the Lynch affair.

For many years, the merchants of Baghdad had been able to send their goods down the Tigris either by using the paddle-steamers of the British-owned company Lynch Brothers or by the Ottoman steamer line, the *Nahriyya*, and the competition which the *Nahriyya* provided had compelled Lynch Brothers to keep their freight rates at levels generally accepted as satisfactory by the Baghdad merchants. However, in early December 1909 news reached Baghdad that the Chamber of Deputies in Istanbul was proposing to privatise the *Nahriyya*, selling it to Lynch Brothers. For the merchants this meant only one thing: a British monopoly of river transport and, sooner or later, much higher freight charges.

On receiving news of this proposal a group of leading Baghdad notables, including not only Sunni and Shi'i traders but also Jewish and Christian merchants, launched an unprecedented campaign against it, a campaign which soon took on the appearance of a turbulent local uprising.[5] One of the participants in this campaign was the grandson of a leading Baghdad cereal merchant, a young man named Ja'far Abu al-Timman, who would later play an important role in opposing the British occupation of his country after the end of the Great War in November 1918.

Soon the movement spread to other Iraqi cities including Mosul and Basra and began to raise fears for their safety among the British residents of Baghdad. Rumours spread that three members of the Ottoman cabinet had accepted a bribe of £50,000 from Lynch Brothers to promote the Lynch concession and on 20 December J. G. Lorimer, the British consul general in Baghdad, telegrammed his superior in Istanbul reporting a mass meeting of between five and ten thousand local people which appointed a fifty-strong committee of leading Muslims, Jews and Christians to lead the fight against the proposed privatisation. On 26 December, so strongly were feelings running that the authorities were compelled to reinforce police guards near the British Residency and the premises of Messrs Lynch Brothers. In the event, the Lynch affair was one of a number of issues which brought about the collapse of the first post-revolution elected Ottoman government in 1910, and with it the proposal to sell the *Nahriyya* also perished for the time being. But in the succeeding years before the outbreak of war there were further manifestations of opposition to the economic policies of the Young Turks which were equally grounded in fears of further British encroachment. So when the British exacerbated this underlying fear of foreign capitalist penetration by actual invasion, there was little appetite for pro-British collaboration against their Turkish co-religionists among the Arabs of this part of the Ottoman Empire.

Meanwhile, the fatwa of 14 November 1914 issued by the Sheikh al-Islam on behalf of the Ottoman sultan, calling for jihad against the British and French, was read out in every Sunni mosque in Iraq. The Shi'is of Iraq did not acknowledge the authority of the Sunni caliph. According to the precepts of the Shi'i, the true successor of Muhammad had to be a descendant of the Prophet's closest male relative, his cousin and son-in-law 'Ali ibn Abu Talib. Moreover, some of the Shi'i religious leaders intensely disliked the more secular policies of the Young Turks. Nevertheless, they heeded the call to jihad, recognising that the events now unfolding constituted a threat to the whole Muslim world.[6] Their response was also a reaction to the anguished appeal for help from their fellow countrymen facing invasion in the south of the country. Three days after the British seizure of Fao, the leading citizens of Basra sent an urgent telegram to the 'ulema' (clergy) of the holy shrine cities of Najaf, Karbela' and Kadhimayn, urging them to mobilise the tribes:

> Port of Basra. The infidels are encircling us. We are all in arms. We fear for all the other Muslim towns. Help us by demanding that the tribes defend us.[7]

In Najaf, the 'ulema' were among the first to declare jihad against the British invaders; but they did so on one condition. Before the outbreak of war, the Turkish authorities had imprisoned a number of important local sheikhs suspected of 'nationalist' tendencies on various trumped-up charges and these men, the clergy of Najaf demanded, must be released before they would issue a fatwa calling upon the tribesmen to join the colours and prepare to march south.[8] The Turks rapidly agreed, and so the leading clerics of this holy Shi'i shrine city issued a call to arms.

The impact of the Ottoman fatwa was particularly strong among the Shi'i tribes of the mid-Euphrates in closest contact with Najaf and Karbela' – the al-Fatla, the Bani Hasan, the Bani Huchaym and the Khaza'il and those tribes in the marshy territory of the Lower Euphrates dominated by the Muntafiq confederation. Around 18,000 volunteer mujahidin from these areas responded to the call and joined the Ottoman colours.[9] They were led by men like Sayyid 'Alwan al-Yasari, one of those released from prison, Muhsin Abu Tabikh, a leading sayyid and wealthy landowner, and Sayyid Hadi al-Mgutar – notables who would form the backbone of a second great struggle against the British, six years later.[10]

Members of the sada (plural of sayyid) were especially well placed to act as recruiting agents for the jihad. They occupied a distinctive position within the social stratification of the Shi'i world of the Middle and Lower Euphrates. A sayyid might be rich or poor – his social distinction came not from his position in the socio-economic structure but from the fact that the sada were a caste: one which traced its descent from the family of the Prophet Muhammad, specifically through the line of Husayn, one of the two sons of the Prophet's daughter, Fatima. As a member of the caste, a sayyid was entitled to claim one-fifth of the income of his non-sayyid neighbours within a certain, traditionally circumscribed territory. But this seemingly parasitic arrangement was rarely seen as such by those who paid since, in addition to the general sense of reverence towards the sada, the richer members of the caste had certain important duties, as well as rights. In particular they acted as intermediaries between the 'ulema' of the holy cities and the rural, tribal population, often carrying out minor religious and judicial functions such as the settlement of land disputes, divorces and quarrels over inheritances. Moreover, in times of crisis like the present one, the richer sada took up leadership roles in mobilising the local population at the behest of the 'ulema', a role also requiring them to provide financial and material support.

One such tribal dignitary, the thirty-six-year-old sayyid Muhsin Abu Tabikh, was to play a particularly important role in the unfolding jihad. His forebears had originally come from Hasa in the Arabian peninsula around a hundred years ago and had subsequently acquired rich rice-producing lands in the Shamiyya, the area to the east of the city of Najaf, watered by the two channels of the Hindiyya branch of the Euphrates.[11] It was from these fertile lands that Abu Tabikh derived his considerable wealth and he now committed a considerable proportion of that wealth to financing the jihad.

On 21 December 1914 a huge flotilla of sailing ships carrying Abu Tabikh and a large contingent of his tribesmen set off downriver on the Shamiyya channel of the Euphrates, heading for the town of Samawa, en route for Nasiriyya, the major concentration point for Ottoman forces. However, on arriving at Samawa, Abu Tabikh found the local military governor struggling to deal with a major logistical crisis.[12] Thousands of tribesmen had been pouring into the town to join the jihad but many of them – and the governor singled out the Bani Huchaym tribe in particular – were entirely lacking in food supplies, or even the cash to purchase food. Since the governor knew Abu Tabikh to be not only a wealthy individual but also a sayyid, he appealed to him to provide the resources to feed this growing army of would-be mujahidin, to which Abu Tabikh readily agreed.

Landowning sada like Muhsin Abu Tabikh were by no means the only wealthy Arab notables who committed their own resources to the struggle against the British invasion. In Baghdad Haji Daud al-Timman, an eighty-one-year-old Shi'i cereals merchant, spent much of his remaining capital to outfit and equip a band of volunteers to fight alongside the regular Ottoman troops. In spite of his age, he accompanied his mujahidin as they headed south towards the British front lines in late November 1914.[13] In his absence, Haji Daud al-Timman left Ja'far, his thirty-three-year-old grandson, to manage the family business as his own son had long since deserted his family and fled to Persia. On 7 December Haji Daud was captured in a skirmish with British troops near Qurna. Having learned that his grandfather had been taken prisoner to Basra, Ja'far wrote to the British authorities seeking permission to visit him on grounds of his age, but his request was refused and the subsequent death of his grandfather in captivity in 1917 would leave Ja'far deeply embittered.[14] Three years later it would be Ja'far Abu al-Timman who would come to play a leading role in Baghdad's emerging campaign for full national independence.

Whereas the jihad was generally well supported among the sheikhs and urban notables of Iraq, the same could not be said of all the neighbouring Muslim territories. In the Arabian peninsula and the Arab lands on the Persian side of the Gulf, the call to jihad produced great uncertainty as to where their best interests lay. For example, on 19 November Sheikh Khaz'al of Muhammara, ruler of much of Persian Arabistan, received the following telegram from the aged Grand Mujtahid, Muhammad Kadhim Yazdi, the most senior Shi'i cleric of Iraq, urging him to join the jihad.

To his honour Sheikh Khaz'al Khan, from Najaf

Salaams to the Exalted Sirdar of the Esteemed Sultanate, Sheikh Khaz'al, may His Majesty remain in perpetuity.

In the Name of God, the Compassionate, the Merciful.

It is well known that one of the most important duties towards the domain of Islam is the defence, at all costs, of the Muslims' sea ports against attack by the Infidels, and since yours is one of the most important of those ports hence it is your duty to protect that port to the utmost that you are able. Likewise you have a duty to lead the local tribes in that region and it is required of you to inform them that it is forbidden for any Muslim to assist the Infidels and that their support must be for the Muslim war effort. We trust in your zeal and sense of honour to make every effort to repel the Infidels: and if God so wills it, may he support you in vanquishing his enemies.

Muhammad Kadhim al-Tabataba'i al-Yazdi

1 Muharram 1333 h.

(19 November 1914)[15]

But Sheikh Khaz'al, now drawing considerable revenues from his lease of Abadan to the Anglo-Persian Oil Company, ignored the Grand Mujtahid's appeal and by now, had thrown his full support behind the British invaders.

Meanwhile, in the Hejaz, hundred of miles away on the western flank of the Arabian peninsula, another Arab potentate, who had already decided against joining the jihad, was contemplating active support for the British. Before the outbreak of war between Britain and the Ottoman Empire, the deeply conservative Emir Husayn ibn 'Ali al-Hashimi, the Sharif of Mecca, had made it known to the British, via a meeting between his second son, the thirty-two-year-old Emir 'Abdallah and Kitchener's oriental secretary, Ronald Storrs, that he was fearful that the CUP government in Istanbul was planning to replace him by a candidate more favourable to their somewhat more progressive social and economic policies, and that under certain circumstances he might rebel against his Turkish overlords.[16] So on 24 September 1914, Kitchener telegrammed Cairo with instructions that a secret letter should be sent to the Emir 'Abdallah to ascertain whether, in the event of the Turks entering the war on Germany's side, 'he, his father and Arabs of the Hejaz would be with us or against us'. Moreover, he closed his message to Mecca with these crucial words: 'It may be that an Arab of true race will assume the Caliphate at Mecca or Medina and so good may come with the help of God out of all the evil that is now occurring.'

Whatever Kitchener meant by his curious reference to the caliphate – and it seems that he probably thought of the caliph only as some kind of Islamic pope – to Sharif Husayn it meant only one thing: that, should he join them, the British were willing to make him the sole ruler of a vast Arab empire whose boundaries would broadly coincide with the historic territories of the medieval caliphs, stretching from Palestine and Lebanon, through Syria and Iraq to the border with Persia and as far south as the Yemen.[17] Needless to say, this was not at all what Kitchener and Sykes had contemplated when they mused over the possibility of a creating a loose collection of pliant 'friendly native states' under the protection of the British Empire. But from this point on, Britain was drawn into an increasingly labyrinthine exchange of communications with Husayn which slowly but surely committed it to accepting a much greater degree of 'Arab independence' in the Middle East than had ever been contemplated by either Kitchener or Sykes.

So, in Mecca al-Mukarrama, the revered city of the Ka'aba, the sixty-year-old diminutive white-bearded Sharif Husayn must have read the words of Kitchener's message with growing pleasure. In his small plain white turban and black outer robe, he retired to his private chamber where he could make himself comfortable on his couch and study the communication in more detail.

Small white turban and black robe – it hadn't always been like that. This modest attire of the Sharif had been an innovation of one of Husayn's predecessors, his uncle Sharif 'Awn al-Rafiq, at a time when the old uncontaminated oriental life was beginning to be replaced and the bravura of the Sharif's court reduced in tone. Husayn could still remember those earlier days. When he was only three years old, already proud in the knowledge that he was a sharif – the Sunni equivalent of a sayyid – he had travelled from Istanbul to Mecca to witness the investiture of his grandfather Muhammad ibn 'Awn. Then, the Sharif had been dressed in a scarlet and gold gown with huge hand-concealing wide sleeves and a gigantic turban. Ostrich-feathered fans, armoured black slaves, swordsmen and trumpeters paraded to announce the Sharif's rising for the dawn prayer. A phalanx of pikemen before him, blind reciters of the Qur'an intoning around him, the Sharif paraded before his people throwing largesse as he rode by, followed by his fearsome black-faced executioners.[18] Now the age-old panoply had gone – for good, Husayn had no doubt; but today not only the panoply but the wealth, power and prestige of the Sharifate were under threat.

Husayn's appointment as sharif by Sultan Abdul Hamid in November 1908 had occurred in the very midst of the fractious political manoeuvring of the Young Turk revolution. The military officers who had led that revolution had shied away from deposing the old sultan while he, in turn, had originally feigned acceptance of the return of a liberal constitution, parliament and a free press. A failed counter-revolution in April 1909 saw Abdul Hamid sent into exile and replaced by his more pliable younger brother, Mehmet, but in the intervening period, Abdul Hamid had been able to continue exercising many of his traditional powers of patronage. Among these was his right to appoint the Sharif of Mecca, and when the existing incumbent had been chased out by the local CUP and Abdul Hamid's first choice of replacement unexpectedly died, the sultan chose Husayn. In doing so he ensured that the Sharifate rested in the hands of someone he knew to be a social and religious conservative like himself.

Over the next six years, Sharif Husayn grew increasingly hostile to the government in Istanbul. All his instincts were contrary to the innovative spirit of the movement which now held power there and he suspected that they intended to abolish shari'a law and the powers of the Sharif's courts. Husayn also feared for his wealth. The income of his stony, unproductive fiefdom depended crucially on the subsidies which, from time immemorial, had flowed from Istanbul – subsidies which reflected the honour and prestige of the Sharif's office and the recognition throughout Sunni Islam that the ashraf (plural of sharif) were the nearest thing to an aristocracy of the blood which existed in their theoretically egalitarian Sunni Muslim world. Yet the signs were growing unmistakably that the CUP, with their reforms and railways, were seeking to undermine his power and privilege, might reduce his subsidies and even replace him by a rival candidate from the ashraf, something that had happened on numerous occasions in the past. So now he was seriously considering rebellion.

But Husayn was an extremely cautious player of power politics and he pondered long over the appropriate reply to Kitchener. Eighteen years at the court of Sultan Abdul Hamid – eighteen years in a condition of comfortable but unmistakably compulsory residence, verging on imprisonment – had taught him some valuable lessons in politics and diplomacy. He had to judiciously balance his grievances against the government with his fears that rebellion against it might be seen by the Muslim world as a rebellion against Islam. Successfully appropriating the caliphate would do much to allay that criticism, but how certain was he of success? If the English really did help him – with guns and gold – that would be a different matter, but the *Ingliz* were cunning and duplicitous.

So, when war commenced between Britain and the Ottoman Empire, Husayn equivocated. He conferred with his four sons. 'Abdallah was the most enthusiastic for rebellion; Faysal, his third son, was reluctant to break with the Turks; 'Ali, the eldest, and Zayd, the youngest, were indifferent. So the Sharif waited, and in March 1915 he sent Faysal to Damascus to talk with a group of anti-Turkish Syrians known as Jam'iyyat 'Arabiyya al-Fatat (The Young Arab Society) who had recently approached him, and also to seek out the leaders of a secret organisation of Arab officers in the Ottoman army called al-'Ahd (The Pledge), of which he had recently learned and whose exact intentions – once they were fully clarified – might help him decide whether to respond positively to what he believed to be Kitchener's offer of a vast, independent Arab state.

IRAQ, WITHIN ITS POSTWAR MANDATE BORDERS,
AND NEIGHBOURING REGIONS OF SYRIA, TURKEY AND PERSIA

The Jihad Defeated

In Iraq, the flotilla carrying the Arab tribesmen, which had been steadily gathering strength since the call for jihad, left Samawa in late December 1914 and sailed south, into the lands of the great Muntafiq tribal confederation, eventually reaching the agreed concentration point at Nasiriyya. By now the vessels carrying the mujahidin were packed with fighters; some – the larger safinas with their lateen sails – were between fifty and eighty feet in length and could carry up to a hundred men; others – the mashufs and flat-bottomed bellums – were little more than punts which were paddled or poled along in the shallows, carrying no more than twenty; and along the right bank of the river the fleet was accompanied by a swelling army of Arab horsemen.

However, as this Arab host was about to leave Nasiriyya the governor of the region received an order from the Ottoman Sixth Army Command in Baghdad that they should await the arrival of regular troops who were marching to support them.[1] Recognising the extremity of the military situation around Basra, the High Command in Istanbul had ordered the 35th (Mosul) Division, which had previously been moved to Aleppo, to return to Iraq by forced march.[2] The army chief in Baghdad had also been replaced by Lieutenant Colonel Sulayman al-'Askari, a stout-hearted Turkish officer who had been wounded in fighting near Qurna earlier in the campaign and sent to Baghdad for medical treatment.

After a delay of forty days, some Turkish regulars arrived but to the disappointment of the Arab leaders they numbered only 1,000, albeit they were crack 'Firebrigade' troops armed with the latest German rifles.

The fleet of safinas and bellums then transported the combined force down the Euphrates until they reached the great Hammar lake. From there they crossed over the waters, arriving at a village called Nukhayla, halfway between Ghabashiyya and Shu'ayba, where, on 23 January 1915, they made camp on the banks of a great area of marshland. A few days later they were joined by Sheikh 'Ajaimi al-Sa'dun and his Muntafiq tribesmen from the lands to the north-west of Basra and 'Umran al-Haj Sa'dun, paramount sheikh of the Bani Hasan, whose men had travelled more than 200 miles from the Hilla region adjacent to the holy city of Karbela'.

At this point, the vagaries of Mesopotamian hydraulics intervened. As the mujahidin awaited further reinforcements of regular Ottoman troops, the water level in Lake Hammar rose unusually early and in February flooded south, inundating a vast area between Shu'ayba and the outskirts of Basra itself. The rising water level compelled both the Arabs and the British to virtually halt operations in the vicinity of Basra and it would be another two months before major hostilities in this area resumed.

For the British, the initial phase of the invasion had been successful in protecting the Abadan refinery. However, the problem of defending the remainder of the industry – the pipeline and oilfield on Persian territory – remained; and now unexpectedly the whole area surrounding Anglo-Persian's operations suddenly became intensely hostile. The call to jihad had also fallen on fertile ground in the Middle Tigris region, where, in January 1915, the son of the Grand Mujtahid Yazdi arrived to preach resistance.

Especially receptive were the Bani Lam, a proud and warlike confederation of tribes of great antiquity who could trace their lineage back over twelve centuries and whose lands stretched from the left bank of the Tigris to the Persian border.[3] Their leading section was the Bunayya, led by Sheikh Ghadhban, a long-standing enemy of Britain's client ruler, Sheikh Khaz'al of Muhammara. The Bani Lam were joined by the Bani Turuf of the Karkha marshes, who also had scores to settle with Sheikh Khaz'al, their nominal overlord and tax-collector. Soon, all the Arabic-speaking tribes between the great Huwayza marsh north and east of Qurna and the Persian town of Ram Hormuz in the territory of the Bakhtiaris were in arms and sending contingents to join Turkish regulars who had advanced into Persia and seized the town of Illa only thirty miles north of Ahwaz. On 5 February 1915 raiders from another hostile tribe, the Bawi, succeeded in cutting Anglo-Persian's pipeline and telephone wires above and below Ahwaz and looted the company's stores. The position of the eighteen Europeans at the oilfield became precarious and only the loyalty of the company's Arab guards prevented the pumping stations from being destroyed.

The British commander, Lieutenant General Barrett, was therefore compelled to send a 'reconnaissance in force' to Ahwaz consisting of two battalions of Indian troops supported by thirty men of the 2nd Dorsets, thirty of the 33rd Cavalry and two 10-pounder mountain guns. The column of about 1,000 men reached Ahwaz on 15 February 1915. Unfortunately, the small detachment which General Barrett had sent to Ahwaz was ill prepared for the kind of resistance which had been fanned to an intense heat by the call to jihad. On 2 March, in some low hills north-west of Ahwaz, the small Anglo-Indian force was badly cut up by a combined force of Turkish regulars and Arab horsemen led by Ghadhban of the Bani Lam, losing 62 killed and 127 wounded and abandoning both its mountain guns. The Arab tribesmen attacked confidently, waving their green, red and white banners, and British officers later reported how they were particularly shaken by the speed of the Arab horsemen, who easily outpaced their own troopers. Indeed, it was reported that in some cases Arabs on foot had been able to run faster than the mounted Indian cavalry and their British officers. This was amply demonstrated by the experience of an Indian cavalry officer. He was on a polo pony which had been a reserve mount for the international polo match with the USA, but he found that as he fled the field, the Arabs on foot were catching up with him; he was lucky to escape.

Others were not so fortunate. Sheikh Ghadhban had offered a reward of several gold pieces for every invader's head brought to him and those of the British and Indian wounded who fell into Arab hands were therefore killed. One such British officer, brought down by an Arab lance, lay wounded and unarmed on the ground. He was surrounded by Arabs who indicated to him that he must soon have his throat cut. The officer then motioned them to wait until he had removed his boots. Puzzled, and thinking that it was perhaps incumbent upon the British to bare their feet before making their final peace with the Almighty, they waited. Then, with unerring aim he threw his boots at the faces of his foes as they closed in to finish him off.[4]

The original motive of the British invasion had been primarily to defend the oil industry; but this situation was not to last for long. In March 1915, with Turkish reinforcements moving south towards the army's positions, the government of India decided to reinforce its troops in southern Iraq to army corps strength and accordingly to replace Lieutenant General Barrett by a more senior officer. The choice fell upon General Sir John E. Nixon, who arrived on 9 April with the following orders:

1) Retain complete control of the lower portion of Mesopotamia comprising the Basra Vilayet and including all outlets to the sea and such portions of neighbouring territories as may affect your operations.

2) Without prejudicing your main operations, endeavour to secure the safety of the oilfields, pipelines and refineries of the Anglo-Persian Oil Company.

3) Submit plans for the effective occupation of Basra Wilaya and a subsequent advance on Baghdad.[5]

So although some part of the original objectives of the invasion remained (protecting the oil facilities), there were now clear indications that a more ambitious campaign was contemplated – today we would call it 'mission creep'. Occupying the whole of the Basra vilayet would mean advancing further up the Tigris, and although only a 'plan' for an advance to Baghdad was requested, the general impression given by High Command was that orders for such an advance would not be long in following. Indeed, both General Nixon and Sir Percy Cox openly advocated such an attack.

Cox had been urging an advance as far as Baghdad since the initial invasion. On 23 November 1914, the day after the capture of Basra, he had privately telegraphed the Viceroy of India, Lord Hardinge, that he did not see how 'we can well avoid taking over Baghdad'. His telegram was prompted – as he later admitted – by 'urgent representations from the Heads of the British Mercantile community'.[6] One 'Head' appears to have been particularly vociferous in this respect. A month later, the redoubtable Lord Inchcape, someone with substantial commercial interests in the Gulf ranging from shipping to oil, wrote to Sir Edward Grey, the foreign secretary, urging an advance on Baghdad as soon as practicable, and went on to say:

> Now is our chance to get hold of the Baghdad-Basra section of the Baghdad railway, to permanently secure our position in the Persian Gulf, that highway to India ... British and Indian trades are greatly interested in Mesopotamia and there are enormous developments possible there if the country is properly and honestly administered.[7]

However, in the meantime, more urgent considerations engaged the new British commander-in-chief. In spite of the fact that his wounds had not yet healed, the new Turkish commander, Lieutenant Colonel Sulayman al-'Askari, had decided to return to the front.

The British had established a forward defensive position around the town of Shu'ayba, about fourteen miles south-west of Basra on a ridge facing towards the desert, manned by five British and Indian infantry battalions, a battery of Royal Field Artillery and some Indian cavalry; but much of the area between Shu'ayba and Basra which had been inundated was still under water and reinforcements could reach the British forward position across the marshes only via a precarious raised causeway or by bellums, a few men at a time.

Realising that the British position at Shu'ayba was virtually cut off from their remaining forces around Basra, Colonel al-'Askari decided to attack and destroy it while it remained isolated. So, carried on a litter because of his wounds, the Turkish commander and his men made a forced march down the right bank of the Euphrates, eventually joining up with the army of mujahidin at Nukhayla on 10 April.[8]

The battle of Shu'ayba is probably the least-known battle in the least-known theatre of the First World War; but it was significant for two reasons: firstly, the strategic one – because if the British had lost, Basra would almost certainly have fallen, and with it their whole bridgehead in Iraq – and secondly, while it is customary in the few military accounts of the battle to refer to the enemy as 'Turks', in fact the majority of combatants on the Ottoman side at Shu'ayba, probably around 17,000, were irregular Arab tribesmen, while the regular Ottoman troops, of whom only half were Anatolian Turks, numbered between 6,000 and 7,000.[9] The mujahidin from the middle and southern Euphrates, who had flocked to the Ottoman colours earlier in the year and were now brimming with confidence and martial fervour, were at last about to confront the invading infidels.

Probing attacks by Turkish and Arab troops began on 11 April and were held off without great difficulty until nightfall, but it was reported to Major General Charles Mellis, the most senior British officer at the front, that the Ottoman troops around Shu'ayba were increasing by the hour and that a major offensive was threatened. The following morning, Mellis, who until then had been stuck on the eastern side of the flooded area, was able to cross over to Shu'ayba with his HQ and a battalion of his 30th Infantry Brigade in a fleet of bellums, followed by the remainder of the brigade and a battery of mountain guns.

Many years later, in his memoirs, Sayyid Muhsin Abu Tabikh, a commander of the mid-Euphrates tribesmen and one of the leaders of the great anti-British uprising of 1920, gave the following account of the Ottoman débâcle at Shu'ayba. Having explained that their regular troops were deployed in the centre, he went on to describe the tribal deployment and the ensuing battle.

Our right flank was composed of tribesmen from the Basra region together with a section of tribes from the Muntafiq, at the head of which was 'Ajaimi Sa'dun Pasha. The left flank was made up of the remainder of the Muntafiq tribesmen and tribes from the mid-Euphrates and other regions, under the command of 'Abdallah Sa'dun Bey. At dawn on the 12 April, Sulayman al-'Askari ordered an all-out attack which lasted until the forenoon. The English then directed their artillery fire at our right wing and launched a counter-attack. They inflicted heavy losses upon it and forced it back to the point where its advance had begun. Then they focussed their attack upon our left flank and I myself was wounded in the forehead by a shrapnel splinter. All this occurred during the first hour of the battle and I left the battlefield as we were all forced to retreat, leaving behind the dead and all the wounded who could not be moved, including one of my cousins, Sayyid Radi Abu Tabikh ... With the retreat of the mujahidin, our left wing scattered and it played no further part in the battle leaving the English to concentrate their fire upon the Ottoman regular troops who were engaged with heavy artillery and some lighter armed troops. The English charged towards the Ottoman troops in a counter-attack with all their men, compelling them to retreat, inflicting heavy losses upon them ... And when news of the rout of the Ottoman troops reached the Commander in Chief, Sulayman 'Askari Bey, whose HQ was situated in the Barjishiya woods together with his general staff, he chose death rather than life.[10]

Gathering the remainder of his officers around him, the despairing Lieutenant Colonel al-'Askari drew his pistol and blew his brains out, after which the remains of the Ottoman army and tribal mujahidin streamed back to Nasiriyya in complete disorder, some of the Arabs even pillaging the baggage and rifles of the fleeing Turkish regulars.

Much has been made of the fact that after their initial encounter with the British, the tribal mujahidin played no further part in the battle of Shu'ayba.[11] Later, they were even accused of treachery by the Turks. But it is not difficult to understand their reluctance to re-engage in the fighting after their first, doomed assault. The Ottoman losses at Shu'ayba amounted to around 3,000 dead and wounded,[12] but probably the majority of these were Arab tribesmen, cut down within the first hour of fighting in their near-suicidal frontal assault.[13] The tribesmen had absolutely no experience of modern warfare – only sporadic tribal raiding in which casualties were typically very low. At best, the mujahidin would have been armed with elderly Martini-Henry rifles and in all probability many carried nothing more than a lance or spear. They stood little chance against a modern army with modern weapons and their reluctance to renew their attack is understandable.

Pacifying Arabistan

If General Nixon was going to protect not only the 138-mile pipeline to Abadan but the Persian oilfield itself, he was also going to have to send more troops up the Karun river into south-west Persia. This was fast becoming a matter of some urgency. Telegrams from the India Office had informed Nixon that the Admiralty were getting worried. Rapid repair of the pipeline was essential. 'The oil question is becoming serious,' they complained.[1]

After the victory at Shu'ayba, General Nixon was able to detach a division-sized force under the command of Major General George Gorringe to cross into Persian Arabistan to avenge the defeat of their earlier incursion, conduct a large-scale pacification campaign against the tribes and ensure the permanent safety of Britain's Persian oilfield. Lieutenant Wilson was attached to the force as a political officer (PO).

Let us picture Lieutenant Wilson as he presents himself for duty. He is now thirty-one years old, of above average height, broad shouldered and still sunburned even after some weeks in cloudy England. His moustache is thick but neatly trimmed, his eyes dark and commanding; above them, beetling black eyebrows and close-cropped hair. He wears the old-fashioned Indian Army tunic with a high collar buttoned to the neck, eschewing the new-fangled collar and tie which even his superior, Sir Percy Cox, has now adopted. Equally and characteristically conservative is his sidearm belt with two parallel shoulder straps instead of the now more customary Sam Browne, and holstered on his left hip is his service revolver. Round the brim of his

Captain Arnold Wilson in the uniform of a Political
Officer of the Imperial Indian Army, 1916

cap is a white band and on his collar the two white chevrons indicating unmistakably that he is an officer of the Indian Political Service.

Over the past few years Wilson's social and political views have become more aligned with his sartorial conservatism. As he has matured in age, his opinions have narrowed and hardened. In a letter to his parents he states, 'The more I see of eastern races and western races in the East the more I feel that racial differences are deep and ineradicable ... Education makes the points of difference sharper and harder to conceal.'[2] He disagrees profoundly with the views of those he refers to as 'Liberals', like the orientalist Professor E. G. Browne, who believe that democratic constitutional self-government should be the objective of British policy in the East. Indeed, he is equally antipathetic to the progress of democracy and social justice in Britain, attacking the extension of the suffrage to women, co-education, redistributive taxation, state old age pensions and trade unions. 'Radicalism', he pronounces, 'is the creed of the half-educated,' adding rather ominously, 'We want Order and Law, not Law and Order.' And now he is about to have his first experience of large-scale military action.

Major General Gorringe had made sure that his force was certainly not going to suffer the indignity that had befallen the earlier column that had entered Persian Arabistan, and his force therefore consisted of six squadrons of cavalry, seventeen guns, six infantry battalions and a bridging train. Its supplies were carried by some 900 mules supplied by the Anglo-Persian Oil Company. 'A sledgehammer to crack a nut,' thought Wilson.

By chance, Wilson was familiar with the marshy territory between the Karun and Karkha rivers into which the troops were now advancing. He had reconnoitred the area in 1911 and early 1914 when mapping the border for the commission which was attempting to delineate the boundary between Ottoman Iraq and Persia. That task had become essential to the interests of Anglo-Persian, whose vast concession covered territory straddling the previously undefined boundary. Only when the frontier had been finally settled and agreed between the Ottoman and Persian governments would it be possible for Anglo-Persian to sign contracts with the relevant authorities and begin further oil-exploration operations in the disputed region. Just before the outbreak of hostilities, the Turks had given assurances that any oil discoveries 'moving' from Persian territory to Ottoman Iraq as result of the boundary changes would continue to belong to the Anglo-Persian Oil Company.

On that earlier journey in Persian Arabistan, in January 1914, Wilson and the other members of the Border Commission had travelled along the edge of the vast Karkha marshes, passing through villages precariously protected from inundation by small mud ledges, barely sufficient to keep out the waters fed by the melting snows of Luristan's distant mountains. For parts of the journey they travelled in a mashuf, the typical light marsh boat of the region with a long projecting prow, cautiously paddling their way between dense thickets of mardi reeds as tall as a house. Eventually they had arrived at Khafajiyya, the principal village of the Bani Turuf.

On arrival at Khafajiyya's collection of reed-built houses they were warmly received. The two leading sheikhs of the Bani Turuf, Sheikh 'Asi and Sheikh 'Aufi, offered coffee to Wilson and his companions, served to them by 'Asi's qahwaji, his coffee-maker and chief attendant, and they provided Wilson with useful information in furtherance of his map work. Later, after they had left Khafajiyya and journeyed to Bisaitin, another village of the Marsh Arabs, they encountered a party of 150 Bani Turuf who had apparently been sent out to protect them from Bani Lam raiders active in the area. The Bani Turuf tribesmen had made a fine display, carrying rifles, swords and fishing tridents as weapons, and they held aloft their tribal standards, one of which was a fine piece of salmon-pink satin eight feet square with green edges, carrying in the centre the crescent of Islam and a single star. 'Fine-looking men,' Wilson thought.

But now they were the enemy. The Bani Turuf had fallen under the spell of jihad and they would have to be punished. On the evening of 13 May 1915, the Anglo-Indian punitive column advanced towards Khafajiyya on both sides of the Karkha river with Wilson, mounted on an Arab mare, acting as guide. The assault on the village commenced with the artillery firing incendiary shells into the village, setting its reed huts alight and burning alive a number of horses and water buffalo abandoned by their owners. In spite of the overwhelming force brought against them the Bani Turuf put up a strong resistance, replying to the artillery and machine-gun fire of the British and Indian troops with a fierce fusillade from their rusty Martini-Henry rifles.

The bombardment of Khafajiyya went on for three days. At the end 150 Arabs lay dead while most of the women and children had fled into the marshes. Only a few tribesmen remained holding out in the village's small mud-brick fort. Wilson got close to the fort and tried to get its defenders to surrender but with no success. Finally, a company of the 76th Punjabis stormed it, bayoneting most of its dwindling band of survivors, Eleven prisoners were taken: short ragged men with long plaited hair, they sat on the ground surrounded by the Punjabis whose bayonets still dripped with the blood of their enemy. Wilson recognised one of them: it was Sheikh 'Asi's qahwaji. The coffee-maker looked up at Wilson.

> O Wilson, why have you brought this on us? It is you who have led these men here. Was it for this that you ate our bread and wandered in our marshes and made maps? Treachery, treachery was in your heart and lies on your lips, and now the blood of our brothers is on your head. May God pardon you![3]

Reflecting on this episode many years later, Wilson admitted that 'it was not without inward misery that I saw the blazing village and the dead bodies of the cheerful scoundrels whom I had known in earlier years ... and I was witnessing the slaughter of men whom I had come to regard as friends.'[4] Wilson was not a heartless or brutal man: indeed, his obsession with 'order' partly reflected his belief that it was the 'poor and humble' who suffered most from the kind of disorder he had witnessed during the periods of civil war and economic chaos in Persia. He comforted himself with the knowledge that once hostilities in Iraq had ended, men like himself, the 'politicals' in the service of the government of India, would have an opportunity to demonstrate to such 'cheerful scoundrels' that while 'order' and obedience to the representatives of the British Empire would certainly be required of them, in return they would receive security, progress and prosperity.

In the meantime, the lesson taught to the erring Bani Turuf was having a salutary effect not only upon the remaining warlike tribes of Persian Arabistan but also on the potentially hostile Marsh Arabs on the Iraqi side of the border. The rice-growing Al Bu Muhammad tribe on the Tigris below 'Amara could hear the fearsome artillery barrages which Gorringe's force laid down upon Khafajiyya and soon learned from fleeing Bani Turuf of the overwhelming force which the British were now prepared to unleash on any who opposed them.

After the successful punitive expedition into Persian Arabistan, Major General Gorringe learned that the town of 'Amara on the Tigris had been captured on 2 June by an amphibious force under General Townshend and he was ordered to dispatch three battalions, a cavalry regiment and a field battery there, sending the remainder of his force back to Ahwaz to protect the oilfield. Wilson accompanied the patrol heading for 'Amara, acting as a guide for the advancing column stretching out several miles, marching along the northern edge of one of the world's most extensive marshes, through territory invested by potentially hostile Arab tribes. Wilson visited their camps accompanied by a handful of Indian troopers, often at great personal risk, taking coffee with their sheikhs, giving assurances and warnings. After reaching 'Amara on 14 June, Wilson was ordered to return to Basra, where for a few days he was plunged back into the routine of office work; but on 23 June Gorringe asked him to rejoin his staff and he set off up the Tigris by launch.

Gorringe had now been ordered to swing his division to the west to capture Nasiriyya on the Euphrates, crossing Lake Hammar accompanied by a formidable flotilla of gunboats and armoured launches, negotiating its way through treacherous marshes and unmapped canals. Once again, Wilson scouted for the expedition, often up to his neck in muddy water, shot at by Arab and Turkish snipers, searching out weak points in the enemy lines and suitable routes for the passage of Gorringe's amphibious column. After eventually reaching the outskirts of Nasiriyya with a force depleted by heatstroke and disease, a fierce and bloody action took place on 22 June 1915 in which Gorringe's force of 4,600 infantry and twenty-six naval and field guns completely overwhelmed a Turkish force of almost equal size supported by a host of Arab auxiliaries. Wilson was in the thick of the fighting in spite of the fact that he was now suffering from a raging fever. The town was entered on the 25th and Wilson was immediately appointed assistant to its military governor. Sometime later Gorringe's chief of staff told him, 'You are damned lucky to have survived; a good many of us were expecting each evening to be your last.' Wilson also learned that he had been recommended for the DSO or MC, either of them unusual for a PO. In the event he received the DSO.

While the capture of Nasiriyya and the virtual elimination of Turkish and Arab forces in the vilayet of Basra signified a major success for the Anglo-Indian invasion force, the operations of the remainder of Gorringe's forces in Persian Arabistan also ensured the success of what had been the primary objective of the invasion. By June 1915, the pipeline from Ahwaz to Abadan was fully repaired. Never again would Anglo-Persian's oil production operations be threatened by hostile forces during the war. In spite of the disruption caused by Arab raiders in early 1915, output rapidly recovered during the remainder of that year resulting in a total annual production of 3.8 million barrels – around 10,000 barrels per day, a 25 per cent increase over the previous year. By 1916, this had increased to nearly 13,000 barrels and by 1918 – the end of hostilities on the Western Front – Anglo-Persian's refinery at Abadan was processing nearly 25,000 barrels per day.[5] And although the company's operations only provided around a fifth of the Royal Navy's requirements, as the French prime minister Clemenceau put it to President Woodrow Wilson, 'Every drop of oil secured to us saves a drop of human blood.'[6]

Imperial Objectives in the East

On Monday 12 April 1915, Sir Mark Sykes took his usual early morning stroll from his four-storey town house in Buckingham Gate to Westminster Cathedral, where he heard Mass, and then returned home for breakfast. No. 9 Buckingham Gate had not been his first choice as a London base for his parliamentary work. Having inherited his father's huge estate in 1913, valued conservatively at £290,000, he had originally considered renting a furnished house in Mayfair at £1,200 per year; but his wife Edith had put her foot down at this extravagance and, in the end, Sykes had to agree that the Buckingham Gate house at £500 per year was not only much more economical but was ideally placed for his work as an MP. And since his recent appointment by Kitchener to the War Office, Buckingham Gate was eminently suitable – a short walk through St James's Park took him to Whitehall and Horse Guards Parade. But on this particular day he was heading for the Foreign Office, and at 11.00 a.m. Sykes strode purposefully into the designated committee room carrying a large briefcase packed with notebooks, diaries, maps, gazetteers, travel brochures and photographs and settled into one of the comfortable chairs surrounding the huge table in the centre of the room.

The committee to which Kitchener had dispatched Sykes as his personal representative had been established by the prime minister, Herbert Asquith, charged with advising the cabinet on 'British Desiderata in Turkey-in-Asia': in effect, what to do with the vast non-European territories of the Ottoman Empire once it had been defeated;

and at that particular moment, few Englishmen had any doubts about the rapid defeat of 'the Turk'.

Indeed, 'the Turk' already seemed to be on the brink of defeat. In December 1914 an Ottoman army of 90,000 had advanced into the Caucasus, initially causing widespread panic among its Russian defenders. In early January 1915, in a raging blizzard and with temperatures dropping to minus 30°F, they had thrown themselves against the Russian army defending the town of Sarikamish. But the plan had not taken account of the atrocious weather conditions and in an attempt to outflank the Russians, Enver Pasha's troops had floundered in the snowdrifts and over 30,000 men froze to death. Most of the survivors were forced to surrender and only 12,000 of the initial attacking force escaped the catastrophe.

Also in January 1915, Djemal Pasha; commanding the Ottoman Fourth Army based at Damascus, had sent 20,000 men of the VIII Corps, including the Arab 25th Division, to attack British forces defending Egypt's eastern frontier. After a ten-night march across the Sinai peninsula, they had mounted attacks against British posts at Qantara in the north and Kubri, seven miles north of Suez, in the south. According to Djemal Pasha, 'The Arab fighters who constituted the bulk of the 25th … performed splendidly.'[1]

Djemal Pasha had hoped that the success of an Ottoman force would trigger an Egyptian Muslim uprising. On 3 February his troops mounted a major attack at Tussum at the southern end of Lake Timsah, six miles south-east of Ismailia. But it was another disaster; they simply did not have sufficient strength to make a breakthrough. The few Ottoman troops who succeeded in crossing the Suez Canal were all killed or captured and Djemal Pasha was forced to order a retreat to Beersheba, having lost about 1,400 men.

Meanwhile, the government of India had successfully established a bridgehead in Southern Iraq, captured Basra and Qurna and were currently taking steps to defend the Anglo-Persian Oil Company's facilities in south-west Persia. Reinforcements were arriving daily from India and it could only be a matter of time before an advance further up the Tigris commenced.

True, the recent naval assault on the Dardanelles had been disappointing. Between 19 February and 13 March Vice-Admiral Sackville Carden had attacked the forts at the mouth of the Dardanelles and attempted to sweep the mines which the Turks had laid further up the straits. But heavy gunfire from the Turkish forts, gun emplacements and 6-inch mobile howitzers on the northern, peninsular side of the channel had made it impossible for his minesweepers to carry out their task. Overwhelmed by the difficulties of trying to force a way through, Admiral Carden had a nervous breakdown and was replaced by his second in command, de Roebeck. On 18 March Admiral de Roebeck, under strong pressure from Winston Churchill to demonstrate progress, began a major naval advance into the straits. Unfortunately, a number of capital ships, *Irresistible*, *Inflexible* and *Ocean*, and the French battleships *Bouvet* and *Gaulois* were sunk by mines or seriously damaged by coastal shellfire and de Roebeck was obliged to call off a plan to force his way through to Istanbul. However, a formidable land army under General Sir Ian Hamilton was now being assembled at Mudros on the Aegean island of Lemnos and there was a strong expectation that within a few days a major amphibious assault on the Gallipoli peninsula would be mounted. Then the combined naval and land forces would sweep through to the Ottoman capital.

The committee to which Sykes had been summoned was to be chaired by Sir Maurice De Bunsen, formerly British ambassador in Vienna, who had brought together representatives of all the government departments whose views would have to be taken into account in putting together the committee's final report: the War Office, the Admiralty, the India Office, the Board of Trade and of course, the Foreign Office itself. As Sykes glanced around the table he would have seen a group of elderly men – in their sixties or older – with only two exceptions. There was George Clerk of the Foreign Office, whom Sykes had met once or twice and who was in his mid-thirties, and sitting to the left of the chairman was a very short bald man whom Sir Maurice introduced as 'Lieutenant Colonel Maurice Hankey, secretary of the Committee of Imperial Defence'. As yet Sykes knew him only by reputation.

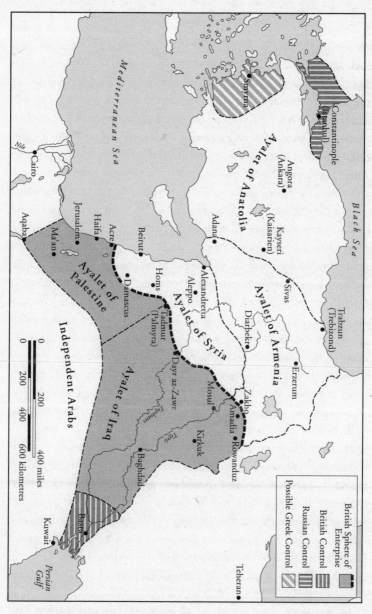

SYKES'S 1915 PROPOSED SCHEME FOR THE 'DECENTRALISATION'
OF THE OTTOMAN EMPIRE'S EASTERN POSSESSIONS

Calling the meeting to order, Sir Maurice reminded the assembled officials of their remit. The cabinet had already agreed to the tsar's demand for Istanbul and the Turkish Straits together with the islands of Imbros and Tenedos in the northern Aegean, and in return the tsar's government had assured Britain that it would respect the 'special interests' of Britain and France in Asiatic Turkey. Sir Maurice made it clear from the start that the 'special interests' they were being asked to define were 'the primary economic and commercial interests of Great Britain and the policy it would be desirable for H.M. Government to adopt to secure those ends'.[2] Doubtless Britain also had a 'civilising mission' east of the Dardanelles and eventually the 'white man's burden' would have to be taken up; but for the moment it was 'economic and commercial interests' which were the overriding focus of the committee's deliberations. Accordingly, the first civil servant called upon by Sir Maurice to address the committee was Sir Hubert Llewellyn Smith, permanent secretary of the Board of Trade.

Sir Llewellyn stated that HM Government had three principal economic and commercial objectives in the Asiatic territories of the Ottoman Empire: firstly, obtaining a free and open market for British manufactures; secondly, the acquisition of secure sources of food supplies and raw materials; and thirdly, to create a field for the employment of British capital and an outlet for the surplus population of Britain's Indian Empire. The first of these desiderata implied ensuring that neither the Turks nor Britain's allies should, in occupation of portions of the Ottoman Empire which they might retain or acquire, be allowed to impose any tariff barriers which would obstruct British trade. The second objective should be based on the recognition that Iraq was of particular interest to Britain as it could be an important source of foodstuffs when major irrigation works were carried out and of oil resources when they were developed. Both the oil and irrigation possibilities fell mainly within the Baghdad vilayet, Llewellyn Smith stated, and so 'they must clearly be included within a British controlled area'.[3] However, although he believed that British interests in Upper Iraq were not as great as in Baghdad and Basra, Llewellyn Smith added that 'an important oil region lies in the Mosul Vilayet ... and it therefore seems desirable that Mosul too should fall within the British sphere of influence.'

The following day the committee reconvened and under the direction of its chairman moved on to discuss the strategic implications of the economic interests which had formed the principal topic of the previous day's deliberations. De Bunsen opened the session by stating that, in his view, if Basra was going to be incorporated into the British possessions – and the government of India now seemed determined that this should be so – then it would also be necessary to control the Baghdad vilayet. Baghdad must not fall into the hands of any other power or its possession by a potential enemy would threaten Britain's position at Basra and the head of the Gulf. To this, the representative of the India Office, Sir T. W. Holderness, agreed, adding that British control up to a line north of Baghdad, from Hit on the Euphrates to Tikrit on the Tigris, should be sufficient and would almost certainly satisfy the government of India.

In fact, the views of the government of India itself were already set out in two telegrams from the viceroy to the secretary of state for India, received in February and March and now placed before the Committee.[4] In the first, Lord Hardinge had asked,

> How far the safety of the oilfields in the upper valley of the Karun river could be permanently secured if the Vilayet of Baghdad were to remain under foreign and possibly hostile control?[5]

adding,

> It is assumed that the administration of the Vilayet, when it comes definitely under British rule, will be carried out by the government of India.

However, in a further telegram in March, the viceroy somewhat modified his remarks about the future administration of Baghdad, stating,

> Our interests are at Abadan and in Karun Valley by (*sic*) the oil works

... it is essential that for this and other reasons we should remain in permanent occupation of Basra Vilayet and that on political, economic and religious grounds, the Baghdad Vilayet should also be ceded by Turkey and a native administration under our protection and control established there.[6]

But Llewellyn Smith thought control of Basra and Baghdad alone was insufficient. If Britain was going to become involved in negotiations with the French on the future of 'Turkey-in-Asia', as was probably inevitable, it would be necessary to ask for something more. Britain, he argued, must also have Mosul. Only by taking the line of defence up to this mountainous northern area would it be possible to construct a strategically sound defensive position in the event of future hostilities with either the remnants of Ottoman power or one of Britain's current allies. And he concluded by saying, 'May I also remind you gentlemen, that it must not be forgotten that there is a valuable oil region in the Vilayet of Mosul.'[7]

Sykes agreed. 'If the Baghdad Vilayet is to be incorporated it will be necessary as well to take the Vilayet of Mosul.' Major General C. E. Callwell of the War Office also threw his weight behind the demand for Mosul: in his opinion the 'Hit–Tikrit line would be unsuitable as a defensive position.' However, he added a further consideration. If Britain was going to control all three of the Iraqi vilayets this newly acquired addition to the empire would have to have an outlet to the Mediterranean, either at Haifa in Palestine or further north at Alexandretta.

Admiral Sir H. B. Jackson added that, whereas he had no objection to including Mosul in the list of desirable acquisitions, he felt obliged to say that from the Admiralty point of view the essential thing was to control the vilayets of Basra and Baghdad. 'Both these Vilayets are of first importance owing to the oil supplies which the Admiralty draws through those regions.'[8]

By the time the third meeting of the committee was convened on Thursday 15 April it had become clear that the observations which a number of members had already made in relation to the question of oil resources called for a more detailed exposition of the subject than any of the permanent appointees – even Sykes – could offer. Sir Maurice De Bunsen therefore opened the meeting by reminding the committee, 'It is known that there are extremely rich oil deposits in Mesopotamia and in view of our commitment as regards the Anglo-Persian Oil Company, it is important to know what steps we should take to safeguard those interests.'[9]

De Bunsen therefore informed the committee that he had invited Rear Admiral Sir Edmond Slade, reputed to be the country's leading oil expert, to address the meeting. Slade had led the Admiralty's investigating commission which spent three months in Persia between October 1913 and January 1914 studying the operations of the Anglo-Persian Oil Company and which had declared the company's concession to be potentially of great value and capable of supplying the Royal Navy's requirements for a long time. Behind his bluff, grey-bearded nautical exterior he possessed a shrewd analytical mind with a personal fascination for the facts and figures of fuel logistics and the emerging geopolitics of oil. It had been Slade who had urged the government to obtain some form of control over Anglo-Persian, paving the way for Churchill's dramatic move to partially nationalise the company.[10] Subsequently, Slade had been chosen as one of the two government-appointed directors on the board of Anglo-Persian and at the beginning of hostilities in the East it was Slade who had strongly urged the defence of the Abadan refinery and Anglo-Persian's pipelines.[11] So when the admiral took his place at the table and began his exposition the committee members would have listened to him very attentively indeed. Slade explained to the committee that there were,

large deposits of oil throughout Asiatic Turkey. A strip of oil-bearing regions is known to run from the southern extremity of Arabia along the west coast of the Persian Gulf, through the valley of the Tigris and Euphrates and so on to the northern coast of Asia Minor almost to the European end.

If the Eastern possessions of the Ottoman Empire were partitioned, Slade argued,

> it would be sufficient if we secured the Vilayet of Mosul as that district comprises some very rich oil-bearing lands, connecting with the Persian oil fields, which it is essential we should control to prevent undue competition with the Anglo-Persian Concessions.[12]

Now here was a consideration which had not, as yet, entered the minds of the committee – it was not, apparently, just a question of acquiring access to Iraqi oil in order to supplement Britain's military oil requirements currently being developed in Persia, but given the apparent abundance of oil in 'Asiatic Turkey' to which the admiral had alluded, it was also a matter of preventing any other power – or company – acquiring oil resources in Iraq, developing them, and undermining the monopoly which the partnership of state and private interests had obtained in Persia and at Abadan. Oil was going to become a major world commodity and when production of that commodity began to take on the scale that he envisaged, Slade, for one, had no intention of allowing competition from other large oil companies (and here, both he and the committee members most probably thought of Shell) to force down prices and undermine the returns on the heavy investment which not only British taxpayers but also British capitalists had made in southern Persia.

Slade concluded his presentation by urging that once the Iraqi oil-fields were acquired it would be necessary to 'connect the fields by a pipeline with the Mediterranean' and Haifa was again mentioned as a possible oil terminal. De Bunsen then expressed his satisfaction that 'Admiral Slade's views as to our requirements in regard to oil practically coincide with the views that the Committee has taken in regard to the inclusion of the Mosul Vilayet in the territory to be acquired by us.'

Although this was the first time they had met, as the deliberations of the De Bunsen Committee proceeded, Sykes and the thirty-eight-year-old secretary of the Committee for Imperial Defence, Lieutenant Colonel Hankey, became close friends. They met, they dined, they discussed. It wasn't just their similarity in ages: Hankey as well as Sykes was an 'Easterner'. It was Hankey who, on Boxing Day 1914, had issued a memorandum to the War Council proposing a major attack on

Turkey. Contrary to the views of the majority of the British general staff, Hankey argued that 'no increase in men would enable us to break the front in the West', urging that victory was only to be obtained in the Eastern theatre of operations.[13] And by now, Hankey had won the enthusiastic support of both Churchill and Kitchener: the assault on the Ottoman Empire had begun. Moreover, of all the members of the De Bunsen Committee, it was Hankey who seems to have paid closest attention to the repeated mention of oil in the Mosul vilayet. Three years later it would be Hankey who turned all his subtle intelligence and guile to the task of ensuring that Mosul and its oil remained firmly in the grasp of the British Empire when the war ended.

By the time of the fourth meeting of the committee on 17 April, the rest of its members had become duly impressed by Sykes's seemingly comprehensive knowledge of Turkey-in-Asia, its peoples, geography and resources. No doubt interspersing his detailed factual observations with amusing anecdotes based on his travels, Sykes began to introduce his own schemes for dividing up the conquered Ottoman Empire. The first of these called for the Allies to partition all but Turkish Anatolia among themselves with Russia receiving a northern, France a central and Britain a southern part of the Asian provinces. As an alternative he proposed keeping the area 'nominally independent but under effective European Control' within Allied 'zones of political and commercial interest'. Both of these schemes – 'partition' and 'zones of interest' – would involve the construction of a British-controlled railway stretching over a thousand miles from a new British Mediterranean port, probably at Haifa in Palestine, to the Euphrates. However, the Foreign Office, under Sir Edward Grey, a high temple of self-regarding moral rectitude, worried that the discussion might be developing along far too imperialistic lines. So the committee found itself unable to reach a consensus on either of Sykes's proposals.

At the next meeting, a month later, Sykes came up with yet another scheme for ensuring that Britain's 'desiderata' in Asiatic Turkey were achieved. After the Turks were defeated, their Asian territories should be 'devolved' into five historical and ethnographical ayalets: Anatolia,

Armenia, Syria, Palestine and Iraq. In theory these ayalets would remain provinces owing formal allegiance to a reformed – and much weakened – Ottoman Empire. In practice they would enjoy considerable powers of self-determination, albeit guided by foreign 'advisors'. In the event it was this scheme which the committee decided to recommend in its report published on 25 June 1915.

The report began by first considering the 'direct partition' option and, reflecting the discussion during the committee's first three meetings, it stressed that if partition were to take place, oil would be a major determining factor in deciding the territories Britain would wish to acquire. The report stated:

> Acquisition of Baghdad would guard the chain of oil wells along the Turko-Persian frontier, in the development of which the British Government has an interest. And oil makes it commercially desirable for us to carry our control on to Mosul in the vicinity of which are valuable wells, possession of which by another would be prejudicial to our own interests.[14]

The problem with outright partition, however, was that achieving it might involve prolonging the war in the East as well as changing its character: no longer would Britain be able to claim that the war was merely against the German-dominated clique in Istanbul. And there would inevitably be problems with Britain's allies as to precisely which parts of Turkey-in-Asia would be allocated to which nation. Specifying particular 'zones of interest' would be preferable to partition, but might still raise some of the same problems. In the end the committee decided to recommend Sykes's scheme of 'devolution'. Its principal advantage was its flexibility and the fact that in the longer term it could be just as advantageous to Britain as the alternatives.

According to the 'devolution' scheme, while a reformed Ottoman government, probably based in the Anatolian ayalet, would be responsible for foreign affairs, the higher courts of justice and certain types of taxation, the individual ayalets would have extensive powers devolved to them: responsibility for agriculture and irrigation, the lower courts of justice, education, roads, the command of regional militia and police and, crucially from the oil perspective, the right to issue mineral concessions. Although each ayalet would have an imperial governor general, his powers would be strongly circumscribed by the fact that each ayalet would elect its own parliament, which in turn would appoint a cabinet of 'Heads of Departments'. Moreover, provision would be made 'to enable the Heads of Departments to employ foreign advisors without reference to the Imperial Government'. This last requirement, coupled with the fact that the five ayalets specified in the scheme were virtually coextensive with those envisaged in both the 'partition' and 'zones of interest' options, meant that, depending on circumstances, the devolved ayalets could easily be transformed into either of those two alternatives. This advantage of flexibility was explicitly stated in the concluding section of the report.

> We are thus favourably placed, in the event of the complete breakdown of the scheme, for securing our political and commercial interests and indeed there seems to be no valid reason why the division of Turkey into these Ayalets need necessarily preclude an understanding among the Allies as to the areas in which each of them claims to have special interests.[15]

Indeed, as if to already anticipate this eventuality, the map attached to the report showing the geographical extension of each of the five ayalets was already marked with a red line drawn around the ayalets of Iraq and Palestine (including most of the present state of Jordan), delineating what was described as the 'British Sphere of Enterprise'.

In reality, given that the five ayalets could employ foreign advisors 'without reference to the Imperial Government', the 'British Sphere of Enterprise' might well be expected to be even larger. Britain might gain influence in *all* of the ayalets without interference from the Turks, Germans, Russians or French. In short, 'devolution' was a solution very close to the old idea of 'friendly native states' so dear to the hearts of both Sykes and Kitchener.

However, by the time the De Bunsen Committee presented its report to the prime minister listing the various alternative methods for sharing out the eastern possessions of the 'Sick Man of Europe', the Sick Man himself was unexpectedly beginning to show signs of recovering from his earlier indisposition. On one point Sykes had always been relentlessly emphatic in both his written and spoken commentaries on the Ottoman Empire. Commenting on the behaviour of Turkish troops who had been sent to fight in the Yemen before the war, he observed:

> The Turk as a soldier shows a heroism that no other race can boast: willingness to face any danger is nothing compared with that stubborn sense of duty which makes a man ready to endure eight years of misery in a climate of hell, unpaid, unclothed, ill-fed. Continually at war, with no hope of reward, no bounties, no banquets or encouragement. We who pride ourselves on our army having borne the South African campaign with endurance and fortitude must reverence and respect the Turks who bear ten thousand times more, and consider it as nothing but their ordinary duty.[16]

However, for some reason, Sykes's appreciation of the Turkish fighting man had not filtered down to Kitchener, Churchill and the British High Command currently embarking on a major escalation of their campaign in the Dardanelles: an amphibious attack on the Gallipoli peninsula. The conventional wisdom to which they subscribed was summed up by one British staff officer: 'It will be grim work to begin with, but we have good fighters ready to tackle it, and an enemy who has never shown himself as good a fighter as the white man.'[17] Not only did this expression of racial arrogance display a remarkable ignorance of Ottoman history but it also completely ignored the fact that Britain was no longer fighting an army of spear-wielding 'fuzzy-wuzzies' but a resourceful enemy equipped with all the accoutrements of modern technological warfare: breech-loading rifles, machine guns, artillery, both heavy and light, and even aircraft.

Nevertheless, on 25 April 1915, General Sir Ian Hamilton launched a major amphibious assault on the Gallipoli peninsula. Under his command he had 74,800 men in five divisions. The plan was to occupy the southern part of the narrow peninsula and then sweep across to the

Dardanelles taking the Turkish forts and gun emplacements in the rear. Eliminating the forts would allow Admiral de Roebeck's minesweepers to clear the way for the Fleet unimpeded by fire from the shore batteries and then the Fleet would be able to pass through the Dardanelles into the Sea of Marmara, from where it would sail on to bombard and capture Istanbul.

The plan was deeply flawed at all levels. There was no unified command: the army and navy operated separately. The army commander, General Ian Hamilton, personally a brave and experienced soldier, was unable or unwilling to stamp his own authority on his subordinates, leaving them to make tactical decisions which he often knew were mistaken; in fact some of the field officers under his command were clearly incompetent while those lower down the chain of command frequently received orders which were unclear or self-contradictory. Supplies of every kind were inadequate and in particular there was a serious weakness in field artillery. There was virtually no intelligence or accurate maps to clarify the sort of terrain over which the army would have to fight and which turned out to be a nightmare patchwork of steep escarpments, winding gullies and ravines, small scrub-covered plateaus and sharp-edged ridges. Above all, there was no advantage of surprise. The Turks had been forewarned by the original naval attack and had been able to assemble 80,000 men spread around the peninsula. Given that the standard military maxim of the day was that an amphibious force attacking an enemy entrenched on their own shoreline needed at least a superiority in numbers of 4 to 1 to have any hope of success, the fact that the British troops and Ottoman forces were approximately equal in numbers made the enterprise virtually doomed from the start.

Perhaps, if the first assault had been carried out with more vigour at those landing points where Ottoman resistance was relatively light, it might have been possible to achieve the initial objectives of the attack – the high ground overlooking the Dardanelles – before the Turks had a chance to regroup and concentrate their scattered forces; but this didn't happen. Instead, the inexperience and disorganisation of many of the units, once they had landed, allowed the Turks time to bring up reserves and mount ferocious counter-attacks which penned the invaders into two small enclaves, one at Cape Helles and the other at Ari Burnu, where Mustafa Kemal, commander of the Ottoman 19th Division, had hurled his men, two-thirds of them – the 72nd and 77th Regiments – Arab troops from Syria, against the invaders, very nearly throwing them back into the sea.[18]

As a result of the bravery of both Turkish and Arab Ottoman troops and their own tactical failures, the British were forced to dig in and establish defensible perimeters at the beachheads. Thereafter, the campaign inevitably became just as bogged down and attritional as the war on the Western Front.

The Menace of Jihad and How to Deal with It

While the carnage at Gallipoli mounted day by day, Sykes was dispatched by the War Office to visit British commanders, diplomats and imperial officials throughout the eastern theatre of war to acquaint them with the general outline of the De Bunsen Committee's report and obtain their reaction to its conclusions – a mission which proved largely unrewarding. Equally unsuccessful was the continuation of his mission to India where the viceroy, Lord Hardinge, was not impressed by the committee's 'devolutionary' proposal for Asiatic Turkey and opined that 'Sykes did not seem to be able to grasp the fact that there are parts of Turkey unfit for representative institutions.'[1]

During his long return sea journey from India Sykes turned his ever-wandering attention to Iraq, concerning which he composed a lengthy memorandum on the political and military situation. However, in the second part of that memorandum entitled 'Indian Muslims and the War', his thoughts returned to the subject which had long been the main preoccupation of both himself and his chief, Kitchener – the ever-present danger of jihad. It was fear of militant Islam which had underpinned his belief that Britain should cultivate those elements of the religion he construed as 'moderate' and susceptible of being won over to the Allied side; and now, having witnessed signs of anti-British nationalism among the Muslims of India during his recent visit, he merged his visceral dislike of 'westernised orientals' with a conceptualisation of the two main tendencies which he believed he had detected in contemporary Islam.

On the one hand there were the intellectual nationalists, devious, half-educated manipulators who were seeking to mobilise the ignorant Muslim masses against Britain and her Allies; and on the other hand there were the traditionalist, 'clerical' and 'conservative' forces whose sincerely held religious concepts were not incompatible with, nor necessarily hostile to, the romantic Tory imperialism he himself espoused. These conservative Muslims were precisely the sort of men who might be trusted to lead the 'friendly native states' which he and Kitchener were advocating; and in the person of the Sharif of Mecca he believed they had found such a promising figure. As for those scheming intellectual Muslim nationalists, Sykes believed they were very much like the leaders of the Turkish CUP. Their objective was to

> engross all political power in the hands of a clique of journalists, pleaders and functionaries, to oust the clerical element, but to retain its power to excite an ignorant mob to massacre or rebellion when necessary ... An 'intellectual' with an imitation European training, with envy of the European surging in his heart ... sees in Islam a political engine whereby immense masses of men can be moved to riot and disorder ... The Muslim 'intellectual' uses the clothes of Europe and has lost his belief in his creed, but the hatred of Christendom and lust for the domination of Islam as a supreme political power remains.[2]

Supremely confident of his penetrating understanding of the 'oriental mind', Sykes therefore advocated a policy of 'educating' the contemporary Muslim upper classes in their own traditions and religious precepts in order to steer them away from those pernicious Muslim 'intellectuals' whose 'ill-assimilated European education' was polluting the noble cultural heritage of their forebears. And he concluded, characteristically, 'As a rule it will be found that conservatism or orthodoxy is on our side and modernism and ignorant fanaticism is against us.'

Sykes's view about Jews was moving in a similar direction. His original anti-Semitism appears to have been primarily aimed at assimilated, 'cosmopolitan' Jews, a group of whom he described in a letter to his parents in 1900 as 'these beasts' and 'Jews of the most repulsive type'.[3] By now he was

also convinced that what he conceptualised as 'Great Jewry' was a threat to
Britain's war effort. However, after meeting a number of Zionist leaders he
became strangely convinced that they represented a different, traditional
and conservative, kind of Jew – an individual more akin to his notion of
those 'conservative Muslims'.[4] With this in mind he began to support the
Zionists' campaign for a 'National Home' in Palestine in the belief that
this would win 'Great Jewry' to the Allies' side. Therefore it was Sykes – in
consultation with an important Russian Zionist – who was the author of
the first draft of what became known as the 'Balfour Declaration' promising just such a Jewish 'National Home' in Palestine and which would
eventually be published in the press in November 1917.[5]

After leaving India, Sykes's first stopover was Basra where he arrived on
19 September 1915. It was his intention to meet Sir Percy Cox, the chief
political officer, as part of his programme of discussions around the De
Bunsen report, but on his arrival he discovered that Cox was 'up country'
accompanying 'Townshend's Regatta', the Anglo-Indian expeditionary
force commanded by General Townshend which was now advancing
further up the Tigris intending to capture the town of Kut al-'Amara. So
instead, Sykes was informed that Captain Arnold Wilson, Cox's assistant
responsible for the Basra vilayet, would be pleased to meet him.

The meeting was not a happy one. By now, the recently promoted
Wilson had returned to full-time political duties and was living in a
cramped office at Ashar, the old Turkish customs post on the banks
of the Shatt al-'Arab where the Ashar creek meets the Shatt and leads
up to the old city of Basra. Although he was by now quite ill, suffering
intermittently from malaria and a form of beriberi, his appetite for work
remained undiminished. 'AT', as he was now commonly known, had
recently acquired a great enthusiasm for paperwork, taking great pride
in multiplying files, assembling card indexes and firing off telegrams
at every opportunity. Sykes found him in full cry, dashing through an
enormous pile of waiting papers and disposing of them one after another
like a threshing machine.

Sykes could be tactless when he was expounding one of his many
enthusiasms or prejudices and on this occasion he made it abundantly

clear to Wilson that in India he had acquired a dim view of that country's administration and he took an equally dim view of the government of India's predominance in Iraq. There was no understanding, Sykes insisted, that Iraq was an imperial concern, not just an Indian one, and therefore the views of London and Cairo must always be taken into account when deciding military and political policy in this particular theatre. Moreover, Sykes couldn't understand why so little effort was being made to win the Iraqi Arabs round to actively supporting Britain. Surely the Civil Administration could be more active in the propaganda line, leaflets in Arabic, that sort of thing? And couldn't they make greater efforts to win over local sheikhs, raise guerrilla bands to attack the Turkish flanks and so on?

In spite of his position of authority in the Civil Administration, Wilson was still only a relatively junior officer and he must have felt constrained to suffer this tactless onslaught from his aristocratic and distinguished official visitor. But he was later to comment with ill-concealed bitterness that Sykes was 'too short a time in Mesopotamia to gather more than fragmentary impressions', and that 'he had come with his mind made up and he set himself to discover the facts in favour of his preconceived notions, rather than to survey the local situation with an impartial eye.' In particular, Sykes seemed overly concerned to do 'justice for Arab ambitions and satisfy France'.

Arab ambitions and French satisfaction: the two concepts seemed hardly compatible; that was precisely what was beginning to trouble Sykes as he travelled back from India. Over the last few months he had begun to appreciate that the French also had 'desiderata' in the Middle East. Indeed, according to intelligence he was receiving it was clear that they had expectations of planting the tricolour at the eastern end of the Mediterranean to accompany their colonies in North Africa. But since Britain's interests would be best served by a 'devolved' Ottoman Empire of 'friendly native states', these two national objectives were clearly contradictory. Perhaps there would, after all, have to be some kind of agreement on 'zones of control' with France, regardless of the De Bunsen Committee's desire to avoid any such explicit commitment.

On 17 November 1915 Sykes arrived in Cairo, the next leg of his journey home. Here he was shown some important correspondence between the British high commissioner of Egypt, Sir Henry McMahon, and the Sharif of Mecca in which the former, on behalf of the British government, appeared to be offering some kind of independent Arab state to the latter if the Sharif and his four sons launched a revolt in the Hejaz against the Turkish government. In spite of continuing disagreements about the exact boundaries of this new Arab state – and Husayn was angling for a kingdom of vast proportions – all the signs pointed to an eventual revolt by the Sharif and his sons.

Sykes now realised that the conclusions of the De Bunsen report would require major revision. For not only was Britain's principal ally clearly eager to fall upon the carcass of the Ottoman Empire but now a new predator apparently wanted to join the feast, demanding his very own and very substantial piece of flesh. Sykes himself had certainly looked forward to the day when Arabs, Kurds or some other ethnic group within the Ottoman Empire turned to Britain for support against the Turks, but he had never imagined such a group would be so bold as to strike out for full independence and on such an ambitious scale – this was not at all his vision of a 'friendly native state'. Nevertheless, the die had now been cast and Britain would have to try to patch up an agreement with the French which somehow or other satisfied both countries while at the same time leaving Husayn with something for which he and his Arab movement would still be willing to fight. There was no question about it: it was going to be very difficult.

Then, out of the blue, the first hint of a solution emerged – if not a solution at least a step in the right direction. An Iraqi Arab deserter from the Ottoman army at Gallipoli, a certain Lieutenant Muhammad Sharif al-Faruqi, was brought in to see him and, during a long interview, Sykes must have begun to feel somewhat more confident of finding a way out of the maze into which he had somehow stumbled.

The Lieutenant from Mosul

Sykes was informed that Lieutenant Muhammad Faruqi had deserted shortly before the latest major Allied offensive against Ottoman positions on the Anafarta Ridge at Suvla Bay (an offensive which had failed, like all its predecessors). He had told his initial military interrogators that he was a mulazim awwal (first lieutenant) in the 142nd Infantry Regiment, that he was twenty-six years old and had been born in the city of Mosul. The al-Faruqi, so he informed the British, were a branch of the al-'Umari family, one of the leading Muslim families in Mosul who claimed descent from the caliph, 'Umar ibn al-Khattab. After education at elementary and high school in Mosul, he had entered the Military Academy in Istanbul in 1909, where he enrolled in the infantry officers' course. He had graduated in 1912 and was originally stationed with the 12th Faylaq (Corps) of the Fourth Army at Mosul, which was later moved to Aleppo. There he was appointed ADC to 12th Faylaq commander Fakhri Pasha.

But then, to the surprise of his interrogators, Faruqi informed them that he was part of a wide conspiracy whose ultimate objective was to bring about an uprising of Arab troops in Syria. He was a member of a secret organisation of Arab officers within the Ottoman army called al-'Ahd, which he had originally joined in Mosul; but after his unit had moved to Syria he had also become a member of another, somewhat older secret organisation of Arab nationalists known as Jam'iyyat 'Arabiyya al-Fatat – the Young Arab Society. Al-Fatat had been founded by a small group of civilian Arabs in Paris in 1911 and had recently moved its headquarters from Beirut to Damascus while al-'Ahd had been established in October 1913 in Istanbul.[1] In January 1915, the leaders of both al-Fatat and al-'Ahd had joined forces in Damascus where they decided to send a message to Sharif Husayn of Mecca stating that they were ready to start a rebellion in Syria under his leadership.

On receiving this dramatic information, Faruqi's interrogators informed British Intelligence in Cairo, whose chief, Brigadier Gilbert Clayton, immediately issued orders for the Arab lieutenant to be sent to Egypt for further interrogation. He arrived there on 1 September 1915 and the following day was introduced to Na'um Shuqayr, a Lebanese Christian who worked for British Military Intelligence and who was to be his 'minder' and translator. Shuqayr lived in a small house in the old al-Qahira district and Faruqi was instructed that, for the time being, he should live with Shuqayr.

Each day they walked the two miles from Shuqayr's home to the HQ of the British Army at the Savoy Hotel, where Faruqi was ordered to begin writing a detailed account of all he knew about the activities and plans of al-'Ahd. By 12 September Faruqi's long statement, describing the situation of the 'Arab movement' in Syria prior to his desertion, the aims of the movement and his own role within it, was completed and typed up, ready for analysis. It was immediately passed to Brigadier Clayton and was to be the catalyst which would culminate in a dramatic turn in British policy towards the Arabs and the Middle East.

Over the next few days Clayton read and re-read Faruqi's statement with a mixture of concern and excitement. Faruqi stated that, having met with the leaders of both al-Fatat and al-'Ahd in Damascus, he had 'thought of uniting the two societies in order to gain strength by union and to avoid mistakes in politics which history teaches us might occur from the military if left alone', and indeed, it was he himself – so Faruqi claimed – that united the two organisations.[2] The newly united body then carried out propaganda among Arab units and his organisation agreed that they were prepared to give Britain, in return for its help, 'all concessions and privileges which do not touch the essential resources of our country and our independence'.

The first action of the new Arab organisation had been to send an officer to the Sharif of Mecca, after which they discovered that the Sharif
was already in communication with the high commissioner in Cairo and
that 'the English have given their consent for the Sharif establishing an
Arab Empire, but the limits of his Empire were not defined.'

Faruqi then went on to describe the circumstances of his subsequent
arrest in Aleppo, his imprisonment during which the Turkish commander Djemal Pasha had tried – but failed – to get him to reveal what
he knew about 'the secrets of our society'. He and the other officers imprisoned with him were then released but 'sent to Istanbul'. During the
journey he and some of his companions tried to escape to Cyprus and
from there to travel to Mecca and join the Sharif, but they failed as 'we
were under close surveillance'. On arrival in Istanbul they again 'tried to
escape but we could not get a chance of doing so', after which Faruqi 'was
detailed as a commander of an infantry company fighting at Gallipoli'.
He deserted at Gallipoli because he did not want to fight 'my friends'
or do 'service to my enemies ... the Turks – who wish to kill me and my
party'.

Some parts of the statement must have sounded rather odd to
Clayton. Could this young lieutenant have really had the authority to
unite the two secret Arab organisations? And the circumstances of his
arrest and imprisonment – was he 'released'? But if so, why was he then
'sent to Istanbul'? As a punishment? And if he was sent there as some
kind of punishment, did he or did he not actually try to 'escape'? If the
only thing that prevented him was that he was 'under close surveillance',
he didn't seem to have tried very hard.

Nevertheless, as he read on, Clayton began to push these doubts
into the back of his mind as Faruqi's statement became more and more
interesting. 'Ninety per cent of the Arab officers in the Ottoman Army'
were 'members of our society', he claimed, and not only Arabs but 'a part
of the Kurd officers'.[3] Al-'Ahd had carried out acts of open propaganda
among the troops, telling them that 'the British are our friends and our
support for our independence' and in April they had 'raised revolt at
Homs of the 107th Regiment and two battalions of Kurds and Arabs

of the 30th Division of the 12th Corps'. He himself would 'guarantee to go to Mesopotamia and bring over a great number of officers and more especially from the 35th Division at Mosul who all know me'. And as if to emphasise the strength of the Arab movement of which Faruqi was, he claimed, a leading member, Shuqayr recorded that Faruqi had told him that if Britain did not agree to support the Arabs, they would get their independence by themselves.[4]

In the days that followed Clayton and Shuqayr elicited further information from Faruqi which added more depth and detail to his initial written statement and, rather unexpectedly in the light of that document, indicated that Faruqi appreciated Britain's difficult relationship with its French ally with respect to *their* interests in the Middle East. Faruqi insisted that in return for their help, the Arab movement would insist upon an independent Arab state including the Arabian peninsula, Palestine and Iraq, but that they understood that France had ambitions in Syria. They expected Britain to help find a satisfactory solution to the Syrian problem but at the very least, they would insist that the Syrian inland cities of Damascus, Aleppo, Hama and Homs would be included in the Arab confederation to be established at the end of the war.

Then Faruqi injected a trace of menace into the discussion. The membership of al-'Ahd, he claimed, was so powerful that in spite of the fact that both the Turks and Germans knew about their pro-British aims, neither dared try to suppress them. In fact the Turks and Germans had already turned to the leaders of al-'Ahd and practically promised to fulfil their demands if al-'Ahd and its followers threw its full weight behind them. The Arabs, Faruqi assured Clayton, would much prefer to ally themselves with Britain, in whom they had greater trust, but time was pressing: unless the British gave the Arabs a positive reply to their request for arms and assistance within a few weeks at the most, they might be forced to return to the Turks and Germans and obtain from them the best possible terms available. The British should not prevaricate. The Arabs could not delay indefinitely. Fortunately he, Faruqi, was now here in Cairo and had been authorised by al-'Ahd to receive the British response.

On 11 October, Clayton wrote a lengthy memorandum for the

high commissioner in Egypt, McMahon, offering his own evaluation of the situation. He also copied the memorandum to General Sir John Maxwell, the C-in-C of the British Army in Egypt. Clayton pointed out that Faruqi's reports, together with other information he had received about the 'Arab movement' during the year, had convinced him that a crisis point was fast approaching. Britain needed all the help it could get in the Middle East, especially if it would help sway Muslim opinion away from the continuing menace of jihad. Clayton also underlined the fact that the objectives of the Arab movement as stated by Faruqi were remarkably similar to those which Sharif Husayn had made to the British in recent correspondence, but that both Faruqi and the Sharif were insisting on a clear statement as to the borders of a future Arab state. This was the key issue.

McMahon received the memorandum the following day along with advice from Clayton that he should contact the Foreign Office to get clear instructions about how they should now proceed. The memorandum was forwarded immediately to Sir Edward Grey, the foreign secretary. At the same time General Maxwell cabled Kitchener at the War Office, insisting that a powerful organisation of Arab officers and tribal sheikhs had decided that the time had come to act. The pressure was on, and it was being applied at a particularly crucial moment. The previous day Kitchener, faced with mounting evidence of failure at Gallipoli, had asked Sir Ian Hamilton for an assessment of the losses which might be incurred should an evacuation have to be carried out. In other words, Britain was now facing the real possibility of humiliation at the hands of an army of 'orientals'.

The next day, 13 October, Kitchener authorised Maxwell to open discussions with 'the Arabs', giving him full powers to do anything that would ensure their adherence to the Allied cause and asking him to report immediately what the Arabs' demands were. Three days later – the day on which Kitchener was finally compelled to dismiss Hamilton from his command at Gallipoli – General Maxwell replied that Iraq (except perhaps the vilayet of Basra), and the Syrian districts of Damascus, Aleppo, Homs and Hama, would have to be included in whatever new Arab state was established. And he further emphasised the urgency of the situation, informing Kitchener, 'In my opinion the time is passed for vague generalities ... we may have a united Islam against us unless we make a definite and agreeable proposal to the Sharif at once.'[5]

Meanwhile, further discussions were taking place with Faruqi and on 18 October McMahon cabled the foreign secretary stating that it was now absolutely clear that, unless Britain gave a firm promise to Sharif Husayn that Britain would help the Arabs establish an independent state including the Arabian peninsula, Syria, Palestine and Iraq – except for Basra where Faruqi had apparently conceded that Britain would enjoy 'special measures of control' – the Arabs might throw their weight behind the Germans and create a pan-Islamic union against the Allies.

That was sufficient. Sir Edward Grey immediately drafted a telegram to McMahon stating, with some qualifications about the exact extent of British control in Iraq and the need to respect existing treaties with Arab chieftains, that 'the important thing is to give our assurances that will prevent Arabs from being alienated, and I must leave you discretion in the matter as it is urgent and there is not time to discuss exact formula'. Grey then passed the draft telegram to Kitchener for his approval, which, given with alacrity, ensured that High Commissioner McMahon assumed ultimate responsibility for launching the 'Arab movement'.

The Peculiar Origins of an Infamous Agreement

There are no minutes of Sykes's meeting with Lieutenant Faruqi, so we do not know how or when the discussion between them first began to take the turn it did; nor can we be certain about exactly who led whom along the winding path which at some point clearly began to stray further and further from the destination Faruqi had specified in his previous interrogations and interviews and which the Sharif himself had clearly mapped out. But we can get a fairly clear idea of its tenor from the rather garbled telegram Sykes sent to Sir Percy Cox on 22 November 1915.

First, Sykes informs Cox that 'the following is a resume of situation from the Arab point of view as described to me by Faruqi here'. He goes on to state that 'the Arab Committee here [i.e. in Cairo] and the Sharif are in accord', and also in agreement with 'members among Baghdad Army officers'. This 'Arab Committee' planned to form an independent state or confederation. However, Sykes then adds the following observation, suggesting that their objective of full independence is somewhat less than absolute.

> They are obliged for political reasons to demand absolute independence. That is why members of Committee do not open-up on subject. If they accepted principle of foreign control they would lose the support of the Syrians, however in fact this does not amount to much.[1]

Sykes then lists the territories which would form the new Arab state: 'Vilayets of Damascus, Beirut, Aleppo, Mosul, Baghdad and sanjaks of Urfa, Dayr az-Zawr, Jerusalem.' The form of government will be

'Decentralised Turkish Government under a Parliament sitting in Damascus'. But then, echoing his earlier observation, he adds that the independence of the new state will be

> qualified by agreements made with France and Great Britain ... France to have a monopoly of all enterprise and special educational facilities in region west of the Euphrates as far as Dayr az-Zawr and in Palestine. No Europeans but Frenchmen to be employed by Arab state in that area, but Arab state not to be obliged to employ European Advisors unless it chooses. Great Britain to have same rights in ... Mesopotamia. Basra town and lands south to border with Kuwait and to Fao to be British absolutely. Lands to the north of the line Alexandretta, Aintab, Urfa to be French absolutely.

Sykes then turns specifically to Iraq, Sir Percy Cox's current responsibility.

> Shi'i problem and Karbela' question would to my mind make our cooperation in government in Baghdad and Basra province inevitable. Arabs have agreed they could not take over this region for present and further point out that revenues and development of these provinces will be essential to their economic and financial stability and that these could only be got with our assistance.

He ends with these comforting words:

> If we have a permanent monopoly of enterprise and of European assistance, military and civil, in Mosul, Baghdad and Basra province, and we administer Baghdad and Basra province for the duration of the war, I think that we need not fear for the future. If Pan-Arabism succeeds, and if it does not, we have given nothing away.[2]

The salient points Sir Percy was apparently intended to draw from this confusing telegram were as follows.

1) There exists in Cairo an 'Arab Committee' of considerable importance.

2) The political position of this 'Committee' is identical to that of the Sharif of Mecca with whom they are in communication.

3) the Committee (and by inference, the Sharif of Mecca) are, in reality, willing to accept something less than full independence.

4) They are only demanding full independence 'for political reasons' in order to avoid conflict with 'the Syrians' and might otherwise even 'accept the principle of foreign control' (whatever that means).

5) These 'Syrians' (who, by implication, are more extreme nationalists) are nevertheless less influential than the 'Baghdad officers' and the Sharif's supporters.

6) The form of government to be adopted in the new Arab state is very similar to the model recommended in the De Bunsen report, i.e. 'Decentralised Turkish Government'.

7) They have the option to accept foreign advisors and if they do (and there is the implication that they will) the Arab movement is equally comfortable with a strong French influence in the western and north-western part of its domain as it is with a strong British influence in the eastern and south-eastern part.

8) The Arab movement is willing to concede the lower half of the vilayet of Basra including the city of Basra itself to be 'British absolutely'.

The only problem Sir Percy Cox would have encountered in inferring these conclusions is that, as far as we are able to understand from the available historical evidence, none of it was actually true. In fact, Faruqi was a bit of a fraudster.

By the time Faruqi met with Sykes he had already been living in Cairo in close proximity to leading personages in the military and intelligence community for nearly three months. He seems to have been sharp and intelligent and during this time the numerous interrogations and interviews in which he had been involved would have given him considerable insight into the strategic and political preoccupations of his interrogators. It is also possible that, as a competent linguist (he already spoke Turkish and French), he had considerably improved his knowledge of English. So, having apparently decided that his comfortable and, to an increasing degree, respected status was very much dependent on convincing the British that he was able to 'deliver' to them an Arab movement consistent with their strategic and political preoccupations, he gave them what they – rather than the Sharif of Mecca – wanted.

The lies began almost immediately Faruqi arrived in Cairo. He knew very well that only a tiny proportion of Ottoman army officers belonged to al-'Ahd: his figure of 90 per cent was pure fabrication. He also knew that his claim that al-'Ahd included a 'part of the Kurdish officers' was misleading to say the least – there were perhaps no more than a handful of members who were of Kurdish origin. Faruqi certainly did *not* unite the al-Fatat and al-'Ahd movements: that was achieved by a senior Iraqi officer, Yasin al-Hashimi. Al-'Ahd had never carried out propaganda among the Arab troops: on the contrary, its members had tried as much as possible to conceal their activities. There had been no approach to al-'Ahd by the Turks or Germans offering an alliance, as Faruqi informed Shuqayr (the Germans had never even heard of al-'Ahd). And Faruqi had not been authorised by al-'Ahd, the Sharif or any other part of the 'Arab movement' to 'receive' the British response to their demands.[3]

Furthermore, as regards the 'information' which Sykes obtained from Faruqi during their interview, there was no 'Arab Committee' in Cairo. Neither the (non-existent) committee nor Faruqi himself were in communication with Sharif Husayn – in fact it was to be a further month before Faruqi contacted Husayn and informed him of his existence. And with respect to French influence, although Husayn was later to offer some flexibility over French interests in the coastal region of Syria at Britain's request, at this point in time both he and the majority of al-'Ahd members were strongly opposed to *any* French involvement in a new Arab state, in spite of what Faruqi may have said to Sykes.[4]

So, comforted by the apparent 'reasonableness' of the Arab movement, as relayed to him by Faruqi, Sykes returned to England where, almost immediately, he was thrust into negotiations with M. Charles François Georges-Picot, French counsellor in London and former French consul general in Beirut, to try to harmonise Anglo-French interests in 'Turkey-in-Asia'. For nine months the French had been intermittently raising this question with Britain. So during the first week of January 1916, Sykes and Picot hammered out a draft agreement. Finally, as a result of an exchange of letters between Sir Edward Grey, the French foreign minister, Paul Cambon, and Serge Sasanov, the Russian minister of foreign affairs, a secret agreement was reached among the three Great Powers defining their respective claims on Turkey's Asian provinces. Its terms were embodied in a letter from Grey to Cambon dated 16 May 1916, and in due course it was to become known as the 'Sykes–Picot Agreement'.

The essence of the agreement was that the Ottoman Middle East, excepting the Arabian peninsula and Palestine (which was to be 'internationalised') was to be split in two, roughly on a north-east–south-west axis which would run from a point just north-east of Kirkuk on the border with Persia, across northern Iraq and the Syrian desert, through the present-day occupied Palestinian West Bank and ending on the Mediterranean coast at the Gaza Strip. The central, inland core of each region, designated Area 'A' and Area 'B', respectively, would be a region in which France and Britain agreed 'to recognise and protect an Independent Arab State or Confederation of States ... under the suzerainty of an Arab Chief'. In Area 'A' France would have 'a right of priority in enterprises and local loans', and Britain would have the same right in Area 'B'. Only France, in Area 'A', and Britain, in Area 'B', should supply foreign advisors or officials, if these were requested by the 'Arab State'. However, on either side of this region there would also be a 'Blue' area and a 'Red' area, the former including the Syrian littoral and the southern part of Asia Minor, the latter including the vilayets of Baghdad and Basra. In these areas Britain and France were at liberty 'to establish such direct or indirect administration or control as they may deem fit to establish after agreement with the Arab State or Confederation of States'. In effect these 'Blue' and 'Red' areas would be French and British protectorates. In addition, Alexandretta, on the Syrian coast, and Haifa, on the coast of Palestine, would be free ports with respect to Britain and France, respectively, and Britain would have the right to build, administer, and be the sole owner of a railway connecting Haifa with the 'Red' area.[5]

There was just one matter which may have caused Sykes some unease: in this carve-up Mosul and the surrounding area would form part of the

French-aligned 'A' zone, albeit within a semi-autonomous Arab state. Sykes was well aware of the potential oil wealth which lay in this region, but it seems that broader geostrategic concerns prevailed at this particular juncture. Even in a wartime alliance with the tsar's empire, British policy makers were still playing 'the Great Game': it was apparently thought advantageous that, once the war was won, Britain would have a French-controlled buffer zone between its interests in Basra and Baghdad and the Russian Caucasus. Mosul would have to be part of that 'buffer'.

Nevertheless, in all other respects Sykes had done it – or so he believed. He had squared the circle. He had made an agreement with Picot which satisfied both Britain and France while at the same time believing that he was broadly respecting the wishes of Sharif Husayn and the 'Arab movement' as related to him by their 'representative' Lieutenant Faruqi.[6] Needless to say, neither Sharif Husayn nor his sons had the slightest idea that their objectives had been so seriously misconstrued by the Power to whom they were about to commit their forces and in whose service they were to risk all.

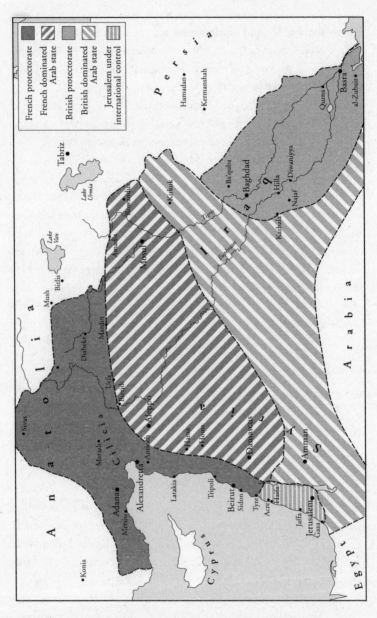

THE DIVISION OF THE OTTOMAN EMPIRE'S EASTERN POSSESSIONS
ACCORDING TO THE SYKES-PICOT AGREEMENT 1916

Two British Defeats but a New Ally

The urgency of inducing Sharif Husayn and his sons to enter the war – even if they provided only a minor distraction to the Turks and a small symbol of Allied–Muslim cooperation to the world at large – was now becoming acute. The war with the Ottomans was not going well – and not just at Gallipoli.

On 21 October 1915 Maurice Hankey, now secretary of the newly established War Council, was lunching with the foreign secretary, Grey, at Churchill's London house, which Grey was currently renting. Later that day a special interdepartmental committee meeting had been arranged specifically to discuss whether the Mesopotamian Expeditionary Force, which had recently advanced up the Tigris and captured the small town of Kut al-'Amara, should continue the advance and take that 'glittering prize', Baghdad. The expeditionary force's commander, General Nixon, was reported to be strongly in favour. Grey asked Hankey what were his views on the matter. Hankey told Grey that the Mesopotamian Expeditionary Force should certainly 'push on to Baghdad without delay', and he added that on arrival, the army should 'issue a proclamation that we had occupied the city temporarily and for military reasons only and that we were favourably disposed towards the formation of an Arab Empire independent of Ottoman rule, to which Baghdad might be handed over'.[1]

Grey agreed, and in the afternoon the special committee, under the impression that the forces at the disposal of General Nixon were greater than they actually were, approved the advance on Baghdad, the decision to authorise the advance being telegrammed to Nixon on the 24th. Nixon was already brimming with optimism. In spite of the fact that his field commander, Townshend, had already complained that his commander-in-chief 'does not seem to realise the weakness and danger of his [Townshend's] line of communication ... 380 miles from the sea', Nixon had already ordered some of his troops to move up from Kut to positions sixty miles upstream. Far away in London the cabinet looked forward to a sparkling victory which would offset the dismal news from Gallipoli and the Western Front.

On 2 November 1915 the prime minister, Asquith, speaking in the House of Commons, gushed with enthusiasm: 'General Nixon's force is now within measurable distance of Baghdad. I do not think that in the whole war there has been a series of operations more carefully contrived, more brilliantly conducted, and with a better prospect of final success.'[2]

By 18 November, Townshend had learned from his handful of reconnaissance aircraft that an Ottoman force of 11–12,000 had taken up position sixteen miles south of Baghdad on the left bank of the Tigris near the village of Salman Pak. The force was commanded by Colonel Yusuf Nur ud-Din Bey, the former police chief of Basra; it was dug in, protected by barbed wire, in two parallel lines of defence terminating in a fortified redoubt. If Townshend was going to take Baghdad, he had no choice but to attack it; but his whole force was no more than 12,000 men and a frontal attack on a fixed position without numerical superiority was doomed from the start.

Four days later, on a battlefield overlooked by the great arch of Ctesiphon – all that remained of the ancient city of the Parthians and Sassanids – Townshend's troops, many of them inexperienced Indian recruits, were thrown against the Ottoman positions. The British appear to have seriously underestimated Nur ud-Din's strength. With a total of 21,000 men with fifty-two artillery pieces and twenty machine guns, Nur ud-Din's army far outnumbered Townshend's. And of the four divisions under Nur ud-Din's command, three – the 45th, the 38th and the 35th – were composed largely of Arab regulars together with some Kurds.[3]

In a straggling and chaotic battle which was fought intermittently over three days, the Anglo-Indian force lost 4,200 dead or wounded. The Ottoman forces fought unexpectedly well, including the Arab 142nd infantry regiment (part of the 35th Division), Faruqi's old unit, which he had previously insisted was seriously disaffected.[4] With the Arab and Turkish troops mounting fierce counter-attacks, on the afternoon of the 25th the decision was taken to retire to Lajj, a small town on the Tigris about ten miles south of Salman Pak. But by now Turkish reinforcements commanded by the energetic but ruthless Khalil Pasha, nephew of Enver Pasha, were arriving and Townshend soon realised that he had no choice but to retreat the hundred miles back to Kut al-'Amara, which he considered to be more defensible than any of the other Tigris towns.

The march back to Kut was a grim ordeal. Pressed hard by the Ottoman regulars in their rear and harassed on their flanks by Arab tribal irregulars who killed and robbed any wounded falling by the wayside, the exhausted remnants of Townshend's force eventually arrived at Kut on 2 December. Initially confident that he could hold Kut until reinforcements arrived, on 6 December Townshend sent his cavalry and transport downriver in order to reduce the number of mouths he would have to feed if the Turks besieged him. Among those ordered to leave was an Indian Army political officer named Captain Gerard Leachman, whom we shall meet again later in this story.

Too late, Townshend realised that, in spite of optimistic reassurances, Nixon would be unable to send a relief column in sufficient strength to lift the siege until after Kut's supplies had run out. By 7 December Khalil Pasha had closed a ring of 20,000 men around Kut, leaving Townshend's 10,000 Indian and British troops, 3,500 Indian non-combatants and around 6,000 Arab civilians trapped in a loop of the Tigris only less than two miles long and a mile wide.

On the very same day that Townshend became trapped in Kut, the cabinet accepted Kitchener's advice – finally given after weeks of dithering – that they had no choice but to evacuate the army from Gallipoli. Winter had arrived early and the beleaguered Allied troops were suffering intensely in their shallow trenches and dugouts huddled under the surrounding Turkish guns on the heights above them. However, the new Allied commander, General Charles Monroe, carefully put together a plan for a staged night withdrawal concealed from the Turks by a variety of clever stratagems such as automatically firing rifles using water-powered weights or candles which burned through strings to pull the triggers of the unmanned weapons. This gave the illusion that his troops were remaining in their positions even while they were being loaded into the boats that would evacuate them. Ironically, the evacuation of Gallipoli turned out to be the greatest – indeed, the only – success of the whole campaign.

While Sykes, in London, was turning his attention to reaching an agreement with the French, McMahon in Cairo was being pressed to come to a final arrangement with Husayn which would bring his Bedouin fighters into the war on the Allied side and provide some limited relief for the accumulating military setbacks on both the Western *and* Eastern Fronts.

Although the Sharif had responded warmly to a letter from McMahon on 24 October 1915 in which the latter agreed to Husayn's request for specific assurances about the frontiers of his Arab state, his reply of 5 November, expressing his 'great gratification' at this sudden change in Britain's attitude, was qualified by continuing disagreement about precisely which territories should be included, in particular the future status of the Syrian region west of the line Damascus–Homs–Hama–Aleppo (i.e. the future state of Lebanon). With respect to Basra and Baghdad, where McMahon had suggested that 'special administrative arrangements' (i.e. some degree of British control) might apply, Husayn reminded McMahon that 'the provinces of Iraq were part of the former Arab Empire and indeed were the seat of government in the days of the Caliph 'Ali ibn Abu-Talib ... and all the Caliphs after him.' However, although Husayn made it clear that 'we should find it impossible to persuade or compel the Arab nation to renounce that honourable association', he was willing to allow those parts currently occupied by British troops to remain so occupied 'for a period to be determined by negotiation' provided that the Sharif's 'Arab Kingdom' was compensated for this temporary alienation by means of 'suitable pecuniary assistance'.

McMahon replied to Husayn yet again on 13 December. But as McMahon's agent arrived in Mecca with the letter, another missive was also delivered to the Sharif – from Lieutenant Faruqi. Eight days earlier, Faruqi had composed a long letter to Husayn informing him, for the first time, of his existence.[5] He introduced himself as an officer in the Ottoman army and as 'the first member of al-'Ahd'. He informed Husayn that he was one of the officers who had met his son Faysal in Aleppo in May 1915 and he told Husayn about how he had decided to desert to the British.

The British, he told Husayn, had explained to him the contents of McMahon's letter of 24 October in which they had accepted Husayn's proposed frontiers but excluded the territory west of the line Damascus–Homs–Hama–Aleppo because of French interests there; British interests in Basra and Baghdad would also have to be recognised, he had been told. However, Faruqi also told Husayn – in sharp contradiction to what he had apparently said to Sykes – that he had made it clear to the British that 'the Arabs would not give up one square foot of land in Syria and that the Arab state must include all of Syria and Iraq', although it would be possible to recognise the purely economic interests of Britain in Iraq and of the French in Syria.

In spite of the fact that McMahon's letter of 13 December added little to their previous exchanges, the fact that it was accompanied by £20,000 in gold with which Husayn would be able to buy the support of many Bedouin chiefs of the Hejaz clearly signalled that the British were now in earnest. In fact, Faruqi had already told him in his own letter that the British felt they had more to gain from Husayn's support than vice versa. Husayn was also pleased to hear of Faruqi's presence in Cairo and his apparently strong influence upon the British – an influence which was seemingly reinforcing Husayn's own representations as to the extent of his desired Arab empire.

After yet another exchange of letters, on 30 January 1916 McMahon replied with what was to be his final missive in the labyrinthine communications which had commenced six months earlier. Implying that the postwar status of the Baghdad vilayet was by no means settled, he promised that Britain would 'examine the question with the utmost care after the defeat of the enemy'. As for the Syrian coastal regions including Beirut, he thanked Husayn for his recognition that they must 'avoid anything that might impair the alliance between Great Britain and France' and, implying that Husayn would eventually be able to count on the support of Britain after the war, McMahon stated that success 'may bind us to each other in a lasting friendship which shall bring profit and contentment to us all'.[6]

Three months later, Britain's defeat at Gallipoli was followed by an even more devastating setback in the war against the Ottomans. By mid-April 1916 it had become clear that all attempts to relieve the siege of Kut had failed. Negotiations on surrender began on 27 April, during which Townshend, with Kitchener's approval, offered Khalil Pasha all his artillery and £1 million in return for his men being allowed to leave Kut on parole. Khalil immediately referred the offer to his uncle, Enver Pasha, who replied, 'Money is not wanted by us.' Townshend then raised the cash offer to £2 million but, insulted by what they considered an attempt to bribe them, Khalil and Enver declined once again. Realising at last that the Turks were intent on unconditional surrender, Townshend resigned himself to the inevitable and on 28 April began destroying his guns.

There was little mercy for the British and Indian 'other ranks' or the local Arab population after the Turks entered Kut. Hangings and torture were the lot of those Arabs who were deemed to have collaborated with the British, and the prisoners themselves were dispatched on a veritable death march to Anatolia, where the survivors were condemned to forced labour. Around two-thirds of the British and Indian troops who surrendered died of disease or maltreatment. General Townshend, on the other hand, was taken to Istanbul, where he lived out the rest of the war in pleasant semi-confinement, convinced to the last that the Turkish commanders were 'Gentlemen'.

For Britain's war leaders, one defeat by 'orientals' had been shocking; two defeats seemed utterly appalling. As far as the war in the East was concerned, there was now 'only one show in town' – a revolt against the Turks by Sharif Husayn and his men. Fortunately, current and future promises of gold in very large quantities were about to produce the desired outcome.

On 5 June 1916 Kitchener, the architect of the 'Eastern Strategy', whose vaguely worded message to the Sharif in September 1914 concerning the caliphate had set in motion the train of events which had since unfolded, drowned in the icy waters of the North Sea when the cruiser HMS *Hampshire* carrying him on a diplomatic mission to Russia was sunk by a German submarine. On the very same day, Husayn's sons 'Ali and Faysal raised the banner of revolt at Medina and five days later the Sharif himself joined the rebellion, having previously been promised a subsidy of £50,000 per month in gold sovereigns, 5,000 rifles and a quarter of a million rounds of ammunition by decision of the British cabinet, a figure which would be raised to £125,000 in gold a month later, and eventually rise to £200,000 per month by mid-1917.[7]

Colonel Gerard Leachman in Arab dress during
one of his adventurous spying missions, *c.* 1912

Colonel Leachman and Captain Lawrence

After the Emirs Faysal and 'Ali raised their standards they led the tribesmen who had rallied to their call to a position south-east of Medina to await the recruitment of further tribal forces. Husayn's own troops attacked the Turkish garrison in Mecca on 10 June 1916 and, at the same time, a force of around 4,000 tribesmen of the Harb confederation launched an attack on Turkish positions at the Red Sea port of Jedda. At Mecca, most of the city was under the control of the rebels within three days, but a major fort and the garrison building held out for a further three weeks. At Jedda, the Arab attack failed when the Turks opened fire upon them with artillery. However, shelling by the elderly British light cruiser HMS *Fox* eventually forced the Turks to surrender on 16 June.

Lieutenant Faruqi, whose presence in the Hejaz had meanwhile been requested by Emir Zayd, accompanied the British on board HMS *Fox* and later recorded his emotions in a report to Clayton: 'I have drunk the cup of happiness for being able to hit the mean Turks actually ... Praise be to God who granted me the means and enabled me to fight against the Turks and smash them ... No better life than is now.'[1] It was, however, the only military engagement against the Turks that Faruqi was to be involved in – if 'involved' is the correct word.

From June to September 1916 further gains were made. Rabigh, an important coastal town, fell to a local uprising led by Husayn bin Mubarak of the Masruh Harb, and Yanbu', another coastal town, was captured at the end of July. Inland, Ta'if was taken by Emir 'Abdallah's forces on 22 September. But there were also worrying indications of problems to come.

T. E. Lawrence posing in Arab clothing for Lowell
Thomas' book *With Lawrence in Arabia*, 1918

The Bedouin tribes who had rallied to Husayn and his sons – mainly
the Juhayna, Harb and 'Utayba – were not jihadi warriors against an
alien invasion like the Arabs of Iraq. Many of them heartily disliked the
Turks and their railway to Medina; but they were essentially mercenaries,
fighting for British-supplied gold and modern rifles. As for their martial
qualities, individually they could be courageous, but up against regular
troops – especially when these were equipped with modern weaponry –
they had a tendency to become disorganised and panic. Moreover, each
tribe was reluctant to move outside its own *dira* – its traditional zone of
pasturage, water-rights and oasis gardens.

Worse still, some tribal leaders soon showed that their loyalty could
not be relied upon when the Turks made them offers of cash which
exceeded those of Husayn. For example, within a few weeks of Rabigh's
capture, its captor, Husayn bin Mubarak, had accepted a Turkish
subsidy and the Ottoman flag was once again flying over the town.

Bin Mubarak later abandoned the town and moved his forces inland but the situation at Rabigh remained precarious because of the Arabs' failure to capture Medina, the second of Arabia's holy cities and the one with a railway link to Damascus. At Medina, Husayn's tribesmen faced a determined enemy commander, Fakhr ed-Din Pasha, who had quickly concentrated 12,000 well-trained Turkish and Arab regulars in the city, from where he was in a strong position to threaten both Rabigh and Yanbu' on the coast and even Mecca itself.

In November 1916, the Emir Faysal's Bedouins were joined by the twenty-eight-year-old intelligence officer, Captain T. E. Lawrence, whose role was to act as liaison officer between the Hejaz Arabs and the British military HQ in Cairo. Lawrence soon became enamoured of the wild tribesmen. Like Sykes, he had a romantic attachment to the country-dwelling 'native' untouched by modern civilisation. (The town- and city-dwelling Syrians he denigrated as 'an ape-like people.')[2] In spite of the fact that his knowledge of Arabic was minimal – a fact which makes his subsequent accounts of delivering lengthy Arabic orations in *The Seven Pillars of Wisdom* highly suspect – he soon won the confidence of the Emir Faysal and his men.[3]

For a while the Arab Revolt in the Hejaz continued in a desultory way, punctuated by a near disaster in December 1916 when Fakhr ed-Din moved against Yanbu' and was only held back by heavy shelling from the 6-inch guns of the Royal Navy's shallow-draught monitor *M31*. But thereafter, the Turks returned to the defensive, concentrating their forces at Medina. This gave Faysal's troops the opportunity to move up the coast to Wajh, from where they could threaten the northern stretches of the Damascus–Medina railway. Even so, it was entirely due to an attack from the sea led by two Indian Army officers, Captain N. N. E. Bray and Captain C. E. Vickery, supported by Royal Navy shelling, that Wajh was captured on 23 January 1917, as the 8,000 strong Bedouin column under Faysal and Lawrence failed to arrive on the day scheduled for the attack. ('A sad lack of initiative,' commented Captain Bray.)[4]

Sykes was now becoming increasingly influential in the new coalition government of David Lloyd George which had replaced Asquith's floundering Liberal administration in December 1916. His friend Hankey had recommended Sykes for the position of chief political assistant to the new War Cabinet of which Hankey remained secretary. In the event, Sykes had to share the new post with Leopold Amery, a former Conservative back-bench MP and a virulent imperialist; nevertheless, Sykes wasted no time in trying to impress his own, frequently idiosyncratic ideas upon the men now running Britain's world-wide war.

Now that the Arab Revolt in the Hejaz had overcome its initial crises, and with Faysal and Lawrence consolidating their position around Wajh, Sykes decided it was time to bring someone over from Iraq to whom he could demonstrate the success of the revolt. He was particularly keen to impress Sir Percy Cox, who remained sceptical about the whole enterprise. However, Cox was in no mood to receive lectures from Sykes, especially since the military situation in Iraq had recently improved considerably. The appointment of a new, energetic C-in-C, Lieutenant General Sir Stanley Maude, supported by major reinforcements and a much improved logistics system, had enabled the British to recapture Kut on 22 February 1917, and with an army now substantially outnumbering Khalil Pasha's they had marched on to capture Baghdad itself on 11 March. So Cox decided that he would send to Cairo one of his best, most battle-hardened POs, moreover one whose experience in dealing with 'the Arab' was second to none. The officer in question was Lieutenant Colonel (formerly Captain) Gerard Leachman. Let Sykes or Lawrence try to upstage Leachman if they dared!

Aged thirty-seven, Leachman was a tall, gangly, big-boned man with a long face and thinning hair, physically very strong, but a rather unprepossessing figure. Lawrence described him as 'a thin jumpy nervous long fellow, with a plucked face and neck'.[5] The son of a country doctor of modest means and the only surviving boy in a family of six children, Gerard was sent to a private boarding school where his teachers regarded him as an indifferent, indeed below-average pupil who showed little interest in either academic or sporting attainments. Eventually, and after a sudden burst of interest in imperial history, he decided to pursue a military career and aided by an intensive burst of 'cramming' he gained entry to Sandhurst, from where he graduated in 1899.

Leachman arrived in Cairo on 24 April and took a room at Shepheard Hotel, which seemed to him 'a great gathering place for M.P.s and sprigs of nobility, for if you go to war from Shepherd's Hotel there is no particular hardship. They are great sticklers for dress and that one should wear a pair of spurs is of much the same importance as beating the Turks.'⁶ Leachman had every reason to be contemptuous. He had spent the last two years living a very dangerous life in Iraq as an Indian Army PO, organising and leading small bands of 'loyal' Arabs, often behind enemy lines, scouting and fighting, rarely out of the saddle, and only very occasionally able to enjoy the fairly spartan comforts of Basra, let alone the fleshpots of Cairo.

After a few days sightseeing and a meeting with the new high commissioner, General Wingate, on 30 April, Leachman sailed for Wajh in order to make a first-hand evaluation of the Arab Revolt's progress. There he was met by Captain Bray, one of the Indian Army officers who had taken a leading part in the capture of Wajh and who told Leachman in no uncertain terms that the operation had been a complete shambles, redeemed only by some accurate shelling by the navy. However, Emir Faysal had now made Wajh his temporary headquarters and both Bray and Leachman were invited to dine with him the following day. They were also informed that Captain T. E. Lawrence, Faysal's liaison officer, would be present.

In the early evening they arrived at Faysal's tent at the rear of which, facing the entrance, stood tall, stately Faysal, 'simple and charming' according to Bray; and to his right a diminutive figure with a pale, smooth, absolutely beardless face, dressed entirely in richly embroidered white Arab robes, a gold dagger at his waist. Lawrence was obviously enjoying himself in his new persona.

Faysal invited his guests to be seated on the Persian carpets covering the floor of the tent while the customary interchange of compliments and courtesies took place. Faysal then asked questions about the progress of the Mesopotamian campaign, but to Bray and Leachman it seemed that he was doing this 'more out of courtesy to his guests than with a real desire to know more than that the Turks were being well beaten'. As for Lawrence, according to Bray, his appearance conveyed an aura of 'unreality' and his behaviour seemed 'servile to Faysal'. However, if Faysal appeared polite, if somewhat cool and distant, during this encounter with the representatives of his powerful new ally, he had his reasons. Because three months previously, Lawrence had privately told the emir what he had discovered about the Sykes–Picot Agreement and both Faysal and Lawrence himself were now deeply worried about the manner in which Britain and France were manoeuvring behind the back of their 'Arab movement'.

After the meal in Faysal's tent was over and Bray and Leachman returned to their billets in Wajh, Leachman recorded nothing of the event. Indeed, he was, generally, a man of few words. Bray, however, writing many years later, gave his own impression of the encounter, noting in particular 'the patent contrast between the two Englishmen' – Leachman and Lawrence. In Bray's opinion, Lawrence had been 'acting the Arab' and 'maintaining his prestige through the medium of his magnificent clothes'. Leachman, on the other hand, 'was so obviously and unashamedly the Englishman, and a masterful one. His sufferings and hardships were mapped on his lean visage and pride showed behind the curtain of his eyes. He had endured five years of toil and danger, and three more still harsher years were in store for him.'[7]

However, Leachman did make known his views as to the effectiveness of the Arab Revolt in the Hejaz – at least to Bray, who recorded that Leachman 'dismissed the whole Arab venture in the west as of little worth'. And back in Cairo on 9 May Leachman had few good words to say about the Hejaz or its inhabitants in a letter to his mother: 'Commend me to the Arabian coast of the Red Sea for absolute hopelessness. Not a blade of grass or bush but miles of volcanic desert and stones. Most vile form of Arab, worse than the worst Mesopotamian specimen.'[8]

As for Leachman's impression of Lawrence, we can only surmise that he was darkly amused by the latter's dressing up as a Bedouin noble. In fact, Leachman would have had every justification in regarding

Lawrence with scorn. In 1910 and again in 1912 he himself had made two daring journeys into the heart of the Arabian peninsula: the first, to the encampment of the great Shammar tribe, whose fratricidal ruling clan, the al-Rashid, were to be loyal supporters of the Turks, and the second to Riyadh, the mud-walled capital of Emir 'Abdul 'Aziz ibn Sa'ud, whose followers were of the puritanical Wahhabi sect. During these journeys Leachman dressed, ate and lived entirely as an Arab – not in the robes of a noble sharif like Lawrence but as a simple Bedouin. On his return from the second journey an officer colleague described him as looking like a 'long, cadaverous and altogether filthy-looking Bedu'.

Later, Leachman would put this earlier experience to good use. As the Mesopotamian Expeditionary Force advanced up the Tigris in the second attempt to capture Baghdad it was Leachman who met with the leading sheikhs and, using his competent Arabic and knowledge of tribal customs, cajoled – and, where necessary, bullied – them into abandoning their allegiance to the Turks. It was he who ventured into the territory of the Bani Lam and with the aid of a 'present' of Rs 10,000, persuaded the redoubtable Sheikh Ghadhban ibn Bunayya to change sides.[9]

While the British under General Maude were advancing towards Baghdad, Sykes had obtained the agreement of the War Cabinet that, on entering the city, Maude should issue a proclamation – in Arabic and English – which, on the face of it, gave a remarkably explicit British commitment to establishing Arab self-rule in Iraq. Sykes had personally composed the proclamation in the flowery language he considered appropriate to the occasion and translation into Arabic had even further enhanced the grandiloquence of the announcement. After much argument among the different branches of government and the civil and military authorities in Iraq, the proclamation was finally published in Baghdad on 19 March, among much hilarity on the part of the British occupying forces.[10]

Britain, the proclamation declaimed, had come as 'Liberator', freeing the Arabs from 'the ancient tyranny of strangers', who had descended upon them since the days of the Mongols. Since those times, 'your palaces have fallen into ruins, your gardens have sunken into desolation

and your forefathers and yourselves have groaned in bondage'. 'Many
Noble Arabs', the proclamation went on, 'have perished in the cause
of freedom at the hands of those alien rulers, the Turks who oppressed
them.' But, the people of Baghdad were assured, 'these Noble Arabs
shall not have suffered in vain', and it concluded, under the signature of
a reluctant General Maude:

> Therefore I am commanded to invite you, through your nobles and elders
> and representatives, to participate in the management of your civil affairs
> in collaboration with the political representatives of Great Britain who
> accompany the British Army, so that in due time you may unite with your
> kinsmen in North, East, South and West in realising the aspirations of
> your race.[11]

And who were these 'Noble Arabs', it was asked by one British officer.
'It's officialese for Beastly *Budoos*,' another British officer is said to have
replied. It wasn't Leachman – but it might well have been, given his
sardonic wit and generally low opinion of those he also referred to
sarcastically as his 'gentle parishioners'. Arnold Wilson, in Basra, took
an equally dim view of the proclamation and its intentions and, knowing
full well who was behind it, he later described it as being 'drafted in
London by a romantically-minded traveller'.[12]

However, educated Arabs in the city of Baghdad had no reason to
be cynical about the proclamation, whatever men like Wilson were
later to claim (arguing that therefore no one *really* felt betrayed when
the British reneged on it). Baghdadis may have had doubts about
how permanent the British presence would be, or whether Iraq might
revert to the Ottoman Empire when the war was eventually concluded,
but in the meantime it seemed clear that the British government was
offering – indeed promising – some form of independence if the Turks
were decisively defeated. Moreover, this was no private letter; no secret
correspondence like that between McMahon and Sharif Husayn. It was
an open public declaration and there were many among the merchants,
government officials, school teachers and students of Baghdad who took
it absolutely seriously.

Maude's proclamation – and a subsequent declaration in an even more explicit vein the following year – soon came to be regarded as firm promises guaranteeing the full independence of the Iraqi people. Indeed, one may gauge the extent to which most Baghdadis accepted the apparent sincerity of General Maude's proclamation and the 'independence' which it appeared to offer by the fact that when the general suddenly died of cholera on 18 November 1917 and the British-controlled Arabic-language newspaper *Al-'Arab* called for suggestions as to how best to commemorate his untimely death, it was no less a figure than Ja'far Abu al-Timman, grandson of the deceased combatant of the 1915 anti-British jihad Haji Daud and a man who now held strongly nationalist views, who proposed a public subscription to erect a memorial building housing a library, reading room and marble statue of Maude himself, and carrying the inscription 'To the memory of General Maude from the citizens of Baghdad.'[13]

Meanwhile, in Cairo, Leachman was in good sprits. An illness which had long been troubling him (and which later was diagnosed as chronic appendicitis) was in remission and to his mother he wrote that he was 'enjoying myself and the good food'. Nor did anticipation of his important forthcoming meeting with Sir Mark Sykes seem to worry him. Indeed, when they did meet they appear to have got on rather well. Leachman describes Sykes as 'most amusing and outstandingly clever' and says that while travelling around with him he had 'learnt many things about the world'. Whether Leachman ever expressed to Sykes his severe reservations about the Arab Revolt in the Hejaz, let alone his extremely dim view of its protagonists, we do not know, but it seems unlikely because the two men apparently parted company on good terms. Yet unbeknown to either, although they would never meet again – Sykes was to die in the great influenza pandemic of 1919 – their lives would further, and fatally, intertwine.

It has been said that the flap of a single butterfly's wing can cause a violent storm on the other side of the world. Be that as it may, a somewhat more direct chain of causation originating in Sykes's highly convoluted and inconsistent policies – oscillating wildly between imperialism and encouragement of 'self-determination' – would soon lead inexorably to a very different kind of storm in the Middle East. And that tempest would envelop Lieutenant Colonel Gerard Leachman, blind him in its fury, and destroy him a few miles outside a small Iraqi town called Falluja.

Mosul and Oil

As the third year of the Great War drew to a close, it was becoming clear to the military and civilian leaders of the belligerent powers that a critical new factor had entered the deadly equation of violence. Hitherto the war had been fought by a combination of manpower and horsepower, with coal-fuelled railways supporting the initial mobilisation and concentration of forces. When the British Expeditionary Force landed in France in August 1914 its motorised logistical support consisted of a mere eighty trucks, twenty automobiles and fifteen motorcycles, most of these attached to GHQ.[1] By 1917, however, large numbers of oil-powered motor vehicles and 'tanks' had become prerequisites for victory.

In fact, the internal combustion engine had already made its debut on the battlefield in September 1914 when the French counter-offensive on the Marne was only made possible by the mobilisation of over 3,000 Parisian taxis to ferry troops to the front; but thereafter, the static nature of warfare on the Western Front slowed the introduction of motor vehicles. Nevertheless, by the end of the war the British Army on the Western Front possessed 56,000 lorries, 23,000 motor cars and 34,000 motorcycles. In addition the USA, which had only entered the war in April 1917, had another 50,000 petrol-driven vehicles in France.[2]

The mechanisation of transportation was accompanied by the mechanisation of warfare itself. Although the use of tanks by the British at the battle of Cambrai in November 1917 yielded disappointing results, lessons were learned and at the battle of Amiens in August 1918 a swarm of 456 tanks finally broke through the German lines.

In the Middle Eastern theatre of war petroleum-powered mechanical transport was less in evidence but by 1918 even here, its advantages were becoming clear. For example, it was calculated that a three-ton lorry could carry the equivalent of between fifteen and thirty camel-loads of supplies and had a radius of action twice that of the camel.[3] By the end of the war, 7,000 motor vehicles, including hundreds of half-ton Ford vans, were being used for army transportation in Iraq and Rolls-Royce armoured cars were being used to good effect in both Iraq and Palestine.[4]

It was a similar picture in the air. A war which had started with a handful of 'stringbags' used primarily for reconnaissance was being transformed by a remarkable increase in the production and deployment of not only fighters but also huge long-range bombers. By the end of the war Britain had produced 55,000 aircraft, France, 68,000, Italy, 20,000 and Germany, 48,000. And during its year and a half of participation in the war the USA produced 15,000.

But it was in naval warfare that the overwhelming advantages of oil had become most apparent, decisively confirming the earlier decisions of Admiral Fisher and Winston Churchill to begin to convert the fleet from coal to oil. A ton of oil could produce the same energy value as 1.4 tons of coal, with obvious advantages in terms of the speed/displacement ratio. While many of Britain's older capital ships still remained coal-fuelled, the Royal Navy's finest vessels, the five battleships of the 15-inch gun Queen Elizabeth class completed between 1913 and 1915, and the latest sleek new battlecruisers, were all oil-fired. But oil consumption was heavy. For example, the battlecruiser HMS *Tiger* consumed 1,200 tons of oil per day when sailing at full speed; and the battlecruisers *Renown* and *Repulse*, completed in 1916, at high speed burned 1,400 tons per day: but that 1,400 tons per day was equivalent to about 85 per cent of the daily output of Britain's only major oilfield in 1916 – the Masjid-i-Sulayman field of the Anglo-Persian Oil Company.

Not surprisingly, therefore, by 1917 the Allies had become increasingly concerned that oil supplies might soon become inadequate to support the war effort. Between 1914 and 1916 world oil production increased by 14.6 per cent, from 58.9 million (metric) tonnes to 67.5 million tonnes; but most of that modest increase took place in the USA, whose production increased from 38.6 million tonnes in 1914 to 43.7 million tonnes in 1916, accounting for 65 per cent of world production. However, a considerable amount of America's production was being absorbed by the rapid increase in domestic motoring: in 1916 there were already 3.4 million registered automobiles in the USA. The only other significant world oil producers were Russia's oilfields at Baku on the Caspian Sea, producing 10.6 million tonnes, Mexico with 5.9 million tonnes, the Dutch East Indies with 1.7 million tons and Rumania with 1.2 million tonnes. But by the end of 1917, and following Russia's Bolshevik revolution in October of that year, the Baku fields were in turmoil as the struggle between the city's local Bolsheviks and other political factions took hold while the Rumanian oilfields and refineries on the Black Sea coast had to be sabotaged by a British raiding party to prevent them falling into the hands of advancing German troops.

As increasing numbers of oil tankers were sunk by German U-boats, concern about the adequacy of oil supplies intensified and it was not just the problem of current supplies which occupied the minds of the Allied leaders. Thoughts were already turning towards a postwar scenario, perhaps one in which Germany survived – cowed, but not decisively defeated. The demand for oil could only continue to grow as more countries joined the race to build oil-fired capital ships and the incipient motor-car industry expanded; but from where was the oil to come?

Not surprisingly, the 'Easterners' among Britain's war leaders had the answer, and used it to emphasise, yet again, how crucial it was to achieve victory in that theatre. In July 1916 Sykes lectured the War Cabinet on the strategic importance of the Middle East to Britain, citing the great value of its 'immense oil areas' to whoever should possess them. The following month he addressed a huge public meeting in London on German war aims, arguing passionately that even though the fields of Flanders might decide the battle, Germany was really fighting for the Middle East and its resources. Admiral Slade, who had addressed the De Bunsen Committee in 1915, also had no doubts about the value of Middle East oil and in a cabinet memorandum of 31 October 1916 he argued that Britain should seek control of all the oil rights not only in Iraq but also in Kuwait, Bahrain and the Arabian peninsula.

The following year, with desperate telegrams being dispatched from London to Washington urging the USA to make more oil tanker tonnage available and the secretary of state for the colonies declaring to Parliament, 'Oil is probably more important at this moment that anything else,'[5] few of those in power in Britain and France had any doubt that, whatever the outcome of the war, the potentially vast oil areas of the Middle East must fall into their hands. And from the British perspective this had direct strategic implications.

On 22 November 1917 Lieutenant General Sir William Marshall took over command of the British Army in Iraq after the death of his predecessor, General Maude, four days earlier. Marshall had a powerful force of 3,500 cavalry, 66,000 infantry and 302 guns and was expecting further substantial reinforcements from India. However, his orders from the general staff were essentially defensive. He was to consolidate his position in the Basra and Baghdad vilayets, continue to ensure the safety of the Persian oilfields and pipelines and, if possible, establish communications and cooperation with the Russian Army of the Caucasus under General Baratoff which was operating in northern Persia.

In response to the first of these instructions, Marshall immediately set about extending his area of control in the Baghdad and Basra vilayets by sending out columns to pacify those areas – mainly on the mid-Euphrates – which had been largely by-passed during the rapid advance to Baghdad and where, since 1915, the Arab tribes had enjoyed freedom from either Turkish or British domination. His troops soon took possession of Musayib, Hilla, Kufa, Abu Sukhair and the important mid-Euphrates dam, the Hindiyya Barrage. On the Lower Euphrates British columns captured Samawa and Darraji. Since there were no reports of any threats to the oil installations in Persia and at Abadan, Marshall next moved troops north-east, to occupy Qara Tepe and Khanaqin on the Persian border; but any hopes of an effective liaison with the Russians was dashed by the virtual disintegration of General Baratoff's forces as his troops melted away under the influence of Bolshevik propaganda,

and on 6 December 1917 Marshall learned that an armistice between the
Ottoman and Russian armies had been agreed.

Meanwhile General Sir Edmund Allenby, who had been appointed
to command the British Army in Egypt on 27 June 1917, won major
victories over the Ottomans on the Palestine front. On 1 November
his troops took Beersheba, on the 6th Gaza, on the 15th Jaffa and on
9 December Jerusalem itself was captured. Lawrence, too, had had his
moment of glory, seizing the Turks' lightly defended Red Sea port of
Aqaba on 6 July 1917 with a band of 300 Howeitat tribesmen, a triumph
marred only by the fact that he accidentally shot his own camel as the
Bedouin charged down upon the town's small group of defenders.

The following year Marshall renewed his offensive in Iraq, sending
columns further north and west up the Euphrates to take the towns of
Haditha and Ana on 27 and 28 March 1918. The attack was notable for
its employment of a mobile force composed of not only cavalry but also
mechanised elements – two Light Armoured Motor Batteries (LAMBs)
of Rolls-Royce armoured cars and a fleet of 300 Ford vans, fuelled by
petrol from the Abadan refinery. After this, the offensive slowed to
a halt as the intense heat of the summer months approached and the
British consolidated their advance on a line from Haditha in the west to
positions just south of Kirkuk.

However, Britain's twin campaigns against the Ottomans now
gained an unexpected advantage as a result of a disastrous strategic
decision by Enver Pasha. With the continuing collapse of the Russian
armies and the beginnings of civil war between the Bolsheviks and
their enemies, he imagined the moment had arrived for a major
diversion of his forces towards the Caspian. On 16 May 30,000 Turkish
troops invaded Russian Armenia, rallying to their cause thousands of
Azerbaijani irregulars under the green banners of Islam. Their first
objective was Baku and its oilfields, but after that, Enver imagined they
would sweep on into Central Asia, a great Turko-Muslim horde which
would eventually threaten India itself. But to pursue this new objective
Enver Pasha had to withdraw some key units from both the Palestine
and Mesopotamian fronts.

Meanwhile, the fact that British troops were now within striking distance of Mosul and the rich petroliferous regions which were believed to surround it began to excite considerable interest among the small group of individuals who were responsible for Britain's incipient oil policy.

They were ensconced in two newly established committees, the Petroleum Executive, which came into existence in December 1917, and its offshoot, the Petroleum Imperial Policy Committee (PIPCO), created in May 1918. The former was originally set up to coordinate the oil-related activities hitherto being undertaken by a number of different government departments – the Board of Trade, the Admiralty, the Colonial Office – without any guiding policy. It was chaired by Walter Long, who by May 1918 was minister in charge of petroleum affairs, and its director was Sir John Cadman, professor of mining and petroleum technology at the University of Birmingham. PIPCO, which itself had representation from the Petroleum Executive, also had members drawn from the Foreign Office, Admiralty, Board of Trade and Ministry of Shipping, and in spite of its rather grand name soon became involved in the specific issue of how the government could ensure that Royal Dutch Shell came under its control in a manner analogous to that of Anglo-Persian Oil.[6]

However, in exactly the same way that Anglo-Persian represented an opaque conflation of private and public interests, so too did these committees – especially the Petroleum Executive, one of whose members was the redoubtable capitalist Lord Inchcape.[7] At the Foreign Office, such a mixture was regarded with some distaste. 'The Petroleum Executive', observed George Kidston, a senior official, 'is largely composed of persons who have a direct personal interest in oil enterprises,' and he and other Foreign Office officials were particularly concerned that the personnel of government departments like his own might be tempted into speculation and the private purchase of oil shares. 'What can one expect,' Kidston asked, 'when private and public interests are inextricably mixed up in a Government body of control?'[8] However, the line of influence could flow in the other direction. Not only might government officials become tainted by commercial motivations but business interests could just as easily come to determine public policy.

So it was that the attention of Maurice Hankey, secretary of the War Cabinet, was 'privately' drawn to the question of Mosul by 'people with knowledge of oil production'. Who they were, Hankey doesn't say, but there are very few individuals to choose from: a reasonable guess would be that they were Charles Greenway, chairman of Anglo-Persian since 1914, and Lord Inchcape.

Meanwhile, with Hankey's support once again, Sykes had recently moved from the War Cabinet Secretariat to the Foreign Office as 'Assistant Adviser on Arabian and Palestine affairs', from where he was bombarding Lord Nathaniel Curzon's newly established Middle East Committee with all kinds of schemes for maintaining British control over the Middle East when the war ended. In January 1918 he sent the committee a long memorandum entitled 'Our position in Mesopotamia in relation to the Spirit of the Age'. In it he argued that 'If America had not come into the war (and) if the Russian revolution had not taken place', then the 'Spirit of the Age' would still be that of the world of 1887, a world of 'Imperialism, annexation, military triumph, prestige, White Man's Burden etc.' But in the changed political circumstances, 'If Britishers are to run Mesopotamia we must find up-to-date reasons for doing so.' Sykes's specific recommendations for achieving this objective included prompting the Christians and Jews of Iraq 'to demand a perpetuation of our administration', providing subsidies to the 'greater Badawi chiefs of the desert', and even subsidising 'an Arab press on Nationalist lines'.

The same memo was also sent to Hirtzel at the India Office, in which Sykes added that the first of a list of reasons why Britain should nevertheless 'run' Iraq – albeit by indirect methods – was that Iraq was a 'storehouse' of oil and agricultural potential.[9] His principal recommendation, therefore, was that Britain should get the United States 'to propose that we should, provided the people of Mesopotamia desire it, assume ... a provisional regime in Mesopotamia ... with the object of setting up a self-governing and independent state in Mesopotamia at the end of twenty-five years.' Sykes seems to have thought that offering Iraq independence after a wait of twenty-five years would be something its inhabitants would accept with alacrity.

If the 'Spirit of the Age' required a less overt pursuit of colonial riches, Sykes's principal adversary on this score was Lord Inchcape. Indeed, at a session of the Middle East Committee in February convened, *inter alia*, to discuss Inchcape's demands to re-establish his shipping monopoly on the Tigris and Euphrates (the project had been aborted by the outbreak of war with the Turks), Sykes openly attacked the arch-imperialist peer:

> If we play our cards well and in accordance with the underlying political principles now current in the world, we should have a good chance of remaining in control of Mesopotamia after the war, but should we be charged with encouraging profiteering or establishing monopolies we should run the grave risk of seeing Mesopotamia pass out of our control at the Peace Conference. The proposal before the Committee is equivalent to handing over the future of Mesopotamia and its inhabitants to Lord Inchcape.[10]

Meanwhile, British understanding of the potential oil wealth of its newly acquired territory in the Middle East was improving considerably. Until the consolidation of the former vilayets of Baghdad and Basra into the British zone of occupation, knowledge of Iraq's oil resources had barely progressed beyond the information acquired by Sykes in 1905. However, in early 1918 one of the Anglo-Persian Oil Company's senior geologists, Mr G. W. Halse, based at Ahwaz, was – in his own words – 'summoned from Persia by GHQ in order to investigate the prospects of discovering oil in the occupied part of Mesopotamia'.[11] Although restricted, for the time being, to the two vilayets in question, Halse's survey, the preliminary report of which was presented to GHQ in March 1918, was very encouraging.

Halse had studied two areas, Naft Khana, on the Persian frontier, about eighty miles north-east of Baghdad, and the Ramadi-Hit district on the Upper Euphrates, approximately eighty miles west-north-west of the capital. With regard to the former region, Halse concluded that it 'so nearly approaches ideal conditions that it must be regarded as an area of the greatest promise', and on the Upper Euphrates, the dome structure identified was similar to those in the USA from which substantial oil production had been obtained. Moreover, Halse's report added that in this region 'the gas pressure and large extent of the seepages ... must be taken as exceedingly favourable evidence'. And although, in general, on the Euphrates 'the conditions are less determinant' than at Naft Khana, nevertheless Halse considered that since 'the indications of petroleum are on so large a scale', a 'practical test' (i.e. exploration drilling) should be carried out.

On the basis of this and other preliminary reports, Wilson telegrammed the Foreign Office, India Office and Sir Percy Cox, underlining its main conclusions and adding – almost incoherent with enthusiasm – his own observation: 'There is not one single item that militates against prospects. It cannot be doubted that oil will be struck. The magnitude of seepages, the gas pressure (especially) at most almost ideal structure render good productions eminently reasonable.'[12]

By the time Halse had completed his final report on the two regions in August 1918, he remained cautiously optimistic about Hit, but even more confident about the prospectivity of Naft Khana, where 'conditions ... are of such an extremely favourable nature that the striking of oil would seem a certainty.'[13]

As knowledge of these geological findings percolated through government departments, Maurice Hankey decided to act. Three years earlier he had been a member of the De Bunsen Committee, and one of its conclusions had been that if outright partitioning of the Ottoman Empire was the option – and in the changed circumstances since 1915, that now seemed inevitable – then it would be desirable for Britain 'to carry our control to Mosul, in the vicinity of which place there are valuable (oil) wells, possession of which by another power would be prejudicial to our interests'.

On 30 July 1918, in the knowledge that the previous day Admiral Slade had submitted a final report on the future petroleum requirements of the British Empire to Sir Eric Geddes, First Lord of the Admiralty,

Hankey wrote to Geddes requesting information on the oil situation. Directly on cue, the following day Geddes sent him Slade's report. Slade, with Geddes's wholehearted agreement, argued that, given the expected shortfall in British oil supplies after the war, Britain should,

> encourage and assist British companies to obtain control of as many oil-producing areas in foreign countries as possible, with the stipulation (in order to prevent control being obtained by foreign interests) that the oil produced should only be sold to or through British oil-distributing companies. These oil-producing areas could be developed to assist in providing our requirements in times of peace whilst our own resources in British territory can be conserved for war.[14]

Furthermore, Britain's war aims should include preventing the enemy from in any way endangering the Persian oilfields, to push forward as soon as possible the development of the Persian and Iraqi oilfields as purely British interests, to encourage and assist the colonies to obtain control of oil-bearing lands, but only sell through British companies, and to exclude all foreign interests from British oil businesses. Hankey immediately wrote back to the First Lord, 'The retention of the oil-bearing regions of Mesopotamia and Persia in British hands, as well as a proper strategic boundary to cover them, would appear to be a first class British war aim ... we should obtain possession of all the oil-bearing regions in Mesopotamia and Southern Persia.'[15]

Since Slade's report of 29 July had not specifically referred to the oilfields around Mosul, Hankey immediately asked Slade for further information on this subject, to which Slade quickly responded, showing Hankey a map on which the potential oilfields were marked. Hankey then asked Slade to send him a further short memorandum and a copy of the map indicating precisely which oilfields still lay north of the line currently being held by General Marshall's forces. Since there was a cabinet meeting the next day, Hankey did not wait for this supplementary information to arrive but wrote immediately to the foreign secretary, Balfour, and the prime minister, Lloyd George. To Balfour, Hankey wrote:

As I understand the matter, oil in the next war will occupy the place of coal in the present war, or at least a place parallel with coal. The only big potential supply that we can get under British control is the Persian and Mesopotamian supply. The point where you come in is that the control over these oil supplies becomes a first class British war aim. I write to urge that in your statement to the Imperial War Cabinet you should rub this in.[16]

And to Lloyd George, having commented on the general staff's current belief that there was little military advantage in any further advance northwards in Iraq, Hankey argued that Admiral Slade's report had suggested to him that 'there may be reasons other than purely military for pushing on in Mesopotamia where the British have an enormous preponderance of force', adding, 'would it not be an advantage, before the end of the war, to secure the valuable oil wells in Mesopotamia?'

The Imperial War Cabinet was due to discuss a final statement on war aims on 13 August. But on 3 August Balfour told Hankey that he considered acquisition of the oil-bearing regions of Iraq 'a purely imperialist war aim'. An infuriated Hankey confided to his diary that evening: 'Fancy allowing such humbug to stand in the way of our vital national interests!'[17]

However, Hankey was not defeated yet. He well knew that Balfour was more concerned with appearance than reality and he soon hit on a means of allowing Balfour to salve his apparently troubled conscience. The day before the war aims statement was to be discussed by cabinet, he wrote again to Balfour.

It appears to me ... that it is almost unavoidable that we should acquire the Northern regions of Mesopotamia ... neither President Wilson nor any one else will wish to place the vast regions of Mesopotamia bordering the Tigris and Euphrates under Turkish control ... The question I ask, therefore is as to whether it is not of great importance to push forward at least as far as the Lesser Zab, or as far as is necessary to secure a proper supply of water. Incidentally this would give us most of the oil-bearing regions.[18]

Balfour presented his views on Britain's war aims to the Imperial War Cabinet on 13 August. Admiral Slade's recommendations were not included, nor was there any explicit reference to Mosul, but Balfour made two significant points. Firstly, the Sykes–Picot Agreement (which had allocated Mosul to the French sphere of influence), was pronounced 'historically out of date'; and secondly, Balfour emphasised that there was a 'vital necessity for the British Empire to secure an (Iraq) settlement which would not endanger our facilities for obtaining oil from this region'. It was as far as Balfour was willing to go, but it was sufficient. From then on, irrespective of whether the acquisition of Mosul and its oil was officially designated as a war aim, the cabinet effectively committed itself to pursuing a policy of acquiring *all* the oil-bearing territories in Iraq; and although there was no official endorsement of the Admiralty's 'oil imperialism', the policies pursued by the government from then on *in practice* took a shape little different from those supported by Hankey, the Admiralty, Inchcape and the other directors of the Anglo-Persian Oil Company.[19]

On 15 September 1918, Enver Pasha's Army of Islam, now swelled to 60,000 men by thousands of Azerbaijani irregulars, finally captured the oil city of Baku. A tiny force of British troops commanded by General Dunsterville (the so-called 'Dunsterforce') had tried, unsuccessfully, to organise the local Armenian and Russian population into an effective defensive force but had been compelled to flee the city by sea. However, for Enver Pasha it was all too late. On 29 September Bulgaria asked for an armistice, its withdrawal from the war isolating Turkey from its two European allies. The following day Australian cavalry followed by Arab irregulars accompanied by Lawrence entered Damascus. The remnants of the CUP government in Istanbul now began to put out peace-feelers.

The clock was ticking: unless General Marshall acted quickly, a peace agreement with Turkey would leave Mosul in Ottoman hands. Consequently, the War Office sent dispatches to Marshall informing him of the Bulgarian collapse and the victories in Palestine and Syria which might, at any moment, lead to a request for a cessation of hostilities. 'It is advisable in these circumstances', Marshall was told, 'that as much ground as possible should be gained up the Tigris. Such action is important not only for political reasons but also to occupy as large a portion of the oil-bearing regions as possible.'[20]

On 7 October the terms of an Allied–Ottoman armistice were settled in Paris and the date on which it was to be signed was fixed for 30 October. The following day Allenby's troops captured Beirut. On 13 October the Ottoman Chargé d'Affaires in Madrid asked the Spanish government to invite President Wilson to take upon himself the task of re-establishing peace. Meanwhile, in Iraq, every effort was being made to advance further up the Tigris before the whistle blew.

By 21 October Marshall was still 140 miles from Mosul and the Turks were strongly entrenched in the Fatha gorge on either side of the Tigris, and on the Lesser Zab river, with 5,500 infantry and 42 field guns. In and around Kirkuk they also had 2,500 infantry and 30 guns. But in a series of hard-fought battles, the numerically superior British infantry and cavalry, supported by armoured cars and aircraft, pushed back the Turkish troops, surrounding and isolating various units as they advanced. By the end of October the Turkish forces were exhausted and demoralised and at daybreak on the 30th the British troops were cheered by the sight of a forest of white flags in the trenches opposite them. At 7.30 a.m., what was left of the Ottoman Sixth Army defending the approaches to Mosul surrendered; all that remained was a force of about 1,650 infantry and 32 guns defending Mosul itself and a further 1,500 infantry and 12 guns on their way to the city, having been dislodged from the town of Altun Kopri north of Kirkuk. A further major advance towards Mosul was halted by a shortage of supplies and munitions, but by the evening of 31 October – by which time news of the signing of the armistice had reached Marshall – a small force of cavalry and armoured cars had penetrated as far as Qaiyara, but still about forty miles distant from Mosul itself.

However, on 2 November 1918 the British authorities in Baghdad received unambiguous orders from the War Office that Mosul was to be captured, coupled with the detailed terms of the Anglo-Ottoman armistice, one of whose clauses required the 'surrender of all garrisons in Hejaz, Asir, Yemen, Syria and Mesopotamia to the nearest Allied Commander'. But what, exactly, was Mesopotamia? Did it include Mosul? The name 'Mesopotamia' was not in current official or diplomatic usage in the Ottoman Empire, and even in British parlance it was an extremely vague expression. However, the day before, Marshall had already instructed his second in command, General Cassells, to push on and seize Mosul. Cassells received this order at midnight of 1 November, only a few hours after he had also received a letter from 'Ali Ihsan Pasha, the Ottoman commander at Mosul, demanding that Cassells withdraw his troops to Qaiyara, the furthest point reached by the British force at the moment the armistice had been signed.

Nevertheless, on the morning of 2 November, Cassells sent Colonel Leachman, under a flag of truce, into Mosul where he informed 'Ali Ihsan that he must withdraw his troops a distance of five miles from the city, leaving only a small number of guards and police to prevent disorder. At midday Leachman returned with the message that 'Ali Ihsan would not leave Mosul but would evacuate the hills south of and dominating the city which General Cassells might occupy if he wished. Although Cassells felt satisfied by this offer, when he informed Marshall the latter insisted that it was wholly unsatisfactory, that his orders were to occupy the city itself and all the surrounding vilayet. At a further face-to-face conference between Cassells and 'Ali Ihsan, the Turkish commander again rejected the British demand, arguing that it was contrary to the terms of the armistice since Mosul was not a part of 'Mesopotamia'.

On 7 November yet another conference took place, in Mosul itself, this time between General Marshall and 'Ali Ihsan. Arnold Wilson was present and recorded how Marshall now threatened to attack if the Turks did not withdraw from the whole vilayet of Mosul within ten days, insisting that if 'Ali Ihsan refused, he would personally be held responsible for any blood that was spilt. The Turkish commander continued to resist for some hours, strenuously protesting that Marshall's demands were contrary to the terms of the armistice, but eventually, worn down by the ceaseless British pressure, he agreed the wording of a document put before him. By the evening of 7 November 1918 Mosul and its environs, including the potentially rich oil-bearing lands, were in British hands and Colonel Gerard Leachman was appointed military governor of the city.

So now the die was cast. Britain had stumbled into a terrible war in the Middle East and in so doing had totally destroyed a vast and venerable empire. But what was to be done with its remains? In late 1918 it looked as though Anatolian Turkey would eventually be sliced up between Greece, Italy and France. For the moment some kind of independent Arab state in Syria seemed a possibility. Palestine's future as a 'home' for European Jewish colonists had already been decided by the Balfour Declaration and, for the moment, the stony desert lands which would later become the state of Jordan were of no particular interest to anyone. But Iraq was a different matter. Within a year three different perspectives would emerge as to what should be done with this huge but unanticipated accretion of imperial territory

Firstly, there were those – especially among the military and civilian authorities currently administering the occupation – who believed that after all the sacrifices in men and resources which the war in Iraq had entailed, it should become an outright colony on the Indian model. Secondly, there was a significant body of opinion, closely associated with the Cairo group of military intelligence personnel who had promoted the 'Arab Revolt' against the Turks in the Hejaz, who believed that Britain did not have the moral authority to establish a fully fledged colonial regime in Iraq but thought it would be possible to retain de facto control by creating some kind of semi-independent Arab state which would remain sympathetic to British economic and strategic interests. Lawrence and Sykes both shared this vision. Thirdly, there were those – probably the majority of the informed British public – who simply thought that any further involvement with Iraq, whatever its form, would be an extravagant waste of money and that, at a time of deepening economic crisis, Britain should simply withdraw all its forces from the country.

But whereas the third of these perspectives almost certainly commanded the greatest popular support, it had one very serious defect. By late 1918 it had become clear to Britain's ruling class that the nature of military technology had been irreversibly transformed and that in any future war the survival of its empire would depend on the availability of substantial quantities of cheap and easily accessible oil. Since Iraq was believed to have large, albeit undeveloped, oil reserves, the country couldn't be abandoned and allowed to fall entirely into the hands of 'irresponsible natives', or worse, the Turks or Bolsheviks. So the 'oil factor' dictated that, in deciding on the most appropriate method of dealing with Britain's territorial acquisitions in the Middle East, the choice could only be between the first and second of the three perspectives outlined above. The proponents of these alternative policies would now begin an acrimonious struggle to determine which method of control – outright colonialism or 'informal empire' via a 'friendly native state' – would predominate.

'Complete liberation'

While the newly victorious British forces were still pushing north up the Tigris, an important addition was made to Sir Percy Cox's political administration in Baghdad, the forty-nine-year-old Miss Gertrude Lowthian Bell.

The granddaughter of a wealthy Northumberland ironmaster, Miss Bell's imagination had been fired by the Islamic East after graduating from Oxford with a first-class degree in Modern History in 1888. It was a time when the 'Romance' of the East – a word she herself would later use frequently in her literature and letters – was fast becoming an imaginative construct to rival the prevalent notion of a 'fanatical' and 'treacherous' East given over to cruelty, decadence and despotism. By the outbreak of war, Gertrude Bell had already become famous for her work in the fields of exploration, archaeology and literature. She had published three books based on her travels in the Middle East as well as a well-received translation of the verse of the great fourteenth-century Persian poet Hafiz and through years of study and many months of solitary travelling she had become a fluent and grammatical speaker of Persian and Arabic. In 1913 she had accomplished a daring journey across northern Arabia to the court of the Al-Rashid at Ha'il, the pro-Turkish Arab dynasty of the great Shammar tribe, and in recognition of this and her previous works of exploration and archaeology, in May 1914 she was awarded the prestigious Gold Medal by the Royal Geographical Society.

In autumn 1915 she had been working in London helping to reorganise the Red Cross operations tracing the families of men killed and missing

Gertrude Bell, Oriental Secretary to Sir Percy Cox, Baghdad, 1921

in action on the Western Front. Then, out of the blue, she received an invitation from the head of Naval Intelligence, a family friend, to go to Cairo and apply her detailed knowledge of Arab affairs to the efforts of a team of Middle East 'specialists' based at the Savoy Hotel. After a short but highly successful few months in this role, the following March she was ordered to move to Basra to furnish the High Command in Iraq with a greater understanding of the population which was now under the control of the military authorities. And having further demonstrated her expertise in this field, in April 1917 Miss Bell received orders that she proceed to recently captured Baghdad to act as oriental secretary to the chief political officer, Sir Percy Cox.

In letters to her father and stepmother she positively gushed with enthusiasm about her new role. Apologising for not being able to re-turn to England for a holiday in the spring of 1917, she explains how she 'couldn't possibly come away from here at this moment. It's an immense opportunity, just at this time when the atmosphere is so emotional ... What does anything else matter when the job is such a big one? ... There never was anything quite like this before, you must understand that – it's amazing. It's the making of a new world.'[1]

As in Cairo and Basra, Gertrude soon established a gruelling daily routine. She would rise and go out riding from 6.00 to 7.30 a.m.; then have a bath, breakfast and go straight to her office, where she frequently continued working until 7.00 or even 8.00 p.m. As the temperature continued to rise towards 100°F she soon found that only the lightest of lunches was required – a bowl of yoghurt and a cup of Arabic coffee. In the evening she delighted in the plentiful supplies of fresh fruit which had been largely absent in Basra – 'excellent oranges' in April, succeeded the following month by 'apricots in masses and small sweet greengages'. Melons were also beginning to appear and she could also look forward to the arrival of grapes and figs during June and July: 'truly a bountiful country', she wrote to her parents.

As to the work itself, she told her parents how much she was 'loving it ... loving my work and rejoicing in the confidence of my chief'. Her duties were numerous and diverse. She tried to take as much as possible of the burden from the shoulders of Sir Percy. It was she who would meet and placate the constant stream of petitioners arriving at his HQ; she who would interview representatives of the various classes and creeds of the city and surrounding areas, gathering intelligence about the political leanings and loyalties of this or that particular notable. She played hostess to important visitors to Baghdad, such as her opposite number in Cairo, Ronald Storrs, who arrived from Egypt in early May, and a young PO, Harry St John Philby, who came up from 'Amara later in the month to be the editor of the official Arabic-language newspaper *Al-'Arab*, which the British authorities had decided would be a suitable concession to what Gertrude rather disingenuously described as 'the new order of Arab liberty'.

In late 1917, one of the fruits of Gertrude Bell's research, *The Arab of Mesopotamia* – a concise monograph prepared especially for neophyte British officers arriving in Iraq – was published by the Government Press in Basra. In it, two very important points were underlined.

The first was that the majority of Arabs in Iraq were no longer nomadic but settled, or, at least, semi-settled, cultivators of one sort or another: in short, the tribesmen were increasingly akin to peasants while their sheikhs were fast becoming landlords. Over many centuries the nomadic tribes of the Arabian peninsula had drifted northwards and eastwards, driven by population pressure and the gradual desiccation of their traditional grazing lands. Although this process had begun even before the dawn of Islam, Gertrude Bell pointed out that many of the tribes now settled along the banks of the Tigris and the Euphrates 'have come in during the last two or three hundred years'.[2] As they slowly migrated, the wandering tribes eventually found themselves upon the very limits of the desert – the great cultivated 'barrier' of the Euphrates. The wide spaces essential to nomadic existence no longer stretched out before them while the pressure of those migrating tribes behind them forbade any return to Arabia. So the great Iraqi tribal confederations – the Muntafiq, Zubayd, Dulaym, Bani Huchaym, 'Ubayd, Khaza'il, Bani Lam, Al Bu Muhammad, Rabi'a and sections of the Shammar – settled down and began to engage in agriculture, fishing and the raising of domestic animals.

In fact, it is now clear that Bell's estimate of the historical proximity of the settlement of the nomadic tribes in Iraq was still too distant: the period of most rapid settlement appears to have been as recent as the late nineteenth century. In 1867 the proportion of the nomadic elements in the rural population of southern Iraq was still 50 per cent, while in central Iraq it was 23 per cent. However, by 1905 these proportions had fallen to 19 and 7 per cent, respectively. As a corollary, during the latter part of the nineteenth century, small rural settlements grew into larger towns. No fewer than twenty major towns including 'Amara and Nasiriyya were either established or expanded from small villages during this period.[3] In the process, certain broad regional patterns of tribal domination became established.

The Muntafiq confederation began to dominate the lands of the Lower Euphrates and the Gharraf river. Gertrude Bell put their number at around 200,000, including women and children, occupying an area which extended sixty-five miles from east to west and fifty miles from north to south. The Dulaym settled on either side of the Euphrates above Baghdad while the mid-Euphrates was occupied by a shifting, unstable patchwork of many tribes including the Zubayd confederation occupying the land between the Tigris and the Euphrates, the Bani Hasan who settled west of the Hindiyya branch of the Euphrates between Karbela' and Kufa, and the Khaza'il confederation whose many tribes were scattered between Kifl, Diwaniyya and Samawa. The al-Fatla occupied the rich irrigated land of the mid-Euphrates along the Mishkab and Shamiyya rivers and along the Hindiyya, while further south the 40,000-strong Bani Huchaym remained a semi-nomadic confederation, raising camels and sheep on the lands between Samawa and Rumaytha, down the Euphrates as far south as Darraji and on the fringe of the great Shamiyya desert.[4]

The Al Bu Muhammad predominated in the great marshlands of the Lower Tigris, where they grew rice and bred immense numbers of water buffalo, while above them on the Tigris and as far as the Persian border were the Bani Lam, still partly nomadic at the time of the British invasion, between February and June moving around with their herds of camels and horses. Around the town of Kut al-'Amara were the Bani Rabi'a and

on the Tigris above Baghdad were the 'Ubayd. To the north-west, the
Jarba' section of the Shammar, also still partly nomadic, occupied the
region between Mosul and the border of Syria, while the Shammar Toqa
were on the Tigris south of Baghdad and the Shammar Zawba' in the
district of Kadhimayn. And out on the western desert fringe, ranging
between the Syrian desert and the right bank of the Euphrates and
regularly at war with the Shammar of Ha'il and its allies, were the still
largely nomadic 'Anaiza confederation, whose number Gertrude Bell
also estimated at around 200,000.

However, as they settled, the great Bedouin tribes had begun to
fracture into smaller units scattered along the cultivated river borders
and they were further split up as new arrivals thrust their way among
them, seeking their own place on the rich agricultural land. For example,
among the great Muntafiq confederation, its principal constituents, the
Bani Malik, al-Ajwad, and Bani Sa'id, effectively became independent
tribes, often warring among themselves; and within each of these tribes,
sections broke away, like the Bani Khayqan and Mujarra which emerged
from the Bani Malik. Even where the tribal confederation remained
broadly intact it was possible to identify numerous tribal sections; for
example, in the case of the Khaza'il, an important tribe of the mid-
Euphrates, Gertrude Bell identified sixteen separate sections, each with
its own sheikh.[5] So at the time of the British invasion the picture was
therefore increasingly one of tribal differentiation and schism while
within the larger tribal confederations the arrival of the British coincided
with a growing tendency among the tribesmen and sheikhs of smaller
tribes and sections to resist the payment of rents to the greater landlord-
sheikhs. As Bell described it, 'three years of war had left tribal cultivators
more independent than ever.'[6]

So, once the British finally established their occupation, many of
the greater sheikhs turned to them for assistance in pacifying their
unruly vassals while the occupiers soon came to realise that reinforcing
sheikhly control would give them the levers of power whereby the
collection of taxes and recruitment of forced labour would be greatly
facilitated. Indeed, regardless of the status of a particular sheikh, if he

failed to comply with British demands for submission, taxation and labour he would be replaced by another candidate supported by British arms. Nevertheless, in many cases this policy of reinforcing sheikhly control or replacing recalcitrant sheikhs with pro-British candidates failed, as Bell herself later admitted.

The second point to which Gertrude Bell drew attention in *The Arab of Mesopotamia* was that whereas in their purely Bedouin era, the tribes had originally been nominally Sunni, after settlement a majority of them converted to the Shi'i branch of Islam.[7] Indeed, in 1919 the British esti-mated that 53 per cent of the Iraqi population (1.5 million out of a total of 2.85 million) was Shi'i.[8]

The conversion to Shi'ism began to develop as the nomadic tribes penetrated the cultivated fringe of the rich Shamiyya region on the Middle Euphrates. The Shamiyya contained the two great Shi'i shrine cities: Najaf, with a resident population of around 30,000 at the beginning of the twentieth century, and Karbela', with around 50,000 inhabitants of which perhaps three-quarters were actually Persian Shi'is who had taken permanent residence there. Their status as Shi'i shrine cities dated from events which occurred in the very earliest days of Islam. In AD 661, the caliph 'Ali ibn Abu Talib, son-in-law of Muhammad and the first Shi'i imam, was murdered at Kufa and his shrine was built at Najaf seven miles to the south-west while that of 'Ali's son, Husayn, the Sayyid al-Shuhada' – the prince of martyrs and third Shi'i imam – was located in Karbela'.[9] The economies of the two holy cities were enriched by the annual presence of thousands of Shi'is who travelled to Najaf and Karbela' to visit the shrines; and outside Najaf lay the vast, ever-growing cemetery, the Wadi as-Salaam, to which the corpses of devout Shi'is were carried from as far away as India, to rest in peace within sight of 'Ali's shrine, a privilege which, naturally, they had to pay for.

However, the Shi'i divines of the two holy cities and their followers were also vulnerable. In 1801 Karbela' had been sacked by an army of Sunni tribesmen from Najd belonging to the fanatical and puritanical Wahhabi sect while Najaf had been twice besieged by them. The Shi'i clergy therefore came to see in the recently settled tribesmen a potential 'home guard' which would protect them against future predatory attacks, so they began to send out religious agents – graduates of the Shi'i madrasas – into the areas of Arab settlement, ostensibly to assist the settlers with such legal matters as inheritance, marriage and divorce but also to convert the tribesmen and bind them in loyalty to the Shi'i cities. In fact, the erstwhile Bedouins' affiliation to the Sunni branch had probably only been nominal – after all, most of them had no mosques in which to worship nor qadis to guide them in religious jurisprudence. Indeed, Lady Ann Blunt, who visited the nomadic tribes which roamed between Syria and Iraq in 1879 considered the true Bedouin to have virtually no religion at all.[10]

So, for the Shi'i mujtahidin and other 'ulema', the religious consciousness of the recently settled tribes was something of a blank sheet of paper on which they assiduously transcribed the tenets of their own version of Islam. They regaled the tribesmen with stirring tales of the heroic Husayn, who laid claim to be his father's rightful successor as caliph, and who in AD 680, with a tiny band of supporters, pitted himself against the overwhelming military might of the rival Sunni forces and perished on the plain of Karbela'. These Shi'i teachings emphasised the courage, eloquence, chivalry and manliness of Husayn and his father 'Ali, often using Arabic poetry to better convey their religious message in a manner which was appealing to the traditional, tribal value systems of the former Bedouin. By 1919 it was estimated that in the Middle Euphrates, the region with the greatest proximity to the two holy cities, 94.7 per cent of the total population of 567,267 were Shi'is while the Sunnis only constituted 3.1 per cent (the remaining 2.2 per cent being Jews, and Christians).[11] For their part, the tribesmen took strength from the knowledge that, after conversion, they were now 'good Muslims' with a proper place in the new social order into which they had migrated. Moreover, the fact that the Shi'is of Iraq – albeit officially tolerated – were nevertheless generally at odds with the government in the shape of the Sunni Ottoman authorities, appealed to their old Bedouin ideals of anarchic freedom and independence.

However, there remained significant groups of tribes and sections of tribes which remained at least nominally Sunni. Generally speaking, the further the distance from the two main Shi'i shrine cities, especially towards the north of Iraq, the more likely the Arabs were to remain Sunni in religious allegiance. Moreover, those tribes which remained largely nomadic – the 'people of the camel', as Bell described them – 'have kept as a rule to the desert doctrine and are almost invariably Sunni'.[12] However, the picture was complicated by the fact that while some sections of a tribe became Shi'i, others, of the same tribe, remained Sunni; and in other cases the mass of the ordinary tribesmen were Shi'i while their leading sheikhs were Sunni: such, for example, was the case of the Muntafiq, whose tribesmen were overwhelmingly Shi'i while their ruling clan, the Sa'dun, were Sunni.

As time went on, Gertrude began to compile tribal lists for GHQ in quite remarkable detail, itemising and naming the hundreds of individual tribes and tribal sections and their leaders. In 1917 she completed a study of the tribes of the Tigris and in the same year two further studies were published by the Government Press, one on the 'Tribes around the junction of the Euphrates and Tigris' and the other on the major tribes of the Lower Euphrates. The following year her enormous erudition resulted in a further volume, *Arab Tribes of the Baghdad* Vilayet. In addition to enumerating and naming tribal sections, estimating their numbers of fighting men and naming their sheikhs and sada, Bell included information as to the economic activity of the tribe, the location of its cultivated areas and animal pastures and any other relevant details she could pick up in conversations with her Arab friends, servants and informers.[13]

Although Bell undoubtedly enjoyed the scholarship involved in this work, its final, instrumental purpose was clear. Writing to her stepmother she observed, 'If you'll take advantage of tribal organisation and make it the basis of administrative organisation ... there is nothing easier to manage than tribes.'[14] And 'managing' the tribes was precisely what the Civil Administration of the new Iraq intended to do.

But perhaps Miss Bell was not so adept at 'managing the tribes' as she thought. Since the occupation of Baghdad in March 1917 and the truce between the British and the Iraqi Arabs, the policy towards their sheikhs had comprised little more than bribery. Muhsin Abu Tabikh, the Shamiyya landowner and sayyid who had fought at the battle of Shu'ayba in 1915, recalled in his memoirs how Miss Bell had written to the sheikhs and notables in April 1917, 'in every district and every Division', asking them to attend Sir Percy's Baghdad office, whereupon they had all received 'presents' in the form of large sums of Indian rupees.[15] Muhsin Abu Tabikh was one of a small number of Euphrates sheikhs and sada who had politely refused and the following month he arranged for a close relative and neighbour to take his letter of refusal to Baghdad; although not wishing to deliberately antagonise Sir Percy, Abu Tabikh merely conceded that 'at a convenient time in the future' he would be happy to pay a visit to the civil commissioner.

A month later, while he was in Baghdad, Abu Tabikh did indeed pay a call on Sir Percy. After the usual exchange of pleasantries, Sir Percy had asked him whether the Euphrates tribes were glad to be free of the Turks and now welcomed the British as their 'liberators from Turkish oppression', to which Abu Tabikh replied that, yes indeed, they *were* pleased to be free of the Turks but they now expected the promises about 'freedom' made in that 'famous' proclamation of General Maude on entering Baghdad, to be fully honoured: not exactly the answer Sir Percy was expecting and who now, rather peremptorily, instructed Abu Tabikh to pay a call on Miss Bell herself. On entering Miss Bell's office, he recalled that he had initially been received with considerable warmth:

> She ordered coffee for me and chatted away about current affairs for some time; but then she began to ask me the same questions, more or less, that Sir Percy had asked and I gave her the same reply. I could tell, then, that she was angry, by her facial expression and when she spoke she expressed herself in a manner inappropriate for a political officer, even if she was a woman. I thought there was something coarse about her and that she only had scorn for the Iraqi people. Before I left I said to her, I'm going to give you some advice, you can take it or leave it, but I just want to add this: if you English want to consider me a friend, as his Excellency the Civil

> Commissioner put it in his letter, I tell you, a friendship only of individuals
> will not suffice: instead you must be friends with all the Iraqi people.[16]

Having politely but coolly said their goodbyes, Abu Tabikh was on
the point of leaving the civil commissioner's HQ when Sir Percy's
Iraqi secretary offered him the same 'present' of rupees that had been
accepted by those other sheikhly visitors to Sir Percy's office. But Abu
Tabikh once more politely refused, apologising that 'he had no need of
it'. As one who considered himself a 'man of honour' he despised those
of his class who – in his own disdainful words – had 'flocked' to get
their bags of rupees. However, Abu Tabikh was still willing to have a
cordial relationship with the occupiers; as yet he had not experienced
the onerous obligations which, sooner or later, would descend upon
the tribal areas, partly as the quid pro quo for those seemingly generous
'presents' (whether accepted or not); and neither he nor Miss Bell had
any idea that in three years' time they would be on opposite sides at the
beginning of a bloody and brutal armed struggle.

While Britain's military situation in the Middle East was transformed
during the late summer and early autumn of 1918, those officials
responsible for determining the political status of the territories whose
ultimate conquest now seemed certain became increasingly bogged
down in trying to untangle the complex web of promises made and
obligations undertaken which had been so casually adopted in the
general struggle to defeat the Turks. Without exception it was agreed
that, with Russia reduced to revolution and chaos, the need for a
French 'buffer' at Mosul against future tsarist territorial expansion had
become irrelevant and therefore this particular element of the Sykes–
Picot Agreement was no longer of any utility; but the problem was that
the French were giving every indication that they had no intention of
abandoning *any* part of the agreement.

At the same time, Sharif Husayn, who by now had learned the full
details of the agreement, which had been widely disseminated by the
Arabic-language press in Cairo following its publication by the Bolsheviks,
was now angrily complaining that its contents bore little resemblance to

the description Sykes and Picot had previously offered when they met him the previous May. Furthermore, news of the Balfour Declaration advocating a 'Jewish Home' in Palestine was now raising anxieties and outright opposition among Arab public opinion from Cairo to Baghdad. The British, it was said, were 'going to give Palestine to the Jews'.

The entry of the USA into the war on 6 April 1917, however welcome from a purely military point of view, also brought with it major complications for Britain's postwar objectives in the Middle East. President Wilson's 'Fourteen Points' address to Congress on 8 January 1918 had spoken unmistakably of the right to 'self-determination' of the subject peoples of the Central Powers when the war was won. What impact would it have upon those 'subject peoples' of the former Ottoman Empire for whom Britain and France had their own plans? Equally threatening was the 'Bolshevik Menace', whose grip on Russia might yet be prised loose, but whose anti-colonial propaganda could meanwhile wreak havoc among the untutored minds of the 'natives' from Egypt to India.

The decision was therefore made that what was needed was some kind of vaguely worded statement which would indicate that Britain and France renounced any overtly imperialist objectives in the Middle East and that any aspirations they had as to incorporating the conquered Ottoman territories into 'spheres of influence' etc. were motivated only by the desire to assist these territories to achieve their ultimate ambition of 'self-determination'. Of course, the reality would be that the Allies would continue to control, but indirectly, behind a façade of native rulers.

So Sykes was now put to work on a declaration of Allied intentions towards the postwar Middle East. His task was to find some form of words which would, more or less, satisfy all parties. After much editing and re-editing and an exchange of notes between the foreign secretary, Balfour, and Cambon, his French counterpart, a joint Anglo-French proclamation was made on 8 November 1918, just over a week after the Turkish armistice. It began by declaring:

> The end which France and Great Britain have in view in their prosecution
> in the East of the war let loose by German ambition is the complete

liberation of the peoples so long oppressed by the Turks and the establishment of national Governments and Administrations drawing their authority from the initiative and free choice of indigenous peoples.

It went on to state that France and Britain were agreed

to encourage and assist the establishment of indigenous Governments and Administrations in Syria and Mesopotamia which have already in fact been liberated by the Allies, and in countries whose liberation they are endeavouring to effect and to recognize the latter as soon as they shall be effectively established. Far from wishing to impose any particular institution on these lands, they have no other care but to assure by their support and effective aid the normal working of the Governments and Administrations, which they shall have adopted of their free will.[17]

'Complete liberation', 'free choice of indigenous peoples', 'Governments and Administrations ... adopted of their free will': this was heady stuff indeed, going even further than General Maude's 1917 Baghdad proclamation, even if it rather obviously omitted any reference to Palestine.

Arnold Wilson was appalled by the declaration. Since Sir Percy Cox had left Baghdad for London on leave in March and had subsequently been seconded to Persia as the British minister, Wilson was now the acting civil commissioner of Mesopotamia. He received the French text of the statement on 8 November with instructions from the India Office to give it the widest publicity, but having read it he immediately concluded that 'nothing in the political situation in Syria or Iraq rendered such a declaration necessary' and that 'its promulgation was a disastrous error, the perpetration of which was forced upon the Allied Powers by President Wilson.'

A few days later, Wilson received another telegram from the India Office informing him that the Inter-Allied Conference was about to assemble in Paris as a preliminary to peace negotiations, that Arab issues might be discussed and that a representative of Sharif Husayn might be present. He was asked to immediately telegram any points relating to Iraq which 'should be borne in mind by the British Representatives'.

Wilson took up the invitation with gusto. Firstly, he felt it his duty to record his conviction that, 'the Anglo-French Declaration ... bids fair to involve us in difficulties as great as Sir Henry McMahon's early assurances to the Sharif of Mecca'. 'In years to come', Wilson pronounced, 'we shall be faced with the alternatives of evading the spirit whilst perhaps keeping within the letter of the Declaration, or of setting up a form of Government which will be the negation of orderly progress and will gravely embarrass the efforts of the European Powers to introduce stable institutions in the Middle East.'

Indeed, the Declaration placed 'a potent weapon in the hands of those least fitted to control a nation's destinies'. According to Wilson it was only 'a handful of amateur politicians in Baghdad' who wanted an independent Arab government in Iraq. In fact he could 'confidently declare that the country as a whole neither expects nor desires any such sweeping scheme of independence'. On the contrary, 'the Arabs are content with our occupation' and 'the world at large recognises that it is our duty and privilege to establish an effective protectorate'. And this point he repeated in his concluding paragraph: 'I submit, therefore, that our best course is to declare Mesopotamia to be a British Protectorate.'[18]

Gertrude Bell, who, in Cox's absence, was now working for Wilson, was equally perturbed by the Anglo-French Declaration. Writing to her father on 28 November, she described how 'The French-British Declaration has thrown the whole town into a ferment. It doesn't happen often that a people are told that their future as a State is in their hands and asked what they would like.' However, she contented herself with the belief that, in reality, the Iraqis 'are all practically agreed. They want us to control their affairs and they want Sir Percy as High Commissioner.' But then, Miss Bell's views about public opinion in Baghdad were formed largely by discussions with people like the Jamil Zadah family, described in a previous letter to her father as 'landowners, very rich, upright honest people, staunchly pro-English'; in other words the wealthiest elements who feared any disruption which might endanger their property rights and social status.[19]

Najaf 1918: First Uprising on the Euphrates

In one respect Arnold Wilson was perfectly correct about Iraqi public opinion. Until the very last year of the war only a very small minority of Iraq's many and varied peoples wanted 'independence'. In the three main cities, Baghdad, Basra and Mosul, educated public opinion still thought of itself as 'Ottoman': its *watan*, its homeland, was the great Islamic state into which they had been born and under whose aegis they had carried on their traditional business, social and deeply religious lives. Outside the three cities – in the countryside and in the two major Shi'i shrine centres of Karbela' and Najaf – the people mostly just wanted to be left alone. And until that final year of the war the people of the mid-Euphrates region in which the two holy cities were situated *had* largely been left alone as the British and Indian troops fought their way up and down the Tigris. Indeed, the only serious attempt to move up the Euphrates beyond Nasiriyya had been defeated. On 14 January 1916 a British and Indian column advancing towards the Shatt al-Muntafiq had been suddenly attacked at a village called Butaniyya by around 17,000 Arabs led by Sheikh Khayyun al 'Ubayd and forced to retreat, losing 183 men dead or 'missing'.[1]

Consequently, for much of the war, a vast area of roughly 180 miles by 80 miles stretching from Nasiriyya in the south to Musayib in the north and encompassing the land surrounding the two main branches of the Euphrates – the Hilla and the Hindiyya – remained largely outside British control. However, since the capture of Baghdad, as the British fanned out, bringing more and more of Iraq under their control, it had become abundantly clear to the settled and semi-settled tribal people under their sheikhs and to the inhabitants of the shrine cities under their mujtahidin that they were no longer going to be left alone but systematically ensnared in the net of control which the British were now casting wider and wider.

In fact, matters had already come to a head in Najaf. In October 1917 the long reach of the British Civil Administration finally brought the Shi'i shrine city within its grasp. A PO was designated for the town and its surrounding region and a pro-British Indian-born notable, Agha Hamid Khan, was appointed as governor while a small detachment of Indian troops was posted at Kufa, seven and a half miles north-east of Najaf on the Hindiyya branch of the Euphrates.[2]

However, the Najafis did not take kindly to this interference in their customary way of life. Since April 1915, when they had driven the Turkish authorities out of the city on account of their overzealous and coercive conscription of their men into the regular army, the citizens of Najaf had run their own affairs. Admittedly, the manner in which they ran their own affairs would have seemed abominably anarchic and 'oriental' to the young gentlemen from the Home Counties who typically made up the personnel of the British Civil Administration in Iraq and who had learned most of what they needed to know about 'handling the natives' in India or the Sudan.

Indeed, the very appearance of Najaf must have seemed strange and daunting to its new rulers. Lying seven miles west of the Euphrates, the ancient city stood on a ridge of reddish sandstone gravel on the very edge of the desert. It was surrounded by massive thirty-foot-high walls, strengthened at regular intervals by rounded bastions fifty feet in diameter and further protected by a moat. To the south-west, the city overlooked an ancient, partially dried-up marsh called the Bahr Najaf lying forty feet below the ridge, and to the north lay the huge, ever-growing cemetery of Wadi as-Salaam.[3] In the centre of Najaf stood the golden-domed shrine of 'Ali, reached by a broad thoroughfare running through a thirty-foot-high covered bazaar from the main gate of the city in the Eastern Wall, the Bab al Husayn. Elsewhere the streets were a maze of narrow huddled alleyways, connecting around 5,000 brick-and-mortar houses as well as some seventy khans providing accommodation to visiting Shi'i pilgrims. Even the houses seemed threatening and mysterious to the British: most of them contained catacomb-like sirdabs, cellars which were sometimes two or three storeys deep, where their occupants could escape the midday heat; and many of these were interconnected by passages, some of which had exits outside the city walls.

Najaf's regular population of around 30,000, lived in four mahallas – self-governing quarters whose organisation strongly reflected the heavily tribalised nature of this city on the edge of the desert. The self-identity and loyalty of the inhabitants of each mahalla were to their quarter and its sheikh or headman, rather than to the city as whole, and they often quarrelled and sometimes even fought against other mahallas. Mahallas even had their own constitutions by which the citizens of the quarter pledged their allegiance to its headman and acknowledged certain rules, in particular the old tribal principle of *fasl*, the settlement of cases involving murder by the payment of blood money.[4]

It was only at the religious level that the city conceived of itself as a united, common entity. Najaf was a holy city; indeed the holiest city of the Shi'is. There resided the most revered of the mujtahidin, some of whom were Persian or of Persian origin and it was the traditional base of the Grand Mujtahid whose religious judgments were endowed with the greatest respect and sanctity. And around the gold-tiled shrine of 'Ali were the madrasas, the religious schools where hundreds of students studied their Qur'ans and keenly debated with their teachers the ethical, political and philosophical topics of the day in the light of their own theological precepts.

To the British, however, the Shi'i shrine cities were the epitome of theocratic backwardness and oriental obscurantism. Major Bray, who spent some months in Najaf's twin city of Karbela' during 1918, considered the city's mujtahidin 'rapacious clerics ... steeped in ignorance', whose 'bigotry' held their followers in 'medieval subservience'. Gertrude Bell often expressed similar opinions: Najaf was 'mysterious, malign, fanatical'.[5]

Among the younger, more recent recruits to the political service in Iraq, Najaf had an even worse reputation. Based presumably, on lurid gossip in the officers' mess, the city was perceived as being barely distinguishable from Sodom and Gomorrah. One clean-living twenty-six-year-old Balliol-educated assistant political officer (APO), Captain J. S. Mann (having arrived in Iraq only a few weeks earlier), wrote to a fellow officer in England that, 'it goes without saying that such a city is unbelievably corrupt, obscene, treacherous and inflammable'.[6] Precisely why such a description should 'go without saying' was not elaborated upon. A few weeks later Captain Mann was writing to his father describing, with considerable relish, that Najaf 'is a city so vicious that the most sober account of it could not be printed in England: one can only say that every vice known to the most unpleasant Greek and Roman authors ... flourishes there publicly'.[7]

In general, the British failed to comprehend that the growing antipathy towards them of Najaf's mujtahidin and other clerics was less a matter of theocratic 'bigotry' than a genuine fear of being incorporated into a foreign European and Christian empire. The two revolutions that had recently occurred in the Middle East – the Ottoman revolution of 1908 and the Persian 'Constitutional' revolution of 1905–11, had strongly politicised certain sections of the mujtahid fraternity. Since many of the mujtahidin were Persian, they naturally took a keen interest in political developments in their original homeland and many of them strongly supported the movement of Persian merchants, clerics and artisans which in August 1906 had compelled Muzaffar ed-Din Shah to agree to sign a proclamation setting up a constitutional assembly. When, the following year, the British and Russians agreed to carve up Persia into zones of control followed by the entry of Russian troops into northern Persia in 1908, the mujtahidin of Najaf and Karbela' protested vehemently and a group of them declared to the British consul that they would issue a call to jihad if Russia did not withdraw its troops.

The Young Turk revolution of 1908 had a broader impact upon the Shi'i shrine cities, affecting not just the mujtahidin but the wider population. By the end of the first decade of the twentieth century, people in those cities were reading journals from Turkey, Persia, Egypt and India. In 1911 it was estimated that between fifty and a hundred different newspapers were available in Najaf's libraries every week. Between 1909 and 1911, Najaf itself published one newspaper and two magazines; one of the latter, *al-'Ilm* (Knowledge) was the first Shi'i magazine to be published in Iraq. It was in the pages of *al-'Ilm* that five leading mujtahidin issued a fatwa in December 1910 addressed primarily to their Sunni co-religionists, calling for the unity of *all* Muslims in the face of the encroachments of the European powers, stating that 'it is obligatory on all Muslims to ... defend the Islamic lands and to guard all the Ottoman and Persian territories against the obstinacy of foreigners and their attacks'. Moreover, as we have seen, during the early stages of the British invasion, Najaf had been at the forefront of organising the mobilisation of the mujahidin, the irregular Arab tribal volunteers who had initially flocked to join the Ottoman colours.[8]

Such, then, was the atmosphere of political awareness around the time when Najaf ceased to enjoy its autonomy and fell under the control of the British Civil Administration of Iraq. Like its sister city, Karbela', it was not so much a bastion of religious obscurantism as a deeply troubled and hostile centre of opposition to foreign rule. Religious feeling and national sentiment were fused into one and focused on the great western power which had so suddenly and shockingly penetrated both the Shi'i world and the greater Muslim homeland of which it was a part. As a result, the arrival of the British in Najaf in October 1917 was followed, one month later, by the formation of a secret Islamic opposition movement – the Jam'iyyat Nahda al-Islamiyya (The Islamic Renaissance Movement) – whose objective was total resistance to the British occupiers and – when the moment was deemed opportune – to bring about an armed revolution which, it was believed, would spread to the remainder of occupied Iraq.

The antipathy of Najaf's citizenry and the inhabitants of its surrounding area towards the British was exacerbated by some specific economic grievances against the occupiers. One of the first actions of the British Army as it moved into the mid-Euphrates area had been to requisition large quantities of wheat for the provisioning of their troops. The result was a steep increase in the price of grain, the impact of which fell heavily upon the poor.[9] The disruption of the local economy was also exacerbated by the ongoing military operations against the Turks which dislocated the local economy from its traditional trading relations with Syria. As elsewhere in the regions occupied by the British, the population was also subjected to a package of new taxes: taxes on housing, water tax, building tax, a tax on abattoirs, animal taxes and taxes on shops were only some of the new and onerous fiscal impositions loaded upon the local population.[10] Indeed, one thing the British were always very clear about in their colonial territories was that in return for enjoying some of the benefits of British civilisation it was only proper that the natives should pay for it.

The troubles at Najaf began in December 1917. First, a British cavalry patrol was fired on from the city walls; then a British aeroplane which flew over the city received a barrage of heavy rifle fire. Next the government offices in the city were attacked and the pro-British governor and his subordinates were forced to flee to Kufa. In response the British imposed a fine of Rs50,000 and 500 rifles on the citizenry and ordered the arrest of two individuals considered the ring-leaders of the disturbance – who promptly escaped from the city. The fine was paid but the rifles handed over turned out to be ancient firing pieces of little practical value. However, the strength of the Indian troops at Kufa was now raised to a battalion and a detachment was posted just outside the city walls.

Events now took a more tragic turn. On 1 February 1918, Captain W. M. Marshall of the Indian Political Service, who was about to go on leave to get married, was sent to Najaf as deputy to Captain C. C. Balfour, formerly of the Sudan Civil Service, who had responsibility for the whole Shamiyya Division within which Najaf was situated. Captain Marshall spoke Persian – but not Arabic, apparently – and whereas in Karbela' the majority of the population were Persian-speaking this was not the case in the predominantly Arabic Najaf. Soon after the arrival in the city of Marshall, who was charged with the task of collecting taxes from its hostile and unruly inhabitants, the movement of opposition to the British flared into widespread civil unrest.[11]

The secret Islamic Renaissance Movement which directed the unrest enjoyed widespread support within the city but its leading members, many of them from the mujtahid fraternity, were divided as to the best way to drive out the British. Some thought it would be reckless to launch an armed revolt against the occupation without some assurances that support would be forthcoming from other cities and from the tribes. Indeed, discussions had already been held with men such as Muhsin Abu Tabikh and other tribal sheikhs of the mid-Euphrates about the possibility of an uprising which would drive the occupying British from Najaf, as had occurred during the war when invading Turkish troops had successfully been driven out of the city; but the sheikhs took the view that any such action would be premature.[12] Sheikh al-Shari'a Isbahani, one of the senior mujtahidin in the city, who had played a leading role in the jihad of 1914–15 and who would later become one of the principal leaders of the 1920 insurrection, was apparently also sceptical about the likelihood of a successful revolt in Najaf and opposed it.

However, there were others, in particular a small group of individuals led by a bazaar trader called Haji Najm al-Baqqal, who had formed what was, in effect, a secret society within a secret society, and it was their belief that by some daring act of violence they could not only spur the broader Islamic Renaissance Movement in Najaf into armed action but also light the spark of a rebellion which would explode throughout the whole country.[13]

For a time the unrest subsided and in March the battalion at Kufa was withdrawn as it was believed by the High Command that the atmosphere in the city had considerably improved, although both Marshall and Balfour expressed their misgivings. Then, on the morning of 19 March, Haji Najm al-Baqqal and a group of his associates, disguised as shabana, the British-paid Arab police, arrived at the khan where Captain Marshall had his HQ. The twenty-seven armed attackers planned to capture and hold the watchtower of the khan, which dominated the surrounding area. Having killed the Indian sentry, they entered the building, heading for the tower. Captain Marshall and his labour officer, who were sleeping at the time, were wakened by the commotion and Marshall tried to reach the office where the telephone was installed but he was shot dead in its doorway.[14] However, by now the Punjabi guards were aroused and after an exchange of fire in which some of the attackers were wounded, Haji Najm and his men were forced to flee, leaving one of their number dead.

As soon as he heard of the attempted coup, Captain Balfour rushed to Najaf with a squadron of armoured cars from Kufa and entered the city. Although he and his escort came under heavy fire they managed to extricate the remaining Indian guards and loyal shabana from the city, although two of them were shot dead as they passed through the bazaar. For the people of Najaf, there was now no turning back: the city had declared open war on the British Civil Administration.

Its response was swift and muscular. The commander-in-chief, General William Marshall, issued a proclamation demanding the surrender of certain named individuals, including some of the leading citizens of Najaf, who were believed to have been complicit in the attack on the khan even though they did not actually take part in the raid. In addition there would be a collective fine of Rs50,000 and 1,000 rifles, and a hundred other persons were to be handed over for deportation to India. Failure to accept these conditions would result in a complete blockade of the city.

The British ultimatum was rejected; and so, four days after the attack on the khan, Najaf was surrounded by barbed wire and all food and water supplies to the city were cut off. Moreover, unfortunately for the Najafis, a few days later, the entire Ottoman army at Ramadi, which had been holding down the British and Indian forces in the west of the Baghdad vilayet, surrendered and Marshall was able to send a full brigade south to reinforce the troops besieging Najaf. For their part, the citizens of Najaf, armed mainly with abandoned Turkish rifles, manned the city walls and bastions and took possession of a group of mounds, collectively known as Tel Huwaysh, which were outside the walls and overlooked part of the city. On these they dug trenches and built barricades.[15]

Over the next two weeks sporadic rifle fire was exchanged between the opposing sides while the British continued to tighten the noose around the city. Meanwhile, the defenders managed to send letters to some of the sheikhs of the surrounding area begging for military assistance.[16] Muhsin Abu Tabikh was one of the recipients; but at the same time he also received detailed information from Kufa about the strength of the British forces surrounding Najaf and in particular the fact that they were fielding heavy artillery. In the circumstances it seemed that any attempt to intervene would only result in the British forces attacking and occupying his, and other, Euphrates towns. Understandably Abu Tabikh was not prepared to take such foolhardy action.

Then, suddenly, on 7 April, the besiegers launched a massive artillery barrage upon the Najafis dug in on the Tel Huwaysh. The defenders were forced to flee behind the city walls and two battalions of Indian troops moved in to occupy the mounds.[17] With the British now in possession of this important vantage point overlooking part of the city, it was now only a question of time before resistance collapsed.

On 9 April 1918, the British commander sent a message to the Grand Mujtahid Muhammad Kadhim Yazdi. The aged and deeply conservative cleric had supported the jihad of 1915 against the invaders but by now was known to be one of a group of mujtahidin in Najaf who were out of sympathy with their city's revolt. General Marshall's message to Yazdi was brutal and unequivocal: he would shortly commence a full-scale bombardment of one of the four mahallas of the city. Without food supplies and, even more critically, without water, the resolution of the Najafis wavered and power fell into the hands of Yazdi and his associates, who promptly offered the capitulation of the city, possibly hoping for some degree of leniency on the part of the British besiegers. By 4 May all the named individuals requested by the British had been surrendered and the other conditions met.

Gertrude Bell, writing to her father, had no doubts about the retribution which the malefactors were due. 'Already a number of the murderers of Captain Marshall have been handed over to us. I expect and hope we'll hang them,' adding that, 'the whole affair has been very successfully managed thanks to Captain Wilson and Captain Balfour'.[18]

A military court was assembled at Kufa to try the offenders. The proceedings of the court resulted in eleven death sentences and nine terms of imprisonment ranging from six years to life. In response, public calls for clemency were issued from all the main Iraqi Shi'i centres. The Persian government also expressed its fears to the British minister in Tehran that Persian religious feeling might be dangerously stirred by the sentences. Letters poured in to Wilson asking him to advise General Marshall that only the two named assassins should be executed and the death sentences on the others commuted on the basis of Islamic jurisprudence, which forbids the execution of more than one man for one murder. It was to no avail. Captain Balfour, the 'man-on-the-spot', insisted on the mass execution. Wilson agreed and so did General Marshall. So on the morning of 25 May 1918, Haji Najm al-Baqqal and ten other Najafis were hanged in public at Kufa, before a cowed but resentful crowd.[19]

To Wilson the outcome was a triumph. The imposition of the harshest of terms on Najaf had been 'a challenge to the fanatical elements throughout Mesopotamia; it was an assertion of our right, our duty, and our intention to govern without too tender a regard for the arrogant claims of the self-appointed oligarchs of the town.'

The Najafis bowed the neck. Eloquent expressions of regret were offered. Extravagant displays of submission were made by those who had been out of sympathy with the revolt including the Grand Mujtahid Yazdi. But meanwhile, the young men of the city, the tribal sheikhs of the nearby villages and a key group of nationalist mujtahidin, brooded over the injustice of the Infidels. They had witnessed Bell's 'making of a new world' and they did not like it. But for the time being they refrained from further open resistance and patiently awaited their opportunity for revenge.[20]

Britain's New Colony

The vast majority of the British military and civilian personnel based in Iraq when hostilities against the Ottomans formally ceased believed that, after all the British blood that had been spilt, Iraq and its resources should remain a British colonial possession and any idea of an Arab state was unthinkable. This was the considered opinion of Acting Civil Commissioner Arnold Wilson, and those officers who joined the Iraq Civil Administration after military service in Europe were quickly converted to the same view. For example, writing to a military colleague on 15 December 1919, Captain J. S. Mann, the APO for the 'Umm al-Ba'rur district of Shamiyya Division (whose strictures on the abominations of Najaf we encountered in the previous chapter), expressed this opinion:

> Any idea of an Arab State is simply blood-stained fooling at present, and this country cannot be handled without some sort of an army in the background ... The well-intentioned self-determinators who know no facts, no Islamic doctrine and no ethnology, have the lives of several British officers to answer for already and they will go on adding to the list I'm afraid.[1]

Like the majority of his fellow POs, Mann was also convinced that 'the Arab' was far too individualistic to respect any kind of organised government and totally unwilling to participate in any activity in which he didn't satisfy his avaricious self-interest. The sort of public-spirited individuals whom one might find in an English village – those who gave their services to the community voluntary – simply did not exist in his experience. As he explained in a letter to his mother, 'One does feel almost awfully in this type of community, the lack of what we call professional gentlemen, the parson, the local doctor and banker, the retired Colonel and the boy scout master.'[2]

Mann did not explicitly attribute the absence of 'boy scout masters' or similarly public-spirited worthies to religious factors, but others had less compunction in doing so. Another member of Wilson's administration, Thomas Lyell, a magistrate in the Baghdad criminal court, made this inference robustly in a book published in 1923, the Preface to which opined, 'The creed of Islam is unprogressive, personally enervating and destructive of any instinct for citizenship, social integrity or national aspirations ... the Muslim, and particularly the Shi'is [are] – and for many years must remain – totally unfit for self-government.'[3]

Wilson would have thoroughly agreed and it had therefore been with considerable irritation that on 19 November 1918 he had received an unexpected and unwelcome telegram from the secretary of state for India, Edwin Montagu. The telegram drew to Wilson's attention the views of an individual who, with considerable impertinence, was now poking his nose into matters of which he had absolutely no experience or knowledge. The views in question were those of Colonel T. E. Lawrence, and although he was not yet the matinée idol he was to become after the showing of Lowell Thomas' extravaganza, *With Allenby in Palestine and Lawrence in Arabia*, Wilson had already heard quite a lot about him. He also knew that Lawrence was fast acquiring influential friends in government, including Winston Churchill.

Apparently, Lawrence had written to the secretary of state for India proposing his own scheme of government for Iraq and Syria which he claimed was consonant with the Anglo-French Declaration, and the secretary of state wished to know Wilson's opinion as to this proposal. Lawrence advocated the division of Iraq into two zones, Lower and Upper Mesopotamia: the former more or less contiguous with the former vilayet of Basra and the latter with those of Baghdad and Mosul. The Emir 'Abdallah would be appointed ruler of Lower Mesopotamia and his brother Zayd would get Upper Mesopotamia. Syria would go to

Emir Faysal. However, this was not exactly a plan for Arab independence since Lawrence also stated clearly, 'It is understood that both the Iraqi states would be in the British sphere and "Lower Mesopotamia" under effective British control.'

In spite of this final caveat, Wilson was incandescent. Not only was he adamantly opposed to even a façade of Arab independence under the sons of Sharif Husayn, but he insisted that the three former vilayets should form one integral unit whose civil administration was now completely in his hands. He immediately fired back telegrams rejecting Lawrence's proposals in their entirety, accompanied by written statements from a number of heavily subsidised British-supporting sheikhs and urban notables claiming they wished only for continuing British rule.

Building on this tactic, he now proposed to the government that there should be a 'plebiscite' of public opinion in Iraq, since 'all agree that the opinion of the country must be taken before any decision can be rightly come to.' Since this sounded perfectly reasonable to the India Office, on 30 November 1918 Wilson was authorised to carry out his plebiscite which should 'render us an authoritative statement of the view held by the local population' focusing on three particular questions:

1) Do they favour a single Arab state under British tutelage stretching from the northern boundary of the Mosul Vilayet to the Persian Gulf?

2) In this event, do they consider that a titular Arab should be placed over this State?

3) In that case, whom would they prefer as Head?

But the telegram containing these instructions was highly ambiguous. On the one hand it insisted that 'in our opinion it is of great importance to get a genuine expression of local opinion on these points and one of such a kind that could be announced to the world as the unbiased pronouncement of the population of Mesopotamia.' On the other hand various remarks in the telegram seemed to indicate a considerable retreat from the principles previously enunciated in the Anglo-French Declaration of 8 November. The intention of the latter, Wilson was informed, was not so much a guarantee of Arab self-determination but rather 'to clear up the existing situation in Syria which Arab suspicion of French intentions had created'. Moreover, 'It should be understood by all that the Peace Conference will settle the ultimate status of all Arab provinces.' Although the British government did not, 'as far as can be seen at the moment', intend 'annexation' or 'to make a formal declaration of Protectorate', Wilson was given to understand that the kind of outcome favoured in Iraq was one similar to 'the position of Egypt before the war', from which Wilson not unreasonably inferred, 'Everything indicated … that the Anglo-French Declaration was not to be taken literally.'[4] Indeed, it seemed clear to Wilson that the first question upon which the India Office required an 'authoritative statement' could easily be used as a means of eliciting not just a view as to the desirability of a 'single Arab state' (as opposed to two or more) but also a more 'satisfactory' response calling for continued British rule.

So on the very same day that he received these instructions, Wilson put into action a plan to ensure that the sounding-out of 'local opinion' came up with such a 'satisfactory' result. In doing so he first discounted altogether the opinions of the rank and file of the 'local population' whose views he was directed to ascertain. The Arab masses – the garden cultivators and date growers of the Tigris and Euphrates, the orange growers of Ba'quba, the shepherds of the Dulaym, the rice cultivators of the Diwaniyya and Shamiyya, the marsh dwellers of 'Amara and Qurna and the craftsmen, traders and former government employees of the towns – all these were considered too ignorant, illiterate or subject to manipulation by 'extremists' to merit any consideration. Instead, the plebiscite would focus almost exclusively on those elements of the population – the more powerful sheikhs, merchants and landowning dignitaries – who by economic status or character were already believed to be favourable to continued British rule, or whose opinions might be influenced by offers of subsidies,

Accordingly, Wilson wrote to the POs controlling the nine administrative areas into which Iraq had now been divided by the occupying authorities, instructing that they should first (and secretly) 'Ascertain … what the trend of public opinion is likely to be.' If – and only if – the response appeared likely to be 'satisfactory', then it was to be communicated to Wilson for submission to the government. On the other hand, 'When public opinion appears likely to be sharply divided or in the unlikely event of it being unfavourable, you should defer holding a meeting and report to me for instructions.'[5]

In spite of this deliberate attempt to influence and, where necessary, distort the outcome of the plebiscite, the response of those 'consulted' was surprisingly mixed.

The 'satisfactory line' of response – that the new Iraqi state should include Mosul and that continued British administration was the best form of government – was duly forthcoming from the sheikhs of the 'Amara Division and those of Qurna, Nasiriyya, Hilla, Kut al-'Amara, Musayib and Khanaqin, many of whom were already on the occupiers' payroll. Similarly in Mosul, where ten declarations were taken from representatives of religious communities, seven of them from non-Muslim groups, there was also a request for British rule directly or British protection. In Najaf, still shocked and demoralised by the tragic events earlier in the year and where an assembly of divines and tribal sheikhs was addressed by Wilson in person, the initial response followed the 'satisfactory' line. The Grand Mujtahid Muhammad Kadhim Yazdi, who had opposed the Najaf rebellion and was now in receipt of a large British subsidy,[6] pronounced that accommodation to British rule was both legitimate and desirable, as did a number of other pro-British notables.

However, two days after the initial declaration of support for continued British rule, a Shi'i emissary from Baghdad arrived in Najaf and persuaded the dignitaries of the city not to send in their declaration. Wilson and his men then pressured Yazdi, to re-run the 'plebiscite', but the final outcome was far from 'satisfactory'. Fourteen declarations from individuals and groups were secured, but while some asked for a British protectorate, others coupled this with the demand for an Arab emir when the country should be ready for him, while others asked outright for an Arab government without an emir, no mention being made of Great Britain.

Then, on 24 December 1918, in Karbela', another senior mujtahid, Mirza Muhammad Taqi al-Shirazi, issued a fatwa of great importance.[7] Approached for guidance on the plebiscite by a group of leading citizens including clergy and tribal sheikhs, he made the following declaration: 'No Muslim may choose and elect any other than a Muslim to an emirate or sultanate over Muslims.' From that point on, effective religious leadership over the majority Shi'i community began to shift decisively away from Yazdi and towards Shirazi, and with Yazdi's death in April, the ascendancy of Shirazi and the nationalist tendency within the Shi'i clergy was assured.[8]

Meanwhile, in Baghdad, an attempt by Wilson to convene an assembly of local dignitaries favourably inclined towards British rule also collapsed. The Christian and Jewish notables wanted British rule, but among the Muslims of both sects there was fierce opposition to Wilson's preferred form of 'consultation' and instead large public meetings were called at which 'inflammatory language' was used and the delegates chosen were mandated to ask for an Arab government without British 'protection'. In the delegates' resolution, passed on 22 January 1919, they declared,

> We being of the Muslim Arab nation and representing the Muslims of the Shi'i and Sunni Communities inhabiting Baghdad and its suburbs resolve that the country extending from northern Mosul to the Persian Gulf be one Arab State, headed by a Muhammadan King, one of the sons of our Sharif Husayn, bound by a local Legislative Council sitting in Baghdad, the capital of Iraq.[9]

The most ominous feature of the resolution was the unprecedented unity of both Muslim sects. But as yet, the significance of this was barely noted by Wilson and his men. Later, however, the implications of this rapprochement would become brutally clear.

Nevertheless, Wilson's final judgement on the outcome of the plebiscite was that 'the majority desired no change of regime, a large minority favoured an Arab Emir under British guidance and control and that no name that we could suggest commanded the acceptance of even a small minority.' Gertrude Bell, agreed. According to her, 'In Mesopotamia they want us and no one else ... They realise that an Arab Emir is impossible, because although they like the idea in theory, in practice they could never agree as to the individual.'[10] So, content that she was in full support of his own position, Wilson dispatched her to London to acquaint the government with more details of 'Iraqi public opinion'. A few days later he himself was called to Paris to report in person to the British Peace Conference delegation and from there to London, where he was requested by Edwin Montagu, the secretary of state for India, to present his own proposals for the future administration of Iraq. On 6 April 1919, these were forwarded by letter to the Inter-departmental Committee on Eastern Affairs chaired by the foreign secretary Lord Nathaniel Curzon.

Wilson was now riding the crest of the wave. The government clearly had no idea what to do with Iraq; so he, with his 'vast experience' of Arab affairs, his detailed knowledge of the region and its resources, his penetrating understanding of the Arab mind, his complete confidence in his own ability to manage and control the situation, would therefore set forth his solution.

There would be no Arab emir, but instead a British high commissioner.[11] Not only would Mosul vilayet be included in Iraq but so too would Dayr az-Zawr, a town on the Euphrates whose control was already being claimed by the embryo independent Arab government in Damascus. The Civil Administration would take over from the army the running of previously military assets such as railways, bridges, docks, electric plant, and irrigation works. Iraq would be divided into four provinces: Basra, Baghdad, Euphrates (including Najaf and Karbela') and Mosul (or five if Kurdistan were to be separated from Mosul). Each of the provinces would have an Arab governor appointed by the British, who would be 'assisted' by a British advisor. In turn, each province would be divided into a number of divisions of which there would be sixteen in total. Each would have a divisional council but it would only be an advisory, not legislative, body and, as to its make-up, 'experience suggests that elective bodies are unsuited to present conditions.' From these divisional councils would be 'selected' representatives to sit on the four provincial councils, but here again, these would 'not at present be made responsible for legislation'.

On 9 May 1919 Wilson received a telegram from Montagu informing him that Lord Curzon's committee had studied his proposals and approved them. A subsequent communication from the India Office added that Wilson's proposals 'were necessarily of a provisional character; but they mark an important stage towards the provision of a definite form of administration for the occupied territories, the ultimate constitution of which must await the conclusion of peace with Turkey and the final decision of the Peace Conference in Paris'. It then went on to praise the 'care and ability' of Wilson and his staff, and stated that 'they had addressed themselves to their task with a zeal that has been as admirable as it has been successful.'

What more could Wilson have wished for? It seemed to him that he was being given the government's authorisation to construct – whatever its name – a new British colony in Iraq. He might have worried a little about the reference to provisionality; he might have wondered whether, perhaps, the decisions of the Versailles Peace Conference might eventually run counter to his scheme; but Wilson was not the man to let such hypothetical eventualities trouble him. Instead he now set about remaking Iraq along Indian lines as he had always desired.

The Oil Agreements

With their armies reeling from a massive and successful Allied attack and facing revolution at home, the Germans were forced to sign an armistice with the Allies on 11 November 1918. As the two great Allied war leaders, the French prime minister Georges Clemenceau and his British opposite number David Lloyd George, strolled side by side in the gardens of the French embassy in London on 1 December 1918, still flushed with joy at Germany's sudden collapse, Clemenceau had turned to Lloyd George and asked him, point blank:

'Tell me what you want?'

'Mosul,' replied Lloyd George.

'You shall have it,' Clemenceau declared, 'And what else?'

'Palestine.'

'You shall have that too.'[1]

In return Lloyd George made three secret reciprocal concessions. The first of these was that Britain would support French claims on the Ruhr, one of Germany's most highly industrialised regions. The second was that when oil production in the Mosul vilayet commenced, France would receive a share, perhaps around 20 per cent. The third was that, as far as Syria was concerned, the terms of the Sykes–Picot Agreement would remain intact, regardless of the promises made to Sharif Husayn and the fact that Emir Faysal was already establishing an independent Arab state in Syria with the tacit support of General Allenby and the British Army of Occupation.[2] Admittedly, the Sharif should have had no illusions about the fate of the littoral part of Syria – the correspondence between McMahon and Husayn had acknowledged that France had 'special economic and political interests' in the Syrian littoral which would have to be protected in some way; but there had been absolutely no suggestion that the remainder of Syria would enjoy anything other than genuine independence within a newly established Arab state, an objective clearly inconsistent with the Sykes–Picot Agreement.

Coincidentally a vehicle was emerging which might bridge the seemingly gaping chasm between the desire of Britain and France to carve themselves out protectorates in the former German and Turkish territories in Africa and the Middle East, and President Wilson's 'Fourteen Points' speech in which he had spoken of 'self-determination' for the subject peoples of the Central Powers.

By January 1919 it was becoming clear that full 'self-determination' in the form of unconditional independence was only considered appropriate for 'civilised' peoples: for example the European nationalities which had belonged to the Austro-Hungarian Empire. It never seems to have occurred to President Wilson and his advisors that the 'semi-civilised' Iraq, Palestine and Syria should become fully independent states. What the Americans wanted was order: order which would put an end to the destructive squabbles over colonies among the European states; and order within the conquered territories which would make them fully receptive to foreign capital.[3] A fundamental codicil to the latter was that in the conquered territories there should be an 'open door' for investment: no dominant power should obstruct the free flow of US capital into these potentially lucrative markets or prevent US capitalists from exploiting their natural resources on an equal footing with the old European states.

So instead of full independence, the Arabs were to be placed under 'mandates' which would be awarded to the victorious powers at the Peace Conference. The mandatory system was first discussed at a meeting of the Allied Supreme Council on 30 January 1919, although no decision about the allocation of the mandates was made. However, the basic concept was clear: the former colonial and other dependent territories of the Central Powers outside Europe would be distributed to the Allies, but not as old-fashioned colonies; for while a mandate necessarily involved the control of territory it also had a façade: it was presented to the world at large as a position of trust whereby the policies carried out by the mandatory power should be aimed at eventually bringing the country in question to a stage where it could become fully independent.

Word of the mandate proposals reached Iraq surprisingly quickly and immediately triggered a hostile response among the informed and educated, not only in Baghdad, Mosul and Basra, but also in the Shi'i shrine cities. And yet there was still a widespread belief that President Wilson would somehow use his great influence to ensure that the former territories of the Ottoman Empire would enjoy the same rights as newly independent European states such as Czechoslovakia and Jugoslavia. Therefore, on 6 February 1919 Mirza Muhammad Taqi al-Shirazi, by now the most influential mujtahid of Karbela', supported by the mujtahid Sheikh al-Shari'a al-Isbahani, wrote to President Wilson via the American embassy in Tehran asking him to help in the establishment of an Arab state in Iraq.[4] In a second letter, sent seven days later, the two senior mujtahidin profusely thanked Wilson for his desire 'to grant the oppressed nationalities their rights and to open the way for their enjoyment of independence' and informed him of the 'desire of all Iraqis ... that we should be free to make our own laws and to elect a King guided by a National Assembly'. As regards the mandate, 'popular opinion' either rejected it or considered that a decision about it 'should be left to the National Assembly after the end of the Peace Conference'.[5] However, if some kind of supportive response to these letters was expected from the US president, it never arrived.

Meanwhile, three months after the Anglo-Persian Oil Company's geologist, G. B. Halse, submitted his report on Iraq's oil prospects to the War Office, discussions about oil commenced between the British and French governments. Between 16 and 23 November 1918 the French commissioner general for fuel, Senator Henri Bérenger, visited London where he held preliminary talks with his opposite number, Walter Long, colonial secretary and minister for petroleum affairs. Discussions were resumed on 17 December but were soon dogged by a peculiarly inconvenient division of labour within the British Foreign Office.

After Lloyd George's triumphant coalition election victory in December 1918, the duties of the Foreign Office were, in effect, split in two. The incumbent foreign secretary, Arthur Balfour, was dispatched to Paris to participate in the peace negotiations, while the remaining functions of the Foreign Office were placed in the charge of Lord Curzon, the government's leader in the House of Lords, who remained in London. Curzon believed there should be no discussions about oil until the question of the mandates was settled at the Peace Conference. But unbeknown to him, Long had already dispatched his emissary in the shape of Professor John Cadman, director of the Petroleum Executive, to settle the 'oil question' with the French as soon as possible. And to add even more confusion to the matter, Lloyd George himself appears to have had no knowledge of the ongoing negotiations between Cadman and his French counterpart, Bérenger. The stage was now set for a classic case of the left hand not knowing what the right hand was doing.

What the French sought at the meeting on 17 December 1918 was actually much wider than the question of Mosul's oil. They wanted a joint Anglo-French oil policy which would encompass a share in oilfield developments not only in the whole of Iraq, but also in Rumania, the Caucasus and Persia. As regards Iraq, they proposed that French interests, either public or private, should acquire Deutsche Bank's share in the old Turkish Petroleum Company, the entity which had been on the verge of acquiring oil rights in Baghdad and Mosul vilayets on the eve of war. That the French were particularly keen to get their hands on as much oil as possible was reflected in a letter from Clemenceau to Bérenger (a copy of which was obtained by the Petroleum Executive and forwarded to the Foreign Office) in which the French prime minister expressed his view that the petroleum question 'appears to be one of the most important economic questions at the Peace Conference. It affects crucially the future of France's national defence and her general prosperity.'[6]

Walter Long considered an agreement with the French to be particularly urgent since he was convinced that the French were already in touch with the Standard Oil Company of New Jersey, and that if Britain didn't rapidly come to terms with the French they would enlist

US support for a fully 'open door' to Iraqi oil.[7] Therefore, on 13 March 1919 what would turn out to be only the first in a series of Anglo-French petroleum agreements was initialled in Paris by Long and Bérenger. The agreement stated that France would receive the German share (25 per cent) of the prewar Turkish Petroleum Company or any other company formed to exploit Iraqi oil reserves, with British interests receiving the remaining 75 per cent. These 'British interests' consisted of the 50 per cent Anglo-Persian share of the original TPC, represented by Anglo-Persian's subsidiary the D'Arcy Exploration Company, plus the 25 per cent share belonging to the Royal Dutch/Shell Group subsidiary the Anglo-Saxon Oil Company. Shell remained partly Dutch-owned, but during the war the company had submitted to British control in order to continue to operate on the high seas. In addition, Henri Deterding, the general manager of the company, became a British subject and the company's HQ was moved from The Hague to London.[8] Moreover, although they eventually were to prove fruitless, negotiations were afoot to ensure that Shell Transport and Trading and a number of other companies in the Royal Dutch/Shell Group were brought under permanent British control.

The price to be paid by the French for the 25 per cent former German share would be that which the British government had previously paid to the public trustees holding the expropriated Deutsche Bank shares in the TPC, plus 5 per cent per annum interest since the date of that transaction. In addition, the agreement provided for France receiving a 50 per cent share of the oil rights which the two countries might obtain in the future in Russia, Rumania and Galicia; France would also receive 34 per cent of the disposable oil in British colonies while Britain obtained the same benefit in French colonies. Finally, Britain would have the right to construct two oil pipelines to the Mediterranean, one from Iraq and the other from Persia, and should one or both of these cross 'territory within the French sphere of influence' France would facilitate their crossing without demanding any royalty or wayleave.[9]

However, when Lord Curzon became aware of the draft agreement he expressed his disquiet to Balfour that he had not been kept properly informed about it and queried whether Balfour himself knew of the

deal. In Curzon's view, the agreement was a mistake. It conceded to
the French a share in Iraq's oil for which the only British compensation
was a promise of pipelines through territory which, as yet, had not
been adjudicated to France and might possibly never be so adjudicated.
So a second version of the Long–Bérenger oil agreement was drawn
up which was now prefaced by the statement: 'In the event of His
Majesty's Government receiving the mandate for Mesopotamia', with an
equivalent form of conditionality applying to the French territory (i.e.
Syria) through which the oil pipeline from Iraq was to pass. Moreover,
following an unexpected intervention by Arnold Wilson, who expressed
concern about the loss of income which would be incurred by Iraq's
puppet government if the oilfields were handed over to what he described
as 'a comparatively small number of shareholders', this second version
of the Long–Bérenger agreement now also included the statement
that a 'native government' of Iraq would have a 10 per cent share of any
company formed to exploit Iraqi oil.

On 29 April 1919 the revised agreement was put to a meeting of an
Interdepartmental Conference of the Eastern Committee called by
Curzon at the Foreign Office, where it was decided that it now broadly
met the previous objections of both the Foreign Office in London and
Wilson in Iraq.

However, just as matters appeared largely settled, Lloyd George
dropped a bombshell. Apparently it was Clemenceau's firm belief that
his secret agreement with the British prime minister in December 1918
committed the latter to support the request of France for a mandate over
the whole of Syria – the inland areas as well as the coastal strip. But all
the signs from Damascus were that some kind of fully independent Arab
state under Emir Faysal was being established there with the connivance
of the British occupation forces. The French prime minister was now
under strong pressure from sections of the press linked to powerful
colonialist elements who claimed that Britain was using Faysal as a front
for their own takeover of Syria.[10] This was completely untrue; but it does
appear that although Lloyd George had no particular qualms about
abandoning Faysal, he wanted to shift the southern boundary of any

future French-mandated Syrian territory further to the north to enable British pipelines and railways from Iraq to reach the Mediterranean without having to cross French-controlled territory. Somehow, at the beginning of May, a discussion on these issues between Clemenceau and Lloyd George blew up into a tremendous row. So when Lloyd George heard about the Long–Bérenger oil agreement – apparently for the first time and in the course of a casual conversation – he furiously ordered it to be cancelled, informing Clemenceau of his decision in a letter of 21 May in which he claimed that the oil agreement did not accord, in certain respects, with his previous private agreement with the French premier.[11]

In London there was consternation, not only because all the laborious negotiations with the French over the preceding months had now, apparently, been a complete waste of time but also because of the prime minister's casual reference in his letter to the secret deal with Clemenceau in December 1918 – an agreement of which the Foreign Office, and indeed, all the other government departments, were in complete ignorance. There was, however, one ray of light in that Lloyd George had now decided Curzon was right – there should be no oil deal until the matter of the mandates had been settled.

Although official negotiations with the French were now stalled, over the summer of 1919 elements within the British government, in particular the Admiralty and the War Office, continued to exert pressure for the restoration of the Long–Bérenger agreement, or its replacement with something very similar.

Throughout 1919 the army continued the geological surveys of Iraq which had commenced in March 1918, using the services of A. H. Noble, a geologist from the Shell subsidiary Anglo-Saxon Oil and another from the Geological Survey of India, E. H. Pascoe. At the conclusion of these surveys – which now encompassed areas of the Mosul vilayet which had been inaccessible before 1918 – Pascoe reported,

> In the area under consideration and probably throughout Mesopotamia the mineral of unique and outstanding importance is petroleum ... My

opinion, based on evidence collected over a fairly extended tour, is that
the country will probably take a not unimportant place among the world's
sources of petroleum. It should rival the Persian fields and collectively
outclass those of Burma.[12]

That the oilfields of Iraq might 'rival the Persian fields' was a truly
dramatic conclusion – precisely the kind of result that the War Office
had hoped for. On 12 November 1919 Churchill, now secretary of
state for war, circulated to the cabinet a number of papers concerning
the situation in Iraq. They included a statement from the general staff
stressing the crucial strategic importance of Iraq as a link in a chain of
contiguous British-controlled areas stretching from Egypt to India.
They also emphasised the particular importance of Iraq's oil potential.
'The future power of the world is oil,' the general staff proclaimed,
adding that although the oilfields of Iraq were not yet 'proved', 'the
Mosul province and the banks of the mid-Euphrates promise to afford
oil in great quantities.' They concluded that a pipeline and railway from
Iraq to the Mediterranean would assure the supremacy of Britain as a
naval power in that important theatre of operations and would lessen
dependence on the Suez Canal.

So, as 1919 drew to a close, and with the British government
increasingly resigned to handing Syria over to the French 'lock stock
and barrel', negotiations on oil were resumed. By 21 December, the
new British minister responsible for petroleum affairs, Sir Hamar
Greenwood, was able to initial a further agreement with his counterpart
Bérenger. In fact, this 'Greenwood–Bérenger' agreement differed only
slightly from its predecessor. Professor Cadman, who, as before, carried
out the actual negotiations, was now able to extract from the French a
further concession: in addition to two oil pipelines running from Iraq
and Persia to the Mediterranean coast through territory which could
now, with some confidence, be assumed to come under French control,
two British-owned railway lines from Iraq to the Mediterranean were
also agreed. The agreement also fixed the French share of the TPC at 25
per cent, although this might fall if 'native interests' were to take up their
putative share.

Finally, the broad outlines of the Iraq oil question were settled at a conference in London on 12 February 1920 at which Britain and France determined the conditions which were to be imposed on the Turkish government in Istanbul, where peace negotiations were about to resume. On the part of the British, negotiations were conducted as before, by Professor Cadman, while on the French side M. Philippe Berthelot, director general of foreign and commercial affairs at the French Foreign Ministry, was now his opposite number.

According to this Cadman–Berthelot agreement, 'native interests' could receive up to 20 per cent participation in any oilfield developments if they so wished. Pipeline facilities would be granted free of any charge when they passed through French-controlled Syria and Britain would offer the same facility to the company operating the Iraqi oilfields if it needed an outlet to the Persian Gulf. The question of what kind of commercial entity would develop the oilfields – private or public – was left open for the time being. Allowing for the possibility that the Iraqi oilfields would be developed 'by Government action', the French would be offered a 25 per cent share of net oil output for which they would pay at current market prices. On the other hand, if the development were carried out by a private company, France would receive a 25 per cent shareholding in that company (with the equivalent investment obligations) but the company in question would be under British control.[13] Finally, the British government agreed to support any arrangements which the French government might make with the Anglo-Persian Oil Company to procure up to 25 per cent of its oil to be piped through French-mandated territory.

Two months later this final oil agreement was ratified at a conference of the Allies at San Remo on 24 April 1920. Lloyd George and Alexandre Millerand, the new French prime minister, confirmed with their signatures a memorandum of agreement on oil on the very same day that the conference assigned the mandates of Syria and Iraq to France and Britain, respectively.

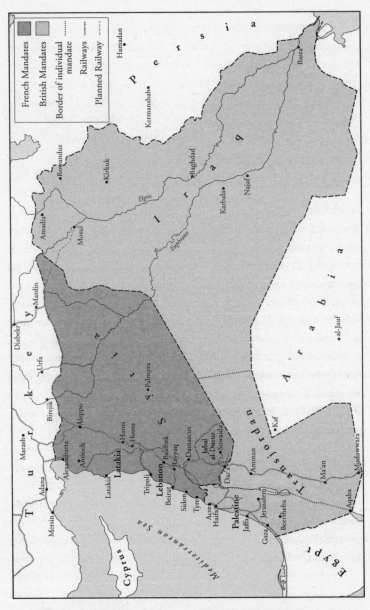

THE DIVISION OF THE OTTOMAN EMPIRE'S EASTERN
POSSESSIONS INTO THE BRITISH AND FRENCH MANDATES 1920

The Independence Movement in Baghdad

When General Maude and his men captured Baghdad on 11 March 1917 they had found a broken city – physically broken and broken in spirit. As the infantry of the 35th Brigade cautiously probed the outskirts of the capital they were confronted with a dismal sight – a vista of rotting corpses and animal bones, fires smouldering, filthy streets commandeered by hundreds of half-starved dogs and crumbling houses spilling rubbish into the streets and alleyways. In what remained of the commercial area Arab and Kurdish looters were at work.

Starvation, cholera and the casual brutality of a retreating Turkish army had afflicted all sectors of the city. So when the British finally arrived there was relief, if not actual jubilation, that the misery of the previous three years had ended. Almost immediately the British set to work on a major programme of restoration and development. A modern boat bridge across the Tigris was constructed. New streets both parallel and perpendicular to the major thoroughfare made by the Turks were built. Other streets were widened and a new system of mapping the city by quarters was devised so that for the first time every house and street had a unique address posted in English and Arabic. Work began on expanding the city's flood protection system and a power station was constructed. The police force was reorganised and the old civil prisons were transformed.

Yet soon, much of this investment and restoration appeared to the citizens of Baghdad as a strong indication that the British were here to stay: these improvements began to be perceived as being not really for *their* benefit; on the contrary, it began to seem that the British were remodelling Baghdad as a *British* city for *British* occupiers. After the armistice these fears increased, as did a growing sense of grievance against the new masters. In particular the requisitioning of private houses by the military – which most Baghdadis imagined would cease at the end of the war – continued and actually intensified, in spite of the fact that the judicial secretary, Edgar Bonham Carter, pointed out that it 'will obviously be a very unpopular step'.[1]

Soon the people of Baghdad began to experience other 'unpopular steps'. With postwar retrenchment in Britain, some investment projects were abandoned; employment of Arabs in government departments was reduced; the outcry for more schools was unmet (with one exception, provided by a group of inhabitants themselves); outside the city military roads and camps blocked canals and damaged vegetable and fruit gardens; some new irrigation works cured neither drought nor floods; price inflation was severe and the insistence on full tax revenue collection on every garden and crop was galling alike to rich and poor. So by early 1920 large sections of the capital city's population had become hostile to the continued British presence.

Meanwhile, a despondent Emir Faysal returned to Syria from the Peace Conference in Paris, where, although supported by Lawrence, he had been unsuccessful in seeking guarantees for an independent Syrian state. On his arrival in Damascus he was faced with accusations that in his attempt to head off an occupation by the French he had compromised far too much with them. Wilder currents of nationalist opinion now flowed through the Syrian capital. Lawlessness and disorder were increasing. There were attacks by Arab Muslim bands on Christian Arab villages and similar raids on some Jewish settlements in northern Palestine. Faysal had to regain the initiative and he did so by resolutely restating his complete commitment to the cause of Arab independence throughout the whole of the Middle East. On 22 January 1920, in a speech delivered at al-Nadi al-'Arabi (The Arab Association) in Damascus, to a great gathering of notables, nationalists and army officers, he declared his allegiance to the supreme aim of Arab independence – not only of Syria but of all the Arab lands.

Then, on 8 March, a 'General Syrian Congress' was convened in Damascus and declared Faysal king of 'a United Kingdom of Syria', including both the Lebanon and Palestine. The flag of the new kingdom was unfurled – a black, green and white horizontal tricolour with a red chevron – and the air filled with the din of hundreds of jubilant rifle salvoes.

Shortly afterwards an equally significant announcement was made: the 'complete independence of Iraq' under the sovereignty of Faysal's elder brother, Emir 'Abdallah. This decision, it was reported, had been taken by an 'Iraqi Congress' meeting in Damascus and working in cooperation with the General Syrian Congress.² This 'Iraqi Congress' was composed largely of the small group of former Ottoman army officers who had deserted to the British during the war and fought alongside the Emir Faysal's Bedouin. By now they had formed a new branch of al-'Ahd, known as al-'Ahd al-'Iraqi, and its membership included two individuals who would come to play an important role in the future politics of their homeland – Colonel Ja'far al-'Askari and his brother-in-law Lieutenant Nuri al-Sa'id.

One such former Ottoman officer was, however, notably missing from this event – Lieutenant Muhammad Sharif al-Faruqi. He had played no part in the final defeat of the Turks in Palestine and Syria and in the meantime had lost the support of Sharif Husayn and the latter's British backers in Cairo. However, he had somehow managed to ingratiate himself with Husayn's youngest son, Emir Zayd, and for a time enjoyed the position of 'senior staff officer' in Zayd's small private army based in Syria.³ However, sometime in 1919 he had fallen ill. Zayd arranged for him to be sent to Paris (at British expense) at a time when the Hashemites could still siphon off a good deal of British gold for their own – or their friends' – personal expenses. After his treatment and recovery, in early 1920 Faruqi travelled to London, apparently under the impression that the emir would finance his stay there in return for some unspecified diplomatic activity. But the money never arrived and Faruqi was compelled to turn to the British Foreign Office to pay off the debts he had meanwhile incurred in England. He also asked the Foreign Office to send him back to Cairo. Presumably glad to be rid of him, the

Foreign Office agreed but it seems that Cairo now had little to offer him and he soon began to plan his return to British-controlled Iraq. It would be a fateful decision.

Meanwhile, Emir 'Abdallah was with his father in Mecca. Precisely what he thought about his 'election' as Emir of Iraq is unknown. Since his initial meetings with Kitchener and Storrs in 1914 he had been an ally – albeit not a particularly active one – of the British. By the time his memoirs were published in 1950 he was King of Transjordan – one of Britain's most loyal allies in the Middle East – and perhaps understandably, in those memoirs there is absolutely no mention of these events. On the other hand there is also no public record of his renunciation of the Iraqi Congress's offer, and with the British seemingly acquiescing in the 'coronation' of his younger brother in Syria, 'Abdallah may have been quietly pleased by this unexpected turn of events.

One might also wonder to what extent public opinion in Iraq favoured one of the Hashemites – hitherto anathematised by many as pro-British traitors – as their new ruler. But the currents of political opinion in Iraq had now become exceptionally fluid; bygones could soon be bygones in this turbulent flow of new political ideas, and a heady mixture of these often incongruent and inconsistent anti-colonial sentiments was now swirling around the country – some of them emanating from Damascus, some from Mustafa Kemal's Turkish nationalist power base in Ankara, others from Bolshevik agents in Persia and yet others from the Shi'i cities invoking a return to an Islamic state. Given the ideological heterogeneity of this anti-colonial movement, wide sections of Iraqi public opinion, both Sunni and Shi'i, had begun to gravitate towards the one political programme that offered some degree of coherence and the possibility of practical implementation – an independent Arab kingdom under the leadership of Sharif Husayn's second son – but with the important proviso that the king would be guided by an elected assembly.

Throughout the summer of 1919, as it had become increasingly apparent that, following Wilson's plebiscite, the British had decided not only to stay in Iraq but also to run it along tight colonial lines, incipient signs of a Shi'i–Sunni alliance began to emerge with a political programme crystallising around the idea of a Sunni Hashemite emir responsible to a popular assembly in which – owing to their numerical preponderance in the population – the Shi'is would have a powerful role. In Karbela' this programme was supported by the new Grand Mujtahid, Taqi al-Shirazi and in Najaf, by Shirazi's opposite number, Sheikh al-Shari'a Isbahani, who had replaced the recently deceased Yazdi as the leading cleric in the city. With Shirazi's blessing, a group of nationalist mujtahidin, urban notables and tribal sheikhs chose Muhammad Ridha al-Shabibi, a respected literary figure and a known supporter of al-'Ahd, to travel to Mecca with a letter for Sharif Husayn – addressed to the 'King of the Arabs' – informing him that the civil commissioner had been informed 'that there should be a constitutional government with one of the sons of Your Majesty as King of Iraq'.[4]

Husayn received Shabibi with due courtesy, but whereas he was no doubt delighted to be addressed by the title he had always coveted (but which his British allies had never conceded), he must have had very mixed feelings about the final part of the emissary's letter. The end of the war had left him in full possession of only the stony wastes of the Hejaz and with a growing threat to his Hashemite state from the east emanating from Ibn Sa'ud and his Wahhabis. Moreover, in the general atmosphere of financial parsimony predominating in London, the Treasury had recently proposed to reduce the subsidy which Husayn had been receiving during the war. The Sharif was now deeply concerned about British intentions and probably had no wish to antagonise London further by making any moves which might appear to challenge the status quo in Iraq. He was also increasingly suspicious that his sons seemed willing to make alliances with local nationalists to further their own interests – in Syria, and now, perhaps, in Iraq – alliances which might undermine his own claim to suzerainty over the Arab world. Consequently, when Sharif Husayn replied on 20 September 1919 – and he addressed his letter to Shirazi himself – it was in a missive replete with compliments, religious references and profuse expressions of sympathy but with little else of substance.[5]

Nevertheless, a campaign for a Muslim King of Iraq heading a constitutional assembly was now well underway and the Damascus Declaration of 22 January 1920 by the 'Iraqi Congress' gave the movement a further impetus. In these circumstances, the reticence of Sharif Husayn (and also, perhaps 'Abdallah himself) could do nothing to dampen the enthusiasm of the campaign's adherents – as illustrated, for example, in a verse written by the Shi'i poet, Muhammad Baqir al-Hilli, recited at public meetings in Najaf:

> Long live 'Abdallah for he is to our people
> a king and his father the Sharif an Imam.[6]

Nevertheless, in spite of some earlier reservations about the mandate concept and the rising tide of complaint about the British Civil Administration, on 3 May 1920 it was a triumphant Wilson who issued a communiqué to the people of Baghdad informing them of the decisions taken at the San Remo conference and conveying his own perceptions of his – and their – future status.

> It is the duty of the mandatory Power to act the part of a wise and far-seeing guardian who makes provision for the training of his charge with a view to fitting him to take his place in the world of men … . And as the guardian rejoices over the growth of his ward into sane and independent manhood, so will the guardian Power see with satisfaction the development of political institutions which shall be sound and free.[7]

'As the guardian rejoices over the growth of his ward …' – Whether he intended it or not, the implications of Wilson's chosen simile would not have been lost on those who read this extraordinarily insensitive declaration. The general tone of Wilson's communiqué was all the more obtuse given that both he and Gertrude Bell had already spent some time trying to find a suitable Arabic translation of the word 'mandate'.

Since the institution had been first mooted, a number of different Arabic translations of the term had circulated throughout the Middle East. Bell herself had originally translated the term 'mandate' as *wisaya*, roughly meaning 'tutelage' and implying a fundamentally paternalistic relationship.[8] However, she soon realised that this had been a serious mistake: *wisaya* had a distinctly pejorative tone. As one pro-British Baghdad notable explained to her, '*Wisaya* implies too much. A man would not be able to alter the course of his canal without reference to the Mandatory Power.'[9] So instead, Wilson and Bell now decided to adopt the much more neutral word *intidab*, meaning little more than 'the government being selected', for official references to the mandate.[10] However, in spite of this semantic change, by explicitly using the analogy of 'guardian and ward' in his public declaration, Wilson made it abundantly clear that, whatever the term used officially, in reality it would be *wisaya*, not *intidab*, that characterised the relationship between Britain and Iraq under the mandate. So Wilson's proclamation could not have been more insulting to the angry and determined men, some of whom, unbeknown to Wilson, were that very day gathering in the city of Karbela' to confer with the Shi'i mujtahidin and tribal leaders of the Euphrates to consider whether the time was now ripe for armed rebellion.[11]

While Wilson and his entourage were focusing their attention on the threat posed by al-'Ahd 'outside agitators' based in Syria, in February 1919 a group of men, some of whom would emerge as the core of opposition to British rule in Baghdad, had been establishing a second party of resistance, calling themselves by the uncompromisingly militant name Haras al-Istiqlal – the Independence Guards.[12] In their party's constitution the second clause committed the organisation to strive for the complete independence of Iraqi territory while the third clause expressed support for one of the sons of King Husayn as ruler provided that the kingdom was ruled constitutionally and democratically.[13]

The founding committee of Haras al-Istiqlal was mainly composed of former Sunni officials and military men of Ottoman Iraq, men like 'Ali al-Bazirgan, one of the founders of a new public school in Baghdad. However, there were others from different backgrounds, including another scion of the highly respected Shi'i Al-Shabibi family from Najaf, Sheikh Baqir al-Shabibi,[14] together with a number of young alumni from the school founded by Bazirgan; and they were later to be joined by four other individuals who, together with Bazirgan, would eventually play a major role in the unfolding political struggle against the British in Baghdad.

The individual who was to become one of the leading nationalists in Baghdad we have already briefly met – Ja'far Abu al-Timman. By now he was thirty-nine years old and since the death of his grandfather during the war he had become head of the family's substantial trading business and one of the few wealthy Muslim merchants in a Baghdad where the large Jewish community dominated most commercial transactions.

As we have seen, General Maude's declaration on entering Baghdad had initially led Ja'far to believe that the British were genuinely offering the Arabs independence and this belief had naturally been strengthened by the Anglo-French Declaration the following year. This optimism about British intentions led him to accept an invitation to join a six-man 'Educational Council' of Baghdad notables to advise a newly established Education Department. Ja'far's qualifications for such a position rested partly on his prewar efforts to improve educational opportunities for young Shi'is. In 1909 he had obtained a fatwa from a progressive Shi'i cleric, the mujtahid Muhammad Sa'id al-Hububi, authorising him to open the first secular educational establishment for Shi'is in Baghdad to teach mathematics and French, a radical departure from the traditional Shi'i education which had hitherto been entirely religious in orientation.[15] The school was known as the Ja'fariyya, and although initially a Shi'i institution it later attracted support from some important Sunni notables including 'Ali al-Bazirgan.[16]

However, the British-sponsored 'Educational Council' to which Ja'far Abu al-Timman was appointed appears to have been little more than a talking shop with no influence over the decisions of the occupying power such as the proposal to impose a British curriculum on all Iraqi schools. It wasn't long before Ja'far resigned from it. A similar experience of being sidelined from effective decision making seems to have been the catalyst for his resignation from another 'Arab' façade for British diktat – a so-called 'Baghdad City Council' in which he was also briefly a member.

By May 1919 the British authorities in Baghdad had given up any hopes of co-opting Abu al-Timman into their apparatus of control and he was being marked down by the police as 'dangerous to the public'. Indeed, for a time he was compelled to move to Tehran after receiving a warning from a friend serving as an interpreter for the British that the authorities were considering arresting him. During his stay in Persia the British PO at Kermanshah was advised by his opposite number in Baghdad that Ja'far's activities should be closely monitored. 'He is a hare-brained, fanatical and clever creature', Baghdad advised, 'and if Tehran could get any information about his political activities in Khurasan it might be of interest to us all.'[17] However, Ja'far was careful to concentrate only on his business activities in Persia and a few months later was back in Iraq, albeit now under close scrutiny by the police and their local spies.

Sometime in early 1920 Ja'far Abu al-Timman made a critical decision: although he had originally stood aside from Haras al-Istiqlal – at any rate he was not one of its founding members – he now decided to join the organisation.[18] Whether this was before or after the announcement of the mandate is unclear, since his biographers do not specify the exact date. Not only did he join the organisation but shortly after his affiliation he also became a member of its eight-man executive committee and its secretary. Three other Baghdad notables who, like Abu Timman, were not among the original founding members of Haras al-Istiqlal also joined the organisation sometime in early 1920.

The first of these was Sayyid Muhammad al-Sadr. He was the thirty-three-year-old son of the mujtahid Sayyid Hasan al-Sadr, over whom he was said to have considerable influence. Although the al-Sadr family home was in Kadhimayn, another Shi'i holy city a few miles north-west of Baghdad, Sayyid Muhammad had established a political base as one of the governors of a new public school in the capital, the Madrasa al-Ahliyya (the People's School), opened in January 1920 largely due to the efforts of fellow Istiqlal member, 'Ali Al-Bazirgan. The establishment of the Ahliyya secondary school had, at first, seemed a laudable enterprise by the British. The Ja'fariyya secondary school, which Abu Timman had founded in 1909, had closed in 1917 and there were no other secondary schools in Baghdad.[19] That a group of wealthy Baghdadis should wish to pay for one, catering for sixty or seventy young men, seemed perfectly acceptable to the British authorities and permission was therefore granted; moreover, when its trustees applied for a grant from the Education Department this too was agreed.

However, it soon became clear to the British that the teaching staff was largely composed of ardent young nationalists whose primary function was to campaign against the continuing occupation. Like Abu al-Timman, although he was not a founder member of Haras al-Istiqlal, Muhammad al-Sadr soon became a member of its executive where he was appointed to the role of president.[20]

The third new member who rapidly became one of Istiqlal's leading personalities was the sixty-six-year-old Yusuf al-Suwaydi, an elderly Sunni of noble (sharif) birth and a senior judge of the shari'a courts, whose family claimed descent from the Prophet's uncle 'Abbas. He had already established his nationalist credentials by his prewar agitation for greater Arab autonomy which had led to his arrest on a trumped-up charge of planning the assassination of a Turkish general in 1913. Although he was later released for lack of evidence he had been exiled to Istanbul during the war, returning to Baghdad only in the summer of 1919. Although a strong opponent of the dictatorship of the Young Turk triumvirate, he had no desire to see that tyranny replaced by a more efficient colonial rule. Consequently, his outspoken opposition to British rule soon brought him to the attention of Wilson and Bell, but mistakenly they did not take him seriously: Yusuf Suwaydi was just 'that old ass Suwaydi', according to Gertrude Bell.[21]

Another Sunni notable, Sheikh Ahmad Daud, who, like Yusuf Suwaydi, had played a part in the prewar movement for greater Arab autonomy, joined Haras al-Istiqlal in 1919 and also soon became one of the key group of activists whom the British regarded as the leaders of the independence movement in Baghdad.

Finally, the thirty-two-year-old Sunni 'Ali al-Bazirgan, whose family name suggests a Turkoman lineage and who had been one of the founders of Haras al-Istiqlal, also now became a member of its executive committee, occupying the role of *mudir idara* in the organisation – a position primarily tasked with the role of maintaining communications between its membership.[22]

So, by the spring of 1920, these five individuals – Ja'far Abu al-Timman, Sayyid Muhammad al-Sadr, Yusuf Suwaydi, Sheikh Ahmad Daud and 'Ali al-Bazirgan – had become the core of the independence movement in Baghdad.[23] Meanwhile, under the direction of al-Sadr and Bazirgan, the Ahliyya school was fast becoming the nerve centre of the independence movement with large protest meetings being held regularly on Monday and Thursday afternoons,[24] while anti-British leaflets were secretly printed and distributed around the city by daring young school students. One such inflammatory missive stated:

> Long live Independence.
>
> Liberty is the daughter of Independence.
>
> No Liberty without Independence and no Honour without Liberty.
>
> We want Independence and we will not have independence except
>
> under the shade of the Arab Flag and with the Arab Union.
>
> The Life of the Arabs is in the Union.
>
> Demand your Independence until death.[25]

Although many of the barely literate citizens of Baghdad could not themselves read the leaflets, their very existence attracted great curiosity. Therefore they were usually taken to one of the hundreds of coffee shops around the city, where someone who could read was called upon to make a public recitation of the subversive patriotic or religious slogans.

In addition to this literature of resistance and rebellion emanating from the nationalists at the Ahliyya school, two additional currents of anti-British propaganda began to swirl around the city. The first of these represented the views of a sizeable body of men who believed that the Iraqi resistance should establish close links with Mustafa Kemal's growing nationalist movement in Anatolia with a view to creating a new, reformed pan-Islamic state. With British, French, Italian and Greek troops occupying large areas of Turkey including the capital Istanbul,

Ja'far Abu al-Timman,
one of the principal
nationalists in
Baghdad, c.1920

between 4 and 11 September 1919, Mustafa Kemal and his allies held a momentous conference at Sivas in south-east Anatolia, where they pledged to free their country from foreign occupation. Among those attending were a number of anti-British Arab notables including the redoubtable paramount chief of the Muntafiq, 'Ajaimi Sa'dun, who had commanded part of the mujahidin at the battle of Shu'ayba and now led a small army of Arab horsemen in the no-man's-land of north-west Iraq.

Any lingering hostility between Turks and Arabs which had developed during the war had, by now, considerably diminished as the two nationalities and co-religionists recognised they once again had a powerful common enemy. In Baghdad the pro-Turkish faction held a number of meetings in May attended mainly by former Ottoman military and police officers, and other former Ottoman government officials. They formally rejected the British mandate and demanded either a Turkish mandate or complete independence and proposed the establishment of a political organisation, Fida' al-Watan (Self-sacrifice for the Homeland), to campaign for these objectives.

However, the pro-Turkish resistance faction in Baghdad faced a number of difficulties. Firstly, the Kemalists had already renounced all claims to former Ottoman territories containing Arab majorities, although the Kurds were specifically claimed as Turks. Since the province of Mosul with a large Kurdish population was therefore designated as 'Turkish', the Kemalists laid claimed to sovereignty over it. This presented a serious difficulty for the pro-Turkish resistance faction and a point of friction with the other resistance groups (and indeed, popular sentiment throughout the other two provinces, Baghdad and Basra). Both al-'Ahd and Haras al-Istiqlal wanted Mosul to remain within a unified Iraq. Secondly, hundreds of miles to the north, in Anatolia, the Kemalists were themselves desperately embattled: even if they had wished to provide military support for an anti-British uprising in Iraq, or in Mosul alone, they simply did not have the resources. Indeed, by early 1920 they were urgently seeking (and receiving) arms from the Bolsheviks, who by now were successfully counter-attacking the White Russian armies and their British, French, American and Japanese interventionist supporters.

It was Bolshevik support for the Turkish nationalists, together with news from Persia of Bolshevik advances in the north in alliance with Persian nationalists, that led to a growing curiosity among some of the younger Iraqi nationalists – not only in Baghdad but also within the Shi'i holy cities – about *balshafiyya* (Bolshevism), this strange new political phenomenon which appeared to be successfully challenging European imperialism throughout the region.

By mid-1919 the Bolsheviks had already established an organisation called Jam'iyyat Takhlis al-Sharq al-Islami (Organisation for the Liberation of the Muslim East) under the aegis of the Eastern Department of Narkomindel (Peoples' Commissariat for Foreign Affairs) with the object of supporting and encouraging the struggle of the Muslim peoples against European domination.[26] The Jam'iyya had a secret base in Anatolia, protected by the forces of Mustafa Kemal and charged with spreading anti-British subversion, a task made considerably easier by the now widely known details of the infamous Sykes–Picot Agreement that the Bolsheviks had published.

By January 1920 the British police in Baghdad were beginning to receive reports of 'Bolshevik talk' in the coffee shops and mosques of Baghdad, and of the circulation of a pamphlet entitled *Bolshevism and Islam*, written by an Indian Muslim with strong Bolshevik leanings called Muhammad Barkatullah. His pamphlet was a curious and discordant mixture of pro-Communist, Pan-Islamist, and pro-Young Turk propaganda whose principal objective was to create sympathy among the Muslim peoples for the Bolshevik revolution. Beginning with an uncompromising declaration of praise for the Young Turk revolution of 1908, it went on to blame the Western Powers for 'extinguishing' it through war, exalting the CUP government for its resistance and denouncing the Sharif of Mecca for treachery. 'Today', the pamphlet stated, 'not a single Muslim state remains independent'. However, 'There is no cause for despair! Following on the long dark nights of Tsarist autocracy, the dawn of human freedom has appeared on the Russian horizon, with Lenin as the shining sun giving light and splendour this day of human happiness.'[27]

Whatever the Muslims of Baghdad made of this remarkable declaration – and as we shall see, there is a evidence to show that at least some among the educated *were* favourably impressed – the British were already becoming near-hysterical about what they saw as a vast Bolshevik–Kemalist threat to their interests in the Middle East. Not only was there a growing fear of Bolshevik agents infiltrating from Persia, but the presence of Bolshevik-armed Turkish nationalist forces in eastern and southern Anatolia, only a few hundred miles north of Mosul, was giving rise to the wildest imaginings of the British authorities in Iraq, such as a report of the presence of a mysterious 'Colonel Koloff' at Kemalist-controlled Diyarbakir, supposedly 'a prominent personage' in something called 'the Bolshevist Green Army'.[28]

Similarly, in the words of the Baghdad magistrate Thomas Lyell, Mustafa Kemal had 'joined the Bolshevik Headquarters in Asia Minor' and 'it is well known ... that no small proportion of the Red Army of Bolshevik Russia is Muslim.'[29] Likewise, for Gertrude Bell, there was 'no lack of evidence to show that a league of conspiracy, organised by the

Sheikh 'Abd al-Wahid al-Sikar of the Fatla Tribe, 1918. One of the principal Arab tribal leaders during the uprising.

Bolsheviks in cooperation with the Turkish Nationalists (has) long been in touch with extremist Arab political societies'.[30]

Perhaps surprisingly, the one source of political influence in Baghdad which appears to have been fading at this time was that of al-'Ahd. Although the party had a branch in Baghdad including civilian members, the organisation had always been stronger in Mosul, partly because of its closer proximity to the al-'Ahd HQ in Damascus.[31] Moreover, the official line of the Baghdad branch of the party that an independent Iraq would seek 'technical assistance' from the British – a position which was strongly opposed by Haras al-Istiqlal – seemed increasingly out of tune with popular sentiment whose antipathy towards the British occupation was approaching the point of explosion.[32] In an attempt to heal the rift between al-'Ahd and the Istiqlal, the Damascus headquarters of al-'Ahd sent two leading Iraqi members, Jamil al-Midfa'i and Ibrahim Kamal, to Baghdad, where, for a time, they managed to bring the two organisations into a common front,[33] but not long after they had returned to Syria, the schism re-emerged.

Although Haras al-Istiqlal was essentially a Baghdad-based organisation, by the spring of 1920 it had established branches in nearby Kadhimayn and in some important localities in the mid-Euphrates – Najaf, Hilla and Shamiyya. On 22 April two emissaries from this region arrived in Baghdad. They were Hadi al-Zwayn, a prominent sayyid from the mid-Euphrates town of Hilla, and 'Abd al-Muhsin Shilash, a leading Najafi merchant with widespread dealings among the Euphrates tribes. Abu al-Timman swiftly convened a gathering of Istiqlal followers and sympathisers including Muhammad al-Sadr, Yusuf Suwaydi and other prominent members of the organisation. As the two messengers related their news the Baghdad nationalists must have listened with growing excitement. The emissaries' report was startling. Only the previous day, most of the leading sheikhs and sada had met with the Grand Mujtahid Taqi al-Shirazi in Karbela' and agreed to take an oath on the Qur'an at the mosques of Husayn and 'Abbas committing them to rejecting British authority.[34] They were ready to take up arms against the occupation provided the religious leadership in Najaf and Karbela' gave the word. Moreover, although the emissaries' bitter complaints against the British – excessive taxation, forced labour, a particularly brutal PO in one division – Diwaniyya – were primarily local grievances, they were now becoming articulated in the language of 'national independence'.

At the close of the meeting at Abu al-Timman's home it was decided that Ja'far himself should be sent to Karbela' to observe and evaluate the extent of the tribal mobilisation in the surrounding region and establish a permanent link between the Baghdad nationalists and the Shi'i holy places.[35]

So on 4 May 1920, in the golden-domed city of Karbela', Abu al-Timman was ushered into a secret congregation of sheikhs and sada in the presence of the Grand Mujtahid Mirza Muhammad Taqi al-Shirazi and his son Mirza Muhammad Ridha.[36] The meeting was held in the Dar al-Hujja (House of Religious Debate) in Karbela'. Shirazi, a diminutive figure in a large white turban, was seated on a low couch supported by pillows and by his side sat Mirza Muhammad Ridha, himself already grey-bearded, wearing a smaller white turban. By now Ridha was the intellectual driving force behind the independence movement in the mid-Euphrates. He was president of Jam'iyyat 'Iraqiyya al-'Arabiyya which advocated collaboration with both the Kemalists and the Bolsheviks and he believed that some, at least, of the political principles of the latter were compatible with the values of Shi'i Islam.[37] In fact, he had already been accused by the British of openly disseminating the contents of an Arabic book entitled *Mabadi' al-Balshafiyya* (The Principles of Bolshevism). According to British police reports, Ridha was actually 'in touch with the Bolsheviks, who, in an open telegram, proclaimed him to be the head of the movement of liberation from the British', and he was 'mentioned by name in a wireless message issued by the Bolsheviks at Resht [in Persia] as working for the Bolshevik cause at Karbela'.[38]

Along each side of the Dar al-Hujja sat the invited mujtahidin, sheikhs and sada, carefully seated on their own low couches with their feet tucked under them; among them 'Abd al-Wahid Sikar, sheikh of the al-Fatla tribe, a thin-faced man with high cheekbones, moustached but beardless, wearing a black cloak and the white kufiyya with black mesh patterning typical of the Shi'is; present also was Sha'lan Abu al-Jun, sheikh of the Dhawalim section of the Bani Huchaym, an older, burly man, black bearded but similarly attired. The contingent of green-turbaned tribal sada, their black cloaks draped over their shoulders in the customary manner, included Sayyid Hadi al-Zwayn, one of the two emissaries to Baghdad, and Sayyid Nur al-Sayyid 'Aziz, both men of high status in a society which accepted and greatly valued their claim of descent from the line of Husayn and the Prophet.[39]

One after the other, the assembled notables expressed their anger at the arrogant and brutal behaviour of the British in the mid-Euphrates region, their belief that the occupiers were nevertheless weakening and withdrawing their forces, the news (some accurate, some exaggerated) of British setbacks in Persia and elsewhere, and the readiness of their men to take up arms if and when the clergy of the holy cities authorised them to do so; the discussion went on well into the night.

At last Taqi al-Shirazi, the Grand Mujtahid, spoke. A judgement on this question was, he said, 'a heavy burden'.[40] He was worried that, for all their courage, the tribes would be unable to stand up to the British and Indian forces with their aeroplanes and bombs. Shirazi was also troubled by the morality of authorising a campaign of violence when peaceful methods of opposition to British rule had not been exhausted. Indeed, at first he insisted that 'keeping the peace is more important than the revolution'. Yet he strongly sympathised with the anger and frustration of the delegates and eventually gave his support to an intensification of the campaign to oust the British. 'If this is your intention and this is your pledge then God will help you,' Shirazi finally declared – provided the rebels' actions were consistent with the maintenance of 'order and peace'. Precisely how this was to be achieved was not, however, resolved.

Nevertheless, as far as Ja'far Abu al-Timman was concerned, the conference in Karbela' had been a revelation. It had opened his eyes to the intensity of anti-British feeling in the heavily populated mid-Euphrates region and the realisation that the political movement in Baghdad now had a powerful constituency outside the capital, moreover one which was armed and ready to move against the British should that eventually become necessary. This was the essence of his report to Haras al-Istiqlal when he returned to Baghdad on 9 May.

The following day the executive committee of the organisation decided to launch a political campaign for independence in Baghdad which would unite both the Sunni and Shi'i communities.[41] The season was approaching when it was customary for the Sunnis to hold a series of celebrations known as mauluds in honour of the Prophet Muhammad's birth; however, on this occasion leading members of the Shi'i community would also be invited to take part. The objective was to hold these joint Sunni–Shi'i mauluds at all the 130 mosques of Baghdad, where the religious festivities would be followed by orations and recitals of poetry in which patriotic and religious themes would be woven together in a rising crescendo of demands for *istiqlal* – independence. As one sheikh who would later play an active role in the armed uprising succinctly put it, the demand for independence would be concealed 'behind a veil of religion' because, although the British authorities had banned political meetings and rallies, it was believed that they would be reluctant to intervene in what were, ostensibly, religious gatherings.[42]

Letters were therefore sent out to all the Muslim notables of the city inviting them to the first of these joint mauluds to be held at one of the city's great Sunni mosques, the Haydar Khana. After supper at six o'clock on the evening of 19 May 1920, the Sunni Mulla Uthman initiated the maulud.[43] This was followed by a recitation of the Shi'i Ta'ziyya – the devotional rendering of the martyrdom of the Imam Husayn – by a Shi'i notable, Muhammad Mahdi al Basir from Hilla.[44] The congregation was also addressed by one of the principal leaders of Haras al-Istiqlal, 'Ali al-Bazirgan. After this remarkable demonstration of solidarity between the two Muslim sects, participants began to stand up and make political speeches and recitations favouring independence and an end to the mandate.

In fact the Shi'is and Sunnis of Baghdad had already begun to draw together the previous year. According to Bell, in her report to Parliament in November 1920,

> For some time past it had been obvious to the nationalists that it would be necessary for them to present a united Islamic front. The deep prejudices which separate the Sunni and the Shi'i sects were temporarily overcome. The first symptom of a rapprochement occurred in the summer of 1919 when on two occasions Sunnis attended the religious meetings which were held in memory of the deceased Shi'i mujtahid Sayyid Muhammad Kadhim Yazdi. But it was not until the following month of Ramadan which began on 19 May 1920 that the political significance of the reconciliation became apparent.[45]

It wasn't long before Wilson's administration realised that a new and potentially highly threatening development was taking place. On 29 May the judicial secretary, Bonham Carter, wrote to Wilson, warning him that 'the drawing together of the Shias and Sunnis, nominally as a religious movement but in reality on political grounds to oppose us shows strong prospects of becoming an accomplished fact.'[46]

Some of the British military based in Baghdad also began to note a general change in the political atmosphere in the city. On 25 May Major General G. A. J. Leslie, commander of the 17th Division, wrote to his wife Edith in India, saying how glad he was that he had sent her and their daughter Kathleen there a fortnight earlier, adding that there had recently been attacks on individual British personnel. 'I am carrying a loaded revolver,' he informed her.[47]

Three days later, he wrote to her again describing the 'clear efforts ... being made to bring an entente between the Sunnis and the Shias'. He related how, on 24 May, the authorities had been forced to intervene. A young man named 'Isa Abd al-Qadir had been arrested after delivering a nationalist poem at the Jalani Mosque which Wilson considered to be 'dangerous to public order'.[48] The following day the young man was bundled off to imprisonment at Basra.[49] However, General Leslie had his own particular slant on this event. At this 'seditious meeting' the arrested man had not only made a speech which called upon Sunnis and Shi'is to unite but he had also 'mentioned a white woman at Clock Tower Barracks in a suggestive way'. True or not, nothing was more likely to enrage a British officer than a report that one of the 'natives' was casting aspersions upon the virtue of a 'memsahib'.[50]

Wilson was under the impression that the arrest of al-Qadir – a relatively restrained response to the campaign of opposition – would be sufficient to cool the ardour of a movement whose significance he was inclined to belittle and sending the prisoner to Basra would also remove a focus for demonstrations. But the leaders of the independence movement saw the action differently – an act of repression: but one so half-hearted that it indicated weakness rather than strength.

So, on the evening of al-Qadir's arrest, the leaders of Haras al-Istiqlal met once again at the house of Abu al-Timman to plan an intensification of the campaign: a protest demonstration the following day and the election of a team of delegates who would confront the civil commissioner with a madhbata – a mass petition demanding among other things the immediate formation of a national assembly to determine the future of the country.

The huge crowd that gathered on 26 May 1920 acclaimed fifteen of their leaders, including key members of the Istiqlal, as the delegation which would demand a face-to-face meeting with Wilson where the madhbata would be formally presented.[51] It was also agreed that the delegation should be headed by the elderly and highly respected Yusuf Suwaydi and would include both Sunni and Shi'i nationalists from Baghdad and Kadhimayn, the latter headed by Muhammad al-Sadr. After these formalities, the mass demonstration began to parade through the main streets of the city chanting anti-British and pro-independence slogans. By mid-afternoon it was becoming extremely hot and, it being the month of Ramadan, the demonstrators had neither eaten nor drunk since before sunrise. The mood of the crowd now became boisterous and unruly. So Colonel Frank Balfour, the military governor of the city, decided to send some armoured cars into the streets as a show of force. Predictably, stones began to fly and in the course of the ensuing mêlée two protestors were injured and a blind man was run over by one of the armoured cars and killed.

Meanwhile, Ja'far Abu al-Timman was sending messages to Karbela' and Najaf describing the growing unrest in Baghdad, the success of the interdenominational mauluds and the decision to confront Wilson with the madhbata. The Grand Mujtahid replied to Ja'far, congratulating him on the campaign but also counselling the need to 'protect your fellow citizens, the People of the Book [i.e. Jews and Christians], and uphold their liberty, property and dignity, respecting the honour of their places of worship as the Prophet advises us'.[52]

That such an admonition was necessary reflected the reality that by no means all the citizens of Baghdad were unsympathetic to continued British control. Indeed, on receiving news of the mandate, the leaders of both the Jewish and Christian communities had sent telegrams to King George V, thanking him for his government's action.[53] The reasons for this are not difficult to understand. In the case of the Christian communities, they were aware of the terrible massacres that fellow believers had suffered at the hands of some Muslims (especially the Kurds) during the chaos of the recent war; many of them feared that without the protection offered by the British mandate, they in turn might fall victim to some form of harassment or persecution by an Islamic state. In the case of the large Jewish community, they had seen their hopes of fair treatment under Muslim rulers dashed during the war and now there was the additional concern that they might, in some way, become scapegoats for the Zionist project in Palestine – in spite of the fact that Zionism was a project for which most of them had little sympathy.

Class and culture were also factors. Although there were thousands of poor Jews and Christian Arabs, the Jewish and Christian communities also included some of the richest citizens in Baghdad. As such they saw the British, with their own rigid and seemingly well-ordered class system, as a natural protector of their interests while, for their part, the British officer class resident in the city had a natural affinity towards the culture of Christians and Jews, many of whom shared their interests in music and literature and possessed a similar general world outlook. As a result, the occupiers generally treated the Jews and Christians with more respect and were more sensitive to their religious beliefs, property rights and economic interests than they were towards the Muslim inhabitants.[54]

However, the Islamic movement for independence continued to work hard to win over, or at least, neutralise, any opposition from the Jewish and Christian communities. On 29 May Shirazi issued the following proclamation which was carried by messengers to all the main towns and cities of Iraq and which ended with a renewed call to respect and protect the interests of Jews and Christians.

To my brother Iraqis,

Peace be upon you and God's mercy and blessings. Let it be known that your brothers in Baghdad, Kadhimayn, Najaf, Karbala' and other parts of Iraq have agreed amongst themselves to unite and to organize peaceful demonstrations. These demonstrations have attracted mass support while also maintaining public order, demanding their rights to an Independent Iraq and, God willing, an Islamic government with one objective – that every part of Iraq sends to the Capital, Baghdad, a madhbata for its rights and agreeing with those who are heading for Baghdad from its surrounding areas. It is the duty of all Muslims to be in agreement with your brothers and their noble principles. But take care not to disturb the peace or to hide yourselves away or to fall into disagreement with each other such that your goals would become sour and your rights, which the moment of achieving is now in your hands, would fall into ruination. And I entrust you with the safe keeping of all the other religious communities and sects which are in your towns, with full regard for their persons, wealth and lands and never do any harm to one of them. May God give you success according to his will. Peace be upon you and God's mercy and blessings.

Muhammad Taqi al Shirazi

10 Ramadan 1338 [29 May 1920][55]

Shirazi's call to respect the interests of the 'the other religious communities' was taken seriously by the independence movement in Baghdad. Wilson reported to the India Office that 'extremists' had been active recently. Not only had great efforts been made to unite the Sunnis and Shiʿis against the occupation but 'effusive demonstrations in favour of native Christians were recently made by Mohammedan religious leaders on the occasion of the Corpus Christi procession in Baghdad'. Also Jewish and Christian coffee shops had been 'inundated' by circulars such as the following:

To all our Brothers, Christian and Jewish fellow citizens.

It is to be made clear to you, our brothers, that we in the country are partners in happiness and misery. We are brothers and our ancestors lived in friendship and mutual help. Do not consider in any way that the demonstrations carried out by the citizens affect, in any way, your rights. We continue to value and respect our friendship. All the demonstrations being made do not indicate a lack of respect for you or any citizen. We have no other object than to claim from the present government the fulfilment of its pledges to the Iraqi nation which it has published many times in the newspapers. We therefore invite you to take part with us in everything that is good for the nation.[56]

However, not all the Muslim citizens of Baghdad were swept up in the growing enthusiasm for Unity and Independence. The venerable Naqib of Baghdad, Sayyid 'Abd al-Rahman al-Gailani, religious head of the Sunni community, expressed his dismay at the prevailing mood of frater-nisation between 'his' people and the Shi'is to Gertrude Bell. 'I tell you', he expostulated, 'beware of the Shi'is,' adding, unconvincingly, that 'I have no animosity against the Shi'i sect ... But turn your eyes on the pages of history and you will see that the salient characteristic of the Shi'is is their levity ... Idolatry and mutability are combined in them.'[57] There were not a few among the Baghdad Sunni ashraf, rich men and great landowners on the Tigris, who shared his opinion; but for the time being they largely kept their opinions to themselves.

On learning of the nationalists' intention to present their madhbata, Wilson agreed to a meeting with the delegates at the Baghdad serai, the headquarters of the British Civil Administration, on 2 June. However, claiming that the fifteen nationalist delegates were merely a group of 'self-appointed politicians', he also invited forty prominent 'moderate' Baghdadis who would, so he hoped, overwhelm radical opinion in a show of pro-British enthusiasm.

On the evening of the great event, Wilson, accompanied by the military governor of Baghdad, Colonel Balfour, the judicial secretary Bonham Carter and Lieutenant Colonel Howell, the revenue secretary, arrived at the serai in their well-pressed uniforms and solar topees. The occasion got off to a bad start: outside the building they were met by a crowd of rowdy school students and townsmen who shouted abuse at them. Inside, the atmosphere, like the actual temperature, was torrid. Over 100°F in the shade, the angry mood of the delegates and their supporters was exacerbated by the Ramadan fast, exceptionally trying when it fell in the summer period.[58] Moreover, once inside the serai, Wilson and his entourage were disconcerted to find that only a handful – nine, actually – of the forty pro-British notables, had dared to turn up. It was clearly going to be a difficult encounter. Nevertheless, undaunted by the evident failure of his plan to pack the meeting, Wilson – whose self-assurance had recently been fortified by the award of a knighthood – proceeded to hold forth at great length and with considerable aplomb in English, followed by an Arabic text which had been prepared by Gertrude Bell.

Firstly, Wilson informed the meeting that he welcomed the opportunity of explaining the British government's policy 'in this matter' and reminded the assembled notables of the Anglo-French Declaration of 8 November 1918 and Article 22 of the League of Nations Treaty, adding, 'These declarations represent the policy of H.M.'s Government from which it has at no time diverged.' Wilson then proceeded to read out *in extenso* the text of these documents, documents which were already perfectly well known to the educated and, in some cases, elderly men who stood facing him in the sweltering early evening heat.

After this colourless preamble, Wilson continued by assuring his sceptical audience that, 'H.M.'s Government's desire is to set up a National Government in this country and it is their intention that this shall be done as soon as possible.' He then declared:

No one regrets more than I do the delay that has occurred. It is due to causes beyond our control – the prolongation of the war, the difficulties of making peace and the disturbed conditions of our borders both towards Persia, towards Turkey, and towards Syria have prevented a Civil Government being established here as quickly as we could wish, but I would not have you believe that this delay could have been avoided.

But then he adopted a harsher tone.

I can assure you that those individuals in Baghdad who have sought from patriotic or other motives to hasten the establishment of a Civil Government here by incitements to violence and by rousing the passions of ignorant men are doing and indeed have already done a great disservice to the country ... Those who are encouraging disorder and inciting men against the existing regime are arousing forces which the present Administration can and will control ... It is my duty as the temporary head of the Civil Administration to warn you that any further incitements to violence and any further appeals to prejudice will be met by vigorous action both from the Military authorities and the Civil Administration.[59]

There had been no 'incitements to violence', as Wilson himself knew; but he apparently thought the Baghdad nationalists and their supporters could be cowed by his stern admonitions and menacing references to 'vigorous action'. And so he went on:

> We have the power and the intention to maintain order in this country until a Civil Government is established. I shall not hesitate to ask the Military authorities to apply any degree of force necessary to ensure this and they will not be backward in meeting my requests. It is my earnest hope that I shall not again have to say this to you and that there will be no further occasion for the use of troops or for the adoption of other special measures to maintain public order.

Then, turning to the question of 'the future form of Government to be established in this country', Wilson announced that 'public opinion' would be 'consulted ... as soon as we can do so', and that his own proposal for a 'Provisional Civil Government', the details of which HM Government had not yet seen fit to authorise him to publish, would include the establishment of a 'Council of State under an Arab President to hold office until the question of the final constitution of Iraq has been submitted to the Legislative Assembly which we propose to call'.

The scheme for a provisional government had been drawn up, two months earlier, by a committee chaired by the judicial secretary and composed entirely of other members of the Civil Administration. It would function 'until we have had time in consultation with you to devise a permanent scheme'. The 'Council of State' would consist of a president and eleven members 'each appointed by the High Commissioner and removable from the Council at his pleasure'. The president would be an Arab – chosen by the British, as would be any Arab members of the council; however, 'we contemplate that, in practice, a majority of the [Council] members would be British.' The provisional government would only be responsible for internal affairs. 'External affairs, foreign relations, including treaties and war should be reserved to the Mandatory Power.' And lest any of his audience thought that the formation of this

British-dominated 'Provisional Civil Government' would swiftly lead to any more meaningful form of self-representation, Wilson concluded as follows: 'Do not be misled by appearances. Iraq has been under an alien Government for 200 years and with the best will in the world an indigenous National Government cannot be set up at once. The process must be gradual or disaster is certain.'

Sitting down, Wilson thanked the Arab delegates and their supporters for listening to him 'so patiently', adding that he would now be 'glad to hear any representations you may wish to make'.

At this, the elderly Yusuf Suwaydi stepped forward. He was a man of average stature, a rather delicate face with a short, neatly trimmed white beard and large, piercingly dark eyes. He wore the dark blue cloak and small conical cap surrounded by a white turban of a Sunni qadi; his general demeanour was calm and dignified and as he prepared himself to speak a total silence fell over the assembled crowd. Addressing Wilson and his entourage directly, he reminded them that he and his fellow delegates had been chosen 'by the people' on the night of 7 Ramadan to represent them in discussions with the occupying power and to 'negotiate with its representatives the implementation of three demands which were considered essential by the mass of the people and the majority of its leaders'.

> Firstly, we demand the immediate establishment of a Convention representing the Iraqi people which will lay out the route whereby the form of government and its foreign relations will be determined. Secondly, the granting of freedom of the press so that the people may express their desires and beliefs. And thirdly, the removal of all restrictions on the postal and telegraph services, both between different parts of the country and between Iraq and neighbouring countries and kingdoms, to enable the people to confer with each other and to understand current world political developments.[60]

Suwaydi then concluded, 'In our capacity as delegates of the people of Baghdad and Kadhimayn, we ask that you agree to the implementation of these three demands as quickly as possible.'

There was, however, one notable omission from Suwaydi's three demands. There was no mention of a request for one of the sons of Sharif Husayn to be installed as Emir of Iraq. Possibly this was simply one of the issues which would be settled by the 'Convention'. But it seems equally likely that the nationalist leaders both in Baghdad and on the Euphrates were fast becoming disenchanted by the lukewarm response they had so far received from Husayn and the absence of any response at all from their hitherto favourite candidate, 'Abdallah.

After Suwaydi had spoken, Wilson politely thanked the delegates for expressing their opinions but informed them that nothing further could be done until he received detailed instructions from London as to how the mandate was to be put into practice. Then he marched out of the serai; but as he did so he was met, once again, by a crowd of rowdy demonstrators, booing and shouting.

The very next morning, Hasan Sukhail, one of Gertrude Bell's circle of pro-British notables, arrived at her office; the news he was bringing was not encouraging. He had not been at the madhbata but he had heard all about it – it was the talk of the town.[61] 'No one will accept the Mandate', he declared and he warned her that there was no point in trying to set up the toothless 'Divisional Councils' which Wilson favoured since no one would serve on them: 'The ashraf here, at present, are all determined to resist the mandate,' he warned. And then, more ominously, Sukhail urged that the British must take the initiative in resolving the crisis immediately:

> They say you have no troops now; that they are all dispersed and you can do nothing. I think it would be very difficult for you if they create disturbances up and down the country, attacking motor cars and cutting railways, You must act now. Today there will be 5,000 people in Kadhimayn; at the next meeting there will be 10,000. Such gatherings are difficult to control.[62]

Nevertheless, in spite of this dire warning, which Bell immediately passed on to Wilson, a few days later both of them were taking a relatively relaxed view of the state of internal security. On 7 June Wilson telegrammed the India Office, with copies to the government of India's Foreign and Political Department at Simla and the high commissioner, Cairo, informing them that 'the situation in Baghdad itself has somewhat improved during the last few days. Moderate opinion condemns the extremists. The public feels itself to be misled.'[63] For her part, Bell wrote to her father on the same day, telling him – in complete contradiction to the report by Hasan Sukhail – that Wilson's reception of the madhbata had been a great success. 'A.T.'s speech took the wind out of the sails' of the delegates and that 'the general talk of the bazaars was that the town had made a fool of itself. This impression continues to grow.'[64] And demonstrating the extent to which she was out of touch with events in the Shi'i heartland, Bell added that at Najaf, 'they had definitely refused to send up delegates to ask for Arab Independence.' In reality, the Najafis had not sent delegates for the simple reason that they feared they would be arrested.

General Aylmer Haldane, British Commander-in-Chief in Iraq, 1921

General Haldane's Difficult Posting

Monday 2 February 1920: it is a bitterly cold winter's day and Winston Churchill, secretary of state for war, with his hands in his pockets and his coat-tails resting on his forearms, is warming his backside, standing before a blazing coal fire in his office in Horse Guards Avenue.[1] Opposite him, seated in a comfortable armchair, is Lieutenant General Sir Aylmer Lowthorpe Haldane, formerly commander of the 6th Army Corps on the Western Front, but who has been languishing on half-pay since the end of the war and for the last twelve months anxiously waiting for 'something to turn up'. A few weeks earlier Haldane was informed that he will be appointed GOC-in-chief in occupied Iraq and now he has been called to the War Office to receive his instructions. But the meeting is not going to be a comfortable one. There is bad blood between the two men going back to an incident during the Boer War.

Churchill and Captain (as he was then) Haldane of the Gordon Highlanders had originally been close friends. On the morning of 15 November 1899, Churchill, who had previously resigned his commission as a lieutenant in the 4th Hussars and was now the war correspondent for the *Morning Post*, had joined Haldane on an armoured train at Estcourt, the most forward position of the British Army in Natal, to carry out a reconnaissance of the enemy positions. This was not a role suited to an armoured train and it was soon ambushed and derailed by a superior force of Boers equipped with artillery and Maxim guns. In the ensuing fighting, during which Churchill distinguished himself trying to evacuate some of the British wounded, he was captured along with Captain Haldane.[2]

They were taken to a prisoner-of-war camp in Pretoria. Churchill and Haldane were both miserable as prisoners and together with a sergeant major named Brockie they began to discuss the prospects for escaping. Soon Haldane came up with a plan. He had discovered a part of the perimeter fence near the latrines where the iron palings were low enough for them all to climb over and jump into the dense undergrowth outside the camp. From there they would make their way to Portuguese-controlled territory.

In the event, Churchill was able to seize an opportunity to escape over the perimeter fence alone while the guards were not watching, leaving behind both Brockie and Haldane and with the result that security was thereafter considerably tightened. Haldane and Brockie were furious. Haldane felt that he had been 'left in the lurch' by Churchill, who had 'walked off with my carefully thought-out plan'. He had 'simply taken the bread out of my mouth'.

After many adventures, Churchill eventually made his way to Portuguese territory and from there returned in triumph to Durban. His role in the armoured train fight, his capture and escape, made him an instant international celebrity as the telegraph and Reuters news service spread his story far and wide. However, Churchill said nothing about Haldane or Brockie, who were now much more tightly supervised by their prison guards, and although in March 1900 they too eventually made their escape they got none of the hero-worshipping publicity which Churchill received.

Regardless of this particular painful recollection, it would be fair to say that, in general, Haldane was not a particularly happy man. He was now fifty-eight and, although still a handsome, six-foot tall and quite sociable individual (he particularly enjoyed singing light opera and reciting poetry), he had never managed to find a wife, increasingly relying on his sister, Alice, for female company.[3] In his own mind this was because he had given his life to the army and sadly neglected his own personal affairs – but the army had scarcely reciprocated. During the first two years of the war, while he had served his country on the Western Front with the rank of Brigadier General, he had been passed over for promotion on a number of occasions. His belated (in his eyes) promotion to the command of the 6th Corps in August 1916 had somewhat assuaged General Haldane's melancholy – a melancholy which bordered on self-pity – but he remained convinced that, in his own words, it had been his fate 'to be born under an evil star'.[4]

So today Haldane is attending this meeting with Churchill with gritted teeth. Meeting him again under these circumstances is somewhat embarrassing to say the least and does nothing to alleviate his general mood of mild depression; nor is he exactly overjoyed at having to accept command of a region captured and occupied during the much denigrated 'side show'. Indeed, Haldane knows absolutely nothing about Iraq – except that among those who have served there the near-unanimous opinion is that the place is an absolute 'shit-hole'.

Churchill is aware of Haldane's antipathy towards him but in recent weeks he has been pestered by some of Haldane's friends to find the man a job. He is also aware that Haldane is generally regarded as a taut and efficient commander, one who is probably well suited to the task in hand; and the task in hand is to reduce the garrison in Iraq as quickly and smoothly as possible, both to save costs and so that the forces deployed there can be moved to other parts of the empire where they are desperately needed. Indeed, while Churchill is by no means unimpressed by the advantages conferred upon Britain by the remarkable accretion of territory in Iraq – not the least of which are the potentially rich oil resources which his own department has extensively researched during the past two years – he is also acutely aware that the additional responsibilities thereby incurred have arrived at an extremely inconvenient time; and, in the circumstances, nobody in government appears to have a clear idea about what to do with this problematic new British colony.

In fact, the circumstances in early 1920 were very dire indeed. The last twelve months had been among the most difficult and threatening ever experienced by the British Empire and its ruling class. Both at home and abroad that experience had been one of almost continuous chaos, disorder and outright rebellion. In January 1919 there had been two mutinies of British troops demanding immediate demobilisation and in Glasgow, a virtual revolution by 35,000 industrial workers had been suppressed only by the deployment of tanks and machine guns. In June, police in Liverpool had gone on strike, resulting in widespread rioting and looting. Throughout the summer and autumn of 1919 mass industrial unrest continued and by the beginning of 1920 the cabinet was anxiously anticipating a revolutionary strike by miners, railwaymen and dockers and had little idea how to combat it. Ministers even received reports that there was 'a considerable amount of revolutionary talk going on in the Brigade of Guards'.[5]

Meanwhile, in Ireland, republican politicians had announced that they were setting up their own independent government in Dublin and on 22 January 1919 convened their first parliament. At the same time they called for volunteers to build up their own armed force – the Irish Republican Army. When Britain attempted to restore control from Westminster a widespread campaign of terror began in which British officials and police were hunted down and assassinated. In response, the British government had been forced to recruit a volunteer militia – the so-called Black and Tans – whose mission, in the words of cabinet secretary Maurice Hankey, was to meet terror 'by a greater terror'.

Abroad, the empire's situation was equally dire. In Egypt the arrest and deportation of the nationalist leader Fuad Zaghlul on 9 March triggered a major uprising. By the summer of 1919 British troops had largely suppressed it but it had cost almost a thousand Egyptian lives and the death or injury of seventy-five British, but sporadic strikes and other disorders were still continuing in the towns. According to the British authorities, the unrest had manifested a clear 'Bolshevik tendency', engaging the sympathy and support of 'all classes and creeds'.[6]

In India, too, nationalist sentiment had become intense, exacerbated by General Dyer's ghastly blunder. On 11 April 1919, faced with large-scale agitation in the Punjab, he had ordered his troops to open fire on a rowdy but peaceful demonstration in the city of Amritsar: 379 men women and children had been killed and over 2,000 injured. It was difficult to imagine anything more likely to inflame nationalist sentiment at a time when Britain was having to rely increasingly upon Indian troops to control the territories of its now vastly expanded empire.

The following month, Amanullah, the new Emir of Afghanistan, abandoning the pro-British neutrality of his late father and seeking to throw off the last vestiges of British-Indian domination of his country, had ordered his army to make an incursion across India's North-West Frontier. The Emir hoped to take advantage of nationalist sentiment in India, the shortage of experienced troops there and war weariness in Britain to compel Britain to recognise the full independence of Afghanistan and the emir's right to be addressed as 'King'. In the event, the Afghan army was defeated but the losses suffered by British and Indian troops during the war were considered excessive for the scale of the fighting and in August the viceroy, Lord Chelmsford, had been forced to accept the emir's original demands. Nevertheless, by the autumn of 1919 fighting was still continuing on the North-West Frontier. Taking advantage of the Afghan attack, there had been a rising of the wild frontier tribes of Waziristan, further stretching the military resources of India. A series of embarrassing reverses had been suffered by the punitive columns sent to deal with the tribesmen and the situation was still by no means under control.

To complicate matters, Britain was now burdened by huge debts to the USA and the country seemed to be sliding into a recession: unemployment was rising and the great coal-mining industry was in a serious economic crisis. In these circumstances the Treasury, the Bank of England and sections of the press were all clamouring for major cuts in public expenditure and Churchill had to admit that military expenditure could not be exempted from the financial stringency demanded by the markets. The real problem, as Churchill saw it, was the Middle East. Currently there were 9,500 British troops occupying Istanbul, 6,000 in Egypt, 9,000 in Palestine and 14,000 in Iraq plus a further 46,000 Indian troops and a veritable host of labourers, officers' wives and children and camp followers, the cost of the whole occupation of Iraq amounting to over £18 million per year. It simply wouldn't do.[7]

So that is why Churchill is now conducting this uncomfortable interview with General Haldane; because, having reviewed all the various demands upon the military from all the various outposts of Britain's far-flung Empire, Churchill has decided that Iraq is one area where significant reductions in troop levels can and must be achieved.

The meeting lasts only twenty minutes. Haldane is to leave for Iraq on or about 15 February, subject to suitable travel arrangements becoming available. He is to take command of all British and Indian troops in the vilayets of Basra, Baghdad and Mosul with the primary objective of reducing the garrison whose expense has become 'an intolerable burden on the British taxpayer'. 'Being one of that suffering class', as Haldane later put it, he found himself 'in full sympathy' with this objective.

Haldane is also to be responsible for the 14,000 Turkish POWs being held in Iraq pending the termination of all hostilities with Turkey and to examine solutions to the problem of the 50,000 Armenian and 'Assyrian' (Nestorian) Christian refugees who have fled into the Mosul region following the collapse of Russian forces in northern Persia. And since the Bolsheviks have recently recaptured the Azerbaijani oil city of Baku and are now rapidly pushing south, threatening the 9,500 British and Indian troops sent to support the newly independent Caucasian republics, Haldane is to ensure that lines of communication across Persia to these troops remain open and protected should it become necessary to evacuate them.[8] However, in pursuing all these objectives, Haldane is to liaise closely with the Civil Administration in Iraq in the person of the acting civil commissioner, Captain Wilson, recently promoted major and gazetted brevet lieutenant colonel.[9]

At which point Churchill politely, but somewhat frostily, thanks Haldane for coming to see him, indicating that the meeting is now over. Haldane in spite of his sympathy with Churchill's intentions, nevertheless would prefer to defer any general policy of troop reductions in Iraq until he has examined the problem on the spot; but it is clear from Churchill's demeanour that – as Haldane would later put it – 'an expression of my views, beyond a general assent, would be of little value, and I refrained from uttering it.' But then, just as Haldane is about to leave the room, Churchill takes his hand and, looking him straight in the eye, tells Haldane, 'I have chosen you for this command, because you are something more than a soldier: write to me regularly – aside from official cables – about how you see things.'[10] And Haldane cannot help but feel some of his enmity towards Churchill evaporating.

Had Haldane known the full extent of Churchill's plans for the imperial control of Iraq he would have been, to say the least, startled. Those plans went much further than a mere reduction in troop numbers. For some time Churchill, under the strong influence of Hugh Trenchard, chief of the air staff, had been studying the possibility of relying almost entirely on air power to administer 'law and order' in Britain's colonial territories and he was increasingly inclined to hand over control of Iraq to the fledgling Royal Air Force, a plan whose realisation would be facilitated by the fact that Churchill now held the office of air minister as well as secretary of state for war. It would be far more economical, he believed, to dispatch a squadron of aircraft to bomb and strafe recalcitrant Arab villages than to send punitive columns of infantry with all the supply and logistics problems which that entailed.

General Haldane, on his own admittance, knew absolutely nothing about Iraq and its current administration. He could have remedied this by visiting the India Office, where voluminous reports on this subject would have been made available to him. Instead he ordered a selection of books from Messrs Hatchard of Piccadilly dealing primarily with the ancient history of Mesopotamia, together with a revised version of the Bible published by Oxford University Press, which he later explained was 'by no means the least valuable of the literary possessions which he took with him'. So instead of briefing himself about the territory whose garrison he was shortly to command, Haldane left London on 9 February and travelled to the South of France, where he enjoyed a short holiday with friends at Cannes. On the 15th he sailed from Marseilles aboard the P&O liner *Devanha*, arriving at Bombay on 2 March. There he received orders that he should proceed to Delhi to meet the current viceroy, Lord

Chelmsford, and to discuss the situation in Iraq with his predecessor as GOC-in-chief Mesopotamia, Sir George MacMunn, who had replaced General Marshall the previous year.

On 10 March 1920 Haldane set off back to Bombay, from where he embarked on the British India ship *Chakdina*, which was to carry himself, his aide and a small number of Indian reinforcements to Basra. After six days steaming along the coast of Persia and up the Gulf, on 20 March they arrived at the mouth of the Shatt al-'Arab, awaiting a tide which would take them safely over the great sand bar. So far Haldane had not been impressed by his first views of Iraq. Not only had the journey up the Persian Gulf been 'devoid of interest', but at the mouth of the Shatt, 'the view of the low-lying coast, with its background of date-palms, and the muddy waters all around which soiled the pale green of the sea, inspired no admiration'. 'The outlook struck me as particularly dreary,' Haldane observed.

At 3.30 in the afternoon, the *Chakdina* finally docked at Basra, where Haldane was received by a guard of honour of a hundred officers and men of the 2nd Battalion of the Manchester Regiment with their regimental colour.[11] Smart enough, Haldane thought, but the 'other ranks' were mainly raw recruits from the slums of that dark northern city and with their pale young faces framed by top-heavy solar topees and bandy legs protruding from long baggy shorts, they looked particularly unsuitable for operations in that miserably hot and humid land. In fact, the battalion's last assignment had been guard duties in Ireland, where they had been mainly carrying out functions which were more of a policing than military nature.

Afterwards, Haldane drove around the city and base which now covered an area of twenty square miles and got his first view of the miles of wharves and riverside buildings which had been built to support the invasion and subsequent campaigns 'up-country'. Reducing this to a more manageable size and making commensurate cuts in the garrison was going to be an 'Augean task', Haldane ruefully concluded.

The next day, at four in the morning, the general boarded a comfortable stern-wheeler and began the journey up the Tigris to Baghdad, arriving at 'Amara two days later. It was the flood season and for miles on either side of the river there was little to see except a vast expanse of water fringed far away to the east by the mountains of the Pusht-i-Kuh. With sadness, Haldane pictured those British and Indian troops plodding their way up the river bank in that first, doomed attempt to capture Baghdad. 'Never could a march have been performed with surroundings less inspiring,' he thought.[12]

Two days later, Haldane disembarked at Kut and continued his journey to Baghdad by special military train along the one-metre-gauge railway which the British had built after Kut had been retaken. It was getting dark as the train pulled into the terminus, Hinaydi station, a few miles south of the city itself, and as Haldane stepped down from his carriage he was very tired after an extremely uncomfortable hundred-mile journey. On the platform stood a large welcoming party of senior military officers, local Arab notables and members of the Civil Administration. As he worked his way down the line, saluting, shaking hands and making occasional polite remarks as seemed appropriate, he eventually found himself face to face for the first time with Acting Civil Commissioner Arnold Wilson.

This first encounter must have brought to mind an incident that had taken place shortly before Haldane's departure from England. He had been dining with an old acquaintance, Sir John Hewitt, at the latter's club. The previous year Sir John had been sent out to Iraq by the War Office to examine whether certain expenditures should have been charged to the military or to the Civil Administration, and on returning to England had produced an official report, some of whose conclusions were unwelcome to the latter. Sir John and General Haldane had spent a quite convivial evening together, reminiscing about the war and enjoying a bottle of good Riesling. Suddenly Hewitt took hold of Haldane's wrist and, leaning forward, whispered, 'Before you go, Aylmer, I must give you a piece of advice – you can take it or leave it, but I'm going to give it to you anyway – Get rid of Wilson.'[13]

Precisely why he was to 'get rid of Wilson' was never made clear, except that Hewitt had apparently found Wilson uncooperative. In any case, Wilson, as acting civil commissioner, was employed by the India Office while Haldane was employed by the War Office and had no direct powers over his civilian colleague. Moreover, as far as Haldane could see in the gathering darkness, Brevet Lieutenant Colonel Wilson was a soldierly looking type of person with no obvious personal defects, and for the time being he decided he would discount his old friend's opinion and form his own judgement of Wilson as he proceeded to carry out the war minister's orders. What he did not yet appreciate was that the orders which Churchill had given him were quite inconsistent with the objectives already decided upon by Wilson and the team of admiring young political officers with whom he had now surrounded himself.

By the time General Haldane arrived in Baghdad, a large part of Wilson's project had already been achieved. The country had been split up into sixteen administrative divisions each ruled by a PO – 'Amara, Arbil, Baghdad, Ba'quba, Basra, Diwaniyya, Diyala, Hilla, Kirkuk, Kut, Mosul, Nasiriyya, Samarra, Shamiyya, Sulaymaniyya and Qurna – these, in turn, being subdivided into forty separate districts, each under the control of an APO. To man this complex structure a force of 534 POs, APOs, departmental officers and other senior staff (of which 507 were British) earning more than Rs600 per month (equivalent, in 'standard of living' terms, to around £2,200 in the UK in today's money) had been recruited to administer the country, supervise the collection of taxes, and run the departments responsible for public works, irrigation, postal services etc.[14] Of these, 106 officers represented the executive staff of divisions, of which fifteen were actually based in Persia. In addition there were a further 515 British and 2,209 Indian Civil Administration staff on a monthly pay scale lower than Rs600. At the apex of this bureaucratic pyramid stood Wilson, who, as acting civil commissioner, drew a monthly salary of £300 (£11,000 in today's money).[15] On the other hand, by October 1919 none of the proposed provincial councils had been set up and only four of the sixteen divisions had been provided with divisional councils, and these met only occasionally to consider matters placed before them by the POs. Even in these cases the Arab notables who were appointed as members soon experienced the high-handed methods of their new masters. For example, at Basra, the PO laid down an elaborate set of standing orders among whose provisions was the rule that no member should speak for more than five minutes, a somewhat onerous imposition upon the local worthies whose traditional eloquence would easily exhaust this time limit merely in making polite introductions.[16]

A far more onerous imposition, but one which was experienced not in the towns but in the countryside, was forced labour. For example, in late 1918 around 1,000 Arabs from the Rumaytha district on the Lower Euphrates had been dragooned into the work of laying steel rails for the new one-metre-gauge railway network the British were building from Samawa to Diwaniyya. Forced labour was also widely employed in the agricultural sector. The staff of the Civil Administration's Irrigation Department had very definite ideas about how Iraq's water resources should be used and developed – ideas which often ran contrary to traditional usage and custom – and they didn't hesitate to call upon their local POs to compel tribes in the vicinity of the irrigation works for which they were responsible to provide labour parties for making or repairing flood banks and other public works; men like Colonel Leachman were always more than ready to assist in this task by means of a few swift blows of his cut-down polo stick.[17]

In their day, the Turks had also used tribal labour for these tasks but they had usually been careful to consult the local sheikhs concerning any new scheme, taking care to point out the benefits that would be likely to accrue to the local population. The British, on the other hand, simply demanded labour, without explanation, whether the works in question were seen as beneficial to the Arabs or not, and there were a good many cases where the 'expertise' of the British irrigation officers proved sadly inferior to the knowledge of the Arabs forced to work on their schemes, resulting in unanticipated and undesired changes to the water flow and similar mistakes.[18]

However, forced labour was only one dimension of the new Civil Administration's passion for control – its other essential element was taxation: those who were the unwilling 'beneficiaries' of British control also had to pay for it – and it was becoming increasingly expensive. Between the financial years 1917/18 and 1918/19 the total expenditure of the Civil Administration in occupied Iraq had already increased by 66 per cent, but between 1918/19 and 1919/20 it increased by a further 177 per cent. Of the total expenditure for 1919/20, nearly a third was attributable to 'Headquarters Administration, Political Officers and the Revenue (Taxation) organisation', in other words the machinery of domination. By way of comparison, Public Works accounted for 10.7 per cent and Education a mere 1.9 per cent.[19]

Under the Turks, the taxation regime had been haphazard in collection, being largely delegated to the tribal sheikhs who received, in return, a share of the income. Tax assessments were highly variable, made on the basis of the estimated profits earned by the tribes which occupied government-owned lands. In other words, allowance was made for the annual vagaries of climate, irrigation, flood control, pests, dust storms and so on.[20] In addition, from time to time, many tribes escaped their obligations by the simple expedient of making life extremely unpleasant for their sheikhly tax collectors. The British changed most of this. Where possible, sheikhs unfriendly to the British were replaced by others who were willing to collaborate.[21] The old Turkish tax-farming system was retained but the element of proportionality in the old regime was gradually replaced by fixed assessments while police and 'levies' – paramilitary forces recruited from among the tribes themselves, backed by regular troops when necessary – enforced collection with an iron hand. And where a tribe prevented the authorities from inspecting their crops for tax-collection purposes, the offending tribe was indiscriminately bombed.[22]

As a result, by the end of 1918 the British tax authorities had collected more land revenues than had the Ottomans in any prewar year. So 'efficient' was the tax-collection regime that in every year of the British occupation the budget of the Civil Administration was in surplus. However, it was in the years of Wilson's incumbency that these surpluses grew most rapidly. Indeed, as Wilson was determined to prove, it was not the expense of the Civil Administration which so burdened the British taxpayer – there was none: it more than paid for itself – it was the continuing cost of the huge military establishment which had been built up to support the war in Iraq. But because, as yet, no peace treaty had been signed with the Turks, and the Kemalists and Bolshevists threatened the security of Mosul and northern Persia, his administration still had need of this military shield.

Unfortunately for Wilson and his colleagues this was not fully understood in Britain. There had recently been some criticism of the alleged profligacy of his administration in the press, notably – and in Wilson's opinion, inexcusably – in the *Times* itself. But Wilson and his men also had their admirers. Such a one was the Revd Joseph T. Parfit MA, of the Church Missionary Society, who had recently visited Iraq and in a few months' time would publish a veritable panegyric on British-occupied Iraq entitled *Marvellous Mesopotamia: The World's Wonderland*. According to the Reverend Parfit, Wilson's regime was 'a masterpiece of efficient administration', which, among other achievements had 'largely succeeded in bringing about the moral reformation' of its 'fanatical inhabitants'. Indeed, under the British Civil Administration, Parfit concluded, 'The most desolate country in the world is being rapidly transformed into something like a paradise.'[23]

General Haldane, on the other hand, whose first impressions of Iraq were more redolent of Hades than Heaven, soon decided that he was not at all happy with the state of affairs in Wilson's satrapy. The total forces under his command – forces which he had been ordered to reduce as quickly as possible – numbered only 73,000, of which 61,000 were Indian.[24] As a junior officer, Haldane had commanded Indian troops during the Tirah Campaign of 1897–8 in the Khyber Pass and he was well aware that, in general, Indian troops, drawn mainly from the Punjab, had usually shown themselves doughty fighters when led by good officers. However, such an exceptionally high proportion of Indian to British troops filled Haldane with unease. To make matters worse, over a third of the troops under his command were tied up in various non-combatant duties, such as guarding Turkish prisoners or working in the various departments of the Civil Administration in the absence of civilian recruits from England. Moreover, around half of his British troops were either hundreds of miles away in Persia – supposedly deployed to deal with any advance by the Bolsheviks – sick, or in transit. So long as the country remained quiet he could probably manage; but if there were simultaneous disturbances in different parts of the country the situation could quickly become critical.

Three days after his arrival at his Baghdad HQ, on 27 March 1920, the new GOC-in-chief set off on a tour of all the garrisons, in particular those which were small and isolated. On his return, he concluded that the quality of the British troops – most of them recruited after the 1918 armistice and who so far had never fired a shot in anger – left much to be desired.[25] Some infantry units consisted largely of half-disciplined, pale-faced boys who were always going sick.[26] The situation was much the same with the British cavalry, many of whom were still in the elementary stages of learning to ride.

He also noticed that the airport outside Baghdad had absolutely no protection: no blockhouses, no barbed wire – any 'thieving *Budoo*' could get in and help himself to whatever loot he fancied. Indeed, he had already noticed that a good deal of pilfering was going on – and it was not just the light-fingered Arabs who were involved. There were far too many temporary and warrant officers who seemed excessively keen to 'shake the pagoda tree', in the old India parlance. As another British officer put it, shortly after his arrival in Iraq, 'One could almost feel the miasma of lethargy, apathy and corruption that pervaded the whole country.'[27]

As for Wilson's 'politicals', Haldane thought they were a pretty mixed bunch. Some of them had only recently been recruited into the Mesopotamian Civil Administration from British junior officers who had joined at the armistice and subsequently been demobilised and were totally lacking in experience in 'handling the Arab'. That sort of thing could cause trouble, and the last thing the general wanted was trouble. And there were others, officers of the railway, public works, irrigation, levies and sundry other employees of the sprawling administration, who were quite unsuitable for their duties. As a British officer in a recently arrived Indian cavalry regiment put it, 'Nearly the whole of these were below the average type of Sahib one meets in India and one or two were frequently drunk. On seeing them one could understand the Arab not thinking much of us.'[28]

But the biggest problem facing General Haldane was the way in which Wilson had scattered his POs all over the country, trying to control the most recalcitrant elements among the natives in every distant corner of his vast domain. Haldane would later record his scathing criticism of this practice:

> The political officer, I have noticed on many occasions, and I refer to the soldier qua-political, seems to lose all sense of military principles soon after he joins the civil administration ... If permitted, he would like to scatter broadcast the forces, often small in number, which are available for the maintenance of order. In fact he sees no harm in being weak everywhere and strong nowhere.[29]

Haldane agreed that control of some kind was essential. Indeed, his philosophy was that 'coloured races in general ... had to be dominated' and that 'it was absurd to regard them as being on the same level as European nations.' The problem was that, including Northern Persia, the total length of communications along which travelled supplies and other requirements and which had to be guarded by his troops, amounted to 2,622 miles, of which 910 were by road, 856 by rail and a similar number by river. This huge dispersal of forces worried Haldane because it left him with only a tiny mobile reserve with which to meet any serious threat that might suddenly emerge at any distant point on this huge area of operations. However, his initial suggestions that some isolated detachments might be withdrawn from peripheral areas were immediately rebuffed by Wilson. In response, when Wilson asked for the dispatch of one company of regulars to support the Arab levies protecting the APO in one of his most distant outposts, Tel 'Afar, about thirty-five miles west of Mosul on the edge of the great western desert, Haldane ignored the request.[30] From that point on, the relationship between the two most senior British officials in Iraq – the one in charge of the military, the other heading the Civil Administration – began to break down.

And then, there was the damnable heat. It was still early in the year and would obviously get much worse. The general had never experienced anything like it. His health demanded some respite from this inferno. Fortunately, there was a solution. As soon as possible he would leave Iraq and ascend into the cooler climes of Persia, where he could spend the summer examining the military situation there – plus a little rest and recuperation, of course.

Trouble on the Frontiers

Long before news that Britain had awarded itself the mandate for Iraq reached Baghdad there had been serious disturbances on the long, straggling frontiers of Colonel Wilson's vast domain. To the north-east of Baghdad, Kurdistan, a vaguely delineated mountainous territory, considered a region separate from the currently occupied Iraq, but under British control, had exploded into resistance in May 1919 under the leadership of one of the leading Kurdish chiefs, Sheikh Mahmud of Sulaymaniyya. It had taken a substantial force of British-commanded Indian troops to crush his small army the following month and capture the wounded Kurdish leader. Sheikh Mahmud was tried by a military court-martial, found guilty of rebellion and sentenced to death. Wilson had wanted him hanged but in the end the decision was taken by General MacMunn, the current GOC-in-chief, to commute the sentence to a long term of imprisonment.

However, it was the ill-defined frontier with Faysal's semi-independent Arab state of Syria which had given Wilson the greatest cause for concern. Particularly galling to Wilson was the knowledge that certain British officers ostensibly 'advising' Faysal were exhibiting considerable sympathy for the largely Iraqi-born military officers of al-'Ahd and were turning a blind eye to their efforts to undermine Wilson's 'Indian' regime. First and foremost among those whom Wilson now considered his enemies was Colonel T. E. Lawrence.

In January 1919 a number of Iraqi officers attached to Faysal's Syrian regime had petitioned the British military authorities to return home.

Wilson was violently opposed to the idea, seeing it as being promoted by Lawrence. In this opinion Wilson was not without support from the India Office, which also took a dim view of Lawrence's increasingly cavalier attitude to official British policy. Even Sir Arthur Hirtzel, head of the Political and Secret Department at the India Office, himself a critic of Wilson's increasingly high-handed behaviour in Iraq, agreed that Lawrence was a 'problem'. Writing to Lord Curzon, the foreign secretary, on 24 June 1919, he attacked 'the propaganda (which) originated with Faysal and Lawrence', adding that 'there will be no peace in the Middle East until Lawrence's malign influence is withdrawn.' According to Hirtzel, Lawrence was now actively advocating that Iraq should be ruled by an Arab emir, 'roaming about Europe on his own sweet will, playing one party off against another. Is it not possible to control him?' he pleaded. But Lawrence would not be controlled and in a minute to the Foreign Office from Paris in July, he complained bitterly about the continuing ban on the Iraqi officers returning to their country of birth because of unfounded allegations that they might be 'spreaders of undesirable propaganda'.

One month later, the transformation of a little-known junior British officer into a matinée idol commenced with a series of public lectures held at Covent Garden by the American journalist Lowell Thomas, who had met Lawrence at Aqaba in 1917. The lectures, which were originally entitled 'With Allenby in Palestine and the Conquest of Holy Arabia', were soon re-titled 'With Allenby in Palestine and Lawrence in Arabia'. They were a tremendous success. They played to the desire of the British public to indulge in a romantic fantasy about a theatre of war far removed from the horrendous conditions on the Western Front – one where 'noble Arabs' were led into battle by an intrepid Englishman in Rudyard Kipling mode who gained the trust of the 'natives' by becoming, or rather appearing to become, 'one of them'.

This sudden national – and international – fame gave Lawrence further licence to engage in the political struggle to salvage something of the wartime British–Hashemite alliance with its vague promises of an independent Arab state throughout the Middle East. On 8 September 1919 he sent a letter to *The Times* in which he described at some length the various wartime agreements concerning the region's future administration, including both the McMahon–Husayn 'promise' of October 1915 and the Sykes–Picot Agreement of 1916. The latter Lawrence pronounced 'unworkable', adding that 'the necessary revision of this agreement is a delicate matter, and can hardly be done satisfactorily by England and France without giving weight and expression also to the opinion of the third interest – the Arabs – which it created.'[1]

What the readers of *The Times* never saw was a further passage – suppressed by the editor – in which Lawrence added that he had originally been led to believe that the British government meant to live up to its promises to the Arabs, and that was why he had encouraged them to fight against the Turks. However, he now wished to inform the Arabs that he regretted what had been done because the government evidently had no intention of living up to the promises it had authorised him to make to them.

However, the following day, Lawrence drafted a second, and very strange, letter to Lloyd George (it was never sent) in which he appears to have suddenly changed his mind and decided that, as far as Syria was concerned, the prime minister intended to keep 'all our promises' to the Arabs and that his 'relief at getting out of the affair with clean hands is very great'. Moreover, as a 'sign of grace' to the PM, Lawrence promised that he would 'obey the F.O. and the W.O. and not see Faysal again'. Thereafter, Lawrence fired off various recommendations as to a prospective 'Arab state' to the Foreign Office and to Lord Curzon himself, recommendations which clearly illustrate the degree to which Lawrence was willing to accept a minimalist interpretation of 'Arab state' but which expressed his celebrated desire that 'the Arabs should be our first brown dominion and not our last brown colony'.[2]

However, the first of these letters also contained two very prescient statements about developments in Iraq. 'I regard the situation in Mesopotamia as disquieting,' Lawrence warned, 'and if we do not mend our ways will expect revolt there about March next.' To this he added the observation that, at present, 'the dissatisfaction against us in Mesopotamia is mostly in the towns: and will become active when the notables care enough to go out and make agreement with the country people.'³ Unknown to the British – and even to Lawrence himself – that day was now fast approaching.

Lawrence was not alone in his view that men like Nuri al-Sa'id and Ja'far al-'Askari, who had changed sides during the war and led the Sharif of Mecca's small contingent of regular troops, should be allowed to return to Iraq to form the nucleus of an Arab government – albeit one which would remain friendly to British interests. In November 1919 Gertrude Bell had returned to Baghdad after a lengthy tour of the Middle East during which she had been introduced to Iraqi members of al-'Ahd in Damascus and concluded that some were considerably more moderate and pro-British than she had been led to believe and that more rapid progress towards independence for Iraq was warranted. In a report presented to Wilson called 'Syria in October' she expounded her new conviction that unless 'moderate' public opinion in Iraq was rewarded by some clear indications that the current pro-consular regime was to be phased out – sooner rather than later – there would be serious disturbances.

Wilson was furious. Although he forwarded her report to the India Office on 15 November, he added a covering letter stating that he entirely disagreed with its contents. Thereafter he was to consider Bell an enemy, although it was some time before she became aware of Wilson's antipathy towards her. But Wilson's stubborn refusal to consider even the slightest degree of Arab participation in 'his' regime was increasingly bringing him into conflict with his own masters in the India Office. On 16 July 1919 Sir Arthur Hirtzel told Wilson frankly, 'You are going to have an Arab state whether you like it or not ... otherwise we shall have another Egypt on our hands', adding that he 'had hoped you would have realized ... that the idea of Mesopotamia as the model of an efficiently administered British dependency or protectorate is dead'. Precisely what Hirtzel did have in mind was clearly expressed in a further communication to Wilson on 2 February 1920:

What we want is some kind of modicum of Arab institutions which we can safely leave while pulling the strings ourselves, something which won't cost very much, something that Labour can swallow consistently

with their principles [Hirtzel was anticipating a future Labour govern-
ment] but in which our influence and political and economic interests
will be secure.[4]

With regard to frontiers, Wilson was firmly of the opinion that a British-
controlled Iraq should encompass the whole of the former vilayet of
Mosul including the Kurdish areas, and in a debate in the House of
Commons on 25 March 1920, Lloyd George came out strongly in favour
of Wilson's position. 'You might abandon the country altogether,' Lloyd
George hypothesised, 'but I cannot understand withdrawing merely
from Mosul, which is the most promising and important part of the
country. Mosul has rich oil deposits.'[5]

However, majority public opinion in Britain continued to be
doggedly opposed to the whole Mesopotamian involvement – with or
without Mosul and Kurdistan. Not that this had much to do with anti-
colonialism. It was simply a matter of expense. *The Times* continued
to rage against what it claimed was a huge waste of taxpayers' money
and Parliament repeatedly made it clear that it would not consent to
incur liabilities with respect to Iraq for more than a very limited period.
Nevertheless, even those who, reluctantly or otherwise, now accepted
a reduction in the level of British involvement and the inevitability of
some kind of Arab-led administration in Iraq, foresaw the danger that
excessive parsimony would result in too rapid a run-down in the Iraq
garrison. For example, in April 1920, Hirtzel complained, 'What the
High Authorities should be brought to realize is that, if what they are
avowedly out for is oil and other commodities, they cannot have them
without public security, and they cannot have public security under an
Arab or any other Government without paying for it.'[6]

At this juncture it is perhaps worth breaking off our narrative briefly
to consider the implications of this quotation from a very senior British
civil servant. When Hirtzel remarks 'if what they are avowedly out for is
oil ...' this is certainly not a hypothetical 'if': Hirtzel is not ruminating
on the possibility that the 'High Authorities' *might* be 'out for oil'.
Quite the contrary: he apparently knows it to be a well-established
fact. What he is saying could just as well be paraphrased as '*Given that*

the High Authorities are out for oil ...' Nor does the addition of 'other commodities' weaken the significance of Hirtzel's casual admittance that the economic objective first articulated in the proceedings of the De Bunsen Committee, five years earlier, remained as cogent as ever.[7]

'Avowedly out for oil' the High Authorities may have been, but Hirtzel himself seems to have been unaware that one of those 'High Authorities' at the War Office was already planning a substantial diminution in the manpower responsible for 'public security' in Iraq in spite of the fact that the preceding six months had witnessed some serious fighting with Arab nationalist bands on the ill-defined frontier with Emir Faysal's semi-independent state of Syria, including a withdrawal of British troops which, as we shall see, had all the appearance – to both Arabs and British – of a defeat.

On 13 September 1919 Lloyd George and Clemenceau had concluded an agreement whereby British troops would start to evacuate Syria, the withdrawal to be completed by 1 November. The British withdrawal took place on schedule, and in the zone which had been controlled by British troops the major inland cities of Damascus, Homs, Hama and Aleppo were handed over to the Arab authorities. Unaware that this brief experiment in Arab independence was doomed and that the French general Henri Gouraud, appointed chef de l'armée du Levant on 9 October, was already drawing up his plans for a full-scale invasion of Syria, some of the former Ottoman army officers of Iraqi origin belonging to al-'Ahd believed they now had an opportunity to compel the British occupiers of their own homeland to leave.

By now, the members of al-'Ahd al-'Iraqi were by no means united as to the manner whereby the British were to be persuaded to accept an independent Iraq. Some, like Colonel Ja'far al-'Askari and Lieutenant Nuri al-Sa'id, felt some residual loyalty towards their former British allies and favoured a cautious, diplomatic approach to achieving their independence objectives. Others, like the twenty-nine-year-old Mosul-born artillery commander Jamil Midfa'i, had also deserted to the British during the war but now had no scruples about using force to drive them from Iraq. And there were other Iraqi officers who had remained in the

Ottoman ranks throughout the war in spite of their membership of al-'Ahd – men like General Yasin al-Hashimi – who continued to remain hostile to the British in spite of their seemingly sympathetic attitude towards Faysal's administration in Syria. So, towards the end of 1919 divisions had begun to appear in the ranks of al-'Ahd al-'Iraqi, the more radical members of which were more inclined to put the resolution of the British to the test.

Some of these radicals decided to begin a series of small-scale operations probing the western borders of Colonel Wilson's new colony. In this they were supported by Emir Zayd, Sharif Husayn's youngest son who was deputising as Syrian head of state for his brother Faysal, currently in Europe.[8] The first target of the radicals was the town of Dayr az-Zawr.

Dayr az-Zawr lies on the Upper Euphrates, 300 miles to the north-west of Baghdad and twenty miles north of the point where the Khabur river flows into the Euphrates from the north-east. In 1919 it was a rather insignificant walled town of around 5,000 inhabitants with flat-roofed mud-brick houses and a skyline punctuated by six white minarets. The town had received some embellishment during the 1860s when an enterprising Ottoman pasha constructed a broad, straight main street through the town with half a dozen two-storey houses and a small public garden. More recently a number of schools had been built, including a polytechnic.

However, Dayr az-Zawr had one particularly important political characteristic. During Ottoman times, the town and its surrounding province, which stretched as far south as 'Ana on the Euphrates, had belonged to neither the vilayet of Baghdad nor the vilayet of Aleppo but constituted a mutasarriflik – a special jurisdiction governed directly from Istanbul. After the armistice with Turkey, the British had rather thoughtlessly added Dayr to Baghdad province and supplied the town with a resident British PO and small bodyguard with two armoured cars; but as a consequence of its uncertain geopolitical status and its apparent lack of economic significance, by September 1919 the British government was signalling that it intended Dayr to eventually pass back into Syrian – and therefore ultimately into French – control.

On 19 November 1919 Wilson received a telegram from the Arab Bureau in Cairo informing him that their agents in Aleppo had reported the departure from that city of a certain Ramadan al-Shallash – reputedly a particularly hot-headed member of al-'Ahd al-'Iraqi – with orders to proceed to Dayr and seize the town and surrounding areas for the Arabs. Before the war he had been one of the leading men in the al-Sarai section of the Aqaidat, a tribe that occupied lands to the north and south of Dayr. He was also distinguished by one other unusual characteristic – a remarkably realistic celluloid nose.

By 25 November Shallash had reached the ancient walled town of Raqqa on the northern Euphrates, where he distributed to the local tribal leaders personally sealed letters from Emir Zayd proclaiming that he had been appointed 'Governor of the Euphrates and Khabur'. From there, in early December, he set out for Dayr with forty camel corps troops. Having got wind of Shallash's approach the APO and governor of Dayr, Captain Chamier, arrested the town's mayor on suspicion of collaborating with the enemy and telegraphed Baghdad and the British base at Abu Kamal, sixty miles to the south-east, for help. Soon afterwards, the telegraph wire was cut by Arab raiders.

As Shallash continued his advance on Dayr, on 11 December its townspeople and around 2,000 local tribesmen, who had been informed of Shallash's approach, rose in rebellion. A number of public buildings were attacked and ransacked including the British Political Office where the safe was blown open and its contacts seized. The petrol dump was also blown up and all prisoners in the local jail were released.

The APO had only the two British-crewed armoured cars and sixty local Arab levies under his command, so he immediately took refuge with his little force in the military barracks to the north of the town. At sunrise one of the armoured cars was sent from the barracks to make a re-connaissance of the town but received heavy rifle fire and had to retreat, its gun damaged beyond repair. Then, at 10.00 a.m., the barracks itself came under attack.

Although machine guns had been mounted on its roof, these were soon put out of action and forty of the Arab levies deserted, having dropped over the wall in twos and threes. Captain Chamier and his men were now forced to surrender and for a time were threatened with execution by the tribesmen. However, by chance, two British aircraft, which had been sent out on a routine patrol from Mosul flew over Dayr, quickly appreciated that the tiny British garrison had been attacked and began to machine-gun the town. Fearing further attacks from the air, the rebels agreed a truce and their British captives were left unharmed.

Ramadan al-Shallash reached Dayr later in the afternoon, proclaimed independence for the region and raised the Arab flag over the government building. Later that afternoon he began negotiations with Captain Chamier. He demanded that the British permanently withdraw from the town and its surrounding area, contending that the Syria–Iraq border should rightfully pass through Wadi Hawran, south of 'Ana. Since he was unable to offer any further resistance, Chamier stated that he was prepared to withdraw from Dayr provided that no reprisals were taken against any locals who had worked for the British. To this, Shallash initially agreed, but the following morning he added his own conditions, demanding assurances from the British that, after being allowed to leave peacefully, British forces would not return and take reprisals against his own men or the townspeople. Without such assurances, Chamier and his handful of British troops would be kept as hostages.

At noon, another aircraft appeared over the town and was persuaded to land. The pilot was instructed by Chamier to return to Mosul with a message from the rebels that he and his men were being held hostage and would be killed if the town were attacked again by British forces. Meanwhile, Shallash began appointing local Arab notables to positions of authority within the town.

Wilson was now in a quandary. He was aware that the political status of Dayr az-Zawr was, to say the least, unclear. He was also aware that General MacMunn, who was soon to hand over his command to Haldane and depart for India, had insufficient troops available to mount a serious counter-attack on this distant and seemingly unimportant British outpost. Meanwhile, on 21 November the War Office had sent a cable to Baghdad informing Wilson that the Allies had agreed that Dayr az-Zawr was not to be included in the 'British sphere of influence' and should be evacuated. Unfortunately, on arrival in Baghdad the telegram was undecipherable. On request, it was telegraphed again but still could not be understood.

Finally, on 20 December Wilson did receive a decipherable version of the telegram from the War Office, *dated 21 November*, informing him that it had been decided at the Paris Peace Conference that Dayr az-Zawr would categorically *not* be included in the British mandate of Iraq. Wilson was furious. If the India Office had telegraphed him directly instead of through the War Office, and if the War Office telegraph service had been more competent, the telegram would not have been delayed by a month and the entire unhappy episode could have been avoided. Instead, British lives had been endangered, property destroyed and a serious 'loss of face' had occurred. But when this wholly justifiable complaint was relayed to both the India Office and the War Office the latter responded angrily, stating that Wilson's attitude was 'particularly unfortunate' and that it hoped that secretary of state for India would 'take such steps as are necessary to correct the attitude of that officer, which, in the opinion of the Army Council is insubordinate'.[9] The India Office did no such thing and the stage was now set for a protracted period of strife between Wilson and the army.

Meanwhile, Wilson had been compelled to send a message by aircraft to Ramadan al-Shallash indicating that if his British hostages at Dayr az-Zawr were released and allowed to travel to the nearest British outpost at Abu Kamal there would be no attempt to retake the town. The prisoners were duly released on Christmas Day 1919.

However, the failure of the British authorities to reoccupy Dayr az-Zawr only emboldened both the Arab government in Damascus and the more radical elements of al-'Ahd al-'Iraqi. The former now demanded that the frontier of their Arab state be pushed even further south-east, to include Abu Kamal itself. The radicals, in the person of Ramadan al-Shallash, went even further, declaring that the British should retire beyond Abu Kamal, to a position fifty miles south of 'Ana. And although this exercise in putting pressure on the British was couched in terms of extending the frontiers of Syria, it was now becoming clear that these moves had a much more ambitious objective – to drive the British from as much of Iraq as possible. Indeed, on 11 January 1920 Shallash's tribal forces mounted a sustained attack on Abu Kamal, where, for a time, they succeeded in entering the suburbs, killing a number of Arabs in British service and looting their houses. And although Shallash was recalled to Damascus in the middle of January, his replacement, Maulud Pasha al-Khalaf, an Iraqi from Mosul, turned out to be an even more militant adherent of al-'Ahd al-'Iraqi. A further attack on Abu Kamal was mounted in mid-February and the British lines of communication on the northern Euphrates were raided as far south as Al Qa'im.

At the end of February 1920 Colonel Leachman returned from England, having been summoned there by the India Office which had offered him the position of head of the Political Agency in Kuwait. However, Leachman had politely refused the offer; he had no liking for an 'office job'. On 3 March Wilson ordered him to Ramadi on the northern Euphrates as PO for the Dulaym Division and to assist a weak British brigade of the 17th Division under General F. E. Coningham in putting an end to the continuing guerrilla raiding parties emanating from Dayr az-Zawr and its tribal environs.

Under his personal command Leachman had a squadron of Rolls-Royce armoured cars of the 6th Light Armoured Motor Battery (LAMB) and some mounted tribesmen of the 'Amarat section of the nomadic 'Anaiza tribe whose paramount chief Fayad Bay ibn Hadhal was in the pay of the British; he also enjoyed the occasional support of a few antiquated two-seater RE8 fighter-bombers. Writing to his parents on 16 March from Abu Kamal, where he arrived by aircraft, Leachman described the British counter-insurgency operations with his usual mixture of sarcasm and casual brutality:

We are now 'learning' the gentle Arabian who caused the trouble. The day I got here we went out 30 miles further up river and found the local Arabs doing the 'peaceful cultivator' stunt. So we burned ten miles of huts, drove in all the cattle, destroyed everything we could see, and incidentally slew a few Arabs who got in the way ... They are the lowest of the low but quite dangerous ... I shall have to stay here until we have got them in hand and shall then go back to Ramadi.[10]

By 30 March Leachman was at Salahiyya, about twenty-five miles upstream of Abu Kamal, informing his parents, 'I am still in the forefront of the battle; in fact I have the honour of being now the in our most advanced post on the Euphrates.' In spite of the widespread unrest Leachman was still insisting on trying to collect taxes from the local tribes, who now declared that they were no longer subjects of the British occupation. Leachman's response was to machine-gun any recalcitrant non-payers, and if that wasn't sufficient to call in bombing raids on their villages.[11]

Eventually, in May 1920, the frontier line with Faysal's Syria was stabilised just south of Abu Kamal, where it remains today. For the time being, the Arabs had achieved control over most of the territory they had been fighting for during the previous three months and Leachman had the unpleasant duty of travelling to Dayr az-Zawr to formalise the arrangements.[12] The general impression given to friend and foe alike was that Britain had suffered a small but significant defeat; that it had been unable or unwilling to resist the Arab encroachments and that this, in turn, reflected the inadequate military resources available to them.

Indeed, as the British brigade withdrew from Abu Kamal they came under fierce harassing attacks. 'The whole country seemed to arise and go for us and we had a very stiff fight all the way back to 'Ana, 70 miles. They are raiding all over the place,' Leachman reported. However, he added, 'But we are in a position to deal with them. I spend hours in the air, bombing camps and Arabs. The brightest spot we have had for many a long day was when early one morning we bumped across 25 Arabians asleep in a hole in the ground. We enjoyed ourselves immensely.' Nevertheless, by now, even the redoubtable Leachman was beginning to show signs of battle fatigue, wearily admitting to his parents that 'I can see no end to this turmoil.'[13]

The 'turmoil' was now increasing. Forty miles west of the city of Mosul, on the ancient trading route with Aleppo, lies the town of Tal 'Afar. In

1920 it had around 10,000 inhabitants, the majority of them Turkmen, probably the descendants of tribes which had migrated from the region of Lake Van in Anatolia and entered Iraq in the late fourteenth century, predating the arrival of the Ottoman Turks. Over the centuries they had become to a considerable extent Arabised, and spoke both Arabic and their native Turki. As in most of the northerly parts of Iraq, in the region of Tel 'Afar the men of wealth and power were known by the Turkish title of agha rather than sheikh, and in Tel 'Afar itself the leading citizen was Agha 'Abdul Rahman ibn 'Usman. As for religion, the inhabitants of Tal 'Afar were both Sunni and Shi'i and relations between the two sects were generally peaceable.

The town itself was situated on four knolls, two on either side of a steep gully running north–south. Its houses were well constructed from local stone and, on the eastern side of the gully, a large, partially destroyed medieval castle crowned the heights of the highest knoll, and from under this eminence emerged a stream which provided the inhabitants with fresh water and irrigated their gardens of figs, olives and other fruit trees.

For the town's new British rulers its location presented some difficulties. Like Dayr az-Zawr, it was a considerable distance from the main northern garrison at Mosul; to the west the stony desert stretched away to the border with Syria and Faysal's unruly new Arab state; and to the north lay the armistice line across which hostile pro-Turkish Kurdish and Arab tribes ranged and raided. Nevertheless, Wilson had thought it important to 'show the flag' in even this distant and isolated spot and accordingly an APO supported by a small troop of British-officered Arab levies had been established in the town.

Since the withdrawal of the British from Dayr az-Zawr the area west and south of Mosul had become the target of Arab raiding parties operating out of the no-man's-land of the Syrian border. Some of these raiders reached as far as the towns of Sharqat and 'Ain Dibbs. On 21 April the first caravan for some months arrived at Mosul from Dayr az-Zawr, bringing more news of the British 'defeat' and inaugurating a spasm of anti-British propaganda. Political meetings were held and anti-British notices were posted on the walls at night.[14]

On 26 May British intelligence staff at Mosul received reports that a force of about 1,000 Arab horsemen, under the command of the militant al-'Ahd member Jamil al-Midfa'i, had established itself at Fadghami on the Khabur river well within striking distance of both Tal 'Afar and Mosul itself.[15] Like Lieutenant Faruqi, the thirty-year-old Midfa'i was a native of Mosul and his plan was to make a striking military demonstration against British power in the region by cutting the occupiers' lines of communication with the south of the country.[16] This was expected to lead to an uprising in the city of Mosul, where Midfa'i was in touch with Amin Effendi al-'Umari, a prominent member of the clan of that name, described in British intelligence reports as 'a young and misguided fanatic' and a 'liaison officer between Kemalists and Sharifians' (i.e. those supporting independence under 'Abdallah).[17]

Midfa'i's troops were accompanied by an approximately equal number of Shammar, Juhaish and Khabur Jubur tribal horsemen, all Sunni tribesmen. The Shammar were under the command of Humaydi Ibn Farhan, hitherto Ottoman *rais* (governor) of the al-Jarba' section of the Shammar; the Juhaish were led by Salih, son of Ahmad al-Khudhayir, sheikh of that tribe; and the Jubur were commanded by its paramount sheikh, Muslat Pasha.[18]

Two days later the British received a report of hostile Arab tribesmen moving towards Sharqat on the Tigris and rumours of an advance by a unit of Mustafa Kemal's Turkish troops on Zakho, Wilson's most northerly outpost. Meanwhile, in Mosul itself, anti-British agitation was continuing to spread throughout the city. On 30 May the PO for the region, Lieutenant Colonel L. F. Nalder, submitted a report to Wilson and to the commander of the Mosul-based 18th Division of the British Army that he believed an attempt to drive the British from the city with the aid of rebel tribesmen was imminent.[19]

At British Military Headquarters in Baghdad it was unclear whether Jamil Midfa'i's group was operating independently or was part of a combined Arab–Turkish manoeuvre. Whichever was the case, Wilson feared a repetition of the Dayr az-Zawr incident and urged General Haldane to send reinforcements to the region. Unfortunately news of these developments came at a particularly awkward moment for the British High Command in Iraq.

Eight days earlier, at 8.00 a.m. on 18 May 1920, Commander F. F. Raskolnikov on the bridge of the Bolshevik destroyer *Karl Liebknecht* was peering through his Zeiss binoculars at the British-held port of Enzeli, two kilometres away on the southern coast of the Caspian Sea.[20] In the bay he could see the anchored ships of General Denikin's White Fleet which had fled there after the Bolsheviks' capture of Baku a few weeks earlier. Onshore, he could just make out the clay-and-gravel houses of the Persian town and the governor's palace surrounded by slender palm trees. To the left of the town lay the British military camp of Kazian.

Signalling to his two shallow-draught gunboats, *Kars* and *Ardahan*, to move closer inshore, he waited a few minutes before giving the order to open fire. Then the 4-inch guns of his own ship and those of the rest of the Soviet Volga–Caspian Flotilla began a heavy bombardment of the British cantonments while Bolshevik sailors in blue jumpers with white collars, the long ribbons of their hats fluttering in the wind, rowed their launches up to the beach, leapt out through the surf and cut the telegraph lines linking Enzeli to the outside world.

The British base was manned almost entirely by Indian troops, in total around 500 men – a company of the 2nd Gurkha Rifles, a company of the 42nd (Deoli) Regiment and the 122nd Rajputs. But by an unfortunate coincidence, Brigadier General Bateman-Champain, commander of the 36th Indian (Mixed) Brigade and GOC of Noperforce, the whole British contingent in northern Persia, was also visiting the base at the time. After a brief and unsuccessful attempt by the Gurkhas to repel the Bolshevik landing parties, General Bateman-Champain opened radio communication with the Soviet commander.

'By whose authority have you come here?' he demanded.

'The Soviet Government bears no responsibility for me. I have come here on my own initiative, on my own responsibility and at my own risk', replied Raskolnikov.[21]

As a matter of fact, on 20 April, Trotsky had insisted that the Caspian must be cleared of the White Fleet entirely. Consisting of ten auxiliary cruisers, seven transports, several smaller vessels and six seaplanes, the White Fleet which lay at anchor in the port of Enzeli had escaped Baku and fled to Persia, where it had been interned. But the Bolsheviks were determined to remove any threat to the movement of oil between Baku and Astrakhan, from where it could be shipped up the Volga to Moscow and Petrograd. So Raskolnikov's orders were to capture that fleet. The British could fight to protect it or withdraw, Commander Raskolnikov informed General Bateman-Champain.

Bateman-Champain replied that he had no authority to surrender Enzeli or the White Fleet. However, he was seeking instructions from Baghdad. Until a reply had been received he proposed a two-hour truce. Raskolnikov agreed. But while the unfortunate British commander desperately tried to restore telegraph communications with Baghdad, Raskolnikov continued to land more and more sailors and marines and since no further radio communication from the British had been received by the expiry of the truce, the Bolsheviks recommenced shelling the British positions. Bateman-Champain now asked for a one-hour extension of the truce, which was granted, but shortly before its termination, realising that he had lost all hope of communicating with Baghdad, he informed Raskolnikov that he was willing to hand over Enzeli and the White Fleet if his troops were allowed to leave the town with their weapons. Delighted, Raskolnikov agreed and sent the commander of his landing parties ashore to settle the details.

The situation of the garrison at Enzeli had always been worrying. Indeed, Churchill himself had urged its withdrawal in February, fearing precisely the kind of humiliation which had now been inflicted. However, he had been strongly opposed by Lord Curzon. The foreign secretary and former viceroy of India had long considered Persia a crucial factor in the defence of the British Empire. He knew the country well; as a young man he had travelled widely throughout its vast territory and had later written a magisterial two-volume account of its people, religion and history. On 9 August 1919 he believed he had achieved a lifelong ambition – a treaty with Persia was signed which, in effect, converted it into a British protectorate. In return for a loan of £2 million (of which £160,000 was, in reality, a bribe to the Persian prime minister and two Qajar royal princes), the young Anglophile Shah Ahmad and his government agreed to hand over control of Persia's finances and military forces to British 'advisors'. The agreement, Curzon informed his colleagues, was essential to avoid 'a hotbed of misrule, enemy intrigue, financial disaster and political disorder' which would have led inevitably to Bolshevik intervention and a threat to the British-owned oilfields.[22]

The British military presence in Northern Persia was therefore an integral element in this new relationship between the two countries. To have withdrawn from Enzeli when the Bolsheviks were consolidating their recent gains in Azerbaijan would surely have looked like weakness and a signal to the Persian nationalist opponents of Curzon's treaty that the British could not deliver on their promises of military support for the shah and his government. Unfortunately for both Britain and the shah, the fiasco at Enzeli had now created even greater embarrassment for the two parties to the treaty.

In a desperate attempt to shore up the rapidly deteriorating situation in northern Persia – with Bolshevik forces and Persian nationalist irregulars pushing on past Resht and threatening to overrun British outposts at the Manjil Pass – on 24 May the War Office turned to the only available source of troops – Iraq. So just two days before news of potentially hostile Arab forces gathering near Tal 'Afar and Mosul began reaching Baghdad, General Haldane received orders to send two battalions to Qasvin, fifty miles south of the Manjil Pass outposts and the HQ of Bateman-Champain's 36th Brigade. By chance there were two weak British battalions, about 600 men in total, currently resting in the Persian highlands at Karind and these were promptly transported to Qasvin by motor lorry. But soon afterwards another, separate demand for military assistance assailed Haldane from Sir Percy Cox, the British minister in Tehran, urging him to send more troops and artillery to Qasvin.

Difficult though the military situation was, the events in Persia held out certain opportunities for General Haldane personally. The weather in Baghdad was now becoming unbearable and the thought of cool Persian climes began to seem irresistible to the heat-tormented GOC-in-chief. He had already announced that the whole of the GHQ would move up to Karind in the Persian highlands for the summer and remain there until October, but until now their departure had been delayed by various engagements including an official visit to Iraq by the shah. Most of the wives and children of the British officers and civilian personnel now lived at Karind, which was 150 miles north-east of Baghdad by air, and the location was well provided with amenities of all kinds. There was even a golf course. And now Haldane could claim that he had a genuine and pressing reason to go immediately to Persia – the Bolshevik threat. Surely it was only proper that he should proceed to Qasvin himself to examine this serious military situation, and after that, perhaps Tehran? He soon made the necessary announcement.

Needless to say, General Haldane's decision was not well received by those whose duties meant they would have to remain in Iraq during the sweltering summer heat. Gertrude Bell, for one, was disapproving. Since his arrival in March she had befriended the general and initially had felt a little sorry for him. MacMunn, his predecessor as GOC-in-chief, had been a popular and sociable commander and by contrast Haldane seemed almost totally lacking in personality. 'I cannot find any real solid person in Sir A.,' Gertrude told her father. 'He is very kind and friendly and most polite, but he doesn't seem to me to have a mind at all ... He is shy and nervous and un-self-confident and of course the poor man is at a drawback from knowing nothing about the people or the country. He is most anxious to do the right thing but he has no means of knowing what it is.'[23]

Nevertheless she had taken him under her wing, frequently invited him to her house and tried to help him by introducing him to various pro-British Arab dignitaries. But now she was beginning to lose patience with him. 'Going up to Karind until October,' she wrote to her father, 'it's very wrong.' She went on,

There's a strong feeling against it both among military and civil. We have
a critical six months ahead of us; we all ought to be on the spot, and after
all Sir Aylmer is still head of the administration – even if he doesn't know
anything about it (and he doesn't) things have to be done in his name ...
We have electric fans and lights, plenty of ice and good houses. No hot
weather is a hardship under such conditions. And if it were a hardship,
many people, including all the civil administration, have got to do it, and
G.H.Q. ought to do it too. And that's what they all feel.

Arnold Wilson agreed. He accepted that the general should, in due
course, leave for Persia – but not now, with reports just coming in of an
outrage at Tal 'Afar and continuing Arab raids out of Dayr az-Zawr. But
Haldane was adamant. Consequently, on 5 June, General Haldane and
his staff left Baghdad by train, their destination the railhead at Quraitu
in Kurdistan and thence by car to the British camp at Karind. En route,
the general hoped to do a little sightseeing and photography – the
scenery at the Tak-i-Girrah Pass was reputed to be very impressive.

After he left, Gertrude Bell recorded a remarkable conversation she
had just had with the general. In a further letter to her father she wrote,

I lunched with Sir Aylmer the day he left. We chatted about common
acquaintances in London over our iced melon and mayonnaise. As I
went away I said: 'I suppose if you hear when you reach Karind that the
tribes have taken Baghdad, you'll – go on to Kermanshah [Bakhtaran]?'
He replied 'Oh I don't feel any responsibility for what happens while
I'm away.'[24]

Meanwhile, sixteen British officers and men had been killed at Tal 'Afar.[25]
On the night of 2 June, one of Jamil Midfa'i's men entered the town
and addressed a meeting of the town's elders organised by Agha 'Abdul
Rahman ibn 'Usman. He told them that a large force of Arab troops and
tribesmen was approaching and that they should either gather together
all their men with weapons and get ready to join them or themselves
immediately attack the small British outpost on the summit of one of
the hills above the town where the APO had his house and office and the
barracks of the levies were situated.

The following morning the local APO, Major J. E. Barlow, contacted his superior, Lieutenant Colonel Nalder, by telephone, informing him that a large Arab raiding party was in the vicinity and that he intended make a reconnaissance towards the suspected location of this force later that night. In the event, while making this brave but perhaps rather foolhardy patrol, Barlow was taken prisoner by some of the Shammar tribesmen on the outskirts of the town. The next day the telegraph line between Tel 'Afar and Mosul was cut.

Meanwhile, two Rolls-Royce armoured cars of the Mosul LAMB had been sent out on a routine patrol heading towards the town. So the officer commanding the Mosul garrison dispatched an elderly two-seater RE8 of 30 Squadron RAF to fly over the armoured cars and drop a message informing their commanding officer that the telegraph to Tal 'Afar had been cut and therefore to proceed with great care. The pilot of the RE8 was also ordered to make a reconnaissance flight over the town. Early on the morning of 4 June the armoured cars were spotted six miles from the town and the RE8 flew over them and dropped the message. It then continued to fly over the town and at first noticed nothing of an unusual nature. A little later, the aircraft's observer spotted a large body of mounted men approaching Tal 'Afar from the west and the pilot flew back over the armoured cars which by now had begun to enter the south-east corner of the town. Another message was dropped to the vehicles warning them of the approaching enemy forces, after which the RE8 flew back over the Arabs intending to machine-gun them.

As the British aircraft made its first pass over the Arab attackers it received a rifle shot which penetrated its fuel tank. The engine cut out but somehow the pilot managed to make a forced landing without either of the crew being injured. Luckily they were able to escape capture and eventually got back to Mosul.

Meanwhile, on the morning of 4 June 1920, Midfa'i's troops entered Tel 'Afar in force and the townspeople, led by Agha 'Abdul Rahman ibn 'Usman, rose up in support.[26] At the time, the officer in command of the levies, Captain Stuart, was conducting a routine patrol of the town accompanied by an Arab mulazim. Unbeknown to the British, their own gendarmes had also joined the conspiracy and Stuart was shot in the back by the mulazim. Midfa'i's men then surrounded the APO's office, which was defended by his chief clerk and the British sergeant of the levies together with one machine gunner. After an exchange of fire during which Salih, son of Sheikh Ahmad of the Juhaish, was killed, the British defenders were wiped out by a hand grenade tossed onto the roof of the building from which they had been engaging the rebels.

By now the two armoured cars were well inside the town and were heading for the levies' barracks. As they did so, it seems they were spotted by Major Barlow, who was being led back into the town by the tribesmen who had captured him. Barlow broke away from his captors and made a dash for the armoured cars but before he could reach them he was shot down.[27]

The armoured car had proved a useful weapon during the latter stages of the war in Iraq. The Rolls-Royce 1920 version weighed 4.7 tonnes, was powered by a six-cylinder 80hp petrol engine and on the flat level surface of the desert it could comfortably reach 45mph. It had 12mm thick armour and its revolving turret carried a .303 Vickers machine gun. It was normally manned by a crew of three, although some photographs show a crew of four, as appears to have been the case at Tel 'Afar. It was not, however, particularly well suited to the type of hilly terrain found at Tal 'Afar. Moreover, during the war, the Turks and their Arab allies had learned that it was possible to disable an armoured car by shooting at its tyres.

The approach to the levies' barracks from the gulley traversed a narrow lane between houses and so steep was the ascent that only a vehicle in perfect running order would be able to negotiate it. As the two cars struggled up this narrow twisting track they came under a hail of fire from the roofs of neighbouring houses. Whether the vehicles stalled, or whether their tyres were shot through, their crews were trapped and all eight officers and men were killed.[28]

News of the raid on Tel 'Afar reached Mosul within the day and many in the city exulted. Rumours abounded that the British were about to depart. British officers and men were jeered at in the street. It was therefore essential that swift retribution was meted out to the inhabitants of

Tal 'Afar to prevent this *coup de main* emboldening potential insurgents in Mosul itself.

The British garrison in Mosul was part of the 18th Divisional Area which also included Tikrit, Baiji and as far north as Zakho. The division's GOC, Major General T. Fraser, had under his command three infantry brigades, the 53rd, 54th and 55th, each mainly composed of Indian troops with a stiffening of one British battalion per brigade. In addition the division had a number of supporting units, field artillery, pack artillery, machine gunners, signals and cavalry. But in Mosul itself General Fraser had just one brigade, some cavalry and a few aircraft. However, it had already been arranged that at Mosul and other localities mobile punitive columns would be established, ready to take action in the event of serious disturbances. So on the afternoon of 5 June General Fraser dispatched Lieutenant Colonel G. B. M. Sarel of the 11th Lancers with 150 cavalry, 500 infantry and a section of 18-pounder field guns with air support to deal with the situation at Tel 'Afar.

As the column advanced along the Tigris in a curving north-westerly sweep towards the rebel town they systematically burned and destroyed all the crops of the Turkoman and Arab farms through which they passed. By the evening the column had reached a point ten miles above Mosul on the Tigris, where they surprised Midfa'i and around 1,200 rebel horsemen who had been raiding in the area. After a skirmish in which the Arab horsemen were bombarded by the light artillery and aircraft, they were put to flight, Jamil Midfa'i retreating to the rebel-held zone at Dayr az-Zawr. Continuing his advance, Sarel reached Tel 'Afar on 9 June and the punitive column entered the insurgent town. But by now the local leaders of the rebellion had learned of Midfa'i's defeat and had also fled, Agha 'Abdul Rahman ibn 'Usman escaping over the armistice line into Turkish territory.

The decision had already been taken to inflict a collective punishment on the rebel townspeople. Two days earlier Gertrude Bell had written to her father recounting the recent events and declaring, 'The inhabitants of Tel 'Afar are going to be turned out ... and every house is to be destroyed. Nor shall we allow the town to be rebuilt. I fully agree with the decision.'[29] Subsequently, the whole population, men, women and children were forced out of their homes at bayonet point and driven into the desert while many of the houses were burned, looted and destroyed.[30]

The incidents at Dayr az-Zawr, Tal 'Afar and Enzeli convinced Wilson that the principal threat to British rule in Iraq came from outside. Even before the raid on Tel 'Afar and the Enzeli débâcle he was urging the War Office to increase the number of aircraft 'to the three squadrons which were promised by middle of April' and replace the obsolete RE8s, because 'there are persistent reports that Abdallah (or Zayd) will shortly reach Abu Kemal.'

> Seizure of Dayr az-Zawr was first step in campaign of penetration from Syria to Mesopotamia. Occupation of Albu Kemal, following on recent agreement is second step. Local representatives of Arab Government have given us verbally and in writing to understand that there will be no cessation of hostilities on this front until we have withdrawn to Wadi Hauran south of Ana ... Occupation of Ana, third step and if made effectively by Arab Government would imperil our position at Mosul.[31]

The telegram then continued in an almost hysterical vein as Wilson poured out his loathing of the 'extremists' infiltrating from across the border:

> There are indications that in future we may be faced with a recrudescence of fanatical pan-Arab activity with aims and methods closely similar to those of their colleagues in Syria and Egypt ... The fact that complete anarchy is imminent is nothing to them. They have grown fat on anarchy in Syria; Syria is exhausted and they seek to revitalize their parasitical existence by fastening themselves on this country.

The telegram ended by warning the War Office that 'unless His Majesty's Government and Parliament are prepared to find and support forces to maintain order in this country ... the coming autumn is bound to usher in a wave of anarchic energy which will swamp us, and with us Persia', to which Wilson added, characteristically, 'Further concession in a constitutional direction will not affect this issue.'

On the other hand, Wilson believed that he had seen off the madhbata episode in Baghdad without too much trouble. To Wilson,

Haldane and even Bell, it still appeared that the main threat came from outside. It could not be denied that the occupation was becoming unpopular among some sectors of the populace; and a few days before the attack on Tal 'Afar, the judicial secretary in Baghdad, Edgar Bonham Carter, had warned Wilson that according to his information, 'the extreme party is gaining ground' and that there was 'distrust of our intentions' and 'a strong desire for the immediate appointment of an Emir'.[32] But as yet, it seemed that the only disturbances likely to threaten British rule in Iraq during the coming months would be those emanating from Damascus and its scheming former Ottoman officers or from Bolshevik agents infiltrating from Persia. However, within six weeks all that would change.

PART TWO

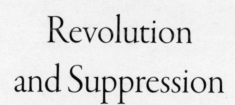

Revolution
and Suppression

The Drift to Violence

On 9 June 1920 Wilson flew back to Baghdad from Mosul in the observer's seat of an RE8. He had been conferring with the civil and military authorities as to the state of security on the northern border in the aftermath of the Tel 'Afar attack. Usually he enjoyed flying – the feeling of freedom and ascendancy: the desert stretched out below him dotted with tiny mud-walled villages; the chequerboard of criss-crossing canals in the cultivated areas; and here and there the turquoise-tiled roof of a Shi'i shrine – but on this particular day these anticipated pleasures escaped him. Wilson was morose and angry: and the object of that anger was the British Army of Occupation and its commander-in-chief.

So far, Wilson had lost six of his political officers. APO Captain Marshall had been murdered at Najaf in 1918, In April 1919 APO Captain Pearson had been ambushed and killed by pro-Turkish tribesmen in the north of Mosul Division followed by the deaths of PO Mr Bill and APO Captain Scott in October 1919 at the hands of rebel Kurds. And now APO Captain Barlow had been murdered at Tel 'Afar. Wilson felt all these deaths keenly. Many of the POs and APOs under his command were in their twenties; they were 'A.T.'s Young Men' and he felt a deep affection for them. 'They are practically all my nominees,' he informed Hirtzel at the India Office, adding touchingly, 'Almost all the friends I have in the world are included in their ranks and I regard Political Officers and Assistant Political Officers as being with the same family as my own brothers.' And what was the army doing to protect these brave young men as they carried out their onerous duties in faraway isolated districts guarded by a handful of regular troops and unreliable Arab levies? Absolutely nothing!

A few weeks earlier he had already complained to Hirtzel that 'the army is growing steadily weaker', that 'it exists apparently almost entirely for the purpose of taking in its own washing' and that at some stations 'all available troops are needed for guarding the married families'. He also complained that, in Baghdad,

> the streets are still crowded at all times of the day with motor vehicles containing officers and wives ... We have an effective strength of about one and half divisions, divided up into two divisions ... all of which have large Staffs and an enormous GHQ on top. It is this which is spoiling my Budget, for it keeps up prices without being of the slightest assistance to us. Any single branch of the army contains more officers than the whole of my HQ.

And now, to cap it all, the GHQ had gone off on holiday to the Persian highlands.

So on his arrival back in Baghdad he fired off a long, rambling and bitter telegram to the India Office. 'Recent developments', Wilson declared, had caused him to 'review the whole situation in Mesopotamia arising out of the grant of the Mandate'. The army, he complained, was incapable of defending the frontier divisions of Mosul and Dulaym and reductions of the garrison had meant it had been forced to abandon areas previously held. Any further abandonment of areas previously controlled would 'eventually involve the evacuation of the whole excepting Basra'. Indeed, in his opinion it was essential to regain possession of Dayr az-Zawr and the surrounding area, but this would require more troops and transport than currently available. Further, 'If His Majesty's Government regard such a policy as impracticable, or beyond our strength (as well they may be) I submit that they would do better to face the alternative, formidable and from local point of view terrible as it is, and evacuate Mesopotamia.'[1]

However, were the government to rule out the evacuation option (as, of course, Wilson fully expected) and follow his advice for consolidating the British position in Iraq, he informed the India Office that 'I should be prepared, in any capacity, to assist in giving effect to the more virile policy outlined.' In addition to stating his own strategic and military view of the situation, Wilson could not resist the temptation to reiterate his own political prejudices:

> Whilst acting in accordance with spirit and so far as may be with letter of mandate, we cannot maintain our position as mandatory power by a policy of conciliation of extremists. Having set our hand to task of regenerating Mesopotamia we must be prepared to furnish alike men and money to maintain continuity of control for years to come. We must be prepared, regardless of League of Nations, to go very slowly with constitutional or democratic institutions, the application of which to Eastern Countries has often been attempted of late years with such little degree of success.[2]

Finally, and very pointedly, Wilson informed the India Office, 'The above telegram has not been shown to or discussed with GOC-in-Chief ... because he is in Persia.'

Wilson's telegram had also been copied to Sir Percy Cox in Tehran, who showed it to Haldane. The general opined that it was 'of an alarmist nature', informing the War Office on 12 June that portions of the telegram 'as worded, may cause undue concern'. He also telegraphed the War Office that he was satisfied with the number of troops he had at his disposal. However, prompted by Wilson's telegram, the War Office – which apparently had no idea that Haldane was no longer in Iraq – cabled the general asking him to explain his absence from his HQ in Baghdad. Seven days later Haldane (who by now must have been fuming at Wilson's intervention) felt obliged to return.

Nevertheless, corporate loyalty at the War Office rallied round General Haldane and Wilson was accused of meddling in purely military matters. So the spat between Wilson and the army continued, prompting the Army Council to send the India Office what must be one of the most prolix interdepartmental communications ever composed. 'The Army Council', it announced, is of the opinion that the time has now come when the Secretary of State India will appreciate an expression of desire on the part of the Council that Mr Montagu may see his way to indicate to Lt.-Col. Sir A. T. Wilson KCIE, the advisability of leaving expressions of opinion on military matters to the responsible authority viz. the GOC in Chief, Army of Occupation.[3]

Consequently, Montagu felt obliged to raise the matter with Wilson, informing him that 'as general practice you should avoid telegramming to me on purely military matters without knowledge and concurrence of GOC'.[4] However, privately Montagu had some sympathy with Wilson's action and did nothing further to dissuade him from making his views on the military situation known to the India Office. For his part, Wilson – who after all, had considerable military experience himself – made it clear to everyone that he had absolutely no intention of refraining from pointing out what he considered the shortcomings of the Army of Occupation and its commander.

Although Wilson was convinced that the main threat to his regime came from outside Iraq, he was nevertheless becoming irritated by the challenge to his authority posed by the political campaign for independence of Haras al-Istiqlal. They had been warned that he would deal firmly with them if they continued their agitation but it was becoming clear that they had chosen to ignore that warning. The military governor of Baghdad agreed that preparations should now be made to arrest some of the leading 'extremists' should the situation require it. Accordingly, on 9 June he informed the head of the Baghdad Police, 'It becomes increasingly certain that we shall have no option but to arrest sooner or later 'Ali Bazirgan, Ja'far Abu al-Timman and Ahmad Daud. Also possible action of some sort will be necessary against Yusuf Suwaydi.'[5]

Meanwhile the movement for Islamic unity was spreading outside the capital and Kadhimayn. On 11 June Major Berry, the PO at Samarra, about seventy miles north of Baghdad, reported the presence of Muhammad Hassan, another son of the Grand Mujtahid, who had given 'a big dinner party to which all the Sunni ashraf of the town were invited' on 8 June. The following day Hassan 'had visited the same class of people, taking coffee with them in their own houses ... In each house he pleaded for unity between the Shias and Sunnis. In several cases he stated that the British were shortly leaving this country ... and that the governments of both Najaf and Karbela' are in the hands of the people.'[6]

Similarly, on 14 June, ehe military governor and PO at Basra reported,

> Efforts are undoubtedly being made from Baghdad to induce certain persons in Basra to raise an agitation in support of that in Baghdad ... These efforts which have increased of late are carried out chiefly by means of letters addressed to individuals by name and sent not through the medium of the post but by hand of persons travelling by train. The object is to cause any form of agitation that may be pointed to as an indication that the people of Basra do not desire British rule in any form.[7]

By now, Wilson was seriously considering ordering the arrest of the Baghdad nationalists, but on 16 June, Bonham Carter, the judicial secretary, wrote to him urging caution. 'The local situation', Bonham Carter explained 'is improving', adding that Colonel Balfour, the military governor, agreed with him and that 'the movement has gone too far for the arrest of a few leaders to stop it.' Therefore, 'Let us get out our Announcement. The extremists will not accept it but I believe it will have a good effect on the moderates.'[8]

The 'Announcement' to which Bonham Carter referred was the latest turn in the British government's meandering Iraq policy. Since the end of April the proposals for a 'Provisional Civil Government' which had been drawn up by the committee chaired by Bonham Carter himself had been slowly chewed over by the Foreign Office, the India Office and the special Interdepartmental Conference chaired by Lord Curzon; but neither politicians nor mandarins were very happy with the proposals emanating from Wilson's administration. The problem with the proposed 'Bonham Carter' constitution – as Curzon had explained at a meeting of the conference on the afternoon of 17 May 1920 – was that instead of providing for an Arab government 'advised' by Britain, the Bonham Carter constitution was little more than a British administration infused with Arab elements. It was simply too openly imperialistic. Eventually, after further meetings, on 1 June it was decided that since Sir Percy Cox would be returning from Tehran to Baghdad and his original post as civil commissioner later in the year, no official announcement about Iraq's future government should be made until Sir Percy himself had reviewed the matter.

However, the following day, unaware of this decision, Wilson had already outlined the main points of the Bonham Carter Committee's report to the Arab delegates at the Baghdad madhbata, giving a strong impression that the matter was a fait accompli. Whether it was for this or some other reason, on 7 June Montagu telegrammed Wilson authorising him to make an announcement about Sir Percy Cox's 'impending return' but also informing Wilson that 'subject to reservations on points of detail your recommendations [i.e. the proposals of the Bonham Carter Committee] are accepted in principle as furnishing generally suitable basis on which to construct provisional institutions such as are postulated by the Mandate'.[9] So understandably Wilson now concluded that he had got his way. The official announcement of the provisional government was to be made after the end of Ramadan, on 18 June.

Equally encouraging to Wilson, in a separate telegram from Montagu on 7 June, the secretary of state acknowledged the 'magnificent work' carried out by Wilson's administration in the 'intermediate period' and that he wished to 'take this opportunity of conveying to you [the government's] most cordial and grateful acknowledgements of the high ability and unflagging zeal with which during the past two-and-a-half years you have devoted yourself with such markedly successful results to your difficult and laborious task.'

However, on 16 June the Interdepartmental Conference met yet again and this time flatly rejected the Bonham Carter proposals. Instead they came down firmly in favour of the 'friendly native state' concept – there would be an Arab government in Iraq, albeit one effectively controlled by British 'advisors'. The conference's decision was ratified by the cabinet the following day and Wilson was instructed to publish in Baghdad an announcement markedly different from the one he was currently preparing – that 'His Majesty's Government, having been entrusted with the Mandate for Iraq, anticipate that the Mandate will constitute Iraq as an independent state under guarantee of the League of Nations'. The mandate would 'contain provisions to facilitate the development of Iraq as a self-governing state until such time as it can stand by itself'. To this end, Sir Percy Cox would be returning to Baghdad 'in the autumn' and would be authorised to 'call into being, as provisional bodies, a Council of State under an Arab President and a General Elective Assembly representative of and freely elected by the people of Iraq'. This new announcement was to be made on 21 June.

Nevertheless, as far as Wilson was concerned nothing had *really* changed. He knew that he would remain in charge of Iraq until some unspecified time in the autumn and he had absolutely no intention of slackening the reins of British power, of conceding anything to the 'extremists', or slowing down the remorseless engine of tax revenue collection. No, indeed: he would continue to run a tight ship as he had always done so that when Sir Percy eventually returned he would be able to hand over to him an efficient, well-run British administration. After that, his lofty task completed, his duty to the empire discharged, he would seek some other role commensurate with his experience and abilities.

Meanwhile, the reliable Colonel Leachman was sending in broadly encouraging reports from the Dulaym Division on the Upper Euphrates which suggested that the situation on the Syrian frontier was becoming more tractable. On 18 June he telegrammed Wilson from Ramadi, having just returned from 'Ana with three LAMB armoured cars. With the exception of one particular sheikh, the Dulaym tribes were 'very quiet'.

In spite of our retirements above 'Ana, inexplicable to the Arabs, and the mass of propaganda at work and the bad example set by the town of Baghdad, the general population of this Division is wonderfully behaved, and every credit is due to the Sheikhs of the Dulaym for this attitude.[10]

However, there was one exception: 'the tribes around Falluja, the Zauba'
especially, are restless owing to their proximity to Baghdad'; consequently Leachman informed his chief that he would be 'visiting them in a few
days'. And being paid a 'visit' by Leachman was the kind of experience
that would soon knock any trouble-makers into shape.

While Wilson's attention had been focused on the threats on the
frontier and political agitation in the capital, resistance to British rule
had been steadily increasing in the mid-Euphrates region, the Shi'i
heartland. So as if to underline his determination that, pending the
arrival of Cox, the status quo would be rigorously enforced, the day after
he had been obliged to publish the new announcement on the future
of Iraq, Wilson authorised the political officer responsible for the Hilla
Division to arrest a group of leading nationalists.

At the time of the British occupation the population of the
mid-Euphrates region represented a mosaic of varying stages of
transformation, from nomadic and semi-nomadic tribes in the west
to settled cultivators in the area around Hilla town. There was a two-
way movement of population: some nomads were moving towards a
more settled life while some settled tribes were moving back to semi-
nomadism by abandoning cultivation for sheep raising, primarily
because of deteriorating land conditions caused by the silting-up of old
irrigation channels and the diversion of river courses which shut off
water supply. The principal tribal confederations in the region were the
al-Fatla with around 7,150 fighting men, the Khaza'il with 2,500, the Shibl
with 3,500, the Bani Huchaym with 12,360 and the 10,000-strong Bani
Hasan, many of whose sections had fallen into poverty as a result of the
deteriorating land conditions and some of whom had reverted to raiding
and plundering their neighbours.[11] The tribes were very conscious of the
reality of the struggle for land and alive to closely related issues of land
tenure and tax collection, and their warlike reputation owed much to
the prevailing socio-economic conditions on the land.[12]

Consider, for example, the Bani Huchaym confederation whose
twelve sections occupied the lands from Rumaytha at the southern end
of the mid-Euphrates to Khidhr in the Lower Euphrates. Describing this

confederation, Gertrude Bell stated that it had 'never been submissive to civil control' and that 'for many years before the war, Ottoman authority had been set at defiance', conceding that 'if we affected a partial pacification, order was never completely established'.[13] Although tax assessments were lighter than some other parts of the Diwaniyya Division within which this region fell, the Bani Huchaym resisted crop measurements by the APO and as a result fell into arrears of revenue payments. When the sheikh of one of its sections, the 1,200-strong al-Sufran, was ordered to present himself at Samawa in September 1919, he refused to go. As a result, the following month his villages were bombed. The British then enticed the sheikh's brother into declaring himself the legitimate head of the section but the majority of the tribesmen refused to recognise him. In an attempt to enforce his authority, the pro-British sheikh entered the village accompanied by a bodyguard of Arab shabana who had been authorised to impose upon the al-Sufran a fine of 500 rifles. But when the shabana attempted to do so, they were set upon and forced to flee, leaving two of their number dead.

Further demands were now made upon the recalcitrant sheikh of the al-Sufran but, owing to a temporary lack of aircraft, the British authorities in the division remained impotent. As a result, the rebelliousness of the al-Sufran spread to the 900-strong al-Barakat, a neighbouring tribe of the Bani Huchaym confederation, and from the Barakat to the Antar, a section of the Albu Jayash.

It was not until May 1920 that aircraft became available. Subsequently, the al-Sufran villages were bombed intermittently for two days, killing and wounding twenty men, women and children and destroying about a hundred sheep.[14] But in spite of this brutal retaliation, the British acknowledged that 'no permanent settlement was effected and the position remained unsatisfactory'.

'The position' also remained 'unsatisfactory' elsewhere. By late May and early June there were attempts to derail trains passing through the mid-Euphrates region. Arabs in government service began to desert their posts. More tribal sheikhs refused to pay their taxes. Then, on 12 June 1920, in Karbela', a massive demonstration was held in the courtyard of the mosque of Imam Husayn in which rousing religious and patriotic poetry was declaimed calling for an uprising, and the following evening a similar mass demonstration took place in the courtyard of the mosque of 'Abbas.[15] On 17 June, the last day of the month of Ramadan, the upsurge of opposition to the continuing occupation spread to Hilla, where notices were posted on the walls of the town calling upon the residents to rise up and defy the British.

The PO for the Hilla Division (which also included Karbela'), was Major H. C. Pulley. Since his arrival in Iraq in June 1917, he had served as APO in a number of different localities including Baghdad, Karbela', Tel 'Afar and Hilla itself. He was an officer of some experience but he had only very recently been appointed to the more senior, political officer post. Faced with an unprecedented breakdown of British control in Hilla Division, he decided that he had to take decisive action to stem the rising tide of resistance. So the leadership of the independence movement in Hilla town was arrested and dispatched to a prison camp on the small barren island of Henjam in the Persian Gulf, a locality described by the official *Gazetteer of the Persian Gulf* as having a summer climate which is 'barely tolerable', the heat being terrific and aggravated by moisture, sandflies and other insects.

Meanwhile, in Karbela', another great demonstration was held in the courtyard of the mosque of Husayn on 21 June at which another mujtahid, Sheikh Muhammad al-Khalisi, gave a rousing speech in which he called upon the assembled crowd to prepare for a jihad against the British which should commence the following day.

By now British forces at Pulley's disposal had blockaded Karbela'. Pulley invited Shirazi's son Mirza Muhammad Ridha and a number of other leading figures in the independence movement of Karbela' to a conference. Whatever his reservations – and some of those invited to attend withdrew, fearing British intentions – Muhammad Ridha apparently felt obliged to meet with Pulley in an attempt to avoid bloodshed; such, after all, was the non-violent strategy which his father had consistently pursued since the beginning of the independence movement. In the event, on 22 June Ridha and eleven companions were seized and also sent to Britain's island prison camp in the Gulf.[16]

Wilson was predictably jubilant. 'Mirza Muhammad Ridha is at Henjam,' he telegrammed to Mr H. Norman, the British minister at Tehran deputising for Cox, who was paying a brief visit to Baghdad. 'We have got the wolf by the ears.'[17] And a few days after the events at Karbela' he was informing the India Office, 'The effect of these arrests has been excellent: agitation has subsided, confidence among chiefs and tribes restored, revenue income in regularly and situation is now once more practically normal on Middle Euphrates.'[18]

In fact all the available evidence pointed in the opposite direction. Wilson was now living in a fantasy world of his own imagining. Meanwhile, a distraught and embittered Shirazi made one more attempt to diffuse the situation and obtain the release of his son. The Grand Mujtahid wrote to Major Pulley demanding a face-to-face meeting with him. Pulley bluntly refused, telling Shirazi that the purpose of the blockade and the arrests was to maintain law and order.

Once more the aged Shirazi wrote to Pulley. The letter began in tones more of sorrow than anger. He expressed his 'surprise' at the contents of Pulley's previous message. He stated how he believed that Pulley had been deceived by influential persons who wished to exacerbate the tension between the Iraqi and British people. He explained how the meeting he had requested had been intended 'to remove your suspicions of us' and that 'our perspectives on matters of state are more sound and practical than the resort to violence.' But then the tone of Shirazi's letter changed.

To use force against the demands of the people and their petitions is incompatible with justice and prejudicial to the good government of the people. If you prevent me coming to meet with you again matters will have reached a state where my advice to the Nation with regard to the maintenance of order will be declared null and void and I will leave the people to their own ends. In this situation responsibility for any evil consequences falls upon you and your masters.[19]

A few days later Shirazi learned that his son had been released from prison but instead of being allowed to return home had been exiled to

Persia. This did nothing to assuage the anger aroused by the treatment of Muhammad Ridha and his colleagues, anger that was now spreading rapidly throughout the mid-Euphrates and further south into the notoriously unruly Muntafiq Division. At this point Shirazi issued another and final fatwa of immense importance. It read as follows:

> It is the duty of the Iraqis to demand their rights. In demanding them they should maintain peace and order. But if the English prevent them obtaining their rights it is permitted to make use of defensive force.[20]

And if further clarification were necessary, replying to questions about the precise meaning of the fatwa, Shirazi said, 'Do as you will. Now is the time to take hold of your rights.'[21] In this feverish atmosphere it would take only a small spark to ignite a much larger conflagration. The fire was lit at the small town of Rumaytha on 30 June 1920.

The Revolution Begins

Rumaytha is situated on both banks of the Hilla branch of the Euphrates, about twenty-eight miles above Samawa. In 1920 it had a population of around 2,500 inhabiting small houses built of sun-dried mud bricks, scattered among vegetable gardens and date palm groves. Rumaytha was also the District HQ of the same name, part of the Diwaniyya Division. Its APO was Lieutenant P. T. Hyatt, one of the more junior and inexperienced officers in the Civil Administration who had only taken up his post the previous October. On 25 June, Hyatt had reported to his divisional superior, Major C. K. Daly, that Sha'lan Abu al-Jun, sheikh of the Dhawalim section of the Bani Huchaym, was 'inciting his people to rebel' and 'causing disaffection' and asked Daly for advice on how further to proceed.[1]

Major Daly – an officer cast very much in the Leachman mould, albeit lacking his aura of natural authority – had no doubts about the way to deal with this type of situation. He had already been informed that same day that the Dhawalim 'had their flags out' (signifying refusal to obey the administration any further) so, with Wilson's authorisation, he ordered Hyatt to arrest the sheikh and dispatch him by rail to Diwaniyya.

Daly took his duties very seriously. The collection of taxes and the mobilisation of forced labour were vigorously pursued with threats of deportation to the prison on Henjam island for those who resisted. For example, in October 1919, when the al-Sufran tribe in the division's Samawa district refused to submit to the demands of the Civil Administration, it was he who called in air support to bomb the tribe's villages. Not surprisingly, Daly was hated throughout the Diwaniyya Division. According to one of Gertrude Bell's close informants, a Baghdad notable of conservative inclination, this was 'because of the hardness with which the people have been treated'.² Even Wilson was bound to admit that Daly 'causes me some anxiety. He is awfully efficient, but he is a hard man and a bit too hard for his Arabs who would like to be treated a little less justly and a little more kindly.'³ Political officer Harry Philby had a somewhat sharper appreciation of his former colleague's qualities, describing Daly as being 'as brutal as he was stupid'.⁴

It is possible Major Daly believed that Sheikh Sha'lan Abu al-Jun and the Dhawalim could be easily intimidated. The intelligence on tribes prepared for political officers by Gertrude Bell describes the Dhawalim as a 'peaceful tribe'.⁵ Certainly, it would appear that neither Bell nor Daly knew that Sheikh Sha'lan Abu al-Jun had attended that crucial conference at Karbela' on 4 May and was pledged to rebellion once it was authorised by the Shi'i clergy. So when the sheikh presented himself at the political serai in Rumaytha at noon on 30 June and was duly arrested, he had already primed his leading men for action. At 4 p.m. the 1,200 tribesmen of the Dhawalim attacked, killing an Arab guard of the shabana, putting to flight the remainder of the Arab police and releasing their sheikh.⁶ Lieutenant Hyatt immediately telegrammed the British bases north and south of Rumaytha for assistance.

In theory, the British Army of Occupation had one considerable advantage in 1920 compared with the situation when they first invaded Iraq. During the war a network of railways had been constructed to facilitate the delivery of men and supplies to the front. The steel rails and rolling stock were brought from India and initially a variety of gauges were in use including some short stretches of line which had been built by the Turks before the war. Most of the latter had been dismantled, but the network as a whole was steadily expanded. While railway construction was focused mainly on the Tigris, in May–June 1916 a one-metre-gauge line up the Euphrates was built from Basra as far as Nasiriyya, along which, for a time, two armoured trains patrolled.⁷

Once the war was over, some semblance of a rational railway system had to be achieved to replace the *ad hoc* pattern which military requirements had dictated. The immediate problem was to connect Basra with Baghdad, and at first sight the solution appeared to be one of filling in a gap which existed in the 2'6" gauge line between the Tigris towns of 'Amara and Kut al-'Amara. However, in the end, the Euphrates route was chosen as it was shorter in total length, passed through more densely populated and better irrigated regions and replaced a water transport system that was more difficult than the Tigris. Thus, with the aid of forced labour, a new metre-gauge railway linking Baghdad with Iraq's principal port city was built during 1919 and completed by January 1920.

Rumaytha was one of a number of stations along this long railway link and on the evening of 30 June Lieutenant Hyatt had every expectation of receiving reinforcements with which order might be swiftly restored. However, the following day Hyatt learned that the railway line south of Rumaytha had been torn up in several places and a bridge destroyed while a train sent north from Samawa to investigate the situation, carrying a few sepoys of the 114th (Mahrattas) Infantry, had come under heavy fire and been forced to return to base.

Later that day, after an urgent appeal from Lieutenant Hyatt, the line was repaired and at 3.45 p.m. another train carrying two platoons of the 114th Infantry managed to reach Rumaytha from Samawa. On 2 July an under-strength company of the same regiment also got through, this time from Diwaniyya, bringing the total strength of the Rumaytha garrison to 140. Meanwhile, all the non-combatant members of the town's local administration were moved into the serai, a two-storey brick building on the left bank of the Hilla-Euphrates channel and fifty yards from the bridge of boats from which the railway station on the opposite bank of the river, about half a mile away, could be reached.

On 3 July a train carrying a company of the 99th (Deccan) Infantry under the command of Captain H. V. Bragg, which had been dispatched from Hilla the previous day, arrived at Rumaytha carrying some railway personnel. But en route the train had been forced to stop to repair the line and had come under fire. There had been a number of casualties among both troops and railway working parties.

On his arrival, Captain Bragg, now the senior officer, took command of the garrison and ordered his own company to occupy two Arab khans, one at each side of the town, while the 114th remained to guard the civilians in the serai. By now Captain Bragg had under his command a total of 527 men, of whom about 40 per cent were railway personnel and other civilians. But the garrison had only enough rations for two days.

By 4 July the insurgents, mainly drawn from other sections of the Bani Huchaym, numbered over 2,500 and – ominously for the defenders – had begun to construct trenches around the town. It was a clear sign that among the rebels there were a number of former Ottoman army officers or NCOs with experience of regular warfare.[8] And there were other regular soldiers, men like Lieutenant 'Abd al-Rahman al-Sharaf, formerly an officer in the Arab army of Emir Faysal, Ahmad ibn 'Abdi Pachahiji, another former Arab army officer and 'Ali Jaudat, one-time military governor of Aleppo after the war ended, who were now in the mid-Euphrates region, 'fomenting disturbances', according to Gertrude Bell's agents, but most probably serving as military advisors to the rebels.[9]

Meanwhile, reports reached Lieutenant Hyatt that the inhabitants of a nearby village, Albu Hassan, were looting Rumaytha's bazaar. Captain Bragg therefore ordered two platoons of the 99th into the bazaar to drive off the attackers but, having successfully achieved this objective, APO Hyatt decided that Albu Hassan should now be burned to the ground as a punishment. By the time the troops had completed this task and were returning to Rumaytha, they were ambushed by around 1,500 rebels. Virtually the whole column was wiped out with forty-three infantrymen reported 'missing in action' and one British officer, one Indian officer and fourteen Indian other ranks wounded – only a handful of unwounded survivors managing to escape back to Rumaytha.

After further casualties at the hands of the growing number of insurgents, the khans were abandoned and all troops and civilians brought into the serai, the defensive perimeter of which formed a walled rectangle around the main building, about 150 by 75 yards. The rebels were left in complete control of the remainder of the town and by the following day the Rumaytha serai was surrounded by rebel trenches and completely under siege.

It was just the beginning. In a little over a month the number of insurgents on the Middle and Lower Euphrates would swell to over 100,000; British forces would be compelled to withdraw from every town and village except Hilla, Kufa and the British base outside Samawa, which were all surrounded and besieged; by mid-August Wilson's administration in the region would completely collapse and revolutionary governments would be set up in the cities of Karbela' and Najaf. The great Arab Revolt – the inevitable outcome of Britain's incoherent policy in the region since 1918 – had begun.

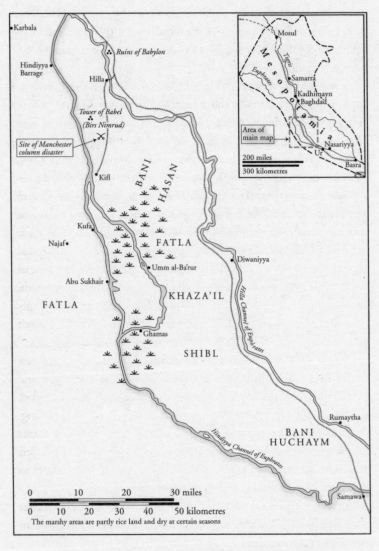

Karbala

Hindiyya Barrage

Hilla

Ruins of Babylon

Tower of Babel
(Birs Nimrud)

Site of Manchester
column disaster

Kifl

Kufa

Najaf

BANI
HASAN

FATLA

Umm al-Ba'rur

Abu Sukhair

KHAZA'IL

Diwaniyya

FATLA

Hilla Channel of Euphrates

Ghamas

SHIBL

Hindiyya Channel of Euphrates

Rumaytha

BANI
HUCHAYM

Samawa

| 0 | 10 | 20 | 30 miles |
| 0 | 10 | 20 | 30 | 40 | 50 kilometres |

The marshy areas are partly rice land and dry at certain seasons

Inset map:

Mosul

Mesopotamia

Tigris

Euphrates

Samarra

Kadhimayn

Baghdad

Area of
main map

Nasariyya

Ur

Basra

| 200 miles |
| 300 kilometres |

THE MIDDLE EUPHRATES REGION, EPICENTRE OF THE 1920
REVOLUTION, SHOWING THE PRINCIPAL TRIBAL AREAS

Discord and Disputation

Having unwillingly returned to Baghdad from his Persian 'hill station' at Karind on 19 June 1920, General Haldane once again began to contemplate escaping Iraq's summer heat, a torment that was becoming daily more and more unbearable to the GOC-in-chief. Indeed, he made no secret of the fact that he 'disliked the idea of remaining in Baghdad throughout the hot weather, where it was not easy, except for an hour or two in the late afternoon, to obtain sufficient exercise to preserve health'. Of course, he was well aware that Wilson was becoming increasingly agitated about threats to his administration. However, he himself considered these to be exaggerated.

By now the greater portion of Haldane's staff had moved to a new Persian HQ at Sar-i-Mil, a few hundred feet higher than Karind and even cooler. So on the night of 24 June, the general again left Baghdad, en route to Sar-i-Mil, arriving there the following day. Before leaving, he assured a none-too-pleased Wilson that 'if there were any matter outside the ordinary routine work with which my staff who were left there were incompetent to deal, I could be at that city [Baghdad] in a few hours by aeroplane'. However, much to Haldane's satisfaction, a few days after his arrival in Persia, on 1 July, he received a private letter from Gertrude Bell which suggested that the likelihood of such an eventuality had considerably diminished.

Apparently unaware that only the previous day a serious attack had been launched against a British outpost at Rumaytha, Bell informed Haldane that, 'the bottom seems to have dropped out of the agitation and most of the leaders seem only too anxious to let bygones be bygones', adding, by way of explanation, that 'I have had many heart-to-heart interviews.'[1] So, understandably, the general spent little time worrying about the size and deployment of his army in Iraq and focused instead upon the social and recreational pleasures of his Persian 'hill station'.

It wasn't long before Wilson got to hear of Bell's letter to the general and understandably he was incandescent. This was not the first time she had gone behind his back, communicating privately with leading British politicians, civil servants and military men, many of whom were personal friends or acquaintances of her rich and well-connected family. Indeed, in retrospect, this pattern of behaviour – which he was now determined to stamp out – had been in evidence since the very beginning of their relationship when Wilson had taken over Sir Percy Cox's position as civil commissioner following Sir Percy's departure to the UK (and later Persia) in April 1918.

In August of that year Wilson had received a letter from Hirtzel at the India Office in which the latter referred, in passing, to a missive from Gertrude Bell containing what Hirtzel described as 'a flaming testimonial' to Wilson's qualities and the 'success of his administration'. Doubtless, at first Wilson was must have been pleased by such a compliment – but then it must also have struck him that here was a woman, considerably junior in rank to himself, who was privately writing to a senior civil servant, offering her opinions as to her superior's abilities. This was not at all the kind of behaviour appropriate to someone in her position and Wilson quickly realised that – as he put it to a colleague somewhat later – Miss Bell was going to 'take some handling'.[2]

However, 'handling' Miss Bell became much more difficult after she returned from Britain via Syria in November 1919, having met Iraqi members of al-'Ahd like Nuri al-Sa'id and Ja'far al-'Askari and become convinced of their moderation. By now, Bell had altogether changed her mind about the 'success' of Wilson's administration and the direction it was taking and was making scant effort to conceal the fact. Indeed, she made it abundantly clear to all that she had been won round to the ideas promoted by Lawrence and the remnants of the old Cairo-based Arab Bureau that Iraq should move to some form of limited independence as soon as possible, with an Arab emir nominally ruling the country supported by a strong team of British 'advisors'.

Nor did she refrain from exploiting her social position and family connections to badger government ministers and higher civil servants with her views as to the correct policy towards Iraq, regularly by-passing Wilson and his administration. While admitting she was 'a minority of one in the Mesopotamian political service', she wrote frequently to Hirtzel and to Montagu, the secretary of state for India (chummily referring to the latter as 'Edwin' in a letter to her father) urging them to recognise the 'political ambitions' of those she identified as moderate nationalists and 'not to try to squeeze the Arabs into our mould'.[3]

However, Wilson and his team of young POs remained utterly opposed to any suggestion of 'independence', no matter how qualified, and it wasn't long before their opposition to Bell's newly acquired views on the viability of an 'Arab government' changed into smouldering antagonism. Although Gertrude remained on friendly terms with Frank Balfour, the governor of Baghdad, and the judicial secretary, Edgar Bonham Carter, the remainder of Wilson's administration grew increasingly hostile towards her. Colonel Leachman, for one, barely recognised her existence; when she lunched in the mess she was met by stony silences, and when Wilson presided over lunch – as he frequently did – he was 'often as cross as a bear so that the only thing is to leave him alone and not talk to him'. Most hurtful of all, she discovered that her small Baghdad house had been dubbed 'Chastity Chase' by some of the younger political and military officers, as though she was some kind of eccentric maiden aunt when, in her own mind, she still longed to find a lifelong soul-mate of the opposite sex.

Convinced that Bell was undermining his own policy, Wilson urged Sir Percy Cox, currently in Persia, to agree to her dismissal, but Cox indicated that he was reluctant to get any further involved in the dispute. So for the time being Wilson resigned himself to her continuing presence. However, for her part, Bell embarked on a project almost

deliberately designed to infuriate Wilson. On 16 May she wrote to her
father mentioning that she had launched a series of 'weekly parties for
young nationalists', the first of which had been attended by 'thirty young
men'. Once Ramadan began, the 'parties' commenced at 8.30 p.m. after
the sundown evening meal. Bell would hold court in her rose garden,
illuminated with old Baghdad lanterns, where her servants offered cold
drinks, fruit and cakes to the invited guests.

Most of these 'young nationalists' were apparently little more than
rich young men flirting with a fashionable notion, flattered to be invited
to Miss Bell's soirées and to chatter with their remarkable female host.
None of the members of Haras al-Istiqlal were invited, as far as can be
ascertained. It is therefore hardly surprising that Bell's 'heart-to-heart
interviews' with such people yielded feeble or misleading information.
Indeed, it was one of Miss Bell's faults that she frequently failed to
understand that, out of politeness, many of her Arab acquaintances
felt obligated to tell her only what she wanted to hear. Nevertheless,
for Wilson, the whole thing was an almost deliberate provocation and
it wasn't long before he found evidence of one of Bell's more serious
indiscretions with which to berate her.

Writing to her father on 14 June, Gertrude recounted how she had
had 'an appalling scene last week with AT'. She had given one of 'our
Arab friends here a bit of information I ought not technically to have
given'. Bell had called to see Wilson in his office and when she absent-
mindedly mentioned disclosing the 'bit of information' he had exploded
in a 'black rage'.

'Your indiscretions are intolerable', Wilson had shouted, 'and henceforth you will never again see a paper in this office.'

A crestfallen Bell offered her apologies, but Wilson, choking with
anger, continued the attack: 'You have done more harm than good here.
If I hadn't been going away myself I should have asked for your dismissal
months ago – you and your Emir!'

Once again, Bell apologised, and having some useful information of
her own to give Wilson she handed it to him, after which he marched out
of the office. She did not see him again for two days, but in the meantime

he appears to have cooled down. On the Monday morning following the confrontation Bell found papers on her desk waiting for her as usual.

For a time, Wilson seemed mollified. However, Bell's letter to General Haldane on 1 July, with its rosy view of the situation, was the final straw. Now, as information flowed into Wilson's office of the growing crisis on the Euphrates, he believed he had something really serious with which to accuse her. Dispensing with the previous game-playing, he came out into the open and urged Cox – currently in London – to dismiss her. 'If you can find a job for Miss Bell at home, I think you would be well-advised to do so,' he wrote, adding, 'Her irresponsibilities are a source of considerable concern to me and not a little resented by Political Officers.'[4]

Yet again, Cox did not accede to Wilson's requests; but it appears that he did do something – he discussed the matter with the secretary of state, Montagu, who, some weeks later, sent Bell a private telegram containing a strong official rebuke, reminding her that 'in the present critical state of affairs in Mesopotamia ... we should all pull together', and that if she had views which she wanted the India Office to consider she should 'either ask the Civil Commissioner to communicate them, or apply for leave and come home and represent them'.

As it happens, Gertrude Bell was not the only individual to receive an official rebuke from the secretary of state for India for a breach of protocol around this time. Wilson himself was accused of committing precisely the same offence. In spite of previous admonitions that he should refrain from criticising the Army of Occupation or its commander (which he had ignored), on 10 July Wilson received a telegram from Montagu informing him that, 'as general practice you should avoid telegramming me on purely military matters without knowledge and concurrence of GOC.'

However, on the very same day, once again Wilson made it abundantly clear that he had no such intention, telegramming the India Office with what was, in many respects, an accurate and damning indictment of the capabilities of General Haldane's army.

This lengthy telegram begins with Wilson's customary analysis of

the causes of the growing unrest, asserting that 'Military position in
Mesopotamia is conditioned by external rather than internal situation.
Principal external factors are Bolsheviks, Turks and Syrians in that order.'
The internal situation is described as 'threatening' but it would 'very
greatly improve so soon as the external situation has been stabilised'.[5]
However, after this risible introduction, Wilson proceeds to identify
the army's deficiencies with a keen eye. The primary requirement
is that 'existing units need to be brought up to strength in personnel
and equipment'. Turning first to the RAF, he points out that currently
it is 'not possible to keep more than sixteen aircraft in the air over
Mesopotamia and Persia or to make more than six available for any
single operation'. On the ground, Wilson complains that 'armoured
cars cannot be sent out of Baghdad owing to weakness or inefficiency
of personnel', reminding the India Office that 'Tanks have been refused
us.' As for the infantry, 'British units in country contain such a large
proportion of immature and almost untrained young soldiers that they
cannot be used for operations during hot weather, whole brunt of which
falls on Indian regiments.'[6]

The latter were, in any case, under-strength and their transport 'worn
out and inadequate'. Finally, he states that, in his judgement, 'GHQ
Mesopotamia should not again leave Baghdad', adding disingenuously
that, 'presuming that Her Majesty's Government required an
independent appreciation of the situation, I have not shown this to
GOC-in-Chief but I am sending him a copy.'

In fact, by the time Wilson sent this telegram, Haldane had already
returned to Baghdad, having arrived on 8 July 1920. Alerted to the critical
situation at Rumaytha a few days earlier, he had reluctantly concluded
that he had little choice but to move his HQ back to Iraq to deal with the
deteriorating situation. Wilson's deliberate refusal to 'clear' his military
observations with Haldane before dispatching his telegram therefore
indicates the extent to which he was willing to completely ignore the
War Office's complaints about his behaviour as conveyed to him by
the India Office. But it also suggests that Wilson knew that the India
Office's reprimand had, perhaps, been little more than 'going through

the motions' and that both Montagu and Hirtzel had some sympathy with his complaints.

And so the antipathy between the head of the Civil Administration in Iraq and the army on the one hand, and between the former and the person who was, in effect, his intelligence chief on the other, continued to smoulder, and it wouldn't be very long before a serious disagreement would develop within the army High Command in Iraq itself. All in all, it wasn't a very propitious start to the campaign to defeat what would turn out to be a far tougher enemy than any of these individuals could have imagined.

General Haldane's Indian Army

While the army objected to Wilson's 'interference' in military matters on grounds of protocol, General Haldane could hardly have disputed the basic facts of Britain's current military weakness in Iraq to which Wilson had drawn attention since he himself had noted many of the same weaknesses on his arrival there. Although Churchill had continued to press him for troop reductions – in April he had demanded that Haldane reduce the garrison of Iraq by 50 per cent by the next financial year – Haldane felt obliged to inform him that, for the time being, any reductions would have to be put on hold until the autumn and that in the meantime it might be necessary to bring some of his weakly manned units up to full strength.

On paper, Haldane's army consisted of two divisions, the 17th commanded by Major General G. A. J. Leslie, and the 18th commanded by Major General T. Fraser, the former with its HQ at Baghdad, the latter, 240 miles to the north at Mosul. In addition, far to the south, there was an under-strength brigade-sized force commanded by Brigadier General H. E. C. B. Nepean composed of three Indian battalions, a cavalry regiment and some support troops scattered around the so-called 'River Area' most of which lay in the vilayet of Basra.

As was customary in the Indian Army, the infantry of each division was organised in three brigades, each containing one British and three Indian battalions. However, in May 1920, one brigade of the 17th Division, the 51st, had lost one of its British battalions – the 2nd Battalion York and Lancaster Regiment – which was one of the two units Haldane had sent as reinforcements to Noperforce in north-west Persia after the Enzeli incident.

At full establishment, a British battalion in the period 1914–20 consisted of 1,007 men, of whom thirty were officers. Battalions were commanded by a lieutenant colonel with a major in second command and each of the four infantry companies of 227 men were commanded by a captain, or sometimes a major. In theory, an Indian battalion would have been organised on the same basis except that fourteen of the thirty officers would have been of Indian nationality.[1] There were also a variable number of 'followers' attached to each Indian unit. However, in reality, the strength of both British and Indian battalions varied considerably. In Iraq, in July 1920, in spite of remarks made previously by Wilson, the Indian battalions appear to have been reasonably well manned with an average strength of 846 men and officers; but the five British ones were seriously under-strength and only averaged 576 men and officers.[2]

Excluding the 3,000 British and 23,000 Indian troops belonging to the Royal Army Service Corps, depot guards, medical services etc. tied up in non-combatant duties, at the beginning of July 1920 the remaining 9,000 British and 38,000 Indian troops under Haldane's command were scattered over a vast area from the armistice line with Turkey to the Persian Gulf – a distance of roughly 600 miles – and from the Upper Euphrates to north-west Persia, a similar distance. Indeed, 3,500 British and 6,000 Indian troops constituting Noperforce were either 450 miles from Baghdad, confronting Bolshevik and Persian nationalist troops in the vicinity of Qasvin, or spread out along the hundreds of miles of mountain road reaching back from Qasvin through Hamadan, Khoramshah and Karind to the railhead at Quraitu in Iraqi Kurdistan. Other troops were resting at the Karind 'hill station', itself 150 miles from the Iraqi capital.

These distances 'as the crow flies' give no idea of the actual time required to travel from one point to another. For example, from Qasvin in north-west Persia to Baghdad required a march of not less than six weeks over difficult mountain roads. In Iraq, the movement of forces could easily be curtailed by a different set of problems: when the Tigris and Euphrates

Indian cavalry on patrol, *c*.1918

were at maximum flow – between April and May – roads could suddenly disappear under the flood waters of the two great rivers and in the winter heavy rains could turn the same unmetalled roads into a soup of alluvial mud. The availability of rail transport only improved matters slightly: for example, travelling by rail from Basra to Mosul could take a fortnight owing to inefficient rolling stock and indifferent railway personnel.

In addition to the troops in Persia currently unavailable to Haldane, 1,700 men were sick and 1,600 in transit. This left Haldane with a mere 4,200 British and 30,000 Indian troops available to meet the outbreak of the insurgency in the Rumaytha region. Of these 26,600 were infantry, 2,900 cavalry and 4,700 gunners: among the infantry the vast majority – 89 per cent – were Indian and excepting two under-strength British cavalry regiments currently 'resting' at Karind in Persia, the cavalry were all Indian while Indians also made up the majority – 72 per cent – of the artillerymen.

The three infantry brigades of the 17th Division were strung out over a vast region from Kirkuk, HQ of the 52nd Brigade on the edge of Kurdish territory, to the Upper Euphrates where its 51st Brigade had been dispatched to counter Arab raiders on the Syrian border, and then south as far as Hilla where the 34th Brigade was the only formation within striking distance of the rebel area.

The three brigades of the 18th Division were also spread out over an equally vast area up the length of the northern Tigris from Tikrit to Zakho in the far north, where the threat of an advance by Mustafa Kemal's Turkish forces had to be contained, while at the same time Mosul and the reoccupied Tel 'Afar had to be protected against the possibility of another raid north by Jamil Midfa'i's men out of Dayr az-Zawr.

Given that the vast majority of Haldane's forces were Indian troops and were to bear the brunt of the fighting against the Iraqi insurgents, what sort of men were they? According to the commanding officer whom Haldane had recently replaced, General George MacMunn, they were predominantly men from the 'martial races of India'. In 1911 this senior Indian Army officer had written a lavishly illustrated work, *The Indian Army*, published by that doyen of Edwardian illustrated books, A. & C. Black.[3] In it he expounded the currently widely accepted opinion that while the European was always ready for war, among 'Asiatics' only specific 'races' were capable of emulating the 'white man', the remainder having become enervated by long periods of exposure to warm, steamy, tropical climates, exacerbated by lengthy periods of peace during which any 'martial' spirit they may have once exhibited had become totally dissipated. As he put it, bluntly, in a later work, 'In India we speak of the martial races as a thing apart and because the mass of the people have neither martial aptitude nor physical courage ... the courage that we should talk of colloquially as "guts".'[4]

Moreover, in accordance with the predominant orientalist thinking there was a rural–urban dimension to the question: whereas the hardy native 'yeoman' working his own farm could make an excellent soldier, the educated or semi-educated townsman had become totally unfit for combat. MacMunn gives as an example a favourite target – 'the people of Bengal ... those with the most-cultivated brain, the trading classes, the artisan classes ...' who, as far as military ardour was concerned, were 'hopeless poltroons', contrasting them with 'the great, merry, powerful

A Rolls-Royce armoured car of the type used in Iraq in the 1920s

Kashmiri'; although MacMunn also warns his reader that physical appearance does not always have anything to with the matter, since 'some of the most manly-looking people in India are, in this respect, the most despicable.'[5] Therefore, 'In India ... certain classes alone do the soldiering and kindred service. These are roughly, in central and northern India, the yeoman peasant, the grazier and the landowner. Very good classes, too, as everyone can see.'[6]

As time went on, British officers in India became increasingly obsessed by the arcane distinctions of race and caste whereby they distinguished 'martial' communities from 'non-martial' and one group of 'martial' troops from another, to the extent that certain communities were held to have developed specific 'racial' characteristics which dictated which particular military function they should perform. For example, the Hazaras (a community of Shi'i Afghans, some of whom had migrated to India) were held to be especially suited to the role of pioneer/sapper – soldiers who could fight as infantry but whose principal role was the construction of roads, bridges and siege works. Thus, we find that the support troops of the 18th Division in Iraq in July 1920 included the 106th (Hazara) Pioneers.

More commonly, segregation by particular 'martial race' was carried

The more modern DH9A which largely replaced the
elderly RE8 towards the end of the uprising

out at the company, rather than the battalion, level. For example, the
86th (Carnatic) Infantry Regiment – in July 1920 just arrived in Iraq
from India as a relief unit – would have had four companies of Madrasi
Muslims, two companies of Tamils and two companies of Pariahs. Yet
others, like the 114th (Mahrattas) Infantry Regiment, whose men were
the first to see action against the Iraqi insurgents, might have a majority
of men drawn from one particular community but depending on the
circumstances, a minority made up of other groups – in this case six
companies of Mahratta Brahmans and two companies made up of other
communities, as circumstances dictated. The same principle ruled in the
Indian cavalry. For example, in the Scinde Horse, who had arrived in
Iraq in March 1920, 'A' squadron was composed of Sikhs, 'B' squadron of
Pathans and 'C' squadron of Derejats.

In reality, many of the fine distinctions and defining characteristics
of race, caste, class and region were largely in the minds of the British
officers who constructed them; but over time, clan or class loyalty among
the Indian troops became self-reinforcing as men returned from military
service to their communities with their turbans tied or beards trimmed
in the regulation manner adopted by their regiments and retained these
fashions in their civil dress. Then, they and their families retained these

distinctions to emphasise their military connections. Subsequently, later generations, both Indian and British, would come to see these fashions as deeply rooted caste distinctions, sanctified by tradition.[7]

Many of the Indian soldiers who were now facing the Arab insurgents had already served in Iraq during the Great War: take Jemadar (Second Lieutenant) Har Chand of the 99th (Deccan) Infantry Regiment, for example.

Har Chand had joined the Indian Army on 8 June 1907 as an ordinary sepoy (infantryman).[8] By religion, he was a Sikh, although in all probability he came from a town or village on the central Indian plateau near Hyderabad which had a large Muslim population – possibly Secunderabad, where the 99th Deccan had its headquarters. Between 15 August 1915 and 15 May 1916, Har Chand fought in Iraq, although it seems likely that this was after being drafted from the 99th to some other unit. On his return to India he rejoined the 99th and from 3 to 23 March 1917 he took part in operations on the North-West Frontier, fighting rebel Mahsud tribesmen in southern Waziristan. In early 1917 the 99th Deccan were at last called to duty overseas, arriving in Iraq on 8 April. The regiment was soon attached to the Euphrates Defence Force, which was assigned lines-of-communications duties along the river. During the course of these, Har Chand was commissioned jemadar on 20 February 1918 and as such, he would have commanded a half-company of two sections, each under a havildar (sergeant). Based at Nasiriyya, the regiment was not at the front fighting the Turks but it took part in two major punitive operations against hostile Arabs around Rumaytha, during which the unit suffered nineteen casualties.

Following the war, the regiment remained in Iraq. So we can picture Har Chand in July 1920 – his parade-ground red tunic having being swapped for campaign khaki – as the HQ and five platoons of his unit form up in a small mixed column with cavalry, infantry and gunners to try to relieve his comrades and others of the besieged Rumaytha garrison. Precisely what he would have thought about having to return to the same region he fought over three years earlier, we shall never know. Nor do we have any specific details of how he conducted himself during this and succeeding actions during 1920. We do know, however, that at the end of these operations Jemadar Har Chand was awarded the Indian Order of Merit, second class, for gallantry in the field.

The loyalty of such men to the British Empire was largely due to the personal and family security which soldiering provided. It was a much sought-after occupation for a peasant farmer and his family who might otherwise fall into utter destitution as a result of the vagaries of weather, crop diseases and ill health. The Indian soldier also enjoyed a certain respect and social status, not only within his own community but even among British soldiers and civilians. For while the former or the latter might freely insult or even harm an Indian civilian with virtual impunity, they would have to answer to an Indian soldier's British commanding officer for any similar acts of disrespect or violence.

And yet this image of absolute loyalty to the flag of the British Empire was beginning to fray a little. Opposition to Indian troops being employed to suppress their 'colonial brothers' in the Middle East was growing in India itself and some of the propaganda emanating from the subcontinent must have begun to percolate the ranks of Indian troops in Iraq. At the same time, it would soon become clear that among the Arab insurgents themselves, distinction was often made between British and Indian captives: whereas the treatment of the latter seems to have been generally favourable the same cannot always be said of the former, a few of whom were shot out of hand; this fate never seems to have befallen Indian captives. Indeed, this expectation of differential treatment may well have triggered a small but notorious mutiny at the height of the fighting against the insurgents, as we shall see.

And what of those British officers in the Indian Army? Consider, for example, Lieutenant Francis Gordon Andersson, of the 86th (Carnatic) Infantry Regiment – in July 1920 recently disembarked at Basra and now awaiting orders to move north. Francis Andersson was born on 1 March 1899 at Formby, a small, rather select seaside town in south Lancashire, the second son of an insurance manager.[9] Between 1913 and 1917 he was educated at Oundle School, situated in the small market town of the same name, one of the smaller traditional public schools to which less-affluent members of the middle classes sent their sons. At school, Andersson already showed an aptitude for military matters and he served in the Officers' Training Corps as a lance-corporal, following which he attended Sandhurst Royal Military Academy, graduating on 24 April 1918. On 29 October 1918 he was admitted to the Indian Army and attached to the 86th Regiment. Subsequently, having studied and become qualified in colloquial Hindustani, Andersson was made a lieutenant in the regiment on 29 April 1919.

Unlike most of the other Indian battalions in Iraq in 1920, the 86th was seriously under-strength with only 554 Indian other ranks, six British officers (including Lieutenant Andersson), twelve Indian officers and sixty 'followers'. However, in the coming months the 86th would see considerable action in both lines-of-communications duties and participation in several moveable columns. The unit would remain in Iraq until May 1921 and as result of his service, Lieutenant Andersson would, in due course, receive the 1918 General Service Medal with 'Iraq' clasp.

To what extent Lieutenant Andersson's social background and route into the Indian Army was typical is difficult to say; but in general, it seems that, like Andersson, A. T. Wilson and Leachman, British officers in Indian Army service tended to be drawn from the ranks of the less affluent middle classes in comparison with those men who were commissioned in the British Army itself.[10] There is also some evidence that British officers of the Indian Army tended to be less well educated in their profession than their British Army counterparts, although this would not seem to be true in the case of the three officers referred to above.[11]

While the majority of the Indian sepoys serving in Iraq in 1920 had some military experience, matters were very different among the roughly 25 per cent of each infantry brigade made up of British soldiers, as Haldane himself privately acknowledged. While a significant proportion of the officers of the five British battalions stationed in Iraq at the beginning of July 1920 had fought in the Great War, most of the rank and file had only been recruited after the end of the war and had never fired a shot in anger.

The 2nd Battalion of the Manchester Regiment, recently arrived at Tikrit on the northern Tigris, provides a not untypical example. Most of the surviving, battle-hardened other ranks, who had served with the battalion on the Western Front during 1914–18, were demobilised in early 1919 and left the regiment. However, in May and June 1919 the battalion recruited seventeen officers and 604 other ranks and on 5 November it was posted to Tipperary in Ireland, where it was involved in police-type actions 'in support of the Civil Power' until the end of the year, when orders were received for embarkation for Iraq.[12]

On 13 February 1920 the battalion commenced its month-long sea journey, arriving at Basra on 13 March before being carried by river steamer and barges up the Tigris to Baghdad. Then, on 16 March the troops were sent by rail to Tikrit, which was to be the battalion's permanent station, as part of the 53rd Brigade.[13] The battalion's young, semi-trained infantrymen, drawn largely from the slums of Manchester, Ashton-under-Lyne and Stalybridge, would have found their new posting very uncomfortable. On arrival there were no wash-houses, dining tents or recreation rooms, so that they had to spend a good deal of time on tedious fatigues.[14] This also meant that further training had to be postponed. To make matters worse, by early June, Arab raids were being made on the railway stations and posts north of Tikrit and the 2nd Manchesters and other units in the 53rd Brigade had to be put to work constructing defences and barbed-wire perimeters.

In addition to the British and Indian infantry there were also artillery, cavalry, pioneers, signals and other divisional support troops in Haldane's army in July 1920. The divisional artillery consisted of two brigades of Royal Field Artillery and two pack (mountain) artillery batteries. Three batteries of each Royal Field Artillery brigade were armed with the Mark IV version of the 18-pounder field gun, with a maximum range of 9,300 yards, an improved version of the weapon which had been in general use by the British Army during the Great War and had come into general service in 1919. A battery usually consisted of six guns, each one – and its limber – pulled by four horses and with a crew of six gunners. In addition, one battery in each artillery brigade was armed with the 4.5-inch howitzer with a maximum range of 7,300 yards but a much higher elevation than the 18-pounder. Howitzers were also manned by six gunners. Unattached to either of the two divisions there was also a battery of Royal Garrison Artillery with 60-pounder heavy guns.

Each division also had a machine-gun battalion and four LAMBs with Rolls-Royce armoured cars; however, all these units were considerably under-strength. Indeed, with regard to the armoured cars, in July 1920 they were having to be manned by men borrowed from infantry units; the cars were old and much the worse for wear, a number always being out of service.

The main British cavalry force, the 7th Brigade, currently at Karind in Persia, was formed by the 1st King's Dragoon Guards and the 7th Dragoon Guards equipped with lance, sabre and rifle. The brigade also contained a battery of the Royal Horse Artillery and was supported by a machine-gun squadron equipped with French-manufactured Hotchkiss guns. However, in July 1920 the two dragoon guards 'regiments' could only muster around a hundred men each.[15] In addition there were a number of under-strength Indian cavalry regiments attached to each of the two divisions

Although it wasn't immediately apparent, air power would come to have a crucial role in the ensuing struggle. By late 1919 two RAF squadrons were based in Iraq, the 6th and the 30th. Both were formed in April 1918 when the Royal Flying Corps and Royal Naval Air Service were merged to form the Royal Air Force. The 30th had arrived first and its three 'flights' were dispersed over a huge area, with one at Mosul, one at Qasvin in the Persian highlands and one at Bushire on the Persian coast.[16] Its main function had originally been to protect the oil pipeline to Abadan. The 6th arrived at Basra with its aircraft in crates in July 1919 and they too were initially distributed over a vast area, between Dayr az-Zawr on the Euphrates, Mosul and Baghdad. Both squadrons were initially equipped with the antiquated RE8 two-seater light bomber and reconnaissance aircraft. During the war it had been the most widely used two-seater British aircraft in service but it had proved unable to defend itself against enemy single-seater aeroplanes. The RE8 had a 150hp air-cooled engine which gave it a maximum speed of 102mph and an operational ceiling of 13,500 feet. It was armed with one synchronised forward-firing 0.303-inch Vickers machine-gun and one, or sometimes two, flexible 0.303-inch Lewis guns carried on a ring over the observer's seat. It could carry two 112lb bombs or an equivalent weight of smaller, 25lb bombs – the most common armament in Iraq in early 1920.

By April 1920 both squadrons had begun to receive more modern replacement aircraft – No. 6 with Bristol Fighters and No. 30 with DH9As. In spite of its name the Bristol Fighter was a two-seater light bomber and reconnaissance aircraft, although during the war it had proved sufficiently manoeuvrable to successfully engage enemy single-seater fighters in combat. Its 275hp water-cooled engine gave it a maximum speed of 123mph and an operational ceiling of 18,000 feet. Like the RE8, it was armed with one synchronised forward-firing 0.303-inch Vickers machine gun and one, or sometimes two, flexible 0.303-inch Lewis guns used by the observer. As a bomber the Bristol Fighter could carry a load of 240lb. The two-seater DH9As had a water-cooled 400hp engine which gave it a speed equal to that of the Bristol Fighter and an operational ceiling of 16,750 feet. The DH9A was armed in the same manner as the Bristol Fighter and RE8, however its bomb load was considerably larger – two 230lb bombs or four of 112lb – and while the maximum operational endurance of the RE8 was four hours fifteen minutes, the DH9A's was an hour longer.

While the replacement of older aircraft by newer and more appropriately equipped machines was very welcome, Haldane's main problem was simply the number of aircraft available. Dust, general wear and tear and illness had rapidly reduced the number of effective aircraft and personnel. For example, by April 1920, No. 6 Squadron had only three serviceable aircraft and seven flying officers available. Matters had improved somewhat by June but at Baghdad, No. 6 still had only eight serviceable aircraft.[17] The following month, Wilson was reporting that the garrison still had only sixteen planes to cover the whole of Iraq and large areas of Persia, of which only six aircraft were fit for service at any one time.[18]

So, when General Haldane first received news of the attack on Rumaytha at the beginning of July he was in a quandary: on the one hand, in spite of his efforts to persuade Churchill to the contrary, his general orders remained broadly the same as when he had departed Britain in February – to reduce the garrison. On the other hand, given the general weakness and scattered disposition of the troops under his command, the intelligence he was now receiving concerning the recent events at Rumaytha was deeply worrying and dictated additions to – not reductions from – the Army of Occupation. In the end Haldane decided that some modest precautionary measures were called for.

On 8 July he began to shuffle his forces into positions nearer to the scene of the uprising, sending an Indian battalion (87th Punjabis) of the 18th Division which had been guarding Turkish prisoners at Baghdad, to Hilla, seventy-five miles north-west of Rumaytha; another Indian battalion (86th Carnatics), which had only recently arrived from India, was also dispatched to Hilla; two Indian battalions and an artillery battery of the 18th Division were sent south from Tikrit to Baghdad; and the 2nd Battalion Royal Irish Rifles, resting at Karind, was also ordered to march to Baghdad, from where it too would be transported by rail to Hilla. On the same day he cabled the War Office that one infantry brigade and one field artillery battery (howitzers) should be made ready for dispatch from India to Basra.

Haldane must have been considerably relieved, therefore, when on 14 July he received a telegram from the War Office indicating that, following the attack on Rumaytha, all plans for troop reductions in Iraq had been abandoned. 'Your difficulties are appreciated', Churchill wrote to Haldane, 'and every effort will be made to complete your force in personnel.'[19] Haldane was now promised the additional men and equipment – signals, armoured cars, more modern aircraft and logistics – which he had requested in early May. In addition the C-in-C of the Indian Army had been asked to send infantry reinforcements to Iraq as soon as possible.

Indeed, news of this change in policy could not have come at a better time, because the very next day Haldane received intelligence that the uprising was no longer a local affair: three major tribal confederations in the Shamiyya Division of the mid-Euphrates – the al-Fatla, Khaza'il and Bani Hasan – were now in arms and had joined the revolt.

'The situation has come to a head'

For Major General G. A. J. Leslie, commander of the 17th Division and Haldane's second in command, the 1st of July commenced much as any previous day in this tedious and uncomfortable posting. In the morning he played polo, after which he returned to his Baghdad office to deal with paperwork; then, after a light lunch, he removed most of his clothing and, for much of the afternoon, dozed under an electric fan until it was time to dress for dinner in the mess.[1]

The fifty-two-year-old Leslie was an Indian Army officer 'born and bred'. Born in Cawnpore, Bengal in 1867, he had obtained his commission in the Royal Engineers in 1887, proceeded steadily up the ladder of command and served in Iraq during the Great War, where he had taken part in General Maude's successful advance up the Tigris in 1916–17. He had recently been promoted from lieutenant colonel to major general.

During the last two weeks of June, Baghdad had been appallingly hot but relatively quiet and in his dual capacity as Chief Steward of the Races and president of the Sporting Club Committee, General Leslie had been able to pursue the project currently closest to his heart. On 15 June 1920 he wrote to his wife, Edith, about his recent success in persuading the Sporting Club to relinquish control over horse racing and agree to the formation of a separate Baghdad Racing Club. He had also managed to establish a new racecourse at Hinaydi, a few miles south of the city. And anticipating a reasonably swift return to normality, which would make their reunion possible, he also informed his wife that he had given 'special orders that the floor of the boxes in front of yours are to be lowered so that you will be able to see over the people in front'.[2]

But two days later, with telegrams flying in with ever more worrying news of events on the Middle and Lower Euphrates, General Leslie had to swiftly postpone these recreational plans, briefly informing his wife that the 'political agents at Najaf and Diwaniyya' had reported 'serious unrest'.

To make matters worse Major General Leslie had a particularly awkward problem at Hilla in the shape of Brigadier General Arthur G. Wauchope, commander of the 34th Infantry Brigade, the unit nearest to the uprising. During the war, the forty-six-year-old Wauchope had served both on the Western Front and in Iraq, for which services he had been awarded the CMG, the CIE and the DSO; but he was now suffering severely from the heat, from the pain of a wound received in 1916 and from what looked increasingly like a nervous breakdown. 'General Wauchope has been hysterical again', Leslie informed his wife on 3 July, and '[has] begun to send the troops at Hilla about in all directions.' Fortunately, Wauchope's doctor had recently forbidden him from remaining in Iraq during the hottest period of the year and a War Office telegram had just arrived on Leslie's desk appointing the unfortunate Brigadier General to the command of a battalion in England. 'So I hope he will soon get away,' Leslie told her.[3]

Meanwhile, the military situation at Rumaytha was deteriorating. By 6 July supplies of food, water and ammunition were running low. A sortie by Indian infantry into Rumaytha's covered souk managed to seize a few days' food and in response to a message sent by heliograph to Samawa, and from there by telegraph to Baghdad, two aircraft flew over the town and dropped three ammunition boxes. One of them fell into the river, one into a date-palm garden outside the serai while the third reached its intended destination but in doing so fatally injured an Indian corporal. Fortunately, through the bravery of a civilian railway official and a sepoy of the 99th Infantry, the other two boxes of ammunition were eventually recovered.

General Leslie had dispatched a train carrying ammunition, food and water for Rumaytha accompanied by a relief column under the command of Lieutenant Colonel D. A. D. McVean, hurriedly put together from various units which had just arrived at Diwaniyya. It consisted of one infantry battalion, the 45th Sikhs, plus five platoons of the 99th Deccan supported by a squadron of the 37th (Indian) Cavalry, a pack artillery battery and thirty Kurdish levies. It was a singularly weak force to achieve its objective and its advance was proving painfully slow owing to the necessity of carrying out frequent repairs to the rail line and removing derailed rolling stock.

By the evening of 6 July the column had reached a point on the railway line six miles to the north of Rumaytha, where it camped for the night. Early the following morning the column began to advance again, but unbeknown to Colonel McVean his men were marching straight into a swarm of around 4,000 insurgents holding positions in a dried-up canal lying directly across the path of the advancing column.[4]

About three-quarters of the rebels were on foot and the remainder were horsemen. Over half carried firearms, of which nearly a third were modern rifles – mainly the ex-Turkish army model 1893 Mauser which was broadly equal in performance to the British Lee-Enfield. The remainder carried older weapons, primarily the single-shot Martini-Henry, a breech-loading rifle firing a black-powder cartridge. Introduced in 1870, it had once been the standard weapon of the British infantry but by 1904 had been replaced. However, although the Martini-Henry had a much slower rate of fire than the Lee-Enfield, its effective range – 600 yards – was comparable. Those insurgents who did not have firearms, including most of the horsemen, carried a variety of other weapons including lance, sword and dagger.

As the column came within range the insurgents opened fire. The Sikhs tried to break through the enemy line but were hurled back. Soon casualties were mounting and Colonel McVean realised that his position was precarious. Breaking through the rebel lines looked out of the question: he simply did not have enough men. Moreover, groups of insurgents were beginning to work their way around his flanks. McVean also knew that his line of communication back to Diwaniyya was only scantily defended. There was a very real chance of the column being completely surrounded and wiped out to a man. Indeed, if it had not been for the timely arrival of a flight of No. 6 Squadron aircraft which joined in the battle, bombing and strafing the Arabs, this would almost certainly have been the outcome. According to Squadron Leader Gordon Pirie's report on the action, 'it is no exaggeration to say that the whole column would have been massacred had it not been for the efforts of those aeroplanes.'[5]

Colonel McVean therefore decided to break off the action and withdraw northwards, and in doing so he had a stroke of luck. At around 11.00 a.m. a savage dust storm suddenly blew up, concealing the column's movements and enabling it to withdraw north for a good mile before the rebels realised what had happened. The Arabs hurried after them and desultory fighting went on until dark, at which point the insurgents gave up the pursuit and the British-led Indian troops formed a protected camp. On the following day the column continued its withdrawal, reaching the village of Imam Hamza, eighteen miles north of Rumaytha, and there it remained for the time being. It had escaped a potential military disaster but it had failed in its objective and, in proportion to the number of troops engaged, casualties had been heavy: One British officer killed and one wounded; forty-seven Indian other ranks killed and 166 wounded. Equally worrying was the fact that the insurgents had shown themselves capable of considerable tactical skill: in effect, they had pulled off a classic guerrilla-warfare manoeuvre – surround and isolate an enemy post and then ambush the troops sent to relieve it.

As soon as Leslie was informed of the failed relief attempt he began to assemble a larger relief column for a second try while putting together a plan to enable the Rumaytha garrison to hold out until this more powerful column could break through. On 13 July, as many aircraft as possible – at least six, he hoped – would carry out a bombing raid on the town and its outskirts, which would give the garrison an opportunity to make a coordinated breakout into the market area and seize as much food and supplies as possible. One of the aircraft – detailed to bomb the centre of the town – would be armed with 112lb bombs (hitherto only 25lb bombs had been used) and Leslie was of the opinion that 'these big bombs should fairly put the wind up the Budoos.'[6]

The intended outcome of Leslie's second relief column, which would follow the bombing raid, would be absolutely critical: if it failed it would almost certainly be necessary to abandon a large stretch of the Middle and Lower Euphrates; success, on the other hand, would give the British a breathing space in which to reinforce their troops in the region affected by the uprising. Consequently, Leslie chose a very experienced officer, Brigadier General F. E. Coningham, commander of the 51st Infantry Brigade, currently engaging Arab raiders on the Upper Euphrates, to command this second and crucial attempt to relieve Rumaytha.

However, messages received from the Rumaytha garrison via Samawa were giving every impression that the besieged soldiers and civilians were already losing their nerve. In a letter to his wife, Leslie complained that, in spite of being informed of his plan to bomb the insurgents, the garrison remained 'despondent'. Indeed, it looked very much as though 'their tails were down so much that they would not make an effort ... and were determined to give-in if they were not relieved at once.'[7]

In spite of the seriousness of the situation, Leslie himself kept his spirits up in the time-honoured traditions of an Indian Army officer, informing his wife on 11 July that he had 'got in four chukkas of polo the day before yesterday and a couple of sets of tennis yesterday', although he did acknowledge that 'things are moving too fast to allow of any recreation for certain.'[8]

Nor was Leslie the only senior British officer unwilling to let the crisis interfere too much with his social and recreational engagements. When Leslie 'dashed in to GHQ' on the evening of 12 July to get permission for his second Rumaytha relief attempt he found General Haldane playing bridge, during which the GOC-in-chief informed an astonished Leslie that he 'would not risk a single man of his reserves' to save Rumaytha and that it was 'the garrison's own fault for getting themselves besieged'.[9]

Somehow Leslie persuaded his commanding officer to agree to his proposal and it was decided that the second relief column should concentrate at Hilla and begin its advance on Rumaytha on 15 July, two days after the bombing raid. In the event, the first part of the plan was successful; nine aircraft took part in the attack and the garrison's sortie managed to seize rations and forage sufficient for it to last out until 23 July. However, Haldane continued to grumble about the dispatch of the second relief column and to Leslie's evident exasperation, at 8.30 p.m. on the same day that the column had set off, he was summoned to GHQ, where Haldane told him that his agreement on the night of the 12th 'was given against his better judgment', and that henceforth he 'refused to jeopardize his whole force in Mesopotamia by making an unready push'.[10]

Meanwhile, Haldane's problems were multiplying. On 14 July it was reported that another garrison, at Samawa, was 'getting itself besieged', that the forty-five levies guarding the railway station at Ibn 'Ali between Diwaniyya and Hilla had now deserted, taking their weapons with them, and that all the tribes of the rich rice-producing Shamiyya region on the Hindiyya branch of the Euphrates north of Hilla had joined the uprising.

South of Rumaytha, the situation was equally threatening. While Brigadier General Nepean, commander of the 'River Area', was trying – largely unsuccessfully – to get reinforcements through from Samawa to Rumaytha, downstream of Samawa insurgents had been ripping up railway lines and attacking trains trying to get through to Samawa from Basra. A train carrying a hundred sepoys of the 2nd Battalion 125th Rifles had reached Samawa on 3 July but an armoured train which was following was derailed twelve miles south of the town. Four days later patrols found the train and with it the bodies of twelve sepoys and the engine driver. It was becoming clear that the rebels understood very well the extent to which the British relied on their railway system. Indeed, by 8 July they had captured or derailed six trains on the stretch of track between Diwaniyya and Samawa, in effect cutting the lines of communication between Basra and Baghdad.[11]

However, the garrison at Samawa was better placed to withstand a siege than Rumaytha. Although the town itself had, by now, gone over to the rebels, the British had four closely linked strongpoints outside the town. The 400-strong garrison was commanded by a capable and experienced officer, Major A. S. Hay of the 31st Lancers, and controlled enough ground for aircraft to land and take off; so, as yet, supplying the defending troops with food and ammunition was not a particular problem. There was also a large stock of bombs at Samawa, so aircraft which flew in with supplies could fly out again with payloads to attack nearby enemy encampments. In addition a gunboat, HMS *Greenfly*, was steaming up to Samawa from Nasiriyya. Consequently, Haldane considered that he could leave Samawa to fend for itself for the time being.

On the other hand, the rising in Shamiyya Division was a much more serious affair, as Haldane's own dispatches to the War Office reveal. Until 8 July Rumaytha dominates the telegraph lines and there is no mention of the Shamiyya. However, on the following day, Haldane informs the War Office that the 'political situation on Shamiyya Division is delicate'.[12] Three days later, the telegram to the War Office notes that the Shamiyya situation continues to be 'unchanged' and a message dispatched at 1400 hours on 14 July also describes the Shamiyya as 'unchanged'.[13]

Then, at midday on the 15th, a four-line telegram simply – but ominously – requests 'that the troops mentioned in ... telegram of 8 July be sent to Basra as soon as possible', continuing, 'I shall probably be compelled, owing to spread of the present risings which are assuming a general form, to ask for the remainder of a full division.'

Three hours later, Haldane sends a much more detailed telegram whose content and wording graphically convey the commander-in-chief's anxiety and his assessment of the rapidly deteriorating situation.

The rising of the Shamiyya Division before the relief of Rumaytha has caused a material change in the situation and adds to the difficulties by exposing my communications between Baghdad and the relief force to increased danger of attack. The rising has become general and may spread ... External intrigue organized and synchronized with recent renewed Bolshevik activity is at the bottom of the disturbances. Tribes who have risen appear to be affected by a wave of fanaticism. Neither they nor their leaders have in any instance formulated any specific grievances and removal of all Government control appears to be their sole expressed object.[14]

Haldane then informs the War Office that he has committed his last reserves to the Rumaytha relief operation, that it is essential that he is able to form another reserve force at Baghdad and that he could withdraw troops from the Upper Euphrates, but 'this action would inevitably lead before long to disturbances in these areas'; therefore 'the only logical decision is to withdraw from Mosul Vilayet ... I propose to order this, possibly within a very few days.' As for the troops in north-west Persia, Haldane observes that their continued presence there 'is ... a matter for the consideration of His Majesty's Government', but suggests that they might be withdrawn to Hamadan, a position nearer Baghdad. The GOC-in-chief also envisages a scenario in which the full pacification and re-occupation of the country will not be possible until the following year.

While events in Shamiyya were coming to a head, the commander of the second relief column, Brigadier General F. E. Coningham, was concentrating all the available troops between Hilla and Diwaniyya at Imam Hamza, where the survivors of the first relief attempt remained. In practice this meant that he would have to command a force made up of units of four different brigades which did not even belong to the same division and was henceforth to be known as RUMCOL. In fact this would be the pattern throughout the campaign as Leslie complained to his wife: 'Everything in this "War" is done in "Columns" – the 17th Division, as such, no longer exists in the minds of GHQ.'[15] But his commander-in-chief had good reason for these unorthodox military formations: 'This organization, though unsound, was unavoidable, not only because, to save time, the troops nearest at hand had to be used, but because ... my reserve brigade, which would normally have been at Baghdad and available to proceed as a whole on any operation required, was, except for one battalion, still on the Upper Euphrates.'[16]

At least, this time, the relief column would be considerably stronger than in the earlier attempt. By 14 July Leslie and Coningham had assembled a force made up of four battalions of Indian infantry, an under-strength British battalion (the 2nd Battalion Royal Irish Rifles), two field artillery batteries and one pack artillery battery. There was also a squadron of the 37th (Indian) Cavalry, some machine-gunners and sappers and an armoured train on which the reserve ammunition, water, rations and medical requirements would be carried. Furthermore, an additional battalion from the 51st Infantry Brigade, the 1st Battalion 10th Gurkha Rifles, had been ordered to join the column and was currently making a forced march from the Upper Euphrates to Baghdad, from where it would be transported by rail to Diwaniyya.

However, in spite of the fact that RUMCOL was considerably larger and stronger than its predecessor, it faced three major problems. First, its line of communications could never be more than scantily defended. Major General Leslie ordered that double platoon posts should be placed every two to four miles from Imam Hamza, the most forward position manned by the 45th Sikhs, to Hilla, a distance of about seventy miles. But to man these posts required the equivalent of two of Coningham's battalions. Even so it was difficult to prevent the rebels from cutting telegraph wires and ripping up railway track under cover of darkness. Second, while this larger column was strung out in marching order, it would be extremely vulnerable to attacks on its flanks or rear by Arab raiding parties. To reduce this risk the column was obliged to proceed south along the railway line in a square formation in which the train and transport wagons were in the middle with companies from the remaining infantry battalions covering the front, rear and sides of the square. Progress in this formation was slow, however, as the column had to make frequent stops to repair track or to transport guns and supplies across the numerous dried-up canals and gullies which criss-crossed their path.

No remedy was available for the third problem: the shade temperature was now reaching 120°F. It was a heat the like of which the British troops in the column could never have imagined: a heat which bore not the remotest similarity to any hot English summer day – a horrible, frightening heat that pressed down upon them like a smothering blanket from which there was no escape. And in these conditions it was inevitable that the military effectiveness of the Royal Irish Rifles, the gunners of the Royal Field Artillery and some of the British officers –

even those who had previously served in Iraq – would soon be reduced by heatstroke casualties.[17]

By 16 July Coningham's force had reached a position sixteen miles north of Rumaytha. Meanwhile, the APO at Rumaytha, Lieutenant Hyatt, had received intelligence that some of the sheikhs of the tribal sections besieging the town were willing to parley. He therefore sent a message – once again using the heliograph link with Samawa – informing Leslie of the Arabs' willingness to negotiate, adding that if an aircraft could be sent to Rumaytha (he would put out a certain sign indicating it was safe to land) he should be flown out of the town to discuss the situation with his superior, Major Daly, who was accompanying Coningham's relief force.

However, General Leslie was not impressed by this proposal and was of the opinion that APO Hyatt's 'tail' was 'between his legs all through'. According to Leslie, the APO 'laid stress on the necessity for an immediate consultation with his boss at Diwaniyya', but was insisting 'that the plane should not bring Daly to him but take him to Daly'.[18] Leslie's response to this request was brutally sharp. He immediately telegraphed General Coningham – knowing that the latter would show the cable to the PO, Major Daly – stating that he considered that the insurgents would be better persuaded to cease hostilities 'if the political officer Diwaniyya [Daly] comes ... with you and your guns than if the political officer Rumaytha comes to Diwaniyya. Proceed with your advance!'

Meanwhile, in Baghdad, GHQ in the person of Brigadier General i/c Administration P. O. Hambro, recently arrived from the Persian hill station, had taken upon himself the task of arranging the transportation by rail of men and supplies to the 'Rumaytha Front'. This was much to the annoyance of Major General Leslie, who was preparing to leave for Diwaniyya and who considered that it was he who should have been making the necessary arrangements. Leslie's irritation rapidly turned to fury when he arrived at the railway station in the late afternoon of 17 July, as he later recorded.

The train to take me and the 10th Gurkhas – recently arrived by forced march from the Upper Euphrates – to Diwaniyya was to leave at 6.30 p.m. When I arrived at the station I found that GHQ [i.e. Hambro] had loaded the whole train with 'comforts for troops' and the 10th Gurkhas could not get on it, nor were there any other rolling stock in the station! I must confess that my temper was really put to the test now. But I might have expected something of the sort from a Staff which turned up to do its job at the last moment and insisted upon relieving me of that job though my staff were perfectly capable of doing it in addition to their own work.[19]

However, Leslie was not the man to be overawed by a GHQ staff officer and he immediately ordered the unloading of the 6.30 p.m. train and the embarkation of the Gurkhas. So by 4.20 p.m. the next day Leslie and the Gurkhas arrived at Diwaniyya and the Gurkhas began yet another forced march to try to catch up with the relief column.

By now it had become obvious to the War Office that recent events in Iraq would have to be fully reported to the cabinet and – in due course – to Parliament. Consequently, on 17 July Churchill informed his government colleagues that 'the situation in Mesopotamia has come to a head.'[20]

Having presented a summary of military events in Iraq since 1 July – an account which did not minimise the difficulties the British were facing – Churchill explained that General Haldane had used his last reserves and that it was essential that a further reserve should be formed. In response to Haldane's request for reinforcements made two days earlier, the general staff had already moved swiftly to commit a full division from India in spite of the fact that Haldane himself had only suggested that it was 'probable' that a full division would be needed. The financial implication of these developments was clear and the secretary of state for war did not hesitate to spell it out: the reinforcements would cost 'millions ... all prospect of reduction is at an end. A very large supplementary estimate is inevitable.' All other objectives must now be subordinated to one single aim. 'Whatever the future policy may be, the rising ... should be stamped out with the utmost vigour.'[21]

However, it would be at least two weeks before any troops from India would begin to arrive in Iraq and a further four to five weeks before the full division completed its disembarkation at Basra. In the meantime it was essential that forces already in the region were redeployed so that the maximum pressure could be brought to bear on the Euphrates rebels. But from which combat zone should these reinforcements be withdrawn?

The situation on the Upper Euphrates and Syrian border had quietened down over the last few months, largely because Haldane had deployed most of his reserves in that theatre. However, news from London suggested it was now inevitable that the French would attack Damascus and crush Syria's nascent Arab government. Churchill thought that if that happened, Emir Faysal might join the Turks, foment trouble for Britain in Iraq and Palestine or even call for a jihad against all Europeans. In other words, withdrawing any more troops from the Syrian border areas would be extremely risky. To the north, Turkish nationalists continued to threaten the British position at Zakho and could even pose a threat to Mosul; it was also possible that Turkish troops would combine forces with the Kurds. It would be extremely unwise to withdraw troops from this frontier, given the continuing failure of the European powers and their postwar puppet government in Istanbul to subdue Mustapha Kemal and his men. Finally, on the eastern flank, Persia continued to be threatened by a combination of Bolshevik troops and local nationalist rebels. Haldane had the equivalent of two brigades in that enfeebled state, propping up a friendly government – should Britain abandon an ally and allow Persia to decline into chaos? The strategic choices were exceptionally difficult; as Churchill himself put it, 'We find, therefore, that we are threatened with possible trouble from the west, the north and east. All the alternatives are disagreeable.'

However, the war secretary was not one to evade the making of difficult choices. 'Persia', he advised the cabinet, 'remains the safest place from which troops can be withdrawn and it is considered that on military grounds the General Officer Commanding should be authorized to withdraw Noperforce.' But would the cabinet agree?

While Churchill and his colleagues were considering these broad strategic issues, General Coningham was approaching the location where the first attempt to relieve Rumaytha had failed. By now the insurgents' position on the banks of the Hilla branch of the Euphrates, where the river curves round in a great loop, had been further strengthened, and now consisted of a series of trenches hidden by scrub in front of parallel lines of dried-up canal beds impassable to wheeled vehicles and lying directly across the column's line of march. The position was a particularly strong one, given that the rebels on the left bank of the Hilla channel could enfilade the British troops as they moved forward to attack the insurgents' main defences on the right bank. Moreover, the insurgent forces had increased to around 5,000 men spread out along a front of 3,500 yards.

By now so many men of the Royal Irish Rifles had gone down with heatstroke that the unit was effectively out of action. Nevertheless, at 1.10 p.m. on 19 July, Coningham's six 18-pounder guns opened up and after the initial bombardment the two battalions leading the relief column, the 45th Sikhs and the 116th Mahrattas, were sent forward against the insurgents' position. But the rebels, instructed by former Ottoman army officers and NCOs, had prepared their position extremely well and the sepoys failed to break through.

However, an hour later the 10th Gurkhas arrived, their commander, Lieutenant Colonel H. L. Scott, having marched towards the sound of Coningham's guns.[22] Coningham and Scott now scanned the battleground with their binoculars, searching for a point in the enemy's defences which could be outflanked. Villages were visible along the line of the river, but from the British position and the flatness of the terrain it was not possible to determine which river bank they were on. Eventually, two objectives were chosen – Umm Nijiris, a small village surrounded by palm trees, and another group of mud-brick buildings a mile further upstream.

So, after a short rest, at 5.00 p.m. 'A' and 'C' companies of the Gurkhas were thrown into an attack on these two points. There followed a bitter struggle to try to occupy both sides of the river. 'A' Company, under its commander Captain Selby Moore, made for Umm Nijiris while 'C' Company provided covering fire supported by a section of British machine-gunners. But after only a few bursts of machine-gun fire, the British gunners collapsed, half-dead with heatstroke. However, although deprived of effective covering fire, 'A' Company advanced grimly towards the river under heavy enemy fire and managed to establish themselves on the near bank.

At this point the river was only forty yards wide but fast-flowing and in places as much as ten feet deep. Nevertheless Captain Moore, with the company jemadar, Panchalal Limbu, led several desperate attempts to cross the river under heavy fire from the insurgents' positions. None succeeded and during one of these gallant efforts both men were killed. So as darkness fell, Coningham was forced to withdraw both companies of Gurkhas to a position 500 yards from the river.

Once again, it appeared that it might be impossible to relieve Rumaytha. The column's advance was blocked. Worse still, as the British attacks petered out, the Arabs began to go on the offensive, mounting sporadic attacks on the 45th Sikhs holding the British forward positions. The situation of the second relief column was now as precarious as that of its predecessor. There was no possibility of further reinforcements yet Coningham remained, facing a strong and resolute enemy in possession of an equally strong defensive position. His men and horses were running short of water and he had insufficient ammunition for a full second day's fighting. There were also a substantial number of sick and wounded with only very basic medical supplies available. He had little choice except to order one more attack.

At dawn the next day, the 10th Gurkhas were again thrown against the right flank of the enemy's position. Two platoons of Gurkhas from 'C' Company, the water reaching up to their armpits – but this time, supported by covering fire from artillery, Lewis and Hotchkiss guns – managed to cross to the left bank of the river on a front of 500 yards. Taken in the flank, the insurgents fell back and the Gurkhas began to advance down the left bank of the Hilla, rolling up the enemy's position. Coningham now ordered the 45th Sikhs to mount another frontal attack on the rebel position on the right bank, but as they advanced they found the enemy trenches abandoned. The rebels had slipped away –

either to avoid being outflanked or because of a shortage of ammunition. So by 6.45 a.m. on 20 July Coningham had three battalions of infantry occupying the insurgents' former position, and two hours later a train from Diwaniyya arrived, bringing water, ammunition and medical dressings which Coningham had ordered to be loaded during the night.

Leaving the 116th Mahrattas to guard the train and transport vehicles, Coningham moved forward without opposition. By 3.45 p.m. word came through that his advance guard of cavalry had entered Rumaytha thirty-five minutes earlier. Rumaytha had been relieved, but at the cost of three British officers and thirty-two Indian other ranks killed and two British officers and 150 Indian other ranks wounded. In addition, since Rumaytha had been first besieged, the garrison had suffered 148 casualties killed, wounded or missing.[23]

Even then, the tribulations of the garrison and relief force were not over. Leslie knew it was folly to continue to leave small numbers of men defending each and every town in insurgent territory and he therefore ordered Coningham to retire with all his men and guns to Diwaniyya. So on the morning of 22 July the column set off northwards. It was not long before bands of Arab horsemen began to appear at the rear and on the flanks of the column. Then, at 7.00 a.m., under cover of a dust storm, a large party of tribesmen fell upon the 87th Punjabis who were acting as rearguard.[24] The 45th Sikhs were ordered to turn about and support the 87th, but as they did so they became hopelessly intermingled with the cavalry who were also trying to come to the aid of the infantry. RUMCOL was now in great danger, especially since its commander could see nothing but dust, and during a chaotic few minutes the 87th Punjabis suffered sixty-nine casualties including two of their British officers.[25] Fortunately, three companies of the Royal Irish Rifles managed to make their way to the rear of the column and eventually succeeded in driving off the insurgents and re-forming the rearguard.

Thereafter, the rebels contented themselves with occasional sniping, with their horsemen ranging round the column but never closing in. At 5.00 p.m. the column was able to halt and make a protected camp alongside the river bank. The column's exploits on 22 July had rivalled its earlier achievements. Having started out at 3.00 a.m. they had marched and fought through the fierce heat of the day, made worse by a dust storm which had raged for several hours. By the time they made camp, both British and Indian officers and men were very nearly at the end of their endurance. Fortunately, after this, Coningham was able to continue his withdrawal to Diwaniyya in relative safety, arriving there on 25 July.

However, the general military situation remained far from satisfactory. The insurgents had been left in control of Rumaytha, the uprising had spread to neighbouring tribes and word was spreading rapidly throughout all the tribes of the Middle and Lower Euphrates that the *Ingliz* had been defeated, that they were too weak to withstand the rebel forces and that they were clearly in the process of relinquishing control over the country.

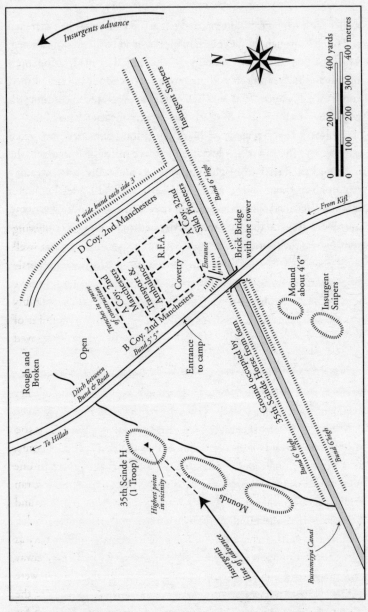

THE SCENE OF THE MANCHESTER COLUMN DISASTER
JULY 1920: THE CAMP ON THE RUSTUMIYYA CANAL

26

The Destruction of the Manchester Column

While General Haldane's attention was focused on the besieged garrison at Rumaytha, the insurgency continued to spread, gathering in more and more tribesmen, their sheikhs swept up in a great swell of religious fervour and primitive patriotism which gave them little room to manoeuvre, even when their sheikhly interests might have been better served by remaining obedient to the British. By mid-July 1920 around 35,000 Arab tribesmen were in arms and the number of British garrisons and outposts at risk of being cut off and destroyed was increasing.[1]

In particular, fears grew for the safety of the British outpost at Kufa, where a small detachment of Indian troops from the 108th Infantry Regiment was keeping a wary eye on the rebellious city of Najaf seven and a half miles to the south-west. Kufa, a town of around 3,500 inhabitants, situated on the right bank of the channel of the same name, lay thirty-three miles south of the British base at Hilla. For twenty-one miles of that distance a narrow-gauge railway, built during the war, ran as far as Kifl, another small British outpost and railway terminus and the point where the Hindiyya branch of the great Euphrates divides, forming two further channels, the Kufa and the Shamiyya. As early as 11 July, the stationmaster at Kifl had reported that attacks on the railway station and telegraph lines were anticipated and the railway staff were authorised to withdraw north to Hilla. However, the following day, the PO for the Hilla Division, Major Pulley, considered it safe enough for the railway staff to return.

Meanwhile, Major P. Fitzgerald Norbury, the PO for the Shamiyya Division, accompanied by his youthful APO, Captain Mann, began a series of visits to the sheikhs of the Khaza'il, Bani Hasan and Shibl tribes, attempting to bribe them to abandon the al-Fatla, who were currently the most actively engaged insurgents. But this was to no avail and on 13 July the al-Fatla and their allies began to threaten Kufa.

The defenders of Kufa totalled 730 men, 486 of whom were Indian troops of the 108th Infantry plus their four British officers.[2] The only other fighting men were a motley force of 115 Arab and Persian levies commanded by six British officers and three British NCOs. There were also 102 Indians and fourteen British employed by the Civil Administration. However, Norbury had selected a strong defensive position of stone buildings on the edge of the town and adjacent to the river and ensured that this strongpoint was well stocked with supplies and ammunition. Moreover the gunboat HMS *Firefly* had just arrived at Abu Sukhair, a few miles south of Kufa, having steamed down from the Upper Euphrates, and could easily return to Kufa in a few hours.

Signs of hostility began to show themselves on 14 July when insurgents opened fire on a British launch carrying supplies which would have certainly been captured without the intervention of *Firefly*, after which the gunboat was ordered upriver to Kufa. Then, on 20 July, the British base in the town came under sporadic rifle fire.

By the following day the British outpost was completely encircled and the attacks grew fiercer. Soon a number of buildings near to the British defensive perimeter were set on fire and Norbury and Mann repeatedly led fire-fighting parties to try to extinguish the flames. On 22 July, in the course of another of these sorties, Captain Mann was shot and killed by the Arab attackers.[3] Wilson had lost yet another of his 'young men'. Meanwhile, insurgent raiding parties began to threaten Kifl and on 23 July its railway station was overrun by a section of the Bani Hasan tribe, and the railway staff, who had been ordered back to their posts on 12 July, were captured and taken prisoner to Najaf.

As the military situation in the Shamiyya Division deteriorated, on Thursday 22 July Major General Leslie, still at Diwaniyya, was summoned to Baghdad for a conference with the GOC-in-chief and the following day was flown up to Baghdad for the meeting with Haldane. Afterwards he paid a visit to his own 17th Division HQ and it was there, later that Friday morning, that he received a telegram from Colonel R. C. W. Lukin, commanding officer at Hilla, who had replaced the 'hysterical' General Wauchope a few days earlier. With Kifl overrun by rebel tribesmen and the Hilla–Kifl railway cut in a number of places, Colonel Lukin informed Leslie that he was under intense pressure from the local PO, Major Pulley, to send out a detachment towards Kifl, in order to 'show the flag' in the hope that this would deter the 'wavering' northern sections of the Bani Hasan from joining the insurgency.[4] The telegram requested authorisation to do so.

The only troops at Hilla available for this purpose were the 2nd Battalion of the Manchester Regiment (less one company), a field artillery battery, a field ambulance section, a company of Indian pioneers and two squadrons of Indian cavalry, in total around 800 men, all units from the 18th Division which had been sent to Hilla, on GHQ's order, to form a column there for the purpose of retaking Kifl and relieving Kufa – but only when a sufficiently strong force had been assembled.

Colonel Lukin's telegram informed Leslie that he intended to send a column made up of the units currently available down the road to Kifl to a point six miles south of Hilla called Imam Bakr, which had been reconnoitred and was reported as having a good supply of water for both animals and men.[5] The objective was to 'show the flag' as requested by the PO. Lukin asked Leslie to approve this move and to authorise a continuation of the advance towards Kifl if circumstances allowed.[6]

Leslie, who by now was fully aware of his commanding officer's strictures about sending out under-strength columns at the behest of POs, decided to pass the request to the GOC-in-chief himself, so he telephoned GHQ and, in the presence of his own two staff officers, he read out Colonel Lukin's telegram to Brigadier General Stewart, Haldane's general staff officer who had taken the call. A few minutes later, Stewart replied, giving GHQ's permission for the Manchester Regiment and other units to advance towards Kifl but, for the time being, to go no further than Imam Bakr, which was to be considered 'an outpost of Hilla'. The commander of the column was also ordered to avoid becoming engaged with superior hostile forces. Leslie then transmitted these instructions to Lukin at Hilla, sending a copy of his telegram by special dispatch rider to GHQ, and later that day he boarded an aircraft at Baghdad to fly back to Diwaniyya.

Precisely why General Haldane authorised the Manchester Column's movement to Imam Bakr is something of a mystery. It was completely inconsistent with his previously stated objections to making an 'unready push' and the manoeuvre had no clear objective. Certainly, there was no reason why GHQ should defer to the judgement of the PO who had been pressing for the column's dispatch. One possible explanation is that Haldane was expecting the arrival at Hilla of some of the units from the Rumaytha relief column he was planning to withdraw north from Diwaniyya and which could then be sent on immediately to reinforce the Manchesters at Imam Bakr. It was this more substantial force which would then advance further towards Kifl and Kufa.

However, when the Manchester Column was sent out on the afternoon of 23 July, neither Colonel Lukin at Hilla nor the officer commanding the column, Colonel Hardcastle, had any idea that reinforcements were en route to them and might be arriving shortly, a communications failure that was to have tragic results.

To better understand the course of events which was now about to unfold, let us first examine the terrain through which the column was to move. Between Hilla and Kifl the landscape was almost entirely flat and featureless except for the ruined Babylonian tower of Birs Nimrud – locally reputed to be the Tower of Babel – which would have been just visible, situated on a mound, about ten miles south-west of the column's point of departure. At that time of year the terrain itself was a mixture of grey-brown desert covered with scrubby 'camel thorn' bushes intersected by a number of half-empty canals which fed off the Hilla branch of the Euphrates. Where these irrigation canals watered the land, rice fields – some of them quite extensive – broke the monotonous vista. Two of these irrigation canals, the Amariyya and the Nahr Shah,

ran roughly north–south, to the east of the road and the 2'6" railway
line from Hilla, while two smaller canals, the Mashtadiyya and the
Rustumiyya lay broadly east–west. Imam Bakr – the position six miles
south of Hilla where Colonel Hardcastle had been ordered to halt, make
camp and water the cavalry and transport teams from local wells – was a
short distance north of the point where the road and railway line crossed
the Mashtadiyya canal. As to the 'road' to Kifl along which the column
would march – it was little more than an unmetalled track.

Let us try to picture the small British force on Friday 23 July 1920 as it
begins its advance into enemy territory under the baking Mesopotamian
sun. A few months earlier the newly planted rice fields and small plots
of winter wheat ready for harvesting would have been bright green and
dotted with spring flowers, but now all has turned to drab dusty yellow.
There is nothing to raise the men's spirits as they set off towards their
equally cheerless destination.

'B' Company of the Manchesters, under the command of Captain
G. M. Glover, are at the head of the column followed by 'A' Company.[7]
But after only a couple of miles these pale young men from Lancashire
in their solar topees and baggy shorts are already in a sorry condition,
sodden with a fine perspiration, like a downy mist, which seems to leak
out of every pore, and desperately thirsty; but the British Army believes
that troops should refrain from drinking water in the heat of the day
while marching, so 'water discipline' is being rigidly enforced.[8] Behind
them march a company of sepoys – strong, lean men of the 1st Battalion
the 32nd Sikh Pioneers, ready in an instant to drop their rifles and seize
their entrenching tools; normally a six-mile march would be nothing
to them but with the shade temperature touching 120°F, even these
tough, experienced soldiers are beginning to suffer. The six horse-drawn
18-pounder guns of the 39th Royal Field Artillery battery are in the
centre of the column together with 150 'Animal Transport' (AT) carts
each pulled by two mules, carrying ammunition and the impedimenta
required for constructing a camp. As their Indian drivers whip them
forward, the animals churn up the fine dust of the alluvial soil, choking

the men of 'D' Company of the Manchesters who are marching behind them. And in the rear, and on either flank, are two squadrons of the 35th Scinde Horse, the pennants of their lances fluttering in the scorching breeze of the shamal as they scan the horizon for enemy tribesmen; but, as often as not, in the shimmering heat, what first appears to be a horseman is just a mirage – or nothing more than a six-foot high clump of wild liquorice or a strangely twisted grey-leaved native poplar tree.

Forty-four-year-old Colonel R. N. Hardcastle, in command of the column, marches with the infantry, alternately on horseback or on foot, resting his mount. The son of a 'gentleman of independent means' of Wakefield, Yorkshire, Colonel Hardcastle joined the army with the rank of second lieutenant in December 1897.[9] By now he is a very experienced soldier. He fought in the Boer War of 1899–1901, serving with the Manchester Regiment's 1st Battalion, and was awarded the DSO for bravery in September 1901. In 1914 his unit formed part of the British Expeditionary Force in France and between 18 and 20 October it saw very heavy fighting at Richebourg-l'Avoué, where Hardcastle, by now a captain, had to assume temporary command of the battalion after its lieutenant colonel was sent to hospital. In April 1915 he was promoted to major and the following year his unit was sent to Iraq, where it took part in the futile campaign to relieve General Townshend's men besieged at Kut al-'Amara and during which Major Hardcastle was wounded. By July 1918 Hardcastle, now with the rank of brevet lieutenant colonel, was commanding the 1st Battalion of the Manchesters in General Allenby's successful campaign against the Turks in Palestine. It was with the same rank that Hardcastle was placed in command of the Manchester Regiment's 2nd Battalion in November 1919.

Many of the column's other officers are equally experienced and decorated. But brave and experienced as they may be, these officers are no less affected by the intense heat than their men and on arrival at Imam Bakr in the early evening all ranks are exhausted and some have already collapsed from dehydration and heatstroke.

At this point events begin to take an unfortunate turn. In spite of the enforcement of 'water discipline', the column has insufficient water

supplies for an operation in such extremes of temperature.[10] Colonel
Hardcastle has been assured that there will be plentiful water supplies
at Imam Bakr but when his cavalry patrols reach the nearby wells it is
discovered that the water is so brackish that even the animals refuse
to drink.[11] However, the column is within a short distance of the
Mashtadiyya canal so the men and animals trudge onwards to that
location. But once again they are disappointed – the Hilla branch of
the Euphrates, from which the matrix of irrigation channels is fed, is
very low this year and there is no water entering the Mashtadiyya canal.
So the weary and despondent British and Indian troops march back to
Imam Bakr.

However, a junior PO accompanying the column who is familiar
with this area, Lieutenant P. H. S. Tozer, is sent out scouting for alternative sources of water and soon returns informing Hardcastle that there
are adequate supplies in another canal, the Nahr Shah, further to the
south-east; there is also a good defensive position at which to make
camp eight miles south of Imam Bakr, where the railway and Hilla–Kifl
road cross another canal with water, the Rustumiyya. So Hardcastle now
sends a message back to Hilla informing Colonel Lukin that he intends
to continue his advance to the Rustumiyya, asking his senior officer to
approve the movement.[12]

On receiving this request, at 00.15 on 24 July, Colonel Lukin sends
a telegram to Major General Leslie at Divisional HQ Diwaniyya informing him of the column's plight and of his intention to allow the column
to advance further southwards towards Kifl, principally to obtain water
but also to continue to 'show the flag' in this unsettled area. Leslie is informed by Lukin that he has authorised the column to set off from Imam
Bakr 'in the morning'.[13]

At this point Leslie is still hours away from his HQ, being flown
back from his conference with Haldane in Baghdad. When he does
eventually receive Lukin's message at 10.40 a.m. on Saturday the 24th,
he is puzzled by the expression 'in the morning' – does Lukin mean he is
intending to order the advance to begin this morning (in which case he
would have already departed) or the following morning – on the 25th?

He therefore telegraphs back to Hilla asking for clarification, at the same time informing Lukin that substantial reinforcements will soon be on their way to him from the units which are expected to return to Hilla from the relief of Rumaytha.

Meanwhile, it has been confirmed that the Nahr Shah canal does indeed contain adequate water supplies and Hardcastle has sent part of the column there with the animals without further authorisation. The operation is successful but because of difficulties leading the horses and mules down the steep banks of the canal, they can only be watered in small batches.

Consequently the party does not return to the camp at Imam Bakr until 8.15 a.m. An hour later, Hardcastle has still not received a reply from Hilla to his telegram of 00.15 as to a further advance to the Rustumiyya canal, so because the temperature is already above 100°F, he decides to give the order to advance without waiting any longer. However, it is not until 4.00 that afternoon that Leslie receives a telegram from Lukin at Hilla informing him that the column has already set off 'that morning, early'. The stage is now set for a tragic denouement.

By midday on Saturday 24 July, Colonel Hardcastle and his men eventually reached the Rustumiyya canal, by which time 60 per cent of the Manchester Regiment troops were so exhausted and affected by the heat as to require, in the opinion of the column's medical officer, a complete rest for twenty-four hours. However, the column was now close to Kifl, whose single white minaret could clearly be seen from the canal bank, and, faced with the possibility of an attack by marauding bands of insurgents, Hardcastle decided that a protected camp would have to be constructed. So after only a few hours' rest the men were set to work preparing a defensible position while two troops of the Scinde Horse were posted as standing patrols on the road and light railway line leading to Kifl.

The spot chosen for the camp was a naturally strong one. It was sited to the east of the road from Hilla to Kifl in the angle between the road and the canal. On three sides there were earthen banks a few feet above the level ground which served on the southern side to retain the ten-foot-wide canal while on the east was an irrigation cut of lesser width. The protection of the third side, which bordered the road, consisted of a dry ditch with a low bank on both sides of it. Beyond this side to the west and making an acute angle with the road, outside the perimeter selected for the camp, ran a line of mounds, possibly the remains of an ancient canal bank of which all other traces had disappeared. Since the highest of these was around ten feet above level ground, and the highest point in the vicinity, these positions were also occupied.

Only on the fourth side facing north-west were there no naturally defensible features and so at 5.30 p.m. those men who were still fit enough were ordered to commence digging trenches along this line. However, a few minutes later an orderly from the cavalry troop stationed on the railway line galloped into the camp with news that a large party of Arabs were tearing up the rails and destroying the culverts. This was followed by the arrival of a wounded cavalryman and then, shortly afterwards, by the remainder of the cavalry with worrying news: at least 10,000 insurgents were said to be advancing on the camp and were only about two miles away. Although this estimate of enemy combatants was later revised down to about 3,000, the British and Indian troops were clearly heavily outnumbered.

A short time later both sides opened fire, although there was some delay in getting the British artillery into action because the British gunners, who were also the column's telephonists, were currently trying to get in touch with Hilla by attaching their instruments to the telegraph line.[14] By 7.50 p.m. the fighting became more intense and the Arabs were seen to be working round the flanks of the encampment, some of them closing to only 150 yards from the camp perimeter. Colonel Hardcastle was aware that he had been ordered to avoid an engagement with superior forces but he was now in a quandary: his orders indicated that the column should probably withdraw to a position of greater safety, nearer to Hilla; but with nightfall approaching he also knew that conducting such a movement in good order would be extremely hazardous. What he did not know, however, was that within the next twenty-four hours reinforcements from the Rumaytha relief force would be available at Hilla ready to be sent on the short distance to support Hardcastle's men. If the Manchester Column had dug in and taken advantage of their superior firepower they would probably have been able to hold their position until those reinforcements arrived.

In the event, Colonel Hardcastle's judgement seems to have failed him. Instead of taking a firm decision as commanding officer, he called all the officers to a council, including the two POs accompanying the column, Lieutenant Tozer and his superior, APO Captain W. E. Hunt. These two urged an immediate withdrawal, claiming that, seeing such a force of British troops pinned down in this manner, all the local Arabs would rise up and even Hilla itself might be overwhelmed and captured. The outcome of the conference was that a decision was taken to abandon the camp and retire northwards towards Imam Bakr and Hilla. 'B' Company of the Manchester Regiment was to act as the advance guard split into two files either side of the AT wagons and artillery. They would be followed by 'A' and 'D' companies; the Sikh Pioneers and the two squadrons of the Scinde Horse would make up the rearguard.

At 8.40 p.m., in a darkness unrelieved by any moonlight, the Manchester Column begins to move off in the direction of Hilla along what is little more than a dirt track. For the first half mile of progress the column holds together well. Morale has now improved somewhat. British and Indian soldiers have enjoyed at least a few hours of rest and they are relieved to be returning to the modest comforts of Hilla after the privations of the march. And for the time being they are able to fend off sporadic attacks by mounted insurgents who are reluctant to come into close combat with their better-armed opponents.

Then, suddenly, there is a commotion among the AT wagons. Something has panicked the mules and horses, which begin to charge off in different directions. In the pitch darkness, the men of 'A' and 'B' companies of the Manchesters have no idea what is happening until careering transport wagons carve through their ranks. In the chaos, the inexperienced young infantrymen who cannot get out of the way are trampled, injured and killed while the rest are split up into isolated groups of men left stranded and in many cases separated from their officers and NCOs.

From now on any sense of there being an organised military formation has disintegrated. Loose horses, led by a white pony, continue to career up and down the road on which some of the Manchesters are endeavouring to make an orderly retreat.[15] The combat degenerates into a scattering of individual fights between little groups of British and Indian troops and a swirling mass of Arab horsemen and foot soldiers. As they retreat, the gunners halt for a few minutes, firing their guns into the Arabs at almost point-blank range, and with drawn swords the sowars of the Scinde Horse make repeated charges into the enemy tribesmen to prevent them surrounding and capturing the guns and gunners. In the course of these charges, all six of the cavalry's British officers have their horses shot from under them; two of their officers are badly wounded and the senior Indian officer, Risaldar Muhammad Azim, who has shown the greatest coolness and bravery throughout the fighting, is shot in the stomach and dies shortly afterwards. And as the struggle to extricate the guns dies down, two-thirds of the cavalry are now fighting on foot.

In another of these close-quarter combats the twenty-six-year-old Captain George Henderson, commanding 'D' Company of the Manchesters, orders his men to fix bayonets and leads a charge into the nearest mass of insurgents.[16] For a while this body of rebels pulls back but within minutes they have recovered and threaten to surround Henderson's men. Once again he leads a charge at bayonet point towards the Arabs but this time he is badly wounded. Nevertheless, after this show of resistance, the insurgents pull back, turning their attention to the substantial amount of equipment, rifles and ammunition in the AT wagons which the Manchester Column has had to abandon. At this point Henderson manages to extricate his men and escape up the road to Hilla. After a few hundred yards the men of 'D' Company halt at a defensible position. It is only now that the severity of Henderson's wound becomes apparent. He asks a sergeant to lay him down on the canal embankment where they are sheltering. His last words, spoken to one of his NCOs are, 'I'm done now, don't let them beat you.'[17] Henderson was later awarded the Victoria Cross 'for most conspicuous bravery and self-sacrifice'.

Meanwhile, Captain Glover and 128 men of 'B' Company of the Manchesters, originally at the head of the column, have become completely disorientated and have veered away from the Hilla 'road' to the left, on a track leading to Birs Nimrud. At some point along this track they are surrounded and attacked by a swarm of mounted insurgents. None of these men would ever be seen again. Glover and his men were later classed as 'missing', but according to a survivor from another unit, they were 'slaughtered to a man', a conclusion broadly confirmed by a subsequent court of inquiry.[18]

By around 6.00 a.m. on 25 July, some men of 'D' Company of the Manchesters and other units had eventually managed to find their way back to Hilla. But what of the remainder of the column? The first Major General Leslie heard of the Manchester Column, since he had been informed of its advance to the Rustumiyya canal, was at 10.30 p.m. the previous day, when he received a telegram from Hilla saying that the column had been in action and was 'withdrawing to Hilla under fire'. As he later described it to his wife, 'I knew only too well what this meant with six guns and a lot of transport withdrawing at night and so few infantry to protect them.'[19]

If Colonel Hardcastle had decided that the Manchester Column remain in its fortified camp it would probably have been able to defend its position until reinforcements arrived, especially since the Rustumiyya canal provided an adequate water supply. Indeed, while the column was beginning its ill-fated retreat to Hilla, Leslie was commandeering as many railway trucks as possible with which to transport the Royal Irish Rifles from Diwaniyya to Hilla from where they could be rushed to support the Manchester Column. Then, at 10.30 in the morning of 25 July, Leslie received the news he had been dreading: the Manchester Column had 'suffered disaster'; only two guns had reached Hilla and the rest of the column was believed to be returning but 'its whereabouts was unknown.'

Leslie had little choice but to continue with the entrainment of the Royal Irish Rifles in the hope that these reinforcements might yet do something to obviate the 'disaster'. So at 11.30 a.m. the train carrying the Irish Rifles, accompanied by Leslie himself, left Diwaniyya station, arriving at Hilla at 6.00 that Sunday evening.

At Hilla Leslie found 'everybody in a state of the utmost gloom'. And to his amazement, instead of retiring to Baghdad as Leslie had ordered, General Wauchope was still in situ, having decided, on his own account, to stay on to 'advise' his replacement Colonel Lukin. Not surprisingly, the scant information being received as regards the fate of the Manchester Column had more or less unhinged him. 'General Wauchope is almost a gibbering lunatic,' Leslie later informed his wife and immediately packed the unfortunate brigadier off to Baghdad.[20]

Indeed, such was the 'gloom' at Hilla that Colonel Lukin – apparently aided and abetted by Wauchope – had begun to turn two large buildings in the town into a fortified position from which to make a 'last stand'. Leslie at once put a stop to this and, going round the outskirts of the town, he selected the best spots for piquets, had them manned and put what Arab levies were available into the most easily defended ones. The remnants of the Manchester Column were placed on the least exposed side of the town and a general night-time curfew imposed on the town's residents.

And as this most depressing Sunday wore on, an account – albeit a very provisional one – of what had happened to the Manchester Column began to emerge. Writing from Hilla in the evening, Leslie described how he intended to set up a court of inquiry into the affair but in the meantime his initial account of the debacle was as follows:

At 8.00 p.m. – i.e. after dark – the Officer Commanding took the fatal resolve to retire on Hilla. Some transport carts stampeded and panic set in. The Arabs closed right in on them and the withdrawal became very much disorganized. I understand that only one squadron of the 35th Horse and a portion of the Pioneers under their British officers continued to conduct an orderly rearguard action. I hear, but don't yet believe, that the men of the Manchester Regiment never recovered the panic. The gunners behaved well, firing their guns at ranges of 80 yards or so. The Arabs got amongst some of the teams stabbing the horses with daggers. They had one gun out of six hopelessly over-turned in a large water channel and it had to be abandoned after the breech block and sights were removed. They also had to abandon some ammunition wagons. The cavalry lost very few men, the Pioneers had 24 missing and 6 wounded out of 141, but the Manchesters account for only about a dozen known killed or rather less wounded, but have nearly 200 missing! They also lost practically all their Lewis guns. It looks bad for them, but one must await the enquiry ... A very bad show of which I do not see the end ...[21]

In fact, as we have seen, some of the Manchesters did put up a strong fight, but overall Leslie's initial views as to the extent of the defeat were largely borne out by the final tally of casualties. The disastrous night action south of Hilla cost the British 178 killed or missing, 150 captured and 60 wounded – a loss of 388 from a total of around 800 men.[22] In addition, considerable amounts of ammunition and an 18-pounder field gun were captured by the insurgents. The loss of the field gun was to have further unfortunate consequences.

It didn't take long before news of the rout of the Manchester Column, and in particular the capture of so many British infantry by the rebels, spread throughout the country. Indeed, it reached the coffee houses and mosques of Baghdad almost as soon as it reached the British GHQ, via the occupiers' own telegraph and telephone system. So panicked were the military authorities in Hilla that they failed to take the elementary precaution of transmitting news of the disaster in code.[23] Since there were many sympathisers and supporters of the insurgency working in the British telegraph and telephone offices, tales of the British mishap – some of them wildly exaggerated – were already sweeping through the narrow streets of the old city by the Sunday afternoon.

Gertrude Bell apparently did not hear about the incident until she arrived at work the following morning. In a letter to her father dated 26 July she begins with some private family matters after which she describes how, 'Things have moved a little since I wrote last week. We have relieved

Rumaytha and at the same time our own minds, for the couple of hundred people who had been shut up there for 3 weeks were a great anxiety.'

But then, after discussing the political situation in Baghdad, the letter continues,

> The above was written before breakfast. When I got to the office I found that the whole complexion on the Euphrates had changed. All the tribes are out ... Whether we can hold Hillah or not I don't know ... But it's a bad business. The military authorities seem to me all through to have been more inept than it's possible to conceive. The crowning scandal was the despatch two days ago of a battalion of the Manchesters from Hillah to Kifl. They were ordered to leave at 4 am and left at 10, with one day's rations and water bottles. You remember that hot and barren road? Think of marching down it in July at midday! 17 miles out of Hillah they were dropping about with heat stroke. The tribes attacked – not viciously, I gather, but it was more than enough for the Manchesters, for there wasn't a kick left in them. The tribes carried off the artillery and ammunition they were convoying down to Kifl ... I believe there are more troops coming from India but unless they send a new higher Command with them, I think they may easily send 20 divisions in vain.[24]

Inept or not, on receiving news of the Manchester Column disaster, any reluctance that General Haldane felt with regard to requests for reinforcements evaporated entirely. However, so far, both Haldane and Wilson had contrived to confuse the War Office as to exactly what reinforcements were required. On 18 July, the day after Churchill announced to the cabinet that, in response to General Haldane's request, an additional full division was being mobilised to reinforce the beleaguered garrison in Iraq, a bemused War Office received a telegram from GHQ Baghdad informing them that they should postpone the dispatch of any more units, except the one brigade which Haldane had originally requested on 8 July. Given that on 18 July the battle for Rumaytha was still in the balance, Haldane's apparent willingness to postpone substantial reinforcements – in his own words 'from motives of economy' – must have seemed inopportune to say the least; and to complicate matters further, the following day, Wilson (as usual ignoring instructions to refrain from commenting on purely military matters) offered *his* opinion that there was no need for any *additional* units – what was needed was to bring all the *existing* units up to strength. While that observation may have had some merit, its impact at the War Office merely added to the general state of confusion. Five days later, any clarity about reinforcements for Iraq further dissolved when Haldane telegrammed the War Office asking that '*divisional* staff and ancillary services' should be sent 'at the earliest opportunity' from which it was inferred that, after all, Haldane was still expecting 'the remainder of the division at an early date'.

Meanwhile, on 21 July, the cabinet had been informed of the military action on the road to Rumaytha. 'The fighting was severe', it was recorded, 'but our attack was successful and a counter-attack by the enemy after dark was beaten off.' After which the cabinet, seemingly reassured that matters in Iraq were not quite so bad as they had expected, moved on to grapple with the host of other problems with which they had been struggling with since the end of the war – the 'Bolshevik threat', Poland, the Irish rebellion, Egypt, strikes etc. etc. And in spite of Churchill's fierce admonition to the contrary, no decision was taken about the withdrawal of British troops from Persia to support the counter-insurgency campaign on the Euphrates. Then, on 26 July, in the aftermath of the Manchester Column disaster, Haldane requested not one, but two divisions of reinforcements.

Replying two days later, Churchill informed Haldane that 'the provision of any such [second] division is extremely problematical and that as regards Ordnance and Royal Army Service Corps personnel we are at the end of our resources',[25] to which he added, more in hope than expectation, that Haldane should consult with the civil commissioner, and decide 'a definite course of policy' but one which would bear in mind the limitation of Britain's military resources.

> Whilst your difficulties in the situation are fully appreciated, we think that it should be possible for the civil and military authorities on the spot to arrive at an agreed appreciation of the political situation on which you can estimate your military requirements and formulate a definite military policy, including the number of days supply reserves considered essential.[26]

What Churchill apparently did not understand was that 'an agreed appreciation' between Haldane and Wilson was simply not possible: these two men had fundamentally different objectives. As the insurgency gained momentum, Wilson's main preoccupation was, more than ever before, the safety of his 'young men', scattered all over the country, facing a very real threat of capture or murder. To counter this threat Wilson believed that the army should be deployed so as to provide as much protection to his young POs as possible. Haldane, on the other hand, was increasingly worried by his lack of any reserve with which to counter a really serious threat – for example a coordinated attack on Baghdad itself. Indeed, in the telegram of 28 July, Churchill had explicitly ordered him to hold 'some reserve in your own hand over and above the troops necessary to meet your visible military requirements at any one time', until more troops arrived from India. The only way Haldane could do this was by withdrawing outlying units and concentrating his forces nearer to the capital while at the same time refraining from responding to each and every request for support from the Civil Administration. A fortnight after receiving Churchill's response to his request for further reinforcements, Haldane therefore issued the following instructions to his officers.

Responsibility of Officers.

On two recent occasions on the advice or recommendation of a political officer, risks quite unwarrantable from a military point of view have been taken by officers in command of troops. Unfortunate results have followed ...

Having described these 'unfortunate results' as involving both losses of men and equipment but also contributing to the spread of the insurrection, the GOC-in-chief,

impresses on all officers in command of troops the responsibility which they incur should they act in a manner not strictly in accordance with sound military principles, more especially in a country such as

Mesopotamia where the climate is in itself our greatest enemy. Political like other information is often untrustworthy and must not be blindly accepted; and to keep his Division quiet at all costs is with the political officer a natural and paramount instinct.

General Haldane, however, was making it abundantly clear to *his* officers that no such 'instincts' should be countenanced.

> The G.O.C.-in-Chief does not wish in any way to cramp the initiative of officers but there is a wide distinction between initiative and rashness. The present situation is such that the least set-back must have harmful results and it is every officer's duty to reflect before acting and realise how great a responsibility he accepts if he is not certain in his own mind that he can fully justify his action.[27]

Haldane could not have made it clearer. Henceforth Wilson's 'young men' were going to be left to fend for themselves until victory over the rebels was in sight. After such an injunction no officer who cared for his military career was going to send troops to the aid of POs unless explicitly ordered to do so by the GOC-in-chief himself. To Wilson, the order was little more than a death sentence for some of those under his command and for whom he had the deepest respect and affection.

And among those to whom General Haldane's order was addressed there were some army officers who would have been equally unhappy with the wording of the order. It contained strong implications – indeed virtually accusations – that one or other senior officer had indeed, been taking 'risks quite unwarrantable from a military point' and behaving in a manner 'not strictly in accordance with sound military principles'. Major General Leslie, for one, would have bitterly resented these words because from the testy encounters with his commanding officer which he had already experienced, he had a strong impression that Haldane was in some way pointing the finger of blame at him for the setbacks of the past few days. For his part, Leslie had taken to referring dismissively to his commander-in-chief as 'the early-Victorian baronet'.

Meanwhile, official opinion fluctuated wildly as to the advisability of withdrawing from the Mosul vilayet in order to concentrate British forces in the vilayets of Baghdad and Basra and hopefully forestall any further catastrophes like the Manchester Column debacle. However, in a telegram of 24 July Sir Percy Cox, recently arrived in Britain to brief the cabinet, weighed in with his own views on the matter. 'I can only contemplate with the greatest dismay the suggestion that we should withdraw from Mosul,' he stated. Apart from the impact upon 'our prestige throughout Mesopotamia',

> I regard the maintenance of our position in Mesopotamia as a factor of enormous importance to our general interests in the Middle East and India. From an economic point of view I think it is common knowledge that the possibilities of Mesopotamia in oil, cotton and wheat make it a great country of promise ... Oil is of course, an uncertain quantity but the prospect is at any rate sufficient to attract to Mesopotamia the interest and capital of very large concerns.

And he continued by pointing out the key importance of holding on to Basra (control of which would be threatened by any withdrawal from more northern parts of Iraq).

> We have previously considered the control of the port of Basra at the head of the Persian Gulf to be most important for the strength of our position in those waters. It is especially so now a days in view of our large vested interested in Abadan and in the oil of Arabistan; but its value would be entirely vitiated were Baghdad in the hands of a hostile Power.[28]

27

'Further unfavourable developments'

Looking back on the twelve days which followed the destruction of the Manchester Column, General Haldane would later conclude that in no other period of his lengthy military career had there been an episode of quite such intense anxiety. His capture and imprisonment during the Boer War; his four-year service on the Western Front – for much of it in command of the Ypres salient under ever-present threat of being overrun by a German assault – these were as nothing compared to the mental strain which the general suffered in that last week of July and first week in August 1920 during which, on 6 August, the mujtahidin of Karbela' had made his task even more difficult by finally declaring the insurgency to be a jihad.[1]

What made matters worse was his sense of the unfairness of it all. Unlike the majority of his fellow senior officers with whom he had served throughout the war, at its end he had no family to return to (except his sister, Alice), no large estate to which he could retire and upon which he could lavish his attention, nor even any close friends with whom he could enjoy the social and recreational pursuits of his class: no, the army was his life, the army was his family – a family for which he had made great personal sacrifices over his many years of faithful service. And now, at a time in his life when he might have expected to be enjoying a comfortable and prestigious posting commensurate with his experience and seniority, instead, he had been handed this poisoned chalice – a thankless assignment in which success would win him few plaudits but failure could mean a shameful and inglorious end to the career to which he had selflessly devoted his whole life.

In his darkest moments, Haldane contemplated a range of miserable outcomes to his present situation. Sometimes his mind dwelt upon the possibility of a steadily increasing number of small-scale defeats in which garrisons up and down the country were wiped out, while in Britain, a furious and vindictive public opinion called for his dismissal and replacement by someone like General Allenby (a bully, whom he detested). In even blacker moods he contemplated the loss of Baghdad itself. Admittedly, he had been flippant about such an eventuality, that day back in June, when he dined with Miss Bell before leaving for Persia; but two months later, when the encirclement and capture of the city by a vast horde of Muslim fanatics – a city for which so much British blood had been spilt during the war – seemed a real possibility, the thought of such a catastrophe brought him to a state of near panic. His only respite from such dismal thoughts was, last thing at night, to take up his Bible and read 'the psalm for the evening of the day'.[2]

Not that he blamed Churchill for his present misfortune. Clearly, when he had offered Haldane the post of GOC-in-chief, Mesopotamia, the war minister himself could have had no idea about how events in Iraq were about to unfold. In fact the person upon whom Haldane most frequently vented his spleen in the days following the Manchester Column debacle was not his chief but his immediate subordinate, Major General Leslie. What on earth had possessed the man to allow his troops to go wandering about in the desert with insufficient water supplies and in the presence of overwhelming numbers of hostile tribesmen? Surely he had made it abundantly clear that the column should advance no further than the position at Imam Bakr, within easy reach of its base at Hilla? Had he not impressed this upon Leslie, when the request for authorisation to send out the column had been communicated to him via his staff officer, Stewart, on the morning of 23 July? At all events, there would have to be a committee of inquiry, but of one thing Haldane was absolutely certain – *he* would not be apportioned any blame for the disaster.

But for now, the commander-in-chief had more urgent matters to attend to. After the retreat from Rumaytha, the bulk of the troops belonging to its garrison and those of RUMCOL, which had rescued them, were still at Diwaniyya, forty-three miles south-east of Hilla, or strung out along the Hilla road, holding small outposts along the line of retreat. In total, this force amounted to two squadrons of cavalry, four batteries of Royal Field Artillery (less two sections), one battery of pack artillery and five Indian infantry battalions plus the elements of four other Indian battalions including some pioneers and sappers. In addition, there were 1,120 civilian railway personnel, 300 cart-loads of ammunition and supplies and 23,000 gallons of water. This brigade-size force under the command of General Coningham, together with the accoutrements, supplies and materiel of a much larger military formation, was now dangerously isolated in overwhelmingly hostile territory with the very real threat of encirclement and destruction.

Haldane decided that extricating Coningham's troops as rapidly as possible by withdrawing them north, to Hilla, was of the utmost importance. However, the road transport available at Diwaniyya for a march back to Hilla was quite insufficient to carry the six days' rations it was believed the retreating column would require. The railway would have to be used, but as each day passed, the rebels were becoming increasingly active and proficient in destroying the track. Haldane faced the very real possibility that 'the Arabs might tear up and damage the railway to such an extent that General Coningham's force might find itself marooned midway between Hilla and Diwaniyya, possibly at some waterless spot where the difficulty of further progress would, for much of it, be insuperable.'

In fact, an initial attempt to use the railway to move more troops back to Hilla had already failed. On 27 July a train en route from Diwaniyya to Hilla had been derailed and isolated at Guchan station, some twenty-eight miles north of Diwaniyya. And on the following day a relief construction train sent out to assist the earlier one had also been attacked by Arabs and failed to reach Guchan. Meanwhile, Haldane began to fret about the slowness of extricating the force at Diwaniyya, blaming this shortcoming, also, on Major General Leslie. Indeed, from that point on, Haldane began to communicate directly with Brigadier Coningham over the head of Leslie, which understandably resulted in a further exacerbation of the ill-feeling between the two men.

Meanwhile Coningham was assembling what must have been, at that time, one the most remarkable military formations in the history of the British Empire – a huge armoured column combining both railway and road transport which would eventually stretch for over a mile in length. Along the railway track, truckage was allotted to each unit and department, together with the railway personnel and some thirteen Armenian lady school teachers who happened to be at Diwaniyya. In the centre of the train a portion was set apart for a hospital for the sick and wounded and at the rear a few trucks and an engine were converted into an armoured train carrying two armoured cars and two machine guns. As night began to fall on the evening of 29 July everything was complete; the men were issued with six days' rations and as much water as could be carried. Then, at 6.30 the following morning, the huge column began to move off.

As this long, snake-like formation slowly trundled northwards, small parties of mounted insurgents followed it at a respectful distance, occasionally loosing off volleys of rifle fire into the column, but without much effect. At the same time, the crew of the train which had been cut off and isolated at Guchan began to re-lay the sleepers and railway tracks in their rear and slowly move south to meet Coningham's column moving north. By 8.00 a.m. on 2 August the two trains were only a mile apart and a couple of hours later they met, with great cheering and general jubilation. After their reunion the combined force proceeded north to Guchan, which was reached at 4.30 p.m. Here, the railway tanks were refilled and an advance force of railway construction workers, protected by the 45th Sikhs, was sent ahead to repair the railway line as they approached the important Jarbuiyya bridge over the Hilla branch of the Euphrates; but news of a large concentration of Arabs in the vicinity of the bridge compelled Coningham to stop the advance and consolidate his position at Guchan station.

On 4 August, the column, now consisting of six locomotives and 250 railway wagons, once again moved off towards Hilla. It was a crucial race against time. The Arabs knew that by destroying the track in front of the column and forcing delays to repair it, they were forcing Coningham's men to use up their food and water supplies. And because the insurgents were now removing the railway sleepers and hiding them in neighbouring villages, the British had to lift the track and sleepers in their rear and carry them forward to replace those which had been removed. All this involved exhausting work for the predominantly Indian labourers upon whom this gruelling task fell and who were toiling in the most excessive heat.

As the force again approached the Jarbuiyya bridge, Arab attackers once more harassed its advance, although a flight of five aircraft from Baghdad helped to drive them off. Still, the advancing column was making only very slow progress and the men were now placed on half-rations, but by 8 August the work of repairing began for the last time and at 9.20 a.m. contact was made by heliograph with a construction train moving south from Hilla to meet them. At 4.45 p.m. the railway line to Hilla was finally restored and by the afternoon of the following day, to Haldane's great relief, the weary British and Indian troops marched into the town.

In many ways the withdrawal from Diwaniyya was a remarkable success. The possibility of an encirclement and the inevitable military disaster had been avoided. But from the insurgents' point of view, the British withdrawal from Diwaniyya – the British *retreat*, as they saw it – was a great propaganda coup. Now a second British military base had been abandoned and another great swathe of occupied territory had been liberated. Even more evidence seemed to point to an imminent British withdrawal from Iraq as a whole, and as news of this second Arab 'victory' circulated among the tribes more and more waverers were drawn to the banners of Islam and independence. By now around 130,000 Arabs had joined the uprising.

While the British GHQ was greatly relieved at the news of the successful withdrawal from Diwaniyya, another piece of news was less welcome: a few days earlier the insurgents had captured the Hindiyya Barrage, the great dam sixteen miles north-west of Hilla at the point where the Euphrates divides into its two main branches, the Hilla and Hindiyya.

Meanwhile, on 14 July, as the military situation in the Kufa–Diwaniyya–Hilla 'triangle' was beginning to deteriorate, the river gunboat HMS *Firefly* arrived at Kufa. *Firefly* was one of sixteen gunboats of the Fly class which had seen active service during the war, mainly on the Tigris, where they had provided valuable flank guards for the British and Indian infantry as they advanced up the river in the campaigns of 1915 and 1917. The gunboats had originally been ordered from the shipbuilders Messrs Yarrow by the Admiralty in February 1915 for the operations in Iraq, but to camouflage their destination they were originally referred to as 'China gunboats'. After construction, they were dismantled and sent out in parts to be re-assembled on slips at the Anglo-Persian Oil Company's concession at Abadan.[3]

HMS *Firefly* had been one of the first to be sent out to Iraq and the first to see serious action. Like the other ships of her class she had a displacement of 98 tons and was 126 feet long and 20 feet in the beam. However, in order to cope with the extreme variations in depth on both the Mesopotamian rivers, her draught was only two feet. Her armament consisted of one 4-inch main gun, one 12-pounder, one 6-pounder, one 3-pounder, one 2-pounder anti-aircraft pom-pom and four Maxim machine guns. The crew consisted of two naval officers and twenty infantrymen.

Firefly and her sister ships were powered by a single oil-fired 175hp engine which gave her a top speed of around nine and half knots. But the gunboats had three main defects. Firstly, their extremely shallow draught made them almost impossible to navigate in strong winds and on the Euphrates they were unable to manoeuvre at all – they could only steam ahead or astern.[4] Secondly, for some reason, in early 1915 the Admiralty had been under the impression that the gunboats' prospective adversaries would only be lightly armed Arab irregulars, not disciplined regular troops with heavy weapons; consequently, the vessels were only provided with armour sufficient to withstand rifle fire. And thirdly, since they had only one boiler, were this to be put out of action for any reason – as indeed might be case if they met up with an enemy equipped with heavy arms – a hit on the boiler by shellfire would leave the ship absolutely helpless.[5]

The gunboat HMS *Firefly*, one of the 'Fly Class'
gunboats used against the insurgents

Indeed, *Firefly* herself had been smashed up by Turkish artillery in
December 1916 during the retreat of 'Townshend's Regatta' following the
battle of Ctesiphon, after which she was captured by the Turks and used to
considerable effect. However, she was later recaptured by the British during General Maude's successful counter-attack the following year. So, since
the British believed that the insurgents of 1920 had neither the heavy guns
nor the military knowledge and experience to use them, news of the arrival
of *Firefly* at Kufa in mid-July was received with great relief and jubilation.

Meanwhile, far to the south, another gunboat of the same class,
HMS *Greenfly*, under the command of Captain Alfred C. Hedger, had
already set off upriver from its base at Nasiriyya with orders to patrol
the Euphrates north and south of Samawa. On 5 July, accompanied
by another defence vessel, *F10*, she arrived at Samawa itself.[6] For the
next month *Greenfly* and her consort steamed up and down the muddy
river, returning fire upon any insurgents who had the temerity to
challenge them and dealing out death and destruction to the reed huts
of the rebels' riverine villages. However, on 10 August, while heading
downriver to help defend the town and railway station of Khidhr,
Greenfly ran aground at a point five miles above its destination.

Had the Hindiyya Barrage still been under British control, *Greenfly*
might have been floated off by closing the Hilla channel and directing
all the water of the Euphrates down the Hindiyya branch. But the
barrage was now in rebel hands. To make matters worse, this was the
season of the year when the Euphrates water level was steadily falling.
Over the next few days intense efforts were made to pull *Greenfly* off
the sandbank. On 15 August, a second gunboat, HMS *Greyfly*, and
another lightly armoured launch, *F11*, joined in the struggle to free
her, coming under intense enemy fire while doing so and suffering
numerous casualties from tribesmen firing from concealed positions
on the river bank. On the 20th another effort was made. On that day
Greyfly, accompanied by two launches, each carrying a company of
Indian troops, managed to reach the *Greenfly* and to their surprise
found that the insurgents had withdrawn. For the next two days
strenuous endeavours were made to free *Greenfly* from the sandbank,
but the mud had now closed further upon her with a vice-like grip. In
the end, the little flotilla of rescuers had to admit defeat and set off
back downriver to Nasiriyya.[7]

The British had no wish to see *Greenfly* captured by the insurgents
so there were now only two options open to them: abandon and scuttle
the gunship or leave the crew on board, well equipped with rations and
ammunition, ready for a second major rescue attempt as and when the
necessary ships and special equipment could be assembled. Eventually
the decision was taken to leave the crew on board; it was a decision
which was later to have particularly tragic consequences.

One of the reasons against scuttling *Greenfly* was that, only a few days
earlier, the British defenders of Kufa had themselves reluctantly decided
to send one of *Greenfly*'s sister ships to the bottom. And this was not an
action anyone wanted to repeat, if at all possible.

After arriving at Kufa in mid-July, HMS *Firefly* had tied up
alongside a small redoubt, part of the British defensive position on
the right bank of the river, and remained at that station guarding the
approaches to the town from the east. On the opposite side of the
river were dense palm groves and once the encirclement and siege of

the town commenced, the gunboat began to receive sporadic rifle fire from groups of insurgents occupying them. Returning fire with its much heavier weapons, *Firefly* soon discouraged these sharp-shooters and for a time fighting at this point subsided.

Then, on the morning of 17 August, the gunboat was suddenly subjected to heavy shellfire from the other side of the river and in a few minutes, during which a British soldier on board was killed and another badly wounded, the ship was set ablaze. After a further battering of shells, *Firefly*'s commander, Lieutenant D. H. Stanley, was fatally wounded and the remainder of the crew had to be taken off.

To Kufa's garrison, the attack came as a terrible surprise. How had the despised 'Budoos' managed to field such heavy weapons against them? For many of the defenders it could only mean they were once again at war with the Turks. What they didn't know was that the shells which were crippling the *Firefly* were fired by the 18-pounder British gun, captured by the rebels during the defeat of the Manchester Column. Haldane and his staff were well aware that this powerful field gun had been lost on the Kifl road; but they were fairly sanguine about it because, a few minutes before its capture, one of the British gunners had managed to remove the breechblock. What the British did not appreciate was that the small number of experienced former Ottoman army officers and NCOs fighting in the insurgent ranks had managed to forge a replacement for the missing part and bring the gun back into service.

As the fire on board the *Firefly* raged from stem to stern, the British and Indian defenders, cooped up within the perimeter of their strongpoint along the right bank of the Kufa channel, realised that the ship's magazine would soon explode, seriously damaging the redoubt and neighbouring positions along the river bank and possibly devastating their occupants. Since they had no wish to abandon those positions the decision was taken, very reluctantly, to scuttle *Firefly*. So several Lewis guns were brought up and the gunboat's plates were swiftly perforated by heavy fire. Within minutes the little gunship tilted to one side and then settled down on the silty bottom of the Hindiyya channel, where she would remain for the duration of the campaign.

While General Haldane's attention was focused primarily on the precarious situation of the troops retiring from Diwaniyya to Hilla, he remained anxious about the fate of the capital. The wholly inadequate size of its garrison and the increasingly truculent attitude of the local Muslim population meant that for a time he was compelled to resort to rather crude ruses – such as marching the same units backwards and forwards across the city – to try to give the impression that the garrison was considerably larger than it actually was. Haldane also began the construction of a number of defensive earthworks around the city's perimeter, which were later to be replaced by high, brick-built blockhouses.

Meanwhile, further bad news arrived. The insurrection was no longer confined to the central and southern Euphrates but had spread north-west, where the 'Azza and other smaller tribes on the Diyala river had joined the revolt.

For some time the Euphrates rebels had been sending out emissaries all over Iraq to try to win the support of the other tribes. In late July a sayyid named Sa'id Sara al-'Azawi reached the 'Azza, whose tribesmen inhabited the lands along the Khalis canal, north-east of the orange-growing town of Ba'quba. Ba'quba itself was the principal town of the Diyala Division, situated on the left bank of the river of the same name, thirty-four miles north-east of the capital. The news that Sayyid Sa'id brought was that the uprising which had begun in the mid-Euphrates was spreading north and south while everywhere the British were retreating from their main strongpoints. He urged the 'Azza to join the uprising.[8]

The paramount sheikh of the 'Azza was the twenty-five-year-old Sheikh Habib al-Khayizran and although he listened respectfully to the sayyid's exhortations, for the time being he held back from committing himself and his tribe to what would clearly be an extremely dangerous venture. However, a few days later, some travellers on the main road to Ba'quba were attacked and pillaged in what was probably a simple act of banditry; but this was not how the local PO, Major Hiles, saw it. Fearing an imminent outbreak of the kind which had occurred on the Euphrates, he immediately called up police and military from Baghdad. On their arrival, Hiles sent out orders to the sheikhs of all the tribes in

the Ba'quba Division, including Sheikh Habib, to assemble in the centre
of Ba'quba town on the pretext that he wished to obtain further information about the robbery. Once they had all arrived, Hiles had them all
arrested. The assembled sheikhs were then lectured on the mandate and
the requirement that they must on no account have anything to do with
the insurgents or try to get in contact with them. Some days later the
sheikhs were released – all but Sheikh Habib – who for some reason had
attracted the attention of Major Hiles.

Years later, Sheikh Habib gave the following testimony of the attempt
by Major Hiles to win him over to the pro-British camp.

> After some days, Major Hiles summoned me and said, 'You're an intelligent
> man; you know very well the military forces which are at the disposal of
> the British Government and the power with which it can ruthlessly crush
> its enemies. Those Iraqis who have rebelled against it including the leaders
> of the tribes will, in the end, be exterminated. However I like you and I'm
> concerned about you; I don't want you to fall into a trap; I'm seeking a
> happy outcome for you. If you follow my advice, without doubt you will
> be viewed by Great Britain as one of the great men of Iraq. Moreover the
> government has ordered me to give you 40,000 rupees for you to spend as
> you wish and is ready to double that when you want it.'[9]

To which Sheikh Habib replied with the following forthright reply:
'Truly, I am in need of such a sum of money; but I am not going to sell
my honour for it.'[10]

For the time being, there the matter rested and, fortunately for Sheikh
Habib, after a few days Major Hiles fell ill and returned to Baghdad for
treatment, after which he was replaced by a Captain Lloyd, political officer
for Daltawa, a town ten miles west of Ba'quba. The sheikh now told Lloyd
that he too was ill and needed to visit Baghdad to see his own physician.
Lloyd eventually agreed to his request and Sheikh Habib set off for the
capital. However, on his arrival he went straight to the 'People's School'
where the Haras al-Istiqlal had one of its main political bases. There, 'Ali
Bazirgan, the school's director, confirmed the information about the
insurgency on the Euphrates and gave him further news of the most recent

defeats and withdrawals suffered by the British. Bazirgan also told the sheikh that Taqi al-Shirazi, the Grand Mujtahid, had issued a statement urging the unity of all Muslims and that the leadership of Haras al-Istiqlal considered the Diyala region critical for the uprising, since if the tribes there joined the insurgency, it would cut the road and rail link to Persia along which the British were trying to get reinforcements.

'In due course, I set off back to Daltawa', Sheikh Habib later recalled.

> There, I made contact with a number of tribal leaders, the foremost of whom were Sheikh Hamid al-Hasan of the Bani Tamim tribe and Sheikh Mukhbir bin Murhaj bin Karim, of the Karkhiya. I related to them what I had heard from the leadership in Baghdad and I asked them to come out in support of the uprising on the Euphrates and its leaders. I also asked each of them to swear an oath on the Qur'an that they would keep their promises and commitment to building a Muslim Arab Government.[11]

On 9 August, the Karkhiya kept their word: they began the revolt on the Diyala by cutting the railway line from Baghdad to Quraitu near the town of Ba'quba and thereby severing all rail communications with Persia.[12] The following morning, the first reinforcements from India, the 2nd Battalion of the 7th Rajputs, arrived in the capital. So later that day, Haldane gave orders for a mixed column under the command of Brigadier General H. G. Young, commander of the 7th Cavalry Brigade, to 'nip in the bud' – as Haldane later described it – the unwelcome and hitherto unexpected extension of the uprising to the Diyala. However, Haldane was still anxious about the safety and security of Baghdad and was reluctant to send troops away from the capital at a time when events seemed to presage a growing threat to the city. Indeed, had it not been for the timely arrival of the 7th Rajputs, he would probably have felt obliged to ignore the problems on the Diyala altogether until he had a much stronger force with which to deal with them.

Brigadier General Young's punishment column consisted of the 1st Battalion of the Rifle Brigade, the 1st Battalion of the 94th (Russell's) Infantry, around one hundred troopers of the 1st King's Dragoon Guards and a similar number of the 7th Dragoon Guards, one section of the 16th Machine Gun Squadron, one section of Royal Horse Artillery and one section of the 50th Pack artillery; there was also a small army medical unit attached to the column. By the evening of 11 August the column had reached Ba'quba after some problems of rail transport had been overcome and was preparing to set out on its mission to 'punish' the rebel villages some eighteen miles distant from Ba'quba railway station. However, later that night, Haldane, still fretting about security in the capital, decided that he needed the Rifle Brigade back in Baghdad. He therefore ordered Brigadier Young to keep the riflemen at Ba'quba and entrain them for Baghdad at 6.00 p.m. on the 12th, apparently the first available opportunity. This meant that as Young's column set off to attack the enemy villages in the early hours of 12 August the only infantry in his column were the five hundred or so Indian troops of the 94th.

It was still dark when the march began and it was not long before the column's Arab guide began to propose repeated changes of direction, suggesting to Brigadier Young that either the man had no real knowledge of the area or he was untrustworthy and could be leading them into an ambush. Sure enough, just an hour before dawn, with the column now strung out over a considerable distance and the head of the column about four miles from its destination, the Indian infantry, who were marching in the rear, were suddenly attacked by a party of mounted Arabs, throwing the sepoys into complete confusion. What followed was almost a repeat of the Manchester Column disaster, as the panic spread to the drivers of the pack artillery and their mules stampeded through the horse artillery and ambulance unit, resulting in many other animals following suit with their vehicles.

Fortunately, the Arab force attacking the rear of the column was only a small one and although the Indian infantry remained in a state of panic for some time, the return of the British cavalry at 5.00 a.m., having burned one of the villages, re-established some degree of order. But as further parties of Arabs now began to harass them, Brigadier Young decided to retreat to Ba'quba, which was reached at around noon.

Soon afterwards the local PO reported that, according to the information reaching him, a heavy attack on Ba'quba itself was imminent and he urged Young to defend the town and protect the resident British and Indian civilians. But when Young passed the request to Haldane he was ordered to immediately evacuate the town and return to Baghdad. By 7 p.m. that evening all the troops and civilians at Ba'quba had abandoned the town which was immediately occupied by tribesmen of the 'Azza who set up their own local government.[13]

Shortly after this small Arab success, an incident occurred which underlines a weakness which was to dog the insurgent movement throughout the remaining months of the uprising. In spite of the Grand Mujtahid's urging that the Arabs should all support the independence movement, keep united and avoid the kind of petty intertribal feuds which had characterised tribal society before the war, there were some who couldn't resist taking advantage of the growing chaos to settle old scores rather than fight the British. A few days after the 'Azza had entered Ba'quba, Sheikh Habib learned that raiding parties from the 'Ubayd tribe, traditional enemies of the 'Azza, were attacking their grazing lands around Dali Abbas, making off with their animals and killing any man who got in their way.[14] So Sheikh Habib was forced to lead his men back to Dali Abbas and, for the time being, withdraw from the fight against the British.

However, this did not provide much consolation for the British. Their abandonment of Ba'quba left only a small party of infantry with ten days' rations to guard the bridge over the Diyala. In effect this meant that the whole of the area east of the Diyala and as far north as the Persian border now fell under the control of the rebels. It also left the town of Shahraban, twenty-seven miles north-east of Ba'quba, with its small British-led garrison of levies, completely isolated from government-controlled territory and in so doing it would sign the death warrant of the town's five resident Englishmen.

With the arrival of the first reinforcements from India on 10 August, Wilson felt the capital was a little more secure and he was now emboldened to crush the dissent which was swelling with every report (some accurate, some not so) of British defeats on the Euphrates. The following day he finally gave orders for the arrest of four of the leading members of

Haras al-Istiqlal – Yusuf Suwaydi, Ja'far Abu al-Timman, 'Ali al-Bazirgan and Sheikh Ahmad Daud. However, the attempt to seize the Baghdad nationalist leaders was bungled. Perhaps because news of the impending arrests leaked out, large crowds gathered in front of the leaders' houses and, in the violent confrontation which followed, three policemen were wounded and six Baghdadis were killed and twelve wounded.[15] In the commotion three of the Istiqlal leaders – Suwaydi, Abu al-Timman and Bazirgan – managed to escape with only Sheikh Daud being captured. Later, the fugitive leaders managed to get out of Baghdad and make their way to the liberated cities of Najaf and Karbela'. Meanwhile Muhammad al-Sadr in Kadhimayn also fled the city and went north to join the insurgents operating around Ba'quba.[16]

Steps were now taken to put an end to the seditious mauluds. On 12 August a proclamation was issued to the people of Baghdad by Brigadier General Sanders, GOC Baghdad, accusing the organisers of the mauluds of 'abusing' their freedom of worship, forbidding any further such mauluds and establishing a military court to try all 'offences against public order'.

Draconian punishments duly followed. Some of those who had played an important part in the mauluds were rounded up and sent to imprisonment on Henjam. Six Baghdadis who had allegedly fired upon the police during the bungled attempt to arrest the leaders of Istiqlal were tried by the military court and hanged. Another four men who were arrested for 'wounding a sentry in Baghdad and taking his rifle' were also hanged.[17] The following month, executions continued. Paid informants denounced those suspected of 'sedition'. For example, 'Abd al-Majid Kana, a member of Istiqlal, was accused of leading a gang whose intention was to assassinate pro-British notables and was hanged on 23 September.[18]

Nevertheless, Wilson now sent an exceptionally dismal and pessimistic telegram to the India Office, copying it to the British authorities at Simla, Tehran, Istanbul, Cairo and Jerusalem. It was as though he was seriously contemplating a major British defeat and wanted to make it clear to as many of his colleagues as possible just how overwhelmingly hostile was the general situation he was facing and, by implication, how unfair it would be to lay any future criticism at *his* doorstep.

There were now, he informed the India Office, 'further unfavourable developments'. The insurgency had spread north. Public buildings in the town of Ba'quba had been sacked by 'riff-raff of the town' assisted by local tribesmen; Shahraban and Qilil Esbat had also been sacked and a PO had been either killed or captured; at Khanaqin near the Persian border, government offices had been burned and a PO and his wife forced to flee; and British detachments at Ramadi and Falluja were now cut off from Baghdad by the rebels. Furthermore, Wilson was now definitely of the opinion that there would have to be a complete withdrawal from Mosul, to which he added that any remaining British women and children in the country should be speedily evacuated.[19] Many of the problems Wilson attributed to 'the perception of our military weakness' since – as he put it in an earlier telegram – 'to kick a man when he is down is the most popular pastime in the East sanctioned by centuries of precept and practice'.[20]

Two days later, Wilson dispatched an additional and unusually brief telegram: it ended with the words 'All civil officers at Shahraban were murdered.' In fact only two of those killed belonged to the Civil Administration but the circumstances in which five British officers and NCOs were killed would further exacerbate the increasingly antagonistic relations between Wilson and Haldane.

The small British colony in Shahraban consisted of the APO and officer in command, Captain W. T. Wrigley, late of the 5th Wiltshires, the commander of the levies, Captain J. T. Bradfield of the 4th Somerset Light Infantry, and two British levy instructors, Sergeant Major Newton and Sergeant Instructor Nesbitt. Bradfield, Newton and Nesbitt had under their charge fifty Arab and Kurdish levies. Also resident in the town was Captain E. L. Buchanan of the Irrigation Department, formerly an officer in the RAF. What neither Wilson nor Haldane knew was that Captain Buchanan was accompanied by his wife, who had ignored the general instructions that all women and children should withdraw to Baghdad pending their removal to either Persia or India.

The small British contingent first began to note a change in the political atmosphere at Shahraban on 8 August, when Mrs Buchanan tried to send her sick Armenian maid to Baghdad by train but found that the line had been cut. At the same time the British officers began to receive various reports of small, hostile incidents, such as the immobilisation of Captain Wrigley's Ford motor car by its former Arab driver and an attack on one of the levies, who had his rifle and ammunition taken from him.[21]

By the evening of the 11th the situation had deteriorated to such an extent that Captain Wrigley advised Mr and Mrs Buchanan to leave their house and sleep in the qishla, the old Turkish fort. The night passed uneventfully and the Buchanans returned to their home at 4.30 a.m. the following day, but it soon became clear that all was not well in the town: the streets around their house were unusually quiet and the nearby coffee shop was deserted all day, even at six in the evening when it was usually full of customers. That night they returned to sleep at the qishla. Then, at 10.30 in the morning of 13 August, an Indian civilian who had been supervising the irrigation works arrived at the Buchanans' house, telling them that the staff there, including his own brother, had been attacked by tribesmen during the night. Half an hour later Wrigley arrived at the Buchanans' house and instructed them to get their servants to collect as much in the way of supplies as possible and take them to his own billet. At 12.30 p.m. Wrigley, who had meanwhile been organising the defences of the qishla, returned to the billet with Captain Bradfield, who straightaway wrote out a message to the PO at Daltawa, some twenty-five miles away on the other side of the Diyala, asking for assistance. The message was entrusted to an Arab in British service but was never delivered.

Meanwhile, the small British contingent at Shahraban still had no idea that they had been abandoned by the GHQ in Baghdad and left to fend for themselves since the last contingents of Brigadier Young's column had withdrawn across the Diyala the previous night.

At around 1.00 p.m. parties of mounted Arabs began arriving in the town and the British hurried into the qishla. In addition to the five

British officers and NCOs and Mrs Buchanan the tiny garrison now included a Mr Baines, manager of the government-run grass farm outside
the town (who was previously unknown to Mrs Buchanan), two of Mrs
Buchanan's servants, a small number of Bengali civilians employed by
the Civil Administration, and the fifty Arab and Kurdish levies. The two
gates of the qishla were now shut and bolted although, while the front
gate was of iron bars, the rear gate was only of wood with a single wooden
bolt. Against it, Captain Wrigley's disabled car had been pushed close-
up for extra security.

Almost immediately around 800 rebels surrounded the barracks and
began an intense fusillade against the defenders. The same could not be
said for the levies, who fired away wildly, without taking aim and heed-
less of their limited supplies of ammunition. Each levy was equipped
with only 200 rounds and while there was a reserve supply of 4,000
rounds, this still only worked out at 280 per levy. Moreover, it wasn't
long before they began to desert in ones and twos and it became clear to
the British – according to the record of Mrs Buchanan – that 'the Levies
... were quite out of hand and would not obey their orders.'[22]

Then, at around 3.00 p.m., a British aircraft was sighted. The delighted
British officers laid out bed sheets on the flat roof of the qishla as distress
signals and as the aircraft flew over them at around 500 feet all the men
on the roof waved and gesticulated, trying to indicate their plight. The
aircraft then flew away and, in the opinion of Mrs Buchanan, 'whoever
were in the plane must have seen in what plight we were, how few were
the garrison and how many the tribesmen.' For a time their hopes were
raised as they imagined the aircraft returning 'bringing Lewis guns and
ammunition'. But the aircraft did not reappear.

After an interval during which the attack subsided, at about 3.45 p.m.
the firing was renewed heavily from all quarters. Wrigley and Bradfield
now proposed a plan whereby, if help had not arrived by 3.00 a.m. the
following day, they would fight their way out on horseback with the
remaining levies and attempt to reach Daltawa. In the meantime they
decided to make an attempt to parley with the rebels. Wrigley believed
he recognised a local notable among the attackers and, calling out to him

by name, he and Captain Bradfield indicated that they wished to discuss terms. For a brief space there was a pause in the fighting as the two sides prepared to meet. Unfortunately some of the remaining levies of Kurdish origin, who failed to understand the situation, suddenly opened fire upon the insurgents who, suspecting treachery, renewed the attack.[23]

By 6.15 p.m. the rebels had begun to scale the walls and some of them broke through the weakened rear wooden gate. It was all over in the next few minutes. Sergeant Nisbett was shot at the gate. Sergeant Major Newton died on the roof. Bradfield and Wrigley lost their rifles in hand-to-hand fighting and retreated into the Buchanans' room, where her husband had armed them both with revolvers, a heavy colt for himself, but with only five rounds of ammunition, and a small Browning for his wife.

Bradfield then turned to Buchanan and said, 'I must try to stop this.' He burst out of the room, shouting in Arabic and was immediately shot dead. A few minutes later Wrigley also left the room and was also killed.

A moment later a crowd of Arabs crashed into the Buchanans' room. According to Mrs Buchanan they were 'short-built men, dirty and repulsive looking. Their *'abas* were tucked in at the belt to keep them out of the way. They were armed with curved knives, daggers and rifles ... the whites of their eyes gleamed horribly.'[24] One of the Arabs seized Mrs Buchanan and her husband fired his revolver at her attacker. Then he himself was shot dead.

Mrs Buchanan was slightly wounded in the fracas, captured, but otherwise left unharmed – in spite of whatever despicable intentions she had inferred from the 'horrible gleaming eyes' of her attackers. She was taken to the house of a local sheikh, who offered her his protection as his 'guest', and she was imprisoned in conditions of relative comfort until her eventual release. As it happens, Mr Baines of the government grass farm was severely wounded during the fighting but survived in captivity until his own release. As far as can be ascertained, none of the non-European members of the garrison were harmed.

When the circumstances surrounding the events at Shahraban were made clear to Wilson he became furious. Haldane would later claim that he had no idea that there were British personnel at Shahraban, an argument easily disposed of by Wilson:

> From Sir Aylmer's account it is equally clear that he was not prepared to send troops from Baghdad to their rescue. Why he should say that he was unaware of the existence of these officers at Shahraban is inexplicable; not only had their names appeared regularly in every printed list of Political, Levy and Irrigation Officers furnished to General Head-quarters, but the decision to retain Levies at Ba'quba, Shahraban, Qizil Robat and Khanaqin under British officers had been reached a few months before after full discussion with the General Staff.[25]

Many of Haldane's subordinates agreed with Wilson, including General Leslie who, a month later, wrote to the civil commissioner expressing his own shock at only recently hearing of the 'abandonment to their fate' of the officials at Shahraban.[26] However, while the loss of the British officers at Shahraban was naturally to be regretted, in Haldane's eyes – and in the eyes of the majority of the army and Civil Administration – a far more serious loss of life had taken place only a few days earlier.

In June, Colonel Leachman had informed Wilson that he was unhappy with the behaviour of the Zauba' tribe whose traditional lands lay between Falluja and Baghdad, and was planning to 'pay a visit' to its chief, Sheikh Dhari ibn Fadara. Actually, Dhari was not known for espousing pro-independence views or having any particular sympathy for the Istiqlal movement in neighbouring Baghdad, although presumably he was aware of its existence. Moreover, as a Sunni, he had little or no relations with the rebellious Shi'i cities, Najaf and Karbela'.

In reality Sheikh Dhari's principal interest was the welfare of himself and his immediate family, regardless of the current holders of power in the country. For example, the Austro-Hungarian explorer and Arabist Alois Musil, who travelled by way of the Falluja–Baghdad road in 1915, relates the following tale of the crafty Sheikh Dhari:

> Our guide explained to us in what manner the Government recruited volunteers. The Wali summoned all the chiefs to Baghdad and when they

were there, he asked them to accept military service voluntarily. Every recruit was to get ten to twelve gold Turkish pounds. Each chief then named offhand the number of volunteers in his clan and received at once the amount due to him. Thus, for instance, Dhari, chief of the Zauba', announced 170 men and was paid, accordingly, two thousand gold pounds. But no one in his whole clan would hear of going to war. Finally, he made ten poor fellows who were indebted to him join the colours as a means of paying him, but only after threatening to take all they had if they persisted in their refusal. And in this way he sent to war ten men instead of 170, keeping, of course, the two thousand pounds all for himself.[27]

By late July 1920 Leachman, like all the POs of the Civil Administration (including Wilson himself), was under great physical and psychological pressure. The rebellion seemed to be gaining ground every day and neither he nor they could understand the failure of the army to protect them or crush the rebels. Leachman wrote to his parents with customary directness, saying, 'I should like to see another two divisions sent out here and a regular slaughter of the Arabs in the disaffected areas. It is the only way.'[28] On 6 August he recorded how 'we are still in the throes of internal strife. The whole of Mespot seem to be fighting.' In the same letter he reported how he was shortly to be sent to Palestine to assist in carrying out a railway survey, apparently on Wilson's recommendation. His response was typical of the man: 'It is madness to leave my district at such a time ... but Wilson is mad ... I have very nearly had as much of this as I can stand.'[29]

These were the last words that Colonel Leachman committed to paper. It seems that even this tough, brutal and sardonic soldier was beginning to crack under the strain. His behaviour thereafter has never been satisfactorily explained. On 11 August the police chief of Leachman's Dulaym Division informed him that 'the country was up in arms'.[30] Later that day Leachman motored to Baghdad from his base at Ramadi to discuss the Palestine assignment with Wilson and to try to find his personal servant and driver, Hassan, who had absconded on a drinking bout. After speaking with Wilson, he informed him that he was returning via Falluja, where he would arrive about 3.00 p.m. and at which time he would telegraph Wilson. However, he also mentioned in passing that he had sent a message to Sheikh Dhari, stating that Dhari should meet him at the Arab police post at Khan Nuqta, midway between Baghdad and Falluja, on his return journey from Baghdad. He also asked Wilson for the authority to waive the repayment by Sheikh Dhari of certain advances made to him for the purpose of seed grain the previous year.[31]

It was a strange, inconsequential matter to attract Leachman's attention at a time when he had only recently been informed that most of the district for which he was responsible was now 'up in arms'. Nevertheless, by the following morning, 12 August, having failed to locate the whereabouts of Hassan, Leachman set off with another driver and reached Khan Nuqta at around 11.00 a.m.

Dhari, his two sons and a strong contingent of his tribal horsemen were waiting to meet Leachman and the two men were beginning a conversation when some Arab merchants arrived on the scene and claimed that their caravan had been attacked and looted. Leachman immediately ordered twelve of the thirteen Arab police at Khan Nuqta to try to intercept the robbers. Then, a short while after the police had departed, the older of Dhari's two sons, by name Khamis, shot and killed Leachman, apparently on his father's orders.[32]

Hard as nails, brave, brutal and a racist, in the casual, conventional racism of the day, Leachman was a man who – in the words of an obituary in *The Field* magazine – 'could shoot a tribesman dead for misdeeds in front of the tribe, and not a hand would be raised against him'.[33] But whatever angry words passed between Leachman and Sheikh Dhari, whatever insults were laid upon the haughty tribal chief, whatever blows may have been inflicted on him by Leachman's cut-down polo stick – in Sheikh Dhari and his clan, the redoubtable Brevet Lieutenant Colonel Gerard Leachman had finally met his match.[34]

Sayyid Muhsin Abu Tabikh, Mutasarrif (Governor)
of the liberated areas, photograph taken *c.*1924

The Structures of Insurgent Power

The majority of British officialdom both inside and outside Iraq never could appreciate the extent to which their Arab adversaries were an organised force: that the insurrection had a formal leadership, structures of control, a press and a political programme, albeit one which was largely grounded in religious belief. On the contrary, to the vast majority of British politicians, military and officers of the Civil Administration the rebellion was mere lawlessness. While they themselves were convinced that they were fighting for 'the very existence of civilisation in the Middle East', a victory for the rebels would mean 'only anarchy'.[1] Indeed, whenever the British witnessed some indication of purposeful organisation on the part of the Arabs or behaviour they could recognise as 'civilised', they immediately attributed it to some sinister outside involvement of European (or sometimes US) origin.

For example, in the aftermath of the destruction of the Manchester Column there was widespread public concern for the fate of the 150 men who had been captured by the insurgents and imprisoned at Najaf. Lurid stories about their treatment began to circulate, causing considerable anxiety about their safety. However, on 9 August Churchill reported to Parliament that General Haldane has received assurances from the rebel leaders that they had 'issued communiqués stating that the Arabs look on prisoners as a sacred trust' and that they were 'ordering the subordinate sheikhs to treat them well'.[2]

Nevertheless, a senior official of the India Office, drawing attention to this report mentioning the issuing of 'communiqués' by the rebels and their desire for the good treatment of their prisoners, opined that if this were true, it would indicate that the leadership of the insurgency must be European, or at least a 'European-trained Oriental'. To support this contention the official in question pointed out that 'both the publication of communiqués and the sentiment expressed [about prisoners] are absolutely un-Arab'.[3]

In reality, by mid-July 1920 the insurgents had rapidly put together a formidable state apparatus to replace that of the occupying power and had little difficulty in mobilising the individuals required to man the structures of governance in the territories from which the British were being steadily expelled. Indeed, given the serious problems of logistics, communications, mobilisation and finance which, from the outset, they had to face, they had little choice.

In Najaf, the transition to insurgent rule had taken place relatively smoothly. The British decided to withdraw their garrison on 9 July as part of Haldane's plan to concentrate his forces in a few highly defensible centres and a few days later, the local police surrendered their weapons and the British flag on the serai was pulled down.[4] On the same day, Agha Hamid Khan, the pro-British governor of the city who had been reinstated after the defeat of the 1918 uprising in Najaf, fled to the nearby town of Tuwairij, his position being taken by a local notable, 'Alwan al-Haj Sa'dun. Soon afterwards an 'Executive Committee' was set up to run the city.

In Karbela', the Grand Mujtahid Taqi al-Shirazi, on learning of the uprising at Rumaytha, first attempted to negotiate with the Civil Administration.[5] He dispatched two emissaries to Baghdad with a letter calling upon Wilson to negotiate in the interests of stopping the bloodshed. Shirazi asked for a cessation of military operations, a general amnesty and a return to their homeland of all those who had been expelled from the country. Wilson, unsurprisingly, refused to meet Shirazi's delegation.

This was the turning point in Karbela'. On hearing of Wilson's rebuff of Shirazi's attempt at negotiation, the leading men of the city assembled in the town hall and summoned Mirza Muhammad Bahadur Khan, the representative of the British authorities, to appear before them. When he obeyed they ordered him to hand over all government property to a special committee set up to administer these valuables.[6]

Bahadur Khan, although himself a Persian, in a city of profound Persian influence, was a loyal supporter of the occupying power, having formerly been the oriental secretary to Sir Percy Cox. He prevaricated and made much of the complexity of responding to their request: it would take at least two days to complete a proper inventory of the government's assets and effects, he informed them. However, in reality he was secretly planning to use this respite to try to arouse opposition to the insurgents.

Although there was no permanent British garrison in Karbela' there was a strong contingent of locally recruited police. Bahadur Khan had already gained pledges of support from the chief of police, Muhammad al-Amin, and a few of his men. His plan was to seize control of the government serai, which was situated on the southern edge of the town, fortify the building and hold out until such time as they could be relieved by British troops from Baghdad.[7] Meanwhile they would issue exhortations to the local population to reject the insurrection and join them in the serai. So as night fell, Bahadur Khan, Muhammad al-Amin and a few police crept into the government building, barricaded the entry points and began to fill sandbags and drill a well to secure adequate water supplies for an anticipated blockade. However, this 'loyalist' rebellion was short lived. The majority of the police, being men of Karbela', knew that their true loyalties lay with their fellow citizens.

The following morning, as a large crowd of police gathered outside the serai, curious to learn what was going on, Muhammad al-Amin saw an opportunity to win more of them over to the British. But when he addressed them, offering all kinds of inducements to join him in the pro-government strongpoint, he received a hostile response. Soon the police began shouting abuse at al-Amin, calling him 'friend of the occupation', 'traitor' and similar insults and refusing to obey his orders, after which the majority of them melted away, back to their homes and families.[8] After this setback the demoralised loyalists soon realised the hopelessness of their position and decided to surrender before the situation became more inflamed. Khan Bahadur, Muhammad al-Amin and a British sergeant who had been training the police handed themselves over to a local notable who subsequently escorted them to the nearest British position on the right bank of the Euphrates, opposite Musayib. Then the leadership of the insurgents in Karbela' took charge of the money, equipment and munitions in the serai.

In Karbela', initially the nerve centre of the insurgency, the uprising against British authority was followed by the formation of two committees. The first, and more important, known as the Higher Military Council, was composed of four senior members of the clergy including Mirza 'Abd al-Husayn al-Ha'iri, second son of Grand Mujtahid Shirazi. In addition Muhammad al-Abtan, one of the leading sheikhs of the Khaza'il confederation, served as advisor to the council.[9]

The second committee was called the Community Council and consisted of seventeen tribal sheikhs and sada, one of the sada, Sayyid Khalil Azami, acting as secretary.[10] The functions of the Community Council comprised the general management of the local government in Karbela' and its environs and it was also responsible for implementing any of the orders of the Higher Military Council; as such, it was therefore subordinate to the latter, but both committees were ultimately responsible to the Grand Mujtahid Shirazi.

In Najaf, the organisation responsible for 'general revolutionary affairs' was the Higher Religious Committee. It was composed of fifteen members with its meetings being chaired by the most senior mujtahid of Najaf, Sheikh al-Shari'a Isbahani. In addition there were a number of other, subordinate committees of which the most important was the City Council composed of eight members, two from each of the four mahallas of the city.[11] Its functions included the collection of taxes and other local dues, the control of public health and internal security.

The death of the aged Taqi al-Shirazi at Karbela' on 13 August initially caused widespread dismay among both leaders and followers of the uprising. But his position as Grand Mujtahid and effective leader of the insurgents was immediately taken over by Sheikh al-Shari'a

Isbahani, Shirazi's widely respected colleague and a man who had stood at his side for many years as virtual co-leader of the politically active 'constitutionalist' faction among the mujtahidin in opposition to Yazdi. From then on, Najaf became the real revolutionary centre, and the Higher Military Council of Karbela' was now transferred to the second holy city, where it took the name Revolutionary High Command, its military leadership being conferred upon Sheikh Abtan of the Khaza'il.[12]

At around the same time the insurgents apparently decided that the time had come to establish a more formal structure of government for the liberated areas as a whole. We must remember that this was a time when the rebel movement was riding high and when a series of success-ful – or at least apparently successful – military actions had given them confidence of an outright victory. As a first step therefore, a conference of all the leading sheikhs and sada of the liberated mid-Euphrates towns decided to set up a provisional national government headed by a mutas-arrif (governor) and the person chosen for this post was the Shamiyya landowner and veteran of the 1914–15 jihad, Muhsin Abu Tabikh.

In his memoirs written many years later, Abu Tabikh recalled, with evident pride and emotion, the circumstances of his elevation to the head of this new government:

> In spite of the fact that it was my desire to continue to remain with my brother fighters on the field of battle, I accepted that important commission and requested permission to go to Karbela' to make a start on that important work on the 18th Dhu al-Hijja [2 September 1920] the auspicious occasion of the 'Eid al-Ghadir' [the festival com-memorating the day on which the Shi'is believe the Prophet Muham-mad appointed 'Ali as his successor]. I set off with a large group of tribal chiefs and Karbela' notables who were present to escort me. By the night of 17 September this assembly reached its destination and as dawn was just breaking the holy city was teeming with delegates who had come from Najaf and nearby Euphrates towns in addition to parties of tribal mujahidin from this region. Also in attendance from Baghdad were those who had fled British harassment, the leading men of the national movement Ja'far Abu al-Timman, 'Ali al-Bazirgan and

Yusuf Suwaydi and many of the officers who had been with us at Kufa. The celebrations were held in the town hall among a throng of tens of thousands and the first Iraqi flag was raised over the building which was adopted as the Government Serai, all the while there were shouts of acclamation ringing out, the ululations of the women and the clamour and rhythmic singing of the people.[13]

However, one particular feature characterised all these structures of power. In addition to the Shi'i clergy, their membership was drawn almost exclusively from the traditional elites of the old society which had seen their influence, prestige, and in some cases financial well-being, suffer as a result of the occupation. The 'revolution' which they espoused was therefore a fusion of the modern cry for 'independence' with a deep yearning to return to the old certainties of the Ottoman era. Indeed, the very title of mutasarrif echoes the title of an Ottoman-period governor of an Arab province.

Consider, for example, Abu Tabikh himself. His forebears had acquired large estates in the Shamiyya region when much of the land of questionable ownership had been converted to *tapu sanad* – a form of tenure barely distinguishable from private ownership – during the Ottoman modernisation reforms of the 1870s. One of the largest landowners and rice-growers in the Shamiyya Division, he was also widely respected as one of the leading sada of the region. Precisely what decided him to join the insurgents in 1920 remains unclear, but while moral and religious ideology clearly played a part, the 'freedom' that Abu Tabikh sought to defend was also the freedom to rule over his estates and peasants in a manner to which he had become accustomed, especially during the years 1915–17, when, by and large, he and the other members of his strata did pretty much as they pleased.[14] But the direct control that the British forced upon his region and the unprecedented regularity and efficiency with which they proceeded to collect taxes was exceptionally galling to a man of his status. As for Abu Tabikh's feudatories – the peasants who toiled on his extensive rice lands – as the ultimate source of those tax revenues and in a world where custom and religion still bound the lowly cultivator to his tribal sheikh, it is by no means surprising that their master's decision to oppose the 'infidel' tax collector found a ready response which overruled any incipient class differences between landlord and peasant.[15]

Another prominent feature of government in the insurgent areas was the role played by age. Seniority and experience were greatly honoured in this society and deference towards the elderly frequently played an important part in determining the structure of decision making. For example, in Karbela', sessions of the Community Council were held under the chairmanship of whoever was the oldest member present.[16] Similarly, age played an important part in determining who should be a member of the Higher Military Council. It is also noteworthy that, although the insurgents clearly made use of the technical experience of the former Ottoman army junior officers and NCOs who took part in their military operations, not one of these men appears to have been co-opted into the actual leadership of the uprising.

Religious authority, social status, wealth and age – these were the attributes widely considered most relevant to determining who should occupy the positions of leadership in the insurgent movement. But they were not attributes necessarily related to military effectiveness or productive of sound tactical and strategic decision-making – except perhaps in one particular respect.

From the very outset of the insurgency, its leaders appreciated the need for communication with their followers throughout the liberated territories both to encourage the fighting men by celebrating their successes and to maintain morale in the major rebel towns by refuting the propaganda emanating from government sources. One of the most active participants in the rebels' own propaganda machine was Muhammad Baqir al-Shabibi, scion of one of the great families of Najaf. Shabibi, now in his forties, had a long history of engagement in Shi'i politics. He had been a member of the progressive, constitutionalist tendency among Iraqi Shi'is which supported the Persian revolution of 1906; he had been active in organising opposition to the British invasion and after the crushing of the Najaf uprising of 1918 he had fled to Baghdad, where, according to some accounts, he was one of the founding members of

Haras al-Istiqlal and at one point served as an emissary from Abu al-Timman to Taqi al-Shirazi.[17]

Throughout the rebellion Shabibi wrote pamphlets which were printed in Najaf. They reported news of the fighting on the different fronts and relayed decisions of the insurgent leadership to the people. They also offered political, religious and military guidance to the rebels, as in the following pamphlet published on 30 July 1920.

The nation which each one of you must defend requires you to heed the following:

1) Every tribal chief must ensure that all its sections understand the objectives of this uprising which is nothing less than the demand for complete independence.

2) On the battlefield every one must cry out for independence.

3) The security of the roads and the maintenance of communications between yourselves and between the insurgent regions is essential.

4) Discipline is essential ... no robbery, no looting, no old grudges, no incitement to hatred.

5) It is essential to make every effort to safeguard ammunition.

6) It is obligatory to take good care of prisoners of war, both officers and men, both British and Indian.

7) The telegraph and telephone systems and the telegraph poles must be maintained because their retention is of great value to the motherland. But yes, you should cut the telegraph wires where necessary so that the communications of the occupying government are disrupted.

8) It is essential to tear up the railway lines and blow up the bridges, particularly those used by the trains.

9) Make sure that you retain any transport vehicles which fall into your hands.

10) Take good care of your artillery and machine guns and do not allow them to be damaged or lost. For these are one of the best means of achieving victory.

11) It is essential to retain captured ammunition, bullets, shells and hand grenades ...

12) If you are obliged to abandon a town or village do not leave it weak and broken. You must arrange a provisional government for it.

13) Do not destroy government buildings except those which are military strong-points and do not destroy their furnishings which may be needed in the future.

14) Take care of hospitals and all their equipment and staff.

15) Show kindness to your opponents' wounded, for nothing deserves kindness and sympathy like a man suffering from the pain of his wounds.[18]

Here we see a combination of clear political guidance (the sole objective is 'independence'), practical advice on military affairs (safeguard ammunition, tearing up railway lines), preserving discipline (no indiscriminate looting, no destruction of government buildings): but also, and most notably, moral guidance on the 'rules of war' (take care of prisoners, look after the wounded). That, in the heat of battle, the rebels themselves did not always heed such moral exhortation does not in any way diminish the intrinsic humanity of this appeal and refutes the oft-repeated assertions of the British authorities and their apologists in later accounts of the uprising that the rebels were simply mobs of savage looters led by cruel fanatics.

It was some time before the transition to real insurgent newspapers occurred and, again, it was Al-Shabibi who led the way. On 15 September the first issue of his paper *Al-Furat* (Euphrates) appeared in Najaf.[19] It was followed, on 1 October, by another paper, *Istiqlal* (Independence), also published in Najaf. Both papers carried news of the fighting on the different fronts and what was happening in the various insurgent towns. *Istiqlal* also offered its readers a clear, concise explanation of exactly why the insurgents were fighting – that the British had been devious and deceitful whereas the Arabs had justice and legitimacy on their side.[20] Both Ja'far Abu al-Timman and 'Ali al-Bazirgan wrote articles for *Al-Furat* and *Istiqlal*.[21]

In the event, only five issues of *Al-Furat* appeared and eight issues of *Istiqlal*.[22] Precisely why *Al-Furat* only appeared five times is unknown, but the demise of *Istiqlal* coincided with the submission of Najaf to British forces on 18 October 1920. Although resistance to British rule continued throughout large parts of Iraq, by then it was entering a more fluid and disorganised type of warfare in which there was little role for organised government and central leadership; ultimately this would contribute to the insurgents' defeat but it would be another three and a half months before that day would arrive.

Although it was not obvious at the time to the Iraqi insurgents, the death of a neighbouring Arab government at the end of July 1920 was probably one of the factors leading to their own ultimate defeat. At dawn on 24 July a rag-tag Syrian army composed of no more than 600 regulars and around 2,000 mujahidin – volunteer townsmen and Bedouin – deployed on high ground at Maysalun, a khan on the road from Beirut to Damascus. They faced an advancing French colonial army composed of Senegalese and French infantry, Moroccan cavalry, tanks and aircraft. By noon most of the Syrian defenders had been killed or put to flight, leaving the Syrian war minister, Yusuf al-Azmah, dead on the battlefield. He had known that defeat was inevitable, yet had bravely taken his place on the front line. The French lost a total of fifty-two men killed and 200 wounded.

That this catastrophe for Arab independence appears to have been shrugged off with remarkable insouciance by the Iraqi insurgents is probably because these events occurred at the moment of one of their great military successes – the destruction of the Manchester Column. Yet in the longer term it would isolate the Euphrates region from a potential source of military supplies and must have eventually damaged the Iraqi insurgents' morale.

The British tut-tutted about the French action but had long since lost interest in fulfilling any undertakings made to the Arabs during the war. Indeed, Churchill's main complaint against the French was that their operations in Syria had been largely conducted 'by black African troops'. In any case, the British already had far more urgent matters to attend to in their own new Arab protectorate where, unlike the French in Syria, they faced a well-prepared and well-armed opponent, imbued with a passionate belief in the rectitude of its struggle for independence and Islam. As we shall see, they were also facing problems at home.

Trouble on the Home Front

It was not until 9 July 1920 that the British public first learned of the Arab uprising in Iraq. On that date, under the title, 'Mesopotamian Arabs' Outbreak', *The Times* carried what it described as a 'semi official statement' concerning 'an outbreak of disorder on the Lower Euphrates valley around Samawa'.[1] Three days later, a 'special correspondent' in Tehran, under the title 'Mesopotamian Rising – Fighting Continues', reported that 'the situation in Lower Mesopotamia remains serious' and that the railway between Basra and Baghdad had been cut. The rebels were described as being under the influence of 'Pro-Turkish agitators'.[2]

Having presumably read the same article the previous day, on 13 July Mr William Ormsby-Gore, Conservative Member for Stafford, asked the war minister in the House of Commons to confirm 'whether an Indian garrison stationed to the west of the Euphrates had been 'cut off by rebel Arabs'; whether several unsuccessful attempts to relieve it had been made; and 'whether the rising is more than purely local in character'. He also asked Churchill 'what was its chief cause?'[3]

He might well have asked. By now the British public, the press and the majority of MPs were becoming both confused and angry about exactly what was going on in British-occupied Iraq. They knew that the government had some kind of plan for local Arab rule; they knew that a considerable number of Arab sheikhs in Iraq and throughout the Middle East generally were receiving hefty subsidies; they also knew that some Arabs were sporadically attacking British soldiers and there had been a number of casualties; and they knew that the whole thing was costing the British taxpayer a huge amount of money.

Since the end of the war the government had done its best to conceal the events in Mesopotamia from the British public. Indeed, Wilson's rejection of Yusuf al-Suwaydi's request for freedom of the press and the removal of restrictions on the postal and telegraph services at the confrontation of 2 June in Baghdad was less out of consideration for local public order than for the purposes of concealing the deteriorating situation in Iraq from British journalists. The only newspapers allowed to be published in Iraq were run by the Civil Administration; had a critical Arab press been allowed to function it would not have been long before unfavourable reports on the situation reached the British press and the swelling number of domestic opponents to what were increasingly seen as the government's covert operations in the Middle East, uncontrolled by Parliament and contemptuous of public opinion.[4]

Moreover, suspicions were growing about the influence of 'oil syndicates'. Those who knew something about the potentially rich oilfields in northern Iraq suspected that continued occupation had something to do with that. Indeed, only a few weeks before news of the insurrection broke, Herbert Asquith, former prime minister and now, in effect, leader of the parliamentary opposition to Lloyd George's coalition, had accused the government of planning to spend over £35 million over the coming year on the military occupation of Iraq and 'for what', he asked the prime minister, 'are we spending it?' The answer, according to Asquith, was, 'There are oil-bearing strata and possibly other mineral resources in Mesopotamia,' although, 'It seems to me that this ... is a fundamental violation of the principles upon which we entered into a covenant with other nations of the world in the League of Nations that those should be considerations which are determining British or any other policy.'[5]

However, Lloyd George was not deterred and later in the debate he acknowledged that 'the administration of Mesopotamia will be an expensive one for some years,' but asked the House, 'Is it not desirable that any natural product of that kind should be developed for the benefit of the whole of Mesopotamia?' adding that, 'the whole of those resources will belong to the Arab State we set up. There are all sorts of suggestions that arrangements have been made with private companies. There is no arrangement of any sort made with any company,' an assertion which was disingenuous, to say the least, since the agreement of the British and French to share Iraq's oil between them, made at San Remo two months earlier, would necessarily involve the participation of British and French oil companies; and on the British side, at least, there were only two such companies capable of the job – Anglo-Persian and Shell, both partners in the old Turkish Petroleum Company. Indeed, even as Lloyd George was speaking, the Petroleum Department of his own government was urging that 'the rights secured by the Turkish Petroleum Company before the war should be recognised' and that in this company a moderate additional participation should be given to the Shell Group 'in order to secure British control over that company'.

Nevertheless, when backbenchers volubly expressed their scepticism, the prime minister reasserted his claim that whatever arrangements about Mosul's oil reserves had been made at San Remo, 'the whole of the property will be vested in the Arab State and will not belong to any company.' The precise size of the oil reserves was uncertain, Lloyd George added, 'but the general opinion is that they are valuable. If that is so, I think it essential for the development of its territory that the Arab State should have these oil wells and deposits at Mosul, not merely for the development of Mosul but for the development of Mesopotamia.'[6]

For the time being the House seems to have been unable to respond to the prime minister's assurances that the oil would belong to the 'Arab State' and that it would 'not belong to any company'. But, here again, Lloyd George was being disingenuous. There never was any question of the sub-surface oil deposits in Iraq 'belonging' to anyone other than the state, Arab or British, which would have rights of eminent domain over them – just as in Persia or in other parts of the oil-producing world (except for the exceptional case of the USA where, for historical reasons, sub-surface minerals were owned by the surface landowner).[7] Indeed, the matter of who 'owned' the sub-surface minerals was largely irrelevant from an economic point of view: the most the 'owner' could ever claim or was expected to claim was a royalty (12.5 per cent *ad valorem* in the US oilfields). It was not in the ownership of oil reserves that the profit lay but in their *extraction* and the terms of access to them. When Iraqi oil did, after a long delay, begin to flow, the Turkish Petroleum Company (later the Iraq Petroleum Company) initially received around 94 per cent of the net profit, leaving the 'owner' – the 'Arab State' – with the tiny remainder.[8]

Yet ultimately the 'oil question' was not so much a matter of private profit as an affair of state. There were those in government and on its periphery who had a financial interest in the Anglo-Persian Oil Company and through that company, in its affiliate, the Turkish Petroleum Company. But for the prime minister, the War Office and the Admiralty what really mattered was the strategic advantage which the control of Middle East oil would confer. They had witnessed the great power of oil on the battlefield and upon the oceans. Oil supplies were now the lifeblood of the British Empire and – as the First Lord of the Admiralty had rather injudiciously put it a few weeks earlier – 'If we secure the supplies of oil now available in the world, we can do what we like.'[9]

But for now, it was the unpleasant reality of the uprising which dominated the debate on Iraq. Answering Ormsby-Gore's question's about the attack on Rumaytha, Churchill – himself clearly uncertain at this stage as to the gravity of the events – confirmed the attack and the fact that the railway had been cut above and below the town. He also confirmed that a relief column had 'suffered some casualties' but he reassured the House that 'the rising appears to be local in character' and was 'probably the outcome of religious agitation in Najaf'.

The anxieties of honourable members were not assuaged. 'Is the garrison in fact surrounded or not? I could not quite gather whether that is so from the reply,' asked Lord Robert Cecil, himself a government minister, to which Churchill admitted that 'it has not yet been relieved' although 'it is still holding out and a considerable column has gone out from Baghdad to join up with the garrison to establish order in the district.'

During the following days, as more news of the uprising appeared in the press, Churchill had to face a battery of questions in Parliament. By 15 July the House of Commons was particularly perplexed and anxious. 'Are rail communications between Basra and Baghdad still cut?' demanded Earl Winterton, an Irish Peer and Conservative Member for Horsham and Worthing; and how many British and Indian casualties had been suffered? How much material and rolling stock had been destroyed by the insurrectionists? And what damage had been done to our armoured trains?

In the circumstances Churchill did his best to present an honest and factual account of the current military situation in Iraq while at the same time presenting a broadly optimistic perspective as to its future outcome. He acknowledged that, to date, six trains had been either captured or de-railed between Samawa and Diwaniyya; that garrisons at Rumaytha and Samawa were currently 'isolated'; that the railway line above Diwaniyya was cut, although not 'seriously cut'; that there had been no report of any British (as opposed to Indian) casualties to date; and that a 'consid-erable force' of British and Indian troops was now 'moving downwards from Baghdad' to relieve the 'isolated' garrisons. Meanwhile, the situa-tion in the Shamiyya region was 'reported to be delicate'.

Not surprisingly, news of the Manchester Column disaster added fuel to the flames of parliamentary disquiet, in particular among those MPs whose constituents included anguished parents of 2nd Battalion men. Attempts to discover what exactly had happened to their sons were met by disconcertingly obvious stonewalling on the part of Churchill and the War Office. Indeed, it was not until 24 September – two months after the event – that the War Office disclosed the names of the casualties, categorising them as 127 missing, 76 prisoners, 2 missing believed killed and 2 dead.[10] This did nothing to assuage the anxieties of the relatives of the prisoners, or those of the suspiciously large number of 'missing'. It took a further two months for the worst fears of these families to be confirmed when, at last, it was acknowledged that all of the 'missing' were actually dead. Such was the fate of the parents of Private J. H. Heathcote (aged eighteen) of Audenshaw, a small cotton-spinning and silk-weaving town five miles east of Manchester, whose death was not reported in the *Ashton Reporter* until 20 November.[11]

As the summer wore on, the pressure on the government to withdraw from Iraq steadily mounted, fanned by a series of remorselessly gloomy headlines in the press. On 4 August, the readers of *The Times* were told of:

> **MESPOTAMIA FIGHTING: SHARP CONFLICT WITH ARABS:**
> **300 BRITISH CASUALTIES**

And on 14 August:

> **BAD TO WORSE IN MESOPOTAMIA: BLOCKHOUSES ON**
> **BAGHDAD ROAD: BRITISH POLITICAL OFFICER KILLED**

On 18 August:

> **LINES OF COMMUNICATION WITH PERSIA CUT**

On 23 August:

> **MESOPOTAMIA: A SERIOUS WAR BEFORE US**

And on 8 September:

> **ANARCHY IN MESOPOTAMIA: TRIBES HOSTILE AND ALERT:**
> **EXTENSIVE DAMAGE TO COMMUNICATIONS**

Meanwhile, on 8 August, in the *Observer*, there appeared the following letter from T. E. Lawrence under the title 'France, Britain and the Arabs'. It began with a bitter attack on the French overthrow of Faysal's 'Arab State' in Syria; but then sarcastically pointed out that the British could hardly complain about French actions when they were doing little different in Iraq, where they were 'fighting battles near Baghdad and trying to render Mesopotamia incapable of self-government, by smashing every head that raised itself among them'. 'These risings take a regular course', said Colonel Lawrence, and continued,

There is a preliminary Arab success, then British reinforcements go out as a punitive force. They fight their way (our losses are slight, the Arab losses heavy) to their objective which is meanwhile bombarded by artillery, aeroplanes or gunboats. Finally, perhaps, a village is burnt and the district pacified.

And then Lawrence switched into the sharpest Swiftian irony:

It is odd that we do not use poison gas on these occasions. Bombing the houses is a patchy way of getting the women and children ...[12]

Thereafter, the letter itemised the huge resources Britain was wasting in Iraq and urged a different policy which would 'save us a million pounds a week'. However, it is at this point that the shallowness of Lawrence's understanding of what the Iraqi insurgents were actually fighting for emerges. Because, for Lawrence, all that was required was to get rid of Wilson and his team and put in the right sort of man who really understood the Arabs and to whom they would readily acquiesce in accepting some kind of neutered semi-independence. Lawrence knew 'ten British officials with tried and honourable reputations' in the Sudan, Sinai, etc. who could 'set up an Arab Government' in Baghdad next month. Whether or not Lawrence thought of himself as one of the ten is beside the point – the fact is that, by this time the insurgents (as opposed to the subsidised collaborators in Baghdad and elsewhere) had absolutely no intention of allowing anyone from Britain to set up any sort of government in Iraq: indeed, as far as they were concerned, they already had an Arab government – at Karbela' and Najaf.

Nevertheless, the letter was an unpleasant blow for Lloyd George and his cabinet. Lawrence was at the height of his popularity in the country and regarded as *the* British expert on the Middle East. It was therefore all the more galling when Lawrence returned to the fray, a fortnight later, but this time in the *Sunday Times*, in which his letter was accompanied by a strongly supportive editorial while the paper's readers were reminded that Lawrence's 'organisation and direction of the Hejaz against the Turks was one of the outstanding romances of the war'.

The people of England have been led in Mesopotamia into a trap from which it will be hard to escape with dignity and honour. They have been tricked into it by a steady withholding of information. The Baghdad communiqués are belated, insincere, incomplete. Things have been far worse than we have been told, our administration more bloody and inefficient than the public knows. It is a disgrace to our imperial record and may soon be too inflamed for any ordinary cure. We are today not far from disaster.

There followed a blistering attack on the 'Civil Authorities' in Iraq, and, without specifically naming him, upon Arnold Wilson. Lawrence went on to claim, 'We have killed ten thousand Arabs in this rising this summer,' something which the bloodstained Turkish sultan, Abdul Hamid, 'would applaud ... The Government in Baghdad have been hanging Arabs in that town for political offences which they call rebellion,' Lawrence declared, and, referring to the British prisoners taken by the insurgents during the attack on the Manchester Column, he asked, 'Are these illegal executions to provoke the Arabs to reprisals on the three hundred British prisoners they hold? And, if so, is it that their punishment may be more severe, or is it to persuade our other troops to fight to the last?'[13]

Not surprisingly Lawrence's dramatic intervention raised even more doubts in the minds of an already perplexed British public as to what precisely was the government's objective in spending millions of pounds in Iraq and at what point Britain's mysterious obligations in that distant territory would end.

The summer of 1920 was particularly cold, wet and miserable in the UK, even by British standards, and as the depressing weather continued through July and into August, Churchill felt more and more worn down by the equally depressing political situation in Britain, the colonies and the world at large, especially in Ireland and in Russia, where the Bolsheviks were now victorious. Moreover, it was not only in Britain that opposition to Britain's involvement in Iraq was becoming deeply unpopular. In India, an article by Gandhi appeared in the Bombay-published journal *Young India*, appealing directly to Muslim sentiment in an attempt to unite Muslims and

Hindus behind his campaign for independence:

> England finds Mesopotamia a tough job. The oil of Mosul may feed
> the fire she has so wantonly lighted and burn her fingers badly. The
> newspapers say the Arabs do not like the presence of the Indian soldier
> in their midst. I do not wonder. They are a fierce and brave people
> and do not understand why Indian soldiers should find themselves in
> Mesopotamia. Whatever the fate of non-cooperation, I wish that not
> a single Indian will offer his services for Mesopotamia whether for the
> civil or the military department.[14]

And in a long article published in the *Bombay Chronicle* on 27 July, the
paper denounced the events in Iraq as, 'A naked act of territorial grab, an
"oil deal" which not only violates the Covenant of the League of Nations
but offends against the high purposes of the Great War – the vindication
of the principle of nationality and self-determination.'[15]

On 13 August, and again on the 19th, Churchill sought to alleviate
his depressed state of mind by physical exercise – playing polo at Rugby.
But by the end of the month, with news from Iraq increasingly grim, his
thoughts turned to the deployment of more ruthless measures against
the rebels. On 29 August he wrote to Air Marshal Trenchard urging a
more rapid development of poison gas bombs, 'especially mustard gas',
which could be dropped on the 'recalcitrant natives'.[16] Two days later, in
a mood of deepening despair, Churchill drafted a long letter to Lloyd
George, a letter with an uncharacteristically self-pitying tone:

> There is something very sinister to my mind in this Mesopotamian
> entanglement, coming as it does when Ireland is so great a menace. It
> seems to me so gratuitous that after all the struggles of the war, just
> when we want to get together our slender military resources and re-
> establish our finances and have a little in hand in case of danger here
> or there, we should be compelled to go on pouring armies and treasure
> into these thankless deserts.[17]

The war minister went on to complain that 'we have not got a single
friend in the Press on the subject', and that 'week after week and month

after month for a long time to come we shall have a continuance of this miserable, wasteful, sporadic warfare.' In all likelihood it would involve numerous minor disasters and the possibility of a major one. The cost of fighting this war would amount to at least £50 million in the current year, which would wipe out any possible commercial advantages Britain might have from holding on to the territory. As for Sir Percy Cox, whom the cabinet had decided to send back to Iraq to replace Arnold Wilson, Churchill confessed that he 'did not feel any complete confidence in him', adding that 'his personality did not impress me.'

Nevertheless, Churchill assured the prime minister that he was 'carrying out the Cabinet directions to the best of my ability' and that 'every possible soldier that we can find is being set in motion for reinforcement to the utmost limits of our available transport.' These reinforcements (and by implication the crushing of the revolt) were 'equally necessary whether we decide to stay or to quit. There is nothing else to do but this and it will take some time.'

In the event, the letter was never sent. Perhaps Churchill recognised its wording was just too revealing of his current state of mind (and, given the widespread antipathy in the country towards him over his 'anti-Bolshevik warmongering', he could no longer be entirely confident of the prime minister's support). Meanwhile, on 26 August, he had written to Haldane assuring him of his absolute determination to help him crush the insurrection:

I take this opportunity of sending you my earnest good wishes for the success of the difficult task you are discharging. The Cabinet have decided that the rebels must be quelled effectively and I shall endeavour to meet all your requirements ... Thus, by the middle or end of October you should be possessed of effective striking forces and a vigorous use of these to put down and punish disaffection combined with the policy of setting up an Arab state should bring about a better situation.[18]

For now, though, there was little more he could do; everything depended on Haldane and the speed with which those reinforcements would arrive. So on 2 September, no doubt pressured by his wife Clementine, Churchill accepted an invitation from his old friend the Duke of Westminster to stay at the Duke's estate at Mimizan, in south-west France. There, he hoped, a fortnight's relaxation under the southern sun might sooth his spirits and invigorate his tired, corpulent body.

The Siege of Samawa

The sun, whose delightful rays gently bathed the British war minister as he stretched out in a deckchair in one of the Duke of Westminster's secluded, box-fringed gardens, presented a fearsomely different aspect 2,400 miles to the south-east and 15 degrees latitude below the Duke's Gascon landscaping. As the 574 officers and men of the 1st Battalion, King's Own Yorkshire Light Infantry clambered down onto the dock at Basra on 8 September 1920, after a trying journey up the Gulf from India, the heat fell upon them like some dreadful beast of prey. While waiting for re-embarkation at Bombay they had become acclimatised to an Asian summer to a limited extent; but the 120°F, accompanied by a fiery desert wind which met them in Basra and lasted for the full nine days they were stationed at the neighbouring military camp, was too much for many of the young men from the industrial and mining towns of Wakefield, Doncaster and Pontefract and heatstroke casualties mounted rapidly.[1]

The battalion had been rushed out to Iraq from India before it had been properly equipped, so the unit was compelled to suffer the heat and flies of Makina Camp while Major A. Barker MC, the quartermaster, did his best to round up the missing stores and equipment.[2] Eventually, on 17 September, the battalion was loaded onto a train and transported to Nasiriyya on the Euphrates, where they were brigaded in the 74th Brigade with three Indian infantry battalions – the 2nd Battalion 7th Rajputs, the 1st Battalion 15th Sikhs and the 3rd Battalion 123rd (Outram's) Rifles – reinforcements which had been rushed to Iraq during the preceding month.

These were but a small proportion of the reinforcements which Churchill had decided to use against the rebels. On 17 August a Pioneer battalion (1/12th Pioneers) had disembarked at Basra together with the 2nd Battalion 96th Infantry, in total 1,518 officers and men, destined to be deployed on the Tigris defending the Kut-to-Baghdad lines of communication. The next day the 3rd Battalion 23rd Sikh Infantry arrived and were ordered to Nasiriyya, followed, two days later, by the 2nd Battalion 117th Mahrattas. Five days later the 2nd Battalion 116th Mahrattas arrived and were dispatched by train to Baghdad and the following day the 2nd Battalion 89th Punjabis disembarked and were also sent north to defend the capital and its communications with Kut. On the last day of August, these were followed by the 3rd Battalion 70th Burmans who were retained in reserve at Basra.[3]

Ten days after the arrival of the King's Own, three more Indian infantry battalions arrived at Basra – the 2nd Battalion 153rd Rifles, the 63rd Palamacottahs and the 3rd Battalion 124th Baluchis; the Baluchis were retained at Basra and the other two battalions sent on to Nasiriyya. They were followed, between 23 and 28 September, by the arrival of four battalions of Gurkhas, totalling 2,547 officers and men; and finally, another Indian unit, the Kapurthala Infantry.

Although two more British units, the Duke of Cornwall's Light Infantry and the 2nd Battalion East Yorkshire Regiment, also arrived in Iraq at the end of September, of the 15,434 reinforcements which Haldane received between 6 August and 29 September, only 16.8 per cent were British. Haldane's 'British' Army was no less overwhelmingly 'Indian' than when he had arrived. Nevertheless, Haldane now considered he had sufficient strength to move decisively against the Arabs.

With no knowledge of these massive British reinforcements, the inhabitants of the liberated areas remained jubilant. Over the previous three months, the insurgents had rejoiced over a series of magnificent victories over the infidel occupation forces – how their heroic tribal armies had inflicted one defeat after another upon the British and their wretched Indian slave-soldiers, driving them from virtually every town and village on the Middle and Lower Euphrates; of the remainder,

British garrisons at Samawa and Kufa were besieged and Hilla was under sporadic attack. On the Diyala, north-east of Baghdad, the Arabs had isolated the British from their troops in Persia; to the west of Baghdad, the insurgent Zauba' tribes held sway and had cut off the British outposts at Falluja and Ramadi from the capital; meanwhile, on the Tigris north of Baghdad, Muhammad al-Sadr, having escaped the attempt to capture him, was personally rallying the tribes in an attempt to seize the old walled city of Samarra. Only the death of the revered Grand Mujtahid Mirza Muhammad Taqi Shirazi in August had somewhat dimmed the insurgents' general mood of exultation.

But among the leadership of the uprising the mood may have been more subdued. In particular, the new Grand Mujtahid, Sheikh al-Shari'a Isbahani, must have been uneasy with the progress of the rebellion. Emissaries from the holy cities had repeatedly been sent out to the tribes on the Central and Lower Tigris – to the Bani Rabia', the Bani Lam and the Al Bu Muhammad – but to no avail. Their sheikhs, now well paid with British subsidies and supported by gangs of heavily armed retainers, dominated their lesser sheikhs and tribesmen and had snuffed out any incipient movements of support for the insurrection. And as yet, there had been no real show of support from the great Muntafiq confederation whose sway extended over the Lower Euphrates and up the Gharraf and Hai rivers.

Like his predecessor, Isbahani was of Persian birth and like Shirazi he was a man of great learning, fluent in classical Arabic; he, too, had taken a strongly constitutionalist position in the great Shi'i religious and political debates at the time of the prewar Persian revolution. But there the similarity ended. The seventy-one-year-old cleric had none of the pacifist tendencies that had made his predecessor initially reluctant to acknowledge the justice and necessity for armed rebellion. Isbahani had long been an advocate of armed resistance to European encroachment into the Muslim world. In 1914 he had been one of the most active mujtahidin in rallying the tribes for the jihad against the British invasion and the hard experience of defeat had done nothing to soften his bitter hostility towards the British. Moreover, unlike most of the other clergy of Najaf and Karbela', Isbahani had a shrewd understanding of military strategy and was particularly conscious of two prerequisites for the insurgency's victory – the utmost unity among the tribes, and the need to counterbalance the occupiers' preponderance in heavy weaponry by seeking every opportunity to capture British artillery pieces and machine guns. He was also a good judge of subordinates and had already sent one of his most able commanders, Sayyid Hadi al-Mgutar, another veteran of the 1915 jihad, to take charge of the tribal forces besieging the British base outside the rebel-held town of Samawa.

In itself, the base was not a great military prize. It had a battalion-sized garrison of British-officered Indian troops, an armoured train and some machine guns and mortars. The real significance of Samawa, however – as Isbahani fully understood – was the impact its capture would have upon the Muntafiq, who could easily add 20,000 armed men to the insurgent forces if they could be persuaded to rally to the cause. And if the Muntafiq joined the insurgency, then some, at least, of the Tigris tribes might do likewise.

Isbahani must also have been puzzled, as well as worried, about the inactivity of the Muntafiq. True, the one man who might have rallied the Muntafiq in support of the insurgency was no longer in Iraq. Ajaimi Sa'dun, the paramount chief of the Muntafiq tribes, who had been one of the key leaders in the 1914–15 jihad against the British invaders, had fled the country at the end of the war and was now with Mustafa Kemal's Turkish Army of Independence, confronting the Allied troops and Greek invaders occupying parts of Western Turkey; and there were other Muntafiq sheikhs, like Khayyun al-'Ubayd who had fought hard against the British even after the defeat of the jihad at Shu'ayba; and after the end of the war, Sheikh Badr al-Rumayidh of the Albu Salih and paramount chief of the great Bani Malik tribe, who had also fought at Shu'ayba, refused to offer his submission to the British and held out until October, 1919 when the sixty-five-year-old leader, harassed by British columns, finally surrendered and was sent into exile in Muhammara.

What Isbahani apparently didn't know was that, in the region of the Muntafiq, the British had an exceptionally brave and able PO –

the twenty-eight-year-old Captain Bertram Thomas. He had fought in Belgium in 1914 before being posted to the Somerset Light Infantry, where he had taken part in General Maude's successful advance to Baghdad. Thomas had then joined the Political Service and, after originally being posted as APO at Suq al-Shuyukh on the Lower Euphrates, in late 1918 he was sent to Shatra on the Lower Gharraf river, perhaps the most isolated and potentially hostile post in the whole Muntafiq-dominated region.

Although Thomas had carried out all the usual functions of a PO, including tax collection and mobilising forced labour, it seems he had carried out these duties – insofar as this was possible – with considerable tact and sensitivity. He was no Leachman or Daly and had never called in aircraft to bomb recalcitrant villages. Above all, he seems to have had the knack of making friends with the local sheikhs so that when, in August 1920, it was decided that it was no longer sensible to leave him isolated and exposed at Shatra and he was withdrawn on a gunboat, he had the assurance of those sheikhs that the region would remain quiet.[4] Nevertheless, as Thomas was forced to admit in a report submitted at the beginning of the uprising, the Lower Gharraf would only remain peaceful so long as its inhabitants could see the British defeating the insurgents. If the tide turned decisively against them – in particular at Samawa – the Muntafiq of the Gharraf would doubtless join the uprising, and with them, the remainder of the Muntafiq tribes.

This was precisely General Haldane's concern. He had originally considered withdrawing from the British base outside Samawa, as he had done at Rumaytha and Diwaniyya. Had he done so, it is more than likely that the Muntafiq would have seen this as a British defeat and joined the uprising. As it happened, by the time he had firmly decided on withdrawal, he was unable to implement it: the base was completely surrounded and under almost daily attack.

By the time the net closed around the Samawa base in mid-August, its garrison consisted of 625 officers and men, the equivalent of a battalion, albeit one made up of three different units – two and a half companies of the 1st Battalion 114th Mahrattas, two companies of the 2nd Battalion

125th Napier's Rifles, and fifty men of the 10th Lancers. The officer
commanding was Major A. S. Hay of the 31st Lancers.

The British-officered Indian troops were actually deployed in four
separate camps. The main camp was situated roughly a mile north-
north-west of Samawa town in a great bend in the Euphrates, accessible
to river supplies and gunboat support. A quarter of a mile further west,
also on the river, there was another position, known as the 'supply camp'.
About a mile west of the supply camp, yet another small post defended
the Barbutti bridge across the river. The supply camp and the main camp
were linked by trenches and barbed wire but the Barbutti position was
not. Moreover, as the defence perimeter was reduced in order to build
these defences, it became impossible for aircraft to land or take off, eliminating one source of supply.

The weakest part of the British defence network lay a few hundred
yards south of Samawa town: here, a long way from the river and more
or less cut off from the rest of the garrison, the British had built a
railway station through which ran the Basra–Baghdad line. In order
to maintain rail supplies from Khidhr station, seventeen miles to
the south, it had to be defended and in August 1920 it was held by a
hundred men of Napier's Rifles and fifty troopers of the 10th Lancers,
under the overall command of Lieutenant Oswald Russell, also of the
10th Lancers. Two other British officers were at this position, known
as Station Camp – Second Lieutenant H. V. Fleming, commanding
the Napier's Rifles and a medical officer, Captain J. W. Pigeon. By
chance, an armoured train with a 12-pounder gun was also parked at
Station Camp.

Although the British were by no means demoralised, the defence of
Samawa had commenced with a number of setbacks, the first being the
foundering of the gunboat HMS *Greenfly*, now stranded with its crew
a few miles downriver. On 12 August the railway line between Samawa
and Khidhr had been torn up by rebel tribesmen and it was reported
to Haldane that a force of around 2,500 insurgents was marching on
Khidhr itself. Since the latter was defended by only three troops of levies
and a handful of Gurkha Rifles, the general decided that it would have

to be abandoned immediately, leaving Samawa isolated, except by river. But even this manoeuvre ended badly.

There were three trains at Khidhr, two of them armoured. The plan was to load all the men and horses at Khidhr into the three trains and transport them south to Ur Junction with the two armoured trains following the leading (unarmoured) train at five-minute intervals. However, as the evacuation procedure began, the rebels began to close in and their attacks considerably hindered the loading of the horses and men. Then, at around 3.30 p.m., as the three trains were pulling away from the station under intense fire, the second train collided with the rear of the first, becoming derailed and blocking the line for the third armoured train. The first train managed to move off and the officer in charge sent orders that the seventeen men of the Gurkha Rifles who were occupying the train nearest to Khidhr should abandon it and jump aboard the one which was escaping. For some reason this message never reached the Gurkhas and they remained behind. All of them were subsequently killed. Tragic though this was, it was not so serious a loss as the 12-pounder gun which had been mounted on the rear armoured train.[5] This was removed by the insurgents and later carried to Samawa, where the small number of former Ottoman army officers and NCOs readied it to bombard the British positions.

Since the only supply route to Samawa now lay on the river, and by the last week in August the defenders were running short of food and ammunition, a supply convoy made up of three Fly-class gunboats and two merchant vessels towing barges was assembled at Nasiriyya and on 26 August it began to steam upriver. The convoy also carried forty-five men of the 2nd Battalion 123rd Rifles as reinforcements.

As it approached Khidhr the flotilla came under heavy rifle fire and one of the merchant vessels in the rear, *S9*, appeared to be in difficulties. The gunboat astern of it signalled, asking whether assistance was required, but when it was replied that all was well, it overtook *S9* and joined the rest of the convoy which, by now, was passing the stranded *Greenfly*. Suddenly ominous clouds of smoke were seen rising from *S9*. One of the gunboats was immediately ordered to return to the stricken vessel but when it arrived alongside it was found that the ship had been abandoned and was in flames. It was later discovered that *S9*'s engines had failed and she had drifted up against the river bank. It had then been boarded by a large group of insurgents who killed its crew and the two British officers and platoon of Indian troops on board.

The remainder of the flotilla continued steaming up to Samawa, continuously under fire from both banks of the river, but two miles south of the town one of the barges being towed by the remaining merchant vessel grounded on a mudbank and had to be abandoned. By evening of 28 August the flotilla reached the supply camp at Samawa but there had been heavy casualties among the crews and escort of Indian troops and a substantial proportion of the supplies had been lost. The only really successful aspect of the operation was that the forty-five men of the 123rd Rifles sent as reinforcements for the garrison arrived unscathed.

By now the situation of the troops defending the railway station was becoming desperate. Lying only 200 yards under the walls of the insurgent-held town, it was possible for the rebels to pour a deadly fire down upon Station Camp and within a short time, they punctured a number of the camp's water tanks. By 3 September it was clear to Major Hay that the position of the men at Station Camp and Barbutti Bridge Camp, was untenable and he therefore ordered them to withdraw into the defensive perimeter surrounding the Main and Supply Camps. The Barbutti Bridge troops accomplished this without incident, but as the men at Station Camp began to move out disaster struck.

The plan was for around half the men of Napier's Rifles, led by Lieutenant Fleming, to march down the railway line in the direction of Main Camp while 200 men of the Mahrattas would sally out to meet them at a point about 400 yards from the station. Meanwhile the remainder of the Station Camp garrison would be loaded into the trucks of the armoured train which would then advance in the same direction. Lieutenant Russell and the medical officer, Captain Pigeon, would accompany the train.

However, as the armoured train pulled out of the station it hit some faulty points and jumped the tracks. Seeing this, around 3,500 insurgents poured out of the town and charged towards it. Lieutenant Russell ordered his men to make their escape towards the Mahrattas' lines as best they could. Led by Lieutenant Fleming, they soon encountered large numbers of rebels and while most of them broke through and joined their comrades, a number were killed while others were forced back into the armoured train, where they rejoined the remaining two British officers who had stayed with the wounded and sick.

From Main Camp, and at distance of about one mile, Major Hay was able to see the derailment of the armoured train through his field glasses and he began to collect every available man to make a counter-attack against the rebels who were now swarming all over Station Camp. But by the time he had mobilised sufficient men, all sound of firing from the vicinity of Station Camp had ceased and the rebels appeared to be dispersing. Again, the commanding officer scanned Station Camp through his field glasses; but an eerie calm had now settled over the scene of the action. Could anyone still be alive on the train? It didn't look like it. Should he therefore sally out towards Station Camp with a force sufficiently large to rescue any survivors and defend itself if attacked, but thus inevitably denude Main Camp and put *that* crucial position at risk of being overrun?

Once more the commanding officer scanned the derailed armoured train and the surrounding desert while he and his fellow officers strained their ears for any sound of firing. However, it now seemed certain that all resistance had ended and, having consulted with his staff, Major Hay decided there was nothing more he could do for the men on the armoured train. By now, they were either dead or taken prisoner.

Tragically, this was not the case. Later reports from a handful of sowars who escaped the train but were later captured by the insurgents told a story of a heroic long-drawn-out resistance on the part of the British officers and Indian troopers who were unable to get away. Lieutenant Russell, Captain Pigeon and some of the remaining troops had barricaded themselves into one of the loopholed armoured wagons, from where they kept up an intense fire upon their assailants. The rebels then poured oil onto the tracks beneath the truck and eventually set it alight. How long this process took will never be known, but at some point the survivors were driven out by the smoke and flames and most were shot down as they tried to escape.

It seems the garrison at Main Camp might have been able to save them had they made the attempt, but Major Hay's predicament, in the face of what appeared to be clear evidence that the train's occupants had been killed at an early stage in the fighting, was understandable. It remains a mystery why no sound of the continuing fighting reached the British officers in Main Camp, but Haldane himself would later observe that 'the atmospheric conditions in Mesopotamia are fruitful causes of deception' and that the summer dust and wind could easily have affected both sight and sound. He also acknowledged that any attempt to make a sally from Main Camp in adequate numbers would certainly have put the latter at serious risk.

Nevertheless, this had been the most serious defeat so far for the Samawa garrison. Fifty men and officers had been killed in the fighting and another 12-pounder gun (the one on the derailed armoured train) had been lost to the enemy. And as the British withdrew into their narrow defensive position along the river bank, the insurgents began to encircle them with a network of trenches while at the same time large groups of rebels took up positions on the left bank of the Euphrates directly opposite Main Camp, from where they began to enfilade its defenders.

As the September days passed, the defenders of Samawa were put on half rations. Meanwhile the enemy trenches crept closer and closer to the British barbed wire and one of the captured 12-pounder guns began a sporadic bombardment of the British trenches around Supply Camp. Indeed, the fact that they were now coming under artillery fire convinced the defenders that they were facing Turkish troops who had arrived to support the Arabs.[6] This belief was reinforced when the gun removed from the armoured train which had been derailed at Khidhr was also brought into service. Moreover, the extent to which the fighting was increasingly taking on the characteristics of regular warfare was highlighted by the fact that the insurgents' trenches were now fortified with sandbagged positions from which they could snipe at the British defenders and from which the rebels launched attacks with hand grenades. For those who had fought in the Great War the situation seemed almost on a par with the Western Front.

Now, believing the British to be unable to keep up their resistance for much longer, the insurgent commander, Sayyid Hadi al-Mgutar, sent an emissary to Major Hay under a white flag. The British commander was informed that his position was surrounded by over 20,000 troops and that the insurgents were aware that the defenders were fast running out of food and ammunition. However, they would be offered generous terms. If they surrendered, each man of the garrison would be allowed to keep his weapon and the garrison would be allowed to march to the nearest British position.

However, throughout the siege, Major Hay had been able to maintain radio contact with Baghdad and by now he was aware that a large relief column was being assembled at Nasiriyya. Although the latter was sixty miles away and it might take three or four weeks to reach them, Hay believed he had just enough food and ammunition to hold out. Hadi al-Mgutar's generous terms were therefore summarily rejected.

Meanwhile the insurgents' attention focused on the stricken gunboat, HMS *Greenfly*, stuck firmly in the mud a few miles south of Samawa. It was now that the British decision to leave the crew and military escort on board until further rescue attempts could be made tragically unravelled. The men of the *Greenfly* were beginning to run out of food but the gunboat had not been left totally unaided. Attempts were made by the Royal Air Force to drop supplies to the ship but so far three-quarters of the provisions had fallen short, into the river. However, on 22 September a Bristol Fighter, crewed by Flying Officer Bockett-Pugh and Flying Officer Macdonald, attempted to drop their food parcels as accurately as possible but were shot down and their aircraft fell into the river about one mile above Khidhr. Both crewmen escaped the wrecked plane but on clambering up the river bank, one of the officers was immediately shot and killed by tribesmen of the Jawabir, a section of the Bani Huchaym. The other officer apparently attempted to negotiate with the tribesmen and promised a large reward if he was given safe conduct to the *Greenfly*, but sometime later the headman of a local village arrived on the scene and shot the remaining officer. The bodies of both aviators were subsequently mutilated. After this incident no further attempts were made to supply the *Greenfly* by air.

By 30 September the situation on board the ship was getting desperate but the *Greenfly*'s captain, Alfred Hedger, managed to get a message out to his commanding officer at Nasiriyya via a friendly local sheikh who had been passing occasional messages between the gunboat and Nasiriyya since it had become stranded.

Political Officer, Nasiriyya

Sir, I am in receipt of your communication dated 20th instant. You will no doubt have seen my letter to the G.O.C. which was sent to the G.O.C. by Sheikh Wannas of El Bab and left yesterday.

Food is the great question on board; but if your arrangements are successful, I expect we shall be able to hang on. The condition of the crew is really very good considering the very severe shortage of rations that we have all experienced. Our spirits are still 'up' altho' at times we have felt very depressed. To get your letter and to know that things are happening helps us all very much indeed. I have lost one Indian and I have one B.O.R. [British other ranks] severely wounded; besides these casualties I have one Indian wounded and 3 or 4 men sick owing to weakness – lack of food ... There are 31 Indians, and you'll know the number of B.O.R.s on board. Give us rations and we will have the heart and spirit to stick it out to the end ... Thanking you for your cheerful letter and again assuring you of our all performing our duties to the best of our ability.

I have the honour to be, sir, your obedient servant,

Alfred C. Hedger.[7]

It was to be the last communication from the *Greenfly*. Precisely what happened to the crew and escort will never be known. Only one body – that of a European – was ever found and none of the crew or escort were ever seen again. It appears that sometime around 3 October, the Indian troops may have mutinied, killed Captain Hedger and the other British and then handed the ship over to the insurgents. The rebels then boarded the ship, stripped it of everything of use including the 12-pounder gun and set it alight. Such was the conclusion of the court of inquiry held some months later, although Haldane would later comment that 'no absolute proof of this has been obtained.'

At Samawa, however, the Indian troops remained loyal. As the siege continued, Arab insurgents who knew a few words of Hindustani began to creep up to the British trenches during the night calling out to the sepoys to abandon the British and come over to their side. Appeals were made, in particular, to the religious sentiments of the Muslim Indian troops, but there was no response. Later, their British officers expressed pride in the loyalty of their 'fighting sons of India', one of whom awarded them what was apparently intended to be the ultimate accolade: 'Black they were, but white inside.'[8]

Meanwhile, Haldane was massing troops at Nasiriyya in preparation for his relief operation. By the end of September he had put together a powerful column composed mainly of the troops that had recently arrived from India. It consisted of the 1st Battalion King's Own Yorkshire Light Infantry, three battalions of the Gurkha Rifles, a battalion of the 23rd Sikhs and two squadrons of the 10th Lancers. The column was supported by a Royal Field Artillery battery, a howitzer battery and two and a half sections of a machine-gun battalion together with a company of sappers, medical corps and transport units. By now Haldane had also acquired another squadron of RAF fighter bombers – the 55th Squadron equipped with the newer DH9As which had arrived at Baghdad West airfield on 23 September.

But while he was deeply engaged in these plans for a major counter-offensive, there was another matter the consideration of which was causing General Haldane frequently sleepless nights: responsibility for the Manchester Column debacle. It was all the fault of Major General Leslie; at least, that was how Haldane saw the matter. From time to time little episodes of self-doubt troubled him. Was it just possible that there had been some ambiguity in his instructions to Leslie when he had telephoned to ask permission for the column to advance so ill-advisedly into enemy territory? Or could Brigadier Stewart, who took and answered the call, have somehow garbled those instructions? However, in the end, the general always managed to suppress such thoughts, returning, with absolute conviction, to the opinion that it was Leslie who was to blame; but would others see it that way? In the end, he decided that the only way to deal with the matter was to confront Leslie openly with his 'serious error of judgement' and if he still refused to accept his responsibility, then he could always remove him from command of the 17th Division – he had the power to do that, after all.

For his part, Major General Leslie was becoming aware of Haldane's antipathy towards him and that he might be preparing some kind of disciplinary move against him. Writing to his wife on 28 August, he told her, 'I gather from General W. who had a long interview with the Chief that I am not in favour there. I am said to be too parochial in my views and think that there is nothing to do but clear the Hilla area.'[9]

And to Wilson, on 17 September, he complained, 'The 17th Division is in great disfavour and cannot do right. I have little hope of many of my recommendations bearing fruit,' adding that the Manchester Column incident was 'at the bottom of my troubles'.[10] The fact that Leslie was now communicating directly with the acting civil commissioner speaks volumes for the acrimony between himself and Haldane, since Wilson's own relations with the commander-in-chief had long since deteriorated to the point where they were now barely on speaking terms. In his letter to Wilson of the 17th Leslie poured out his own bitter feelings about the way Haldane's strategy had effectively condemned some of Wilson's men to a lonely and isolated death:

> Much worse, I think than the Manchester Column was the abandonment to their fate of Ba'quba [Shahraban] and its officials by a force of British cavalry, guns and infantry with station under a mile away, because it was considered essential to save Baghdad from capture. This took place on the 12th of August. I heard of it only on the 2nd September.[11]

Indeed, Haldane was now deliberately leaving Leslie 'out of the loop' of military communications, dealing over his head directly with brigade commanders like Coningham; and commenting on Haldane's failure to inform him immediately of the Shahraban incident and other matters, Leslie tells Wilson, 'It is curious that I, who would have to carry on for the GOC-in-chief if anything happened to him, should have been left in such complete ignorance,' before thanking him for information on 'important military happenings' of which he had been kept in the dark. And he ends the letter by telling Wilson, 'I am very sorry indeed that you are going,' it now having been confirmed that Sir Percy Cox would be returning to Iraq to replace Wilson on 4 October with the new title of 'high commissioner'.

By 1 October all was ready and the Samawa relief column – christened SAMCOL according to the practice of the day – marched up the Euphrates to Ur, where it was joined by one and a half companies of the 114th Mahrattas. In addition to the troops, the column was accompanied by two supply trains each carrying 30,000 gallons of water and all the other necessary provisions, an armoured train with a 12-pounder gun, machine guns and a searchlight, and a blockhouse train with materials sufficient for the construction of ten blockhouses to defend the lines of communication. In this southern region of Iraq the heat was still very oppressive and the march to Ur was particularly trying for the 574 officers and men of the King's Own Yorkshire Light Infantry, who were the only British soldiers in the column, except for the gunners. Although, as usual, 'water discipline' was the rule, the officers and NCOs of the light infantry battalion had great difficulty in enforcing it.[12]

By 6 October the column, commanded by Brigadier Coningham, had reached Khidhr, where a strong body of insurgents was attacked and driven off by the Gurkhas and Sikhs. On 8 October the column reached a point near to the river bank where the *Greenfly* had been destroyed. As yet there was no suspicion of the events which were later discovered to have taken place, although a friendly sheikh offered the information that the British had been murdered while the Indians had been taken prisoner. In reprisal, as they advanced, all the Arab villages the column encountered were burned. By 12 October the column was just four and a half miles short of Samawa.

The insurgents' commander, Sayyid Hadi al-Mgutar, had no choice but to try to block Coningham's advance. He gathered around 7,000 tribesmen, of which about 3,000 were armed with modern rifles, and deployed them in a position straddling the railway line, stretching through palm groves and walled enclosures. It was a strong position but at 8.00 a.m. on 13 October, Coningham launched an all-out attack supported by four aircraft which bombed and machine-gunned the defenders. By 1.30 p.m. the British troops nearest the river reported that large numbers of insurgents were still holding out and blocking their advance. Since the troops were now some miles ahead of the railway supply trains, which were held up, rebuilding the railway line, Coningham called a halt to the attack. However, the following morning it was discovered that the rebel army had abandoned its positions both in front of and surrounding Samawa. By noon the British were in possession of the town, whose entire population had fled except for twenty-five Arabs and the same number of Jews.

Although as yet it was by no means clear to either side, the relief of Samawa was the turning point in the insurrection. Although the fighting would drag on for another three and a half months, it was the beginning of the end. As both sides anticipated, the failure of the rebels to capture the British position at Samawa convinced the Muntafiq tribes that they should remain on the sidelines of the struggle and, as many of the insurgents themselves reluctantly recognised, without the Muntafiq they stood little chance of victory.

Mid-October 1920 was also 'the beginning of the end' for Leslie's command of the 17th Division. Haldane, continuing to brood on the shambles which had led to the Manchester Column disaster, had finally decided to act. On 16 October Leslie received an 'official' communication from GHQ objecting to the statement in one of Leslie's dispatches to the effect that the Manchester Column had set out from Hilla 'with the approval of the C-in-C'. It was stated in the GHQ 'official' that the C-in-C 'knew nothing about the move until it was made'. In response, a furious Leslie informed Brigadier Stewart, Haldane's chief of the general staff, that 'unless his "official" was cancelled I would reply to it officially'.[13]

Stewart promptly telegrammed Leslie cancelling the 'official'. But Haldane had no intention of backing down: a few days later he relieved Leslie of his command, informing the War Office that he had 'lost confidence in Major General Leslie'.[14]

Defeat

At the end of August 1920 Haldane had been facing around 131,000 armed insurgents, of whom nearly half had rifles of one sort or another.[1] Churchill's telegram of 26 August, promising to provide him with every battalion that could be mustered to crush the rebellion, had therefore been of great relief to the general and his reply, two days later, expressed his 'deep gratitude'. 'You can depend on me to my utmost,' he assured the war minister.

However, there was one statement in Churchill's telegram which caused him some unease. It seems he was being asked to couple his military campaign with 'the policy of setting up an Arab Government'. Haldane was vaguely aware that the politicos had a plan to install some kind of puppet Arab regime after the insurrection had been put down; indeed, even Wilson had now apparently accommodated himself to that idea; but the suggestion that he, the GOC-in-chief, should be somehow involved in that process was not one he welcomed – especially since he had already heard that Wilson's replacement, Sir Percy Cox, had ideas about conciliating the insurgents as part of a broad, political settlement. Consequently, the gratitude which Haldane expressed to Churchill in his own telegram of 30 August was coupled with a forthright statement about how Haldane saw his duty.

From recent extracts of Times in Reuters it appears that Sir P. Cox is coming out here as High Commissioner in supreme control of the administration, with intention of securing peace by negotiation. I am convinced that the rising is anarchical and religious though initiated on

political basis, and peace can come only by the sword. The coexistence
of a High Commissioner on these lines and a G.O.C.-in-Chief trying to
carry out wishes of the Cabinet as expressed by you is quite incompatible.
I request that my position may be clearly defined.[2]

Churchill was on holiday in France at the time and Haldane, receiving
no reply, decided that although he would behave towards Sir Percy with
as much civility as he could summon, he would continue to pursue the
campaign against the insurgents as he had always intended.

By now the only British stronghold seriously threatened by the rebels
was Kufa, seven miles north-east of Najaf, which had been under siege
since 21 July. The last time the British had begun an advance south in the
direction of Kufa it had ended in the Manchester Column disaster; this
time Haldane would make sure there would be no mistakes.

Two brigade-strength columns were assembled at Hilla. The 53rd
Brigade column, under Brigadier General G. A. F. Sanders, was composed
of two British infantry battalions – 1st Battalion the Rifle Brigade and
2nd Battalion the East Yorks Regiment – and three Indian battalions;
in addition, the column had three artillery batteries and an escort of
the 5th Cavalry, and a company of sappers and miners completed the
column's strength. The 55th Brigade column, under Brigadier General
H. A. Walker, was somewhat larger. It consisted of two British infantry
battalions – the 2nd Manchesters (now replenished with new recruits)
and the 2nd Royal Irish Rifles – and six Indian battalions, including one
of pioneers. In addition there were three field artillery batteries, one
pack artillery battery, cavalry squadrons from the Scinde Horse and the
37th Lancers and two companies of sappers and miners.

In addition to the ascendancy conferred by this formidable assembly
of military might, this second advance south from Hilla into enemy
territory enjoyed another advantage over the ill-fated Manchester
Column: the climate – although still hot during the daytime – was now
considerably cooler than suffered by the Manchesters, and at night it
was becoming positively chilly.

In fact, the objective of the operation was not just to relieve Kufa
but also to isolate and subdue Karbela', and with this in mind the 53rd

Brigade column was ordered to do a detour towards Tuwairij – strategically, the 'gateway' to Karbela' – while the 55th Brigade column headed directly south towards Kufa. Moreover, along their respective routes the columns were also charged with the task of 'punishing' all the Arab villages through which they passed.

On 7 October, infantry and artillery from the 55th Brigade fought a major action along the Hindiyya south of Hilla, defeating a force of around 3,500 insurgents after which a line of blockhouses was swiftly constructed to protect the communications of the planned advance. By 11 October Haldane considered it safe to launch his main offensive. The 55th Brigade continued south, burning villages of the al-Fatla tribe on their way, and by 13 October had reached the scene of the Manchester Column's camp on the Rustumiyya canal without incident, although according to the commander of the Scinde Horse, 'The mournful relics of the disaster strewed the whole route.'[3] The following day the column reached and captured Kifl, the railway station whose seizure by the Arabs back in late July had been the principal cause of the ill-fated Manchester Column operation.

Meanwhile, the 53rd Brigade pushed on against strong opposition towards Tuwairij, constructing blockhouses as they advanced. The road to Tuwairij was currently defended by men of the Bani Hasan while Tuwairij itself was held by the al-Fatla commanded by Sheikh 'Abd al-Wahid al-Sikar, one of the earliest adherents to the uprising. According to Muhsin Abu Tabikh, at this point the sheikhs of the Bani Hasan treacherously withdrew their men in the night, having been bribed to do so by the British.[4] Whether or not there is any truth in this account – and it seems equally possible that the Bani Hasan tribesmen simply became demoralised and fled – the full weight of the British attack now fell on the al-Fatla, whose bravery was insufficient to withstand bombardment by both artillery and aircraft. On 12 October the insurgents were prevented from burning the bridge of boats over the Hindiyya as they retreated and the subsequent capture of Tuwairij on the right bank of the Hindiyya effectively sealed the fate of the neighbouring city of Karbela'.

On 14 October the revolutionary government in the city was ordered to make its submission and its leaders to present themselves at the British lines, from where they would be taken to Baghdad in captivity. They were given forty-eight hours' grace to do so, otherwise the canal supplying the city with water would be cut off. Among the individuals specifically singled out for arrest were the mutasarrif, Muhsin Abu Tabikh, along with the Baghdad nationalists Ja'far Abu al-Timman, Yusuf Suwaydi and 'Ali Bazirgan, who were believed to be in the city.[5] Ten other prominent citizens duly surrendered, but with the fall of Tuwairij, Abu al-Timman, Suwaydi and Bazirgan had already decided to leave Karbela' and head south to Najaf. As for Abu Tabikh, by now, he too had retreated south with a force composed mainly of Ka'ab and Zayd tribesmen, hoping to unite with the insurgent forces still besieging Kufa.[6]

At Kufa the garrison was perilously close to exhausting its food and ammunition. However, by 17 October, the advanced units of the 55th Brigade column reached the northern outskirts of the town which the insurgents were holding in strength. A wide cavalry flanking movement was then ordered by the column commander in which the Scinde Horse turned the enemy line, forcing the insurgents to flee along the old horse tramway leading to Najaf, and sabring and lancing the retreating rebels as they fled; by 9.30 a.m. Kufa was finally relieved.[7] For the last three weeks of the siege the garrison had survived on rice and horse meat, although casualties during the ninety-day siege had been relatively light – only twenty-five killed (including the PO, Captain Mann) and twenty-seven wounded.

Meanwhile, with the fall of Kufa, Abu Tabikh and his remaining forces had no choice but to continue to flee south. In his memoirs the mutasarrif of the insurgents recalls:

> I gave the order to withdraw under cover of darkness and at the break of day I divided all the men into small groups to avoid the attacks of the aircraft. I myself then headed for Abu Sukhair to join up with those remaining leaders who had sworn oaths of allegiance upon our Sayyid Husayn and our Sayyid 'Abbas (peace be upon them) before the outbreak of the revolt ...[8]

But these 'remaining leaders' no longer included the sheikh of the al-Fatla, 'Abd al-Wahid Sikar. By now, he had decided that the cause to which he had originally committed himself and his tribe was lost, and he 'came in' – as the British liked to put it – sometime around this time.[9]

The Baghdad nationalists had also headed south, hoping that the front could be stabilised around Kufa. Having acquired mules from an uncle of Ja'far Abu al-Timman who traded between Karbela' and Najaf, Abu al-Timman and his fellow Istiqlal leaders left Karbela' by night, heading for Najaf.[10] However, as they journeyed south they learned of the insurgents' defeat around Kufa; clearly, Najaf itself was no longer safe and, like Abu Tabikh, they now fled to Abu Sukhair – only to find that that town was also under fierce attack by British aircraft.

Nevertheless the Baghdad nationalists were correct in their decision to leave Najaf. In the same way that the capture of Tuwairij made the position of Karbela' untenable, so the capture of Kufa determined the fate of Najaf. Indeed, the editor of the Najaf newspaper *Istiqlal* had already acknowledged the deteriorating military situation facing the city and the insurrection as a whole. On 6 October he described the brutal onslaught of the British who had 'attacked the houses of the sheikhs, burned them and their contents. They killed many men, horses and livestock ... the officers had no other interest but in exterminating us.' When the rebels agreed to a truce the British had violated it, and on these occassions, when they allowed the British to withdraw from liberated territory they had treacherously returned to attack them. 'In recent days there has been bloodshed and the destruction of populous towns; places of worship have been violated enough to make humanity weep.'[11]

So on 18 October, representatives of Najaf's revolutionary government arrived at the headquarters of the 55th Brigade column to offer its surrender. They were informed that the first condition would be the handing over of the British and Indians who had been incarcerated there. The following day, seventy-nine British and eighty-nine Indian prisoners were released.

All things considered, the prisoners had been well treated.[12] Those of the Manchester Column had initially been stripped of all their clothes except their shorts and forced to walk to Najaf; on the way they had received considerable abuse from Arab villagers and ominous hand-signs that they would soon have their throats cut. But after some miles they were allowed to rest and given food – boiled rice and tomatoes, which the British had found difficulty in eating. On arriving at Najaf they had been given clothes, housed in reasonable conditions and fed regularly – mainly Arabic flatbread (which the British called 'chapatis') and tea. They had even been given cigarettes. In spite of this, Haldane would later claim that British troops who fell into Arab hands were routinely tortured – a claim which no less an enemy of the insurgents, Arnold Wilson, would later strenuously deny.[13]

For the time being Haldane took no further action against Najaf. At this point in the campaign he apparently thought it unnecessary – or perhaps impractical – to actually enter and occupy the great walled city. This, in turn, seems to have led many among the population of not only Najaf but also Karbela' to believe that it was still possible that the military situation might turn again in their favour. So when Haldane once more focused his attention on the two cities three weeks later, demanding onerous fines of both rifles and cash, they refused. Consequently, Haldane resorted to tougher measures.

For Karbela' the supply of water was cut off while British troops made a very visible demonstration of ravaging the countryside around the city. This had the desired effect and on 8 November the fines were duly paid. Najaf proved a tougher nut to crack, and it was decided to repeat the tactics adopted against the city in 1918. At 10.00 a.m. on 16 November, five British and Indian battalions were drawn up in full battle equipment facing the walled city from the east. Alongside them were ranged three batteries of field artillery while ten aircraft circled over the town. It was made clear to the inhabitants that unless they handed over the rifles and cash which had been demanded they would be subjected to a full-scale bombardment and attack.

Shortly afterwards, a troop of cavalry from the 37th Lancers forced its way into the city and formed up against the serai in which the remaining heads of the revolutionary government were closeted, and the British demands were once more read out to them. Later that day the Najafis agreed to pay the fines and the remainder of the British troops then entered the city and marched through it in a show of force.[14] But there were insufficient troops available to occupy the town permanently, and some weeks later the Najafis had still only handed over one-third of the number of rifles demanded. Given the continuing armed resistance and guerrilla warfare in other parts of the country, for the time being Haldane was in no position to push his demands on Najaf any further.

A Death on the Baghdad Road

A little after dawn on 24 October 1920 a convoy of motor vehicles was setting off from Mosul, heading for Baghdad. There had been little fighting in the area since the insurrection began, partly because, after the abortive Arab raid on Tel 'Afar, the British had made sure they retained a strong grip on the city. But it was also because many of the leading citizens remained loyal to the Turks and had come to believe that the legality of Britain's control of the whole vilayet of Mosul was under question and therefore there was little point in fighting: Mustafa Kemal had let it be known that he considered Mosul to be Turkish territory and would use a combination of military threats and diplomatic activity to try to reintegrate the province into his independent Anatolian bastion on Mosul's northern borders. In short, the idea of Mosul becoming part of an Iraqi 'Arab State' – whether British-controlled or independent – now appeared uncertain.

The convoy of motor vehicles contained mainly civilians – merchants, minor officials of the occupation and others simply making family visits to Baghdad: there was only a small guard of Arab police. But unbeknown to the travellers, the convoy was being shadowed by a strong band of raiders belonging to the Albu Badr section of the Albu Hamad[1] – a tribe which had fled across the ill-defined Turkish border after the unsuccessful raid on Tel 'Afar. Their headman was Agha Bulaybil, a man with strongly Negroid features whose appearance clearly denoted descent from one of the black female slaves of some Albu Hamad forebear. During the war he had been an officer in the

Hamadiyya, the notorious Ottoman militia cavalry: a fierce and brutal fighter, but also 'a man of brains, character and wit' according to Gertrude Bell's intelligence sources.[2]

As the convoy from Mosul continued its noisy advance, Bulaybil positioned his well-armed horsemen on some stony bluffs near Wadi Jahannam, roughly midway between Mosul and the town of Sharqat. There the raiders dismounted and awaited the approaching motor vehicles. Then, as the convoy came into view, the Albu Hamad opened up a deadly fire on the leading car, bringing the whole convoy to an abrupt halt. Most of the occupants leapt out of their vehicles, trying to seek shelter at the side of the road, but one car attempted to escape. It swerved off the road and raced across a patch of stony ground, apparently trying to rejoin the road further away, where there was some cover from the tribesmen's rifle fire. But a group of Albu Hamad remounted and pursued the escaping car, continuing to fire on it from the saddle and aiming at its tyres. Suddenly the vehicle swerved violently and then tipped over in a great cloud of dust. Immediately the tribesmen were upon it, firing round after round from their Mauser rifles through the smashed windows of the stricken vehicle.

While the remaining survivors of the convoy were surrendering, handing over their goods and valuables, Bulaybil rode ahead to examine the contents of the foolhardy vehicle which had tried to escape. Inside he found the bodies of two men. One was apparently just an Arab driver, but the other appeared to be someone of greater importance – and maybe of greater wealth. Although this individual was wearing the Arab kufiyya, the remainder of his dress was European. Bulaybil removed the man's wallet and extracted a disappointingly small wad of rupees. Then he noticed a tattered identity card of sorts. Curious, he gave it a closer look. Although barely literate, Agha Bulaybil was able to recognise it as some kind of military document. At any rate, the photograph clearly showed the dead man in a military uniform, albeit with the same kind of kufiyya headdress which now lay, bloodstained, beside him. And then he just managed to decipher the name underneath the photograph: 'Mulazim Awwal Muhammad Sharif al-Faruqi'.[3]

An hour or so later, having thoroughly looted the remains of the convoy, the Albu Hamad remounted and sped off to their sanctuary on the Turkish border, leaving the corpses of Faruqi and a few other casualties of the attack to be discovered sometime later by a British cavalry patrol.

It seems that, after his short stay in Cairo sometime in mid-1920, Lieutenant Faruqi managed to return to Mosul, the city of his birth. It is difficult to know how he might have been received by his extended family in Mosul. After all, he had deserted from the Ottoman army – hardly honourable behaviour in a city which had largely remained loyal to the Turks throughout the war – and, in the end, he had little to show for it in either money or status. His reception was probably polite but frosty.

And then, suddenly, a new and exciting opportunity materialised. It was reported that Ja'far al-'Askari, a fellow member of al-'Ahd and, coincidentally, the officer who had trained Faruqi in marksmanship before the outbreak of war, had recently returned to Baghdad, apparently in the expectation of playing an important role in a new provisional Arab government which the British were trying to set up. Indeed, on the very day that Faruqi was killed, Ja'far al-'Askari's recent return to Iraq was being recounted to her father by Gertrude Bell:

> Saturday began with a notable visit from Ja'far Pasha. He is a Major General of distinguished service first with the Turks and then with Faisal ... He came to me hot foot from seeing Sir Percy in order to ask me – what do you think? whether it would ruin his reputation as a Nationalist to take a place in the provisional government! on the ground that it would be looked upon as a British subterfuge ... I told him it was his duty as an individual and a Nationalist to assist in establishing Arab institutions in whatever form and that if he and others went boldly forward, relying on our support, they would silence criticism.[4]

In the event, it seems Ja'far al-'Askari needed little further persuasion. As for Faruqi, stuck in an unwelcoming Mosul, without employment, status or money, and after all those unrewarding years trying to find an outlet for his talents, the news that his old commanding officer and colleague in al-'Ahd had returned to Iraq with such outstanding prospects must have seemed an answer to all Faruqi's prayers. He would not only seek out al-'Askari and remind him of their old association but he would also present himself to those who were really running the country. And so he had set off for Baghdad on that chilly autumn morning, full of hope and expectation that, at last, his services to the British would be finally recognised and those largely unrewarding years of wasted wandering now lay behind him.

The Punishment

With the capitulation of the holy cities the Baghdad nationalists and the majority of the rebel sheikhs realised that they had little option but to leave the country; moreover, the only safe haven seemed to be at the court of King Husayn in the Hejaz. In theory there were three possible escape routes to Husayn's capital: through Najd, the emirate of 'Abd al-'Aziz ibn Sa'ud; further north through the emirate of Ha'il, the citadel of 'Abd al-'Aziz's bitter enemy, the al-Rashid; or through French-occupied Syria. Najd was really too risky: there was a strong possibility that they might be captured and the Shi'is among them killed by Wahhabi tribesmen (only a year later, Wahhabi raiders would launch a major attack on Karbela' and the surrounding area). In the event, Sayyid Muhammad al-Sadr, Yusuf Suwaydi and 'Ali Bazirgan chose the route through Syria – as yet the French authorities hadn't completed the full occupation of the country and the borderlands remained relatively free and fluid.[1] Meanwhile, Ja'far Abu al-Timman and some of the leading rebel Sheikhs including Sayyid 'Alwan al-Yasari and Sayyid Hadi al-Mgutar decided to risk the desert crossing to Ha'il, from where they eventually arrived at Medina on 6 March 1921.

Bound by Arab laws of hospitality, King Husayn gave the refugee nationalists sanctuary but the wily old monarch cannot have been too pleased by the arrival of his guests. Although the huge subsidies he had received from the British during the war had now ended, he was still trying to persuade his former paymasters to support his efforts to become caliph with some kind of temporal authority over the remainder of the Arab world and harbouring rebel fugitives from British-occupied Iraq can hardly have been calculated to assist him in that objective. For the time being, however, Abu Timman and his comrades were safe.

Meanwhile, with Abu Sukhair in flames and Abu Tabikh's property in the town destroyed, he and his small band of followers decided to separate and head for their homes. Although Abu Tabikh had a house and warehouses in Abu Sukhair his home village was Ghamas, and it was there that he now sought refuge.

> I set off towards Ghamas with some of my men, taking a route which at times took us through palm gardens and at other times made us plunge into waterways, arriving at Ghamas a little before dawn and avoiding entering the village by the main road because of our fear that the eyes of the British might be upon us. I went further south and then to the palm gardens and from there to my house where my brother Ja'far and my son Kamil took me in, shattered as I was by thirst and exhaustion. I told my brother and son about our situation and that the revolutionaries were scattered and the rebellion had collapsed and I warned them that my open presence among them could put us all into danger of British reprisals since I was a wanted man ...[2]

In the event, Abu Tabikh hid in Ghamas in his son's rice-processing factory, for a while contemplating fleeing to Persia, but in the end he, too, decided to escape to King Husayn's realm in the Hejaz. Abu Tabikh also decided to travel via the Emirate of Ha'il where he arrived with his family and some of his men on 1 January 1921.

Their reception by the current young ruler of the al-Rashid dynasty, 'Abdallah, was far from the generous Arab hospitality they might have expected. It wasn't long before the emir started demanding 'presents' from them and by the fortieth day of their residence at Ha'il, the situation had deteriorated to such an extent that Abu Tabikh decided that they would leave for Mecca and Medina as soon as possible. So on 10 March 1921 they left Ha'il and set off for the Hejaz, reaching Medina on 6 April 1921.

In a number of the brief British accounts of the Arab insurrection of 1920, it is stated that the rebellion ended with the submission of the holy cities in mid-October.[3] This is not correct. Although some tribes submitted, many did not and the fighting – which had previously been characterised by quite large-scale actions of a semi-regular nature – now turned into what Major General Leslie was already describing – in early October – as 'guerrilla warfare'. It would continue until February 1921.

Meanwhile, the arrival of Sir Percy Cox in Baghdad as 'high commissioner' on 11 October, with an official remit to establish what was euphemistically called an 'Arab Government', had been welcomed by Gertrude Bell with gushing enthusiasm. Writing to her father on 17 October she tells him, 'When it comes to the difficult point of dealing with the tribal insurgents on the Euphrates, he will drop all the silly ideas of revenge and punishment which have been current outside my political circle and be guided only by consideration for the future peace of the country under an Arab Govt.'[4]

However, by the end of November Bell had subtly changed her views on this matter. The continuing resistance of many of the insurgents had now convinced her (and Sir Percy Cox) that 'silly ideas of revenge and punishment' would only be dropped once the insurrection had finally been crushed by force. With passing references to their plans for the formation of a puppet Arab government, on 29 November she informs her father:

> We are greatly hampered by the tribal rising which has delayed the work of handing over to the Arab Govt. Sir Percy, I think rightly, decided that the tribes must be made to submit to force. In no other way was it possible to make them surrender their arms or teach them that you mustn't lightly engage in revolution, even when your holy men tell you to do so.

So, in spite of his earlier reservations, Haldane must now have realised that his anxieties that Cox might attempt to make a generous peace with the insurgents were unfounded. The task was now one of 'punishment':

the end of the uprising would indeed, be 'only by the sword'. For an elderly general of the British Empire in 1920 – one who regarded his opponents in Iraq as 'savages' or 'semi-savages' – there would be no feeble concessions to humanity. In Haldane's words, written after his return to England, 'There could be no security for the future peace of Mesopotamia unless the punishment awarded were such as would discourage a repetition of this foolish outbreak.'[5] And a few pages later he adds, 'it should be remembered that we were amongst a people of whom it might be said with truth ...Use 'em kindly, they rebel; / But be rough as nutmeg-graters / And the rogues obey you well.' In short, 'the time for mercy had not yet come and the pound of flesh must be exacted.'[6]

Early in the campaign Haldane had issued a proclamation stating that rebels who were captured in the course of any fighting were to be treated as prisoners of war; however, a different fate would await any rebels who behaved 'treacherously'. Problematically, Haldane had come to his own conclusion in that respect:

> The Arab is most treacherous. He will overpower a small detachment and when a larger force appears he will out up white flags and be found working peacefully in his fields – incidentally with a rifle in easy reach ... [therefore] the white flags and peaceful cultivator's role must not prevent the enemy from being punished later at our convenience.[7]

The implications of this judgement were clear: (1) the assumption that an Arab who was 'working peacefully in his fields' was necessarily a non-combatant should be disregarded and (2) since 'the Arab' was *intrinsically* 'most treacherous', the stipulation that captured Arab combatants should be treated as prisoners of war would apply only in very exceptional circumstances – if at all. In short, it was an open invitation to carry out what Colonel Leachman had advocated before his death – a 'general slaughter' of the Arabs in the insurgent areas.

In practice, the extent and degree of the 'punishment' meted out to the insurgents depended on certain circumstances. In those areas where the tribes refused to submit and carried on fighting the policy would be simply one of 'general slaughter' – although it seems that women and children were not to be *deliberately* included in this policy. In areas where the tribes had formally submitted, they were to be compelled to surrender all their rifles – the quantity required being assessed by the British and frequently at an amount which exceeded the number of rifles actually in the tribesmen's possession; the 'deficit' would then be demanded in the form of cash payments. If the tribe in question refused to surrender their rifles or persisted in handing over only a quantity smaller than the specified number – or old unserviceable weapons – then, after due warning, their village would be burned to the ground, their livestock killed or confiscated and, should there be any sign of resistance – the 'general slaughter' policy would come into play.

In fact there was nothing particularly novel about this manner of dealing with recalcitrant Arab villagers. It dated back to the beginning of the Mesopotamian campaign in 1914. However, for obvious reasons, not mentioned in official military records, the brutality meted out to the despised 'Budoos' was sometimes recorded by individual soldiers who had few reservations about informing their families and friends about what happened.

For example, shortly after the capture of Basra in 1914, a British infantry private related how the army dealt with suspected 'unfriendly' Arab villages. First, the village in question would be surrounded by a strong cordon of troops during the night. Then, at dawn, the troops would storm into the village with fixed bayonets, breaking down doors and searching for weapons. 'Those who attempt to run away are caught by our ring of men outside the village. These are treated as combatants and meet their end on the scaffold.' Similarly, any of the inhabitants who actually put up armed resistance 'are hanged in the market square'.[8] As for minor offences, such as stealing army property, flogging was the usual procedure, one which an Indian Army medical officer described as 'a most pleasant sight'.[9]

Haldane's own account of the manner in which 'the punishment' was carried out in 1920 largely restricts itself to the burning of villages, for which he provides a detailed prescription including the cautionary advice that 'burning a village takes a long time, an hour or more according to the size from the time the burning parties enter'.[10] However, we can get a fairly good idea of the more general *modus operandi* of 'punishment' from Major General Leslie's letters to his wife both before and after the capitulation of the holy cities. On 20 August he writes:

> The column on the railway has been attacking and burning every village within reach ... Walker's column is slowly working its way back here ravaging the country on his way ... Three men with rifles taken. Rifles belonged to headman. Today I had all four tried by a military court and tomorrow they die.

And on 10 October,

> Building blockhouses ... to keep the lines of communication open and unharassed, but the rate of advance is delayed ... so that the column will not actually advance more than four or five miles a day, but they will utilise their leisure time in destroying villages within a couple of miles or so on each side, killing Budoos and generally enjoying themselves.

And on 19 October,

> Killing Budoos and burning villages seven miles to the west and five miles northwest of Hilla ... there was very little opposition ... Meanwhile General Sanders has continued punitive methods from Tuwairij and has laid bare the country almost up to Karbela' ... He has done splendidly.[11]

For the insurgent regions outside the mid-Euphrates we have less verbatim evidence, but we learn from the laconic report of the commander of the Scinde Horse that in a punishment meted out to a certain Arab village on the Diyala, the 45th Sikhs 'bayoneted a few Arabs, but otherwise not much damage was done'.[12] No information is provided as to whether the Arabs bayoneted were putting up any form of resistance, but the contextual information suggests not. Meanwhile, near Falluja, special treatment appears to have been reserved for the Zauba' tribesmen, whose sheikh's son had killed Colonel Leachman. According to Leachman's colleague

Harry Philby, they suffered 'a terrible vengeance exacted by Leachman's fellow soldiers'.[13] Whether this 'terrible vengeance' was more terrible than that inflicted in other rebel villages, and in what manner it was enacted, we cannot tell, but clearly Philby thought it was worthy of mention.

Even if, for a moment, we allow for the fact that in some cases the inhabitants of recalcitrant Arab villages escaped – or were actually allowed to escape – before their dwellings and sources of livelihood were burned to the ground, it is worth considering the impact the 'laying waste' of villages and crops would have had upon the women, children and old people. Autumn was already upon them and cold, wet winter was approaching. Hiding out in the marshes, without shelter or food (and, of course, without even the semblance of medical care), their plight must have been terrible. The casualty figures which the British attributed to the Arab participants in the uprising – around 8,000 – related only to the combatants; but thousands more non-combatants must have perished from this particular counter-insurgency strategy alone. However, Haldane's 'nutmeg-grater' methods – methods which one Iraqi historian has aptly described as 'The English Terror'[14] – involved a lot more than just that.

As we have already seen, the indiscriminate bombing of Arab villages which resisted the various impositions of British rule was already a feature of the Civil Administration's policy even before the uprising (and was one of its causes). However, in the months following the defeat of the insurgent's main forces and the submission of the holy cities, the policy really came into its own, especially since liaison between aircraft and ground forces had now much improved, as Squadron Leader Gordon Pirie described in a staff college lecture at Hendon in 1925:

> At Diwaniyya a halt for a week was made to carry out punitive expeditions in the Daghara and Afej regions. These were spectacular operations. The column would leave Diwaniyya at about 0200 hours. Aeroplanes leaving the base so that they would arrive over the column when its outposts were a quarter of a mile from the village to be attacked, would swoop down on it, drop 30 or 25lb bombs and pour hundreds of rounds of small arms

ammunition into it. Panic-stricken, the inhabitants fled and in a minute the column would enter the village without a shot being fired. The usual procedure then was to drive towards Diwaniyya all the flocks and herds, setting fire to all that was left. This had a most salutary effect on the tribes north of Diwaniyya.[15]

Such 'spectacular' operations, often carried out at night, had the advantage of catching rebel Arabs who had returned home after sniping at British troops during the day. But this also inevitably meant there would be heavy casualties among the sleeping women and children. Indeed, it seems clear that some RAF officers regarded the latter as acceptable targets. For example, in his first operational report after taking command of the RAF in Iraq in February 1921, Air Commodore A. E. 'Biffy' Borton, recorded how, 'The eight machines (at Nasiriyya) broke formation and attacked at different points of the encampment simultaneously, causing a stampede among the animals. The tribesmen and their families were put to confusion, many of whom ran into the lake making good targets for the machine guns.'[16]

Even Churchill's randomly oscillating moral compass could not accommodate such behaviour, and he wrote to Borton's superior, the chief of the air staff, Hugh Trenchard, that he was 'extremely shocked' by this particular report. 'To fire wilfully at women and children is a disgraceful act,' Churchill declared, and he expressed surprise that Trenchard hadn't ordered the officers concerned to be court-martialled.[17] Yet the casual manner in which Borton had reported the incident suggests that events like this were all too common. For Borton – and no doubt for most of his officers and men – this sort of thing was merely routine: 'a vivid, if rather ferocious glimpse of the type of warfare we have to wage', as he commented in a marginal note to his official report.[18]

A 'friendly native state'

Having recently destroyed a genuine Arab government on the Euphrates, and while continuing to hunt down and destroy its remaining supporters, the British plan to establish their own provisional Arab government in Baghdad went ahead with the official announcement of the creation of a 'Council of State' on 11 November 1920. This puppet institution was headed by the venerable and conservative Sunni notable, 'Abd al-Rahman al-Gaylani, the Naqib (head of all the Sunni ashraf) of Baghdad, who had remained loyal to the British since 1917; and, cajoled by Sir Percy Cox and Gertrude Bell, Ja'far al-'Askari accepted the position of defence minister. Each Arab member of the provisional government had his British 'minder'. For example Ja'far al-'Askari was 'advised' by Major J. I. Eadie DSO; the minister of justice, Mustafa Effendi Alusi, was 'advised' by Sir Edgar Bonham Carter; and Sayyid Talib, the minister of the interior, was 'advised' by Harry Philby, recently recalled from a diplomatic mission in Najd.[1]

Meanwhile, around 600 former Ottoman army officers in Syria (the vast majority being Sunni) who had played no part in the uprising were allowed to return to Iraq. They included Ja'far al-'Askari's brother-in-law, Nuri al-Sa'id, who, as early as August 1920, had written to the British announcing his willingness to fight with them against the insurgents.[2] In February 1921 the British appointed the newly promoted General Nuri al-Sa'id, 'chief of staff' of the newly formed puppet Iraqi army. In the same month Sir Percy Cox announced a general amnesty for those who had taken part in the uprising, with the exception of those who had been directly implicated in the killing of British officers in circumstances which could be construed as 'treacherous' – most notably that of Colonel Leachman.

The British knew that the 'Council of State' could only be a stop-gap measure until some more permanent solution was found to the enduring problem of how to hang on to Iraq without expending huge amounts of British taxpayers' money at a time of extreme financial stringency. In the end the solution to this problem would be both military and political. On the political front there was an increasing sentiment that something a bit more 'nationalist-looking' than the Council of State was required to gain a sufficient degree of acquiescence among the populace towards de facto British control. There would have to be an 'Arab Emir' in Iraq after all, and Emir Faysal was now being widely touted as the most suitable candidate – a 'consolation prize' on the part of the British for their acquiescence in the French overthrow of his Syrian kingdom.

As regards the military side of things, Trenchard, the chief of the air staff, had by now convinced Churchill that controlling Iraq should be turned over to the RAF – a far more economic way of ensuring the survival of Britain's new 'friendly native state' than the traditional method of large infantry garrisons. Eight squadrons of aircraft supported by six armoured-car companies should be able to do the job, Trenchard and Churchill believed. In future, all that would be required to subdue troublesome tribes, like those on the Euphrates, would be the sudden appearance of a few fighter-bombers over their villages for them to capitulate to the demands of the central government. After all, as squadron leader Arthur (later 'Bomber') Harris explained a couple of years later,

> The Arab and Kurd ... now know what real bombing means, in casualties and damage; they know that within 45 minutes a full sized village ... can be wiped out and a third of its inhabitants killed or injured by four or five machines which offer them no real target, no opportunity for glory as warriors, no effective means of escape.[3]

Subsequently, on 12 March 1921, forty British delegates were brought together in Cairo to settle the affairs of Iraq once and for all. Although many of those attending were technical and advisory personnel of lower rank, the conference was illuminated by the presence of almost all the dignitaries who had, so far, had an interest in Iraq's affairs including Churchill, Cox, Bell, Lawrence, Haldane, Trenchard, Ja'far al-'Askari and Wilson (in a new role as recently appointed managing director of the Anglo-Persian Oil Company). As expected, the decision was taken to anoint Faysal King of Iraq and the holding of a suitably designed 'referendum' on this fait accompli was agreed. Nobody appears to have recommended Emir 'Abdallah for the job, who was currently occupying the town of Ma'an (on the border between present-day Jordan and southern Syria) with a small contingent of armed supporters, making bombastic threats against the French.

The referendum on Faysal's candidature for King of Iraq was duly held, with, unsurprisingly, a majority of 96 per cent in support of the proposal and on 23 August 1921 he was proclaimed monarch. In October the following year 'Abd al-Rahman al-Gaylani, on behalf of King Faysal and the puppet Iraqi government, signed a treaty with Great Britain whose terms were intended to last for twenty years and which, inter alia, gave Britain the right to station troops in Iraq, to control Iraq's foreign policy, to appoint a 'high commissioner' and a many-tiered phalanx of British officials and police to 'advise' the Iraqi government, and to require Iraq to shoulder a heavy financial burden of repayments to Britain for the latter's current and prior expenditures in the country – but all this behind a façade of sovereignty and self-determination.[4] A 'friendly native state' had been successfully established in the ashes of the Ottoman Empire.

Afterword

If we were to ask the question, 'On whose side did the Arabs fight in the First World War?' most people who know something of the war's history would probably say 'Britain's'. Such a reply would reflect the orthodox account, emanating from the glorification of 'Lawrence of Arabia' and the 'Arab Revolt' of Sharif Husayn and his sons, an episode also burned into our imagination by David Lean's spectacular and immensely popular film on this subject. In both the film and Lawrence's original memoir – *The Seven Pillars of Wisdom* – we see an epic struggle in which 'the Arabs' join with the British in a fight to the death against the former's cruel Turkish overlords. In return, the British promise the Arabs 'freedom', for their contribution to winning the war in the Middle East, a promise which would never be redeemed. This 'orthodox narrative' is also exemplified by the writings of some Arab historians who interpreted the pro-British stance of the Hashemites as part of an 'Arab awakening' after centuries of Turkish domination.[1]

However, over the last two decades, this orthodox narrative has been questioned by a number of historians – not just the role claimed by Lawrence himself, but more fundamentally the assumption that Britain's opponents in the Middle East were almost entirely ethnic Turks, that the Arabs' experience of the Ottoman state was little more than a 'Turkish yoke', and from the outset they were only waiting for an opportunity to rebel against it.[2]

Enemy on the Euphrates has implicitly followed in this questioning of the orthodox account. In reality, the vast majority of Arabs did not 'fight for the British' in the First World War. In 1914 about one-third of the regular troops in the Ottoman army were Arabs, mainly from the towns and cities of the regions which subsequently became Iraq, Syria, Lebanon and Palestine. Numbering around 300,000, they were mainly conscripts (as were their fellow Turks) but, as we have seen, many fought bravely for the preservation of the Ottoman Empire and their religion on the battlefields of Suez, Gallipoli, Ctesiphon and many others. In addition, among the tribal Bedouin there were thousands of Arab volunteers who flocked to the Ottoman colours – not only in Iraq, but also among the Senussi tribesmen of Libya who fought the British across the Egyptian border between 1915 and 1917.

It is true that, as the First World War dragged on with one defeat for the Ottomans following another and Turkish officers responding to those defeats by ever more brutal methods of conscription, many Arab soldiers became demoralised and some deserted to the British.[3] Nevertheless, a study by a US military expert on the Ottoman army has shown that, even towards the end of the war, proportionately, Arab soldiers were no more likely to surrender or desert than ethnic Turks.[4]

It is also worth commenting briefly on the manner in which *Enemy on the Euphrates* has portrayed the role played by Sir Mark Sykes. Another feature of that 'orthodox narrative' referred to at the beginning of this chapter is that Sykes was a typical imperialist and the Sykes–Picot Agreement the epitome of Anglo-French betrayal. However, from our narrative Sykes emerges as a more complex character and the Sykes–Picot Agreement as a somewhat less significant instrument of imperialist double-dealing.

It seems that Sykes may have actually believed that his actions had the best interests of the Arabs at heart: that those 'conservative' and 'traditionalist' Arabs so prominent in his orientalist conceptualisation would be untroubled by a settlement which only offered them a modicum of national independence for the foreseeable future, although whether this was the result of Faruqi's devious intervention or was already part of Sykes's evolving thinking on the subject of 'friendly native states' is unclear. Certainly, his political alignment before his premature death in January 1919 was closer to those like Bell and Lawrence who thought of themselves as being 'enlightened' compared with men like Wilson and Leachman.

At the same time, it is clear that by the end of the war, the Sykes–Picot Agreement no longer had the relevance in Anglo-French plans for the future of the Middle East which it had in 1916. In fact, the ultimate outcome of the Allies' deliberations – the mandate system – was in some respects actually worse for the Arabs than Sykes–Picot, certainly in the case of Syria, which simply became an outright French colony, and Palestine, where the consequences of the Balfour Declaration would eventually have tragic consequences for both Palestinian Arabs and those tens of thousands of Jews who had led relatively secure lives in the old Ottoman Empire.

Indeed, the extent to which Sykes–Picot itself was an egregious 'betrayal' of the Arabs is questionable. This is not to side with those revisionist historians who deny that there was any betrayal at all on the grounds that Sharif Husayn appears to have already known something of its secret provisions before it was signed. The real betrayal of the Arabs was not the abrogation of the Sharif's expectations for a vast Arab empire, but that the Baghdad Declaration of 1917 and the Anglo-French Declaration of 1918 – which openly offered the Arabs 'the aspirations of their race' and 'complete liberation' – were later ruthlessly ignored by the political and military authorities in both Britain and France.

For the Arabs of Iraq, the Great War never really ended. Only ten months after the armistice, the British were already bombing Arab tribesmen and by July 1920 a full-scale revolutionary war against the British occupation had begun. Moreover, as we have seen, it was largely the same Arab tribes and tribal leaders – those of the mid-Euphrates region – who played a leading role in both the Jihad of 1914–15 and the revolution of 1920.

Until the 1970s, the relatively few historians who discussed the 1920 uprising tended to dismiss its importance and denigrate its participants.[5] Two themes had equal importance. The first is that the rebellion was largely the product of agitation and, indeed, direct intervention, by the 'Sharifian' former Ottoman army officers based in

Faysal's short-lived Syrian kingdom. For example, Elie Kedourie, writing in 1956, noted approvingly that Sir Percy Cox, 'knew that the tribal rising of the summer of 1920 had been instigated from the outside'.[6] Similarly, for John Marlowe, whose biography of A. T. Wilson was published in 1967, 'the Rebellion in Iraq was deliberately incited by agents of the Sharifian Government in Damascus.'[7] The same author stated that 'the suggestion ... that the rebellion was a spontaneous rising against British oppression is nonsense.' A similar stress on 'outside' agitation is found in Bell's report to Parliament in December 1920, where the emphasis is upon 'a league of conspiracy organised by the Bolsheviks in cooperation with Turkish nationalists'.[8]

A second and equally pervasive 'explanation' found in a number of official and semi-official accounts – including those of Iraq POs – is that the uprising was mainly 'tribal anarchy' and a pervasive desire to acquire 'loot'. For example, Bell's account of the rebellion also refers to 'anarchy gaining ground' and the tribes being 'out for loot' while the PO and historian of Iraq, Stephen Helmsley Longrigg, headed his list of causative factors with 'tribal recalcitrance, love of freedom and loot ...'.[9]

However, it should now be clear that these explanations are untenable. Not only were the military interventions of the sharifian officers restricted to the Syrian borderlands and had largely evaporated before the real revolution began in July 1920, but some of their number, like Nuri al-Sa'id, were actively opposed to the uprising. As for the claim that Britain's occupation was in no way oppressive, the evidence of our narrative shows that this view is simply risible while the claim that the tribesmen who fought the British were mainly 'out for loot' overlooks the fact that the primary objective of the 'looters' was to acquire modern weaponry in an attempt to counterbalance their enemy's overwhelming superiority in this respect – a perfectly sound military objective.

A much more sophisticated analysis of the 1920 uprising is that of the Palestinian Marxist historian Hanna Batatu, whose monumental work on Iraq's social and political history, first published in 1978, argued that the revolution of 1920 was primarily the reaction of what he termed 'the old social classes', seeking to defend their traditional rights and privileges which the new regime of British colonialism threatened to undermine.[10] There is considerable truth in this analysis: men like the Shi'i landowner Muhsin Abu Tabikh and the Sunni judge Yusuf al-Suwaydi exemplified the traditions, culture and social status of an only recently destroyed Ottoman world; certainly, they would have resented the loss of privileges and prestige which an enduring British domination appeared to herald. On the other hand such an explanation does not adequately account for the mass participation of the predominantly Shi'i Arab peasantry in the uprising, or the fact that, among those who refused to support it – both Sunni and Shi'i – there were many notables and landowners who were subject to precisely the same social and economic pressures as those who did.

Perhaps the most accurate appraisal of the 1920 uprising is that of the historian Amal Vinogradov, in an article in an academic journal published in 1972: 'The Iraqi Revolt was a "primitive", but genuine, national response to fundamental dislocations in the political and socio-economic adaptation of the tribally-organised rural Iraqis. These dislocations were brought about through the direct and indirect encroachment of the West.'[11]

Although it omits any specific reference to the actions of the Baghdad nationalists, this short but succinct paragraph comes very close to explaining the historical 'meaning' of the Great Arab Revolt of 1920.

What, then, were the enduring consequences of the uprising for the British and Iraqis? Although the events of 1920 became progressively erased from official versions of Britain's imperial history, its lessons were not forgotten by the empire's rulers. The 'cost effective' model of repression and control, which had come into its own in the final days of the uprising, became standard policy after 1921. Moreover, in the words of one British politician, Iraq became 'a splendid training ground' for the RAF as it took over responsibility for the security of Faysal's puppet government and its successors.[12]

Henceforth it would be 'friendly native states' led by collaborating elites and buttressed by relatively small numbers of British bombers and armoured cars that would be the chosen method for sustaining the Empire's economic and political interests east of Suez, not only in

Iraq but also in the southern Yemen (the Aden protectorate) and, to a lesser extent, in Transjordan.[13] Even after Iraq was granted nominal independence in 1932, the model which has been described alternatively as 'Informal Empire' or 'Covert Empire' continued as a successful mechanism for achieving British imperial control until the Iraq revolution of 1958.[14]

On the other hand, what was probably the principal original objective of Britain's involvement in Iraq – oil – was to prove something of a disappointment. Between 1905 and 1921 the imperial quest for oil was an abiding concern of Britain's rulers; but by 1925, technical problems and a lack of both capital and oil-industry expertise compelled Britain to 'open the door' to US oil companies. In that year, the old Turkish Petroleum Company (TPC) controlled by Anglo-Persian, Shell and the Compagnie Française des Pétroles was compelled to accept the acquisition of 23.75 per cent of its capital by an entity known as the Near East Development Corporation owned by five major US oil companies.

Over the next three decades Britain performed the role of policeman of the Gulf. But under this Pax Britannica it was the USA which gained most. Already, from 1928, it was American geologists who led the exploration programme of the TPC (shortly to be renamed the Iraq Petroleum Company) and behind Britain's protective shield 'East of Suez', more US oil companies moved into the Middle East. By 1960, five of the seven giant multinational oil companies which dominated the Gulf were American – Exxon (Standard Oil of New Jersey), Mobil (Standard Oil of New York), Chevron (Standard Oil of California), Gulf Oil and Texaco – and between them they controlled 60 per cent of the 164 billion barrels of proven Middle East oil reserves.[15] For all the blood and treasure spent both in the war and in defeating the 1920 uprising, as far as oil was concerned, by the 1960s Britain was very much the junior partner in the business.

According to the historian Eugene Rogan, 'the uprising of 1920, referred to in Iraq as the "Revolution of 1920", has a special place in the nationalist mythology of the modern Iraqi state comparable to the American Revolution of 1776.'[16] A typical example of that 'mythology' can be found in the following passage from the introduction to a book first

published in 1971 and reprinted in 2004: 'The revolt of the Iraqis against
the English in 1920 is one of the most important events in the history of
Iraq during this century. It brought the modern state of Iraq into existence
and opened-up new horizons of progress and development.'[17]

However, while it is true that the uprising convinced the British
that they could not proceed with the explicitly colonial regime in Iraq
favoured by men like Arnold Wilson, and swiftly resulted in a series
of arrangements which provided at least a gloss of independence, it
is difficult to accept the previous writer's rose-tinted vision of 'new
horizons of progress and development'.

Firstly, it should be pointed out that it was not until fifteen years
after the uprising that a historical work by an Iraqi writer was published
which contained an account of this 'most important event'.[18] Indeed, the
puppet kingdom of Iraq, created by the British in 1921 in the aftermath
of the uprising, made sure that the whole topic was swiftly buried. Not
only had its near success at one point been an acute embarrassment to
the British but some of those Sunni Iraqi officers and large landowners
who formed the entourage of the British-installed King Faysal and his
successors had actually opposed the uprising. Consequently, for the next
three decades, newly printed Iraqi school history books omitted any
reference to the uprising and there was no official holiday in celebration
of its anniversary.[19]

And although the revolutionary war of 1920 was eventually to
become rightfully reinstated in Iraq's national history, most of its
participants were not. By the 1980s the predominantly Shi'i affiliation of
those participants had been airbrushed out of its narrative and under the
dictatorship of Saddam Husayn and the Ba'ath Party, marginal Sunni
figures like Sheikh Dhari of the Zauba' became elevated to the pantheon
of martyrs of the 1920 uprising. Indeed, in 1983 a state-financed film
about the revolution focused almost exclusively on Dhari's 'heroic' stand
against the British and in particular against Leachman, inaccurately
portrayed as a drunk, a role played by actor Oliver Reed.[20]

In conclusion, it may be said that, for the Iraqis, the enduring legacy
of the 1920 uprising lies in the consequences of its failure. Although

it resulted in the creation of a 'state' rather than a mere protectorate, the state which came into existence following the defeat of the uprising had virtually no roots among the predominantly Shi'i cultivators who constituted the majority of Iraqi 'civil society' at that time.[21] The British made sure that the machinery of the state was placed in the hands of Sunni Baghdad notables and Sunni 'Sharifian' military officers, many of whom openly despised the majority of their rural fellow countrymen. This is not to deny that many tribal sheikhs, both Shi'i and Sunni, were co-opted into that state machinery – but, in general, their motives were personal and financial advancement rather than to be genuine representatives of their constituencies.

Most importantly, control of the newly formed Iraqi army was monopolised by Sunnis, and from its foundation it was envisaged by both the British and their Iraqi puppets as a force for suppressing internal unrest rather than external aggression. In other words, the 'friendly native state' which Britain had eventually created by defeating the 1920 uprising was 'friendly' only insofar as that state had little or no foundations in the wider Iraqi society: it was entirely based on a small number of individuals from an equally small proportion of the Iraqi population (Sunni Arabs constituted around 19 per cent of the total).[22] Thus, while the British became dependent on this group for the furtherance of their interests, as a minority, the Iraqis' rulers became equally dependent on the British for their survival. Indeed, the policy of favouring a minority to control the remainder of the population was a widespread imperialist *modus operandi* employed, for example, in Syria where the French favoured the Alawites over the majority Sunni population.

This absence of representative state formation at the birth of the Iraqi nation established a dark precedent for the future conduct of Iraqi politics. Since the Sunni military officers who formed the backbone of the regime could rely on bombing by the RAF to 'solve' political problems in the Shi'i (and Kurdish) regions, there was little incentive to develop peaceful democratic methods of conflict resolution.[23] As Toby Dodge has observed, 'Governance was delivered from two hundred feet

... This meant that state institutions never managed to fully penetrate society, mobilize resources or ultimately engender legitimacy.'[24]

At the same time, while the state became predominantly an instrument of violence *against* the population, it also became an arena in which corrupt political cliques and personalities – men who had few or no genuine roots in Iraqi civil society – would struggle against each other to seize the material spoils of power. So, from Iraq's nominal independence in 1932 and throughout successive decades, a queue of military and ex-military 'strongmen' followed each other (punctuated by rigged elections), culminating in the despotism of Saddam Husayn, who became president of Iraq in 1979 (having been de facto ruler since 1976). At the same time, the role of the tribes who had fought and suffered in 1920 became increasingly that of useful pawns to be manipulated as collective weapons against this or that political opponent.[25]

Oil – that object of imperialist interest which first enticed a western power into the Middle East – continued to be a very mixed blessing for the people of Iraq. Although Iraq finally achieved full sovereignty over its oil resources in 1972, the state into whose hands they fell only used them to further exercise its power over civil society and to finance two disastrous foreign wars (against Iran in 1980–88 and Kuwait in 1990–91). Meanwhile, oil has continued to be an enduring source of attraction to foreign powers and foreign companies. Not only did the desire to exercise control over Iraq's huge oil resources provide the principal motive behind the US invasion in 2003, but subsequently the recognition that Iraqi Kurdistan has a much larger endowment of oil and gas resources than previously believed has prompted the involvement of foreign powers in that region – in particular Turkey[26] – while encouraging the forces of separatism and exacerbating already difficult relations with the federal government in Baghdad.

Sadly, that same federal government has studiously ignored the noble aims of the leaders of the revolution of 1920 – the unity of all Iraqis in the cause of independence regardless of religion or sect. Instead the Shi'i politicians have preferred to totally exclude Sunnis from the state apparatus, ensuring that it is now the minority part of Iraqi civil society which is excluded from participation in the governance of *its* country. This failure to follow in the footsteps of their heroic predecessors has undoubtedly fed the barbaric terrorism and near civil-war in Iraq which has followed the withdrawal of US occupation forces and which continues to this day.

Some Biographical Notes

Several of the actors in our narrative were to meet untimely or violent deaths. Sykes's death from influenza in February 1919, aged only thirty-nine, and the violent deaths of Colonel Leachman and Lieutenant Faruqi have already been mentioned. With the accession of King Faysal, Gertrude Bell found her role in Iraq's political life considerably reduced. For a time she found solace in safeguarding the immense archaeological heritage of Iraq and was appointed the first director of antiquities in 1923. She still had hopes of marrying and for while looked to Kinahan (Ken) Cornwallis, chief personal advisor to Faysal, as a future matrimonial partner – only to be rejected. From then on, her increasing loneliness and depression – exacerbated by the death of her brother Hugo from typhus in February 1926 – overwhelmed her. On Sunday 11 July 1926, three days before her fifty-eighth birthday, she retired to bed and took a large overdose of sleeping pills.

T. E. Lawrence died on 19 May 1935 following a motorbike accident six days earlier. The later years of his life are perhaps – like those of his war experiences – far too well known to bear repetition. It therefore suffices to make one further observation relevant to those events in Iraq which have been the subject of this book. By 1921, Lawrence had become a convert to Trenchard and Churchill's doctrine of colonial control via air power. In spite of his previous outrage against the killing of Arab men, women and children during Wilson's administration, he apparently turned a blind eye to events such as the merciless bombing of the Bani Huchaym tribe's villages for non-payment of taxes in 1923, in which 144 men, women and children were killed and an unspecified number were wounded – or perhaps he simply was no longer interested in finding out about such things.[1] Commenting on the later bombing of rebel villages on the North-West Frontier, he claimed that 'destroying those few poor villages hurt no-one', and in a truly damning judgement, Lawrence's biographer, Lawrence James – broadly sympathetic to his subject – was forced to conclude that, 'air control continued in the Middle East until the late 1950s. It was one of Lawrence's lasting legacies to the region.'[2]

Arnold Wilson's employment as local managing director of the Anglo-Persian Oil Company ended in 1932 and two years later he was elected as the National Conservative MP for Hitchin. During the remainder of that decade he was strongly sympathetic to Nazi Germany and the policy of appeasement. However, when the Second World War broke out, he volunteered for the Royal Air Force as a rear gunner at the age of fifty-five. In spite of his age, he was accepted and, on the night of 31 May 1940, flying over northern France near Dunkirk, his aircraft was shot down and Wilson declared 'missing, believed killed'. Although Wilson's record in Iraq and his political opinions during the 1930s are viewed with distaste by many today, when his country was, once again, at war, this old-fashioned English patriot (his biographer, John Marlowe, dubbed him a 'Late Victorian') clearly had no doubt where his duty lay.

Emir 'Abdallah met Churchill on 26 May 1921 in Jerusalem, where he agreed to support the candidature of his brother Faysal for the throne of Iraq. In return he accepted the emirate, later the kingdom, of Transjordan. 'Abdallah ruled as an autocrat under British protection throughout the 1930s and 40s. During the Arab–Israeli war of 1948–9, his British-officered Arab Legion occupied the West Bank and East Jerusalem. However, 'Abdallah had no interest in an independent Palestinian state and these captured areas were annexed to Jordan (newly named as such in May 1949). Distrusted by most other Arab leaders for his continued loyalty to Great Britain and his peace talks with the Israelis, he was shot dead by a Palestinian outside the Al 'Aqsa Mosque in Jerusalem on 20 July 1951.

Iraq in the 1930s witnessed a succession of oligarchic and repressive governments made up of Sunni military officers and rich landowning sheikhs interspersed with military coups and attempted coups. In one of these – in 1936 – Ja'far al-'Askari, who had held the premiership in 1923–4 and 1926–8, was murdered. Nuri al-Sa'id headed a number of pro-British governments during the 1930s, 40s and 50s and was responsible for the violent repression of popular demonstrations against the regime's subservience to British interests. In 1958 the Hashemite monarchy was overthrown in a military-civilian revolution. The royal family were executed and Nuri al-Sa'id was captured while trying to escape; he was killed and his mutilated body dragged through the streets.

At the end of the war, Sharif Husayn was left only with the stony and unproductive Hejaz, in which he imposed a regime of ultra-strict shari'a, restoring punishments such as hand and foot amputation which had fallen into disuse in the region long before the Young Turk revolution. At the same time he began to behave increasingly like the archetypal 'oriental despot', alienating rich and poor alike. In March 1924 Husayn proclaimed himself caliph after the Turkish Nationalist government had formally abolished the role. In response, 'Abd al-'Aziz ibn Sa'ud of Najd sent his feared Ikhwan fighters into Husayn's realm and the king was forced to flee to 'Aqaba in 'Abdallah's Transjordan, from where the British removed him to Cyprus. He later returned to Transjordan's capital, Amman, where he died in 1931.

After returning to Iraq, Sayyid Muhsin Abu Tabikh maintained his opposition to the mandate, the treaty and participation in the elections for a constituent assembly. As a result he was briefly exiled to Syria. On his return, however, he began to pursue a strategy of political involvement of bewildering complexity and opportunism which was to remain his chief characteristic for the rest of his life. He was frequently involved in plots against the government and plans to raise his tribal levies against it, but he was also not averse to siding with whatever clique was currently in power in furtherance of his economic interests. During the long years of conservative governments dominated by the figure of Nuri al-Sa'id between 1941 and 1958, Muhsin Abu Tabikh occupied a variety of political and diplomatic roles, ending his career as leader of the Senate. He survived the 1958 revolution and died in Baghdad in May 1961.

Of the four principal leaders of Haras al-Istiqlal in Baghdad, Yusuf al-Suwaydi played only a minor part in political events after his return to the capital, dying in 1925. Sayyid Muhammad al-Sadr initially campaigned strongly against the treaty with Britain and in August 1922 he was arrested by the British along with a number of other mujtahidin and opposition political figures and exiled to Persia. There is some evidence that in Tehran he had contacts with representatives of the Bolshevik government. However, in May 1924 he returned to Iraq having reached a rapprochement with King Faysal. Thereafter his main objective was to obtain greater political rights for the Shi'is via parliamentary action and loyalty to the Hashemites. In 1929 he was elected president of the Senate and was briefly prime minister between January and June 1948. He died of natural causes in 1956.

The one veteran of the 1920 uprising who remained loyal to the best ideals of the revolution was Ja'far Abu al-Timman. In 1922 he founded a nationalist party, al-Hizb al-Watani, and launched a major campaign against the proposed treaty with Britain. As a result he too was arrested along with a group of fellow nationalists including Sheikh Habib al-Khayizran of the 'Azza, and was sent to Henjam island. He was released the following year and for the remainder of his life he struggled to achieve the two objectives which had motivated his participation in the great uprising – the national unity of the Shi'i and Sunni Muslims and an end to British control, both de jure and de facto. During the 1930s he allied himself with the group of left-wing, anti-imperialist journalists, intellectuals and labour leaders associated with the newspaper *Al-Ahali*. In 1936–7 he was briefly minister of finance and attempted to develop a more egalitarian economic policy with a larger role for the state. In 1941 he supported the short-lived Nationalist government which attempted to end the British military presence in Iraq. He died in Baghdad in 1945 at the age of sixty-four.

General Haldane returned to London in 1921 and for his services in Iraq was invested as a Knight Grand Cross, Order of St Michael and St George (GCMG). Meanwhile he had been writing his own account of the uprising and its defeat, *The Insurrection in Mesopotamia*, in which, on a number of occasions, he strongly criticised the conduct of Wilson's administration. He retired from military service in 1925; he never married and spent the rest of his life living with his sister, Alice. He died, aged eighty-seven, in April 1950.

After returning to India and retiring from the army, Major General Leslie lived quietly with his wife and daughter, moving to England in the late 1920s. In August 1930 Leslie sent Arnold Wilson a copy of some of the letters, originally written to his wife during the 1920 revolution, in which he had recorded his personal experiences, including his fraught relations with General Haldane. In 2003 the letters were deposited in the Asia, Pacific and African Section of the British Library. General Leslie died in Bournemouth, aged sixty-nine, in 1936.

One of Churchill's final acts before the fall of the Lloyd George coalition was to advocate the use of gas bombs against a recrudescence of Kurdish insurgency and continuing outbreaks of Arab tribal resistance in Iraq. Sir Percy Cox and Sir Hugh Trenchard had requested a clear statement of Colonial Office policy on the question and Churchill declared, 'I am ready to authorise the construction of such bombs at once ... In my view they are a scientific expedient for sparing life which should not be prevented by the prejudices of those who do not think clearly.' However, in the event, it was decided that 'ordinary bombing' was sufficiently effective. By now Churchill's popularity in the country had sunk to depths even lower than in the immediate aftermath of the Gallipoli campaign and in the 1922 general election he came fourth in the poll at Dundee. Although he later joined the Conservative Party and in 1925 became chancellor of the exchequer, during the 1930s he became increasingly estranged from many of his party colleagues and, in his opposition to Nazi Germany, widely viewed as a warmonger. In 1940 he replaced Chamberlain as wartime prime minister. The remainder of his career has been recorded by many historians, of which the most comprehensive is the series of volumes by Churchill's official biographer, Sir Martin Gilbert.

Acknowledgements

The origins of this book go back more than twenty-five years. Around that time I developed a fascination for the economics, history, culture and religions of the Middle East and North Africa and, as an avid bibliophile, I set out to build a personal library of this material. There followed innumerable visits to second-hand bookshops and book fairs, during which I was invariably accompanied by my oldest friend, the military historian John Ellis, seeking to add to his own specialised collection. Many of the books I discovered have provided crucial reference material for *Enemy on the Euphrates*. So thank you, John, for being such a companionable fellow book-searcher and long may your own collection flourish.

Having embarked on my quixotic journey, the next step was clearly to learn Arabic. (I suppose it could have been Persian or Turkish but that would have restricted me to those countries only.) After a lonely battle with textbooks of varying utility, I sought out a personal tutor and found one in the person of Haytham Bayasi, formerly of Damascus and now a citizen of Sheffield. Haytham spent many gruelling hours trying to teach me the vocabulary, grammar and syntax of standard Arabic while providing endless cups of his delicious cardamom-flavoured coffee, a taste for which has remained with me to this day. I still retain my notes from those sessions and frequently re-read them. Without the help you gave me I would never have been able to tackle the Arabic texts which made *Enemy on the Euphrates* possible. Let us hope that one day, when the insanity of Syria's civil strife has ended, you and your family may be able to visit your beloved Damascus again in peace.

Remaining with the subject of my bibliography, I must give special thanks to my former PhD student Loriane Yacoub, and her family in Baghdad who furnished me with one particularly rare historical work which has cast light on one of the more obscure corners of the 1920 revolution – the spread of the uprising to the Diyala region of north-east Iraq. Thank you Loriane, and may your own wounded country one day soon return to the ideals of some of those 1920 revolutionaries whose stories I have tried to relate.

Many libraries and archives were invaluable in the assistance they gave me, especially in the area of Arabic texts on the uprising and its historical background. My thanks are therefore extended to the libraries of the School of Oriental and African Studies London University, Exeter University, the Middle East Centre of St Antony's College Oxford, and Sheffield University Library for allowing me to use their inter-library loans system. Needless to say, this book would never have been written without having access to the exceptionally rich archives of the British Library's India Office Collection and the National Archive at Kew. I should also like to thank the librarians at the RAF Museum Hendon and Ashton-under-Lyne public library, which houses the archive of the Manchester Regiment. Finally, I must thank Newcastle University for putting the whole of the Gertrude Bell Collection online thereby saving me both considerable expense and hours of travelling.

Enemy on the Euphrates would never have got into print without the invaluable assistance of four individuals. My literary agent, John Parker, of Zeno Agency Ltd, was the object of a controlled experiment – my very first attempt at writing in a 'popular' style. To my great relief he didn't treat this with derision, although he did advise me to forgo some of my more excessive stylistic endeavours and ridiculously lengthy early versions of the book. Saqi Books' anonymous referee amazed me with some incredibly generous comments on an earlier draft while at the same time disabusing me of the prejudice that academic experts in a particular field are reluctant to accept intruders into their own speciality. Without that support, the book might have ended in the waste-paper basket. Trevor Horwood was responsible for the meticulous copy-editing which went far beyond the customary functions of the profession, providing advice on some important substantive issues and suppressing some of my stylistic infelicities. Finally, I am eternally grateful to my publisher at Saqi, the charming, kind and super-efficient Lynn Gaspard, who somehow finds time to run an international business, reply promptly to every email, read every word of your work more than once and offer invaluable advice about structure and style.

Over many years of writing, so many other individuals helped me that I beg their forgiveness if I have neglected to include their names. My old friend Walter Little cautioned me against an excessive use of Arabic words and reminded me about Britain's long-standing foreign policy towards the Ottoman Empire during the nineteenth century. I look forward to reading the latest fruits of Walter's own labour – a biography of Sir Charles Napier (of Sindh) – when it appears in print. My brother-in-law Peter Hodgson read and commented on one of the key chapters while also assisting in a difficult search for biographical information. But above all, I must thank my wife, Diana Rutledge, not only for helping me with the search for additional biographical data but also for putting up with my frequent dereliction of domestic duties, closeted in my office, in pursuit of an objective which I suspect she frequently doubted would ever come to fruition.

Notes

Preface

1. Until the mid-1970s the only published English-language accounts of the uprising were those of the two senior British officers directly involved in its suppression, Lieutenant General Sir Aylmer Haldane, *The Insurrection in Mesopotamia, 1920*, William Blackwood & Sons, Edinburgh and London, 1922, and Sir Arnold T. Wilson, *Mesopotamia, 1917–1920: A Clash of Loyalties*, Oxford University Press, London, 1931. Mark Jacobsen makes the point that the uprising 'was the largest British-led military campaign of the entire interwar period, but it has escaped the attention lavished upon many smaller scale episodes'. See Jacobsen, '"Only by the Sword": British Counter-insurgency in Iraq, 1920', *Small Wars and Insurgencies*, vol. 2, no. 2, 1991, p. 323.

2. See, e.g., Niall Ferguson, 'This Vietnam Generation of Americans Has not Learnt the Lessons of History', *Daily Telegraph*, 10 April 2004; Robert Fisk, 'Iraq 1917', *Independent*, 17 June 2004; also, before his replacement, Paul Bremner, head of the Coalition Provisional Authority set up to administer Iraq following the invasion, was reported as opining that the great mistake of the Shi'is had been to rebel against the British in 1920.

3. One of these groups called itself the '1920 Revolution Brigades', but see the comments of Abbas Kadhim in *Reclaiming Iraq: The 1920 Revolution and the Founding of the Modern State*, University of Texas Press, Austin, 2012, p. 42, on the dubious credentials of this group.

4. Unfortunately these estimates are also much more vague and regrettably unreliable. For example, 'Abd al-Razzaq al-Hasani in *Al-thawra al-'Iraqiyya al-kubra, sana 1920* (The Great Iraqi Revolution of 1920), 3rd edn, Matba' al-'Irfan, Sidon, 1972, notes that the three divisions of occupied Iraq most seriously affected by the uprising were Diwaniyya,

Shamiyya and Hilla while the Muntafiq and Ba'quba divisions were also affected on a lesser scale. He then suggests that the size of the 'nationalist forces' can be estimated by taking the combined population figures (and therefore including non-combatants) of the Diwaniyya, Shamiyya and Hilla divisions for the year 1920 (567,500), but excluding those of Muntafiq and Ba'quba divisions. By this method, he states, 'perhaps we reach an understanding of the number of rebels' (p. 136). Presumably his assumption is that the over-estimation involved in counting the *whole population* of the three most seriously affected divisions is offset in some way by *not including any* of the population of Muntafiq and Ba'quba. But this cannot be regarded as a satisfactory method.

5. There appears to be no 'official' figure for the number of actual combatants. Estimates range from a mere 30,000 to 120,000; the latter is quoted by onwar.com available at http://www.onwar.com/aced/nation/kay/kenya/fmaumau1952.htm. Although the purely military phase of the uprising occurred between 1952 and 1956, the British repression continued until 1960.

6. Eliezer Tauber, *The Arab Movements in World War One*, Frank Cass, London, 1993, p. 139.

7. The 'mid-Euphrates region' designates an area of roughly 100 miles by 60 miles stretching from the town of Musayib in the north to Samawa in the south and encompassing the land surrounding the two main branches of the Euphrates – the Hilla and the Hindiyya channels.

Chapter 1: Indications of Oil

1. Uriel Dann, 'Report on the Petroliferous Districts of Mesopotamia (1905) – an annotated document', *Asian and African Studies*, vol. 24, no. 3, 1990, p. 283.

2. Ibid., p. 285.

3. Ibid., p. 287.

4. Ibid., p. 291.

5. Roger Adelson, *Mark Sykes: Portrait of an Amateur*, Jonathan Cape, London, 1975, p. 62.

6. Mark Sykes, *Dar-ul-Islam: A Record of a Journey through Ten of the Asiatic Provinces of Turkey*, Bickers & Son, London, 1904, p. 178.

Chapter 2: Lieutenant Wilson's First Mission

1. Quoted in John Marlowe, *Late Victorian: The Life of Sir Arnold Wilson*, The Cresset Press, London, 1967, pp. 22–3.

2. Antony Wynn, *Persia in the Great Game: Sir Percy Sykes, Explorer, Consul, Soldier, Spy*, John Murray, London, 2003, p. 42.

3. Zuhair Mikdashi, *A Financial Analysis of Middle Eastern Oil Concessions: 1901–1965*, Praeger, New York, 1966, p. 293.

4. Arnold T. Wilson, *S.W. Persia. Letters and Diary of a Young Political Officer, 1907–1914*, Readers Union, London, 1942, pp. 33–4.

5. Ibid., p. 42; see also J. R. L. Anderson, *East of Suez*, Hodder and Stoughton, London, 1969, p. 36.

6. Wilson, *S.W. Persia*, p. 211.

7. A point made by Marian Jack, who refers to the whole episode as 'an aberration' in government policy. See Marian Jack, 'The Purchase of the British Government's Shares in the British Petroleum Company, 1912–1914', *Past and Present*, no. 39, 1968, pp. 139–68.

8. There are suggestions of this kind of hypocrisy on pp. 74, 77 and 107 in Stephanie Jones, *Trade and Shipping: Lord Inchcape, 1852–1932*, Manchester University Press, 1989. However, a review of her book criticises the author's timidity in not giving greater weight to this subject. See Gordon Boyce, 'Reviews', *Business History Review*, vol. 63, no. 3, 1989.

9. Stephen Helmsley Longrigg, *Oil in the Middle East: Its Discovery and Development*, Oxford University Press, London, 1954, p. 42. In the event, the field work planned by the company did not take place.

10. Jones, p. 153.

11. Helmut Mejcher, 'Oil and British Policy Towards Mesopotamia', *Middle Eastern Studies*, vol. 8, no. 3, 1972, pp. 377–91; and Helmut Mejcher, *Imperial Quest for Oil: Iraq 1910–1928*, Ithaca Press, London, 1976, p. 15.

12. For a lengthy discussion of the protracted negotiations leading up to the formation of the final version of the TPC, see Marian Kent, *Oil and Empire*, Macmillan, London, 1976, pp. 15–113.

13. For an excellent account of these events see Christopher Clark, T*he Sleep Walkers: How Europe Went to War in 1914*, Allen Lane, London, 2012.

Chapter 3: 'Protect the oil refineries'

1. Arnold T. Wilson, *Loyalties: Mesopotamia, 1914–1917*, Oxford University Press, London, 1930, p. 3.
2. See Clark, p. 250.
3. This very abbreviated account of the events leading to war with Turkey are taken from Field Marshal Lord Carver, *The National Army Museum Book of the Turkish Front, 1914–1918*, Pan Books, London, 2000, pp. 5–7.
4. Wilson, *Loyalties*, p. 6; Carver, p. 10.
5. See the production data in Charles W. Hamilton, *Americans and Oil in the Middle East*, Gulf Publishing Company, Houston, 1962, p. 287.
6. Peter Sluglett, *Britain in Iraq*, 2nd edn, I. B. Tauris, London, 2007, p. 8.
7. A. J. Barker, *The Neglected War: Mesopotamia, 1914–1918*, Faber & Faber, London, 1967, p. 39.
8. Wilson, *Loyalties*, p. 8; see also Stephen Helmsley Longrigg, *Iraq, 1900–1950*, Oxford University Press, London, 1953, p. 77.

Chapter 4: Arab Mobilisation on the Euphrates

1. John Buchan, *Greenmantle*, Kindle edn, Duke Classics, 2012.
2. See the classic work by George Antonius, *The Arab Awakening*, Hamish Hamilton, London, 1938, 1945 edn, ch. 5.
3. See e.g., Jamil Muhsin Abu Tabikh (ed.), *Muthakarat al-Sayyid Muhsin Abu Tabikh, 1910–1960: khamsun 'aman min tarikh al-'Iraq al siyyasi al-hadith* (Memoirs of Sayyid Muhsin Abu Tabikh, 1910–1960: Fifty Years of Iraq's Modern Political History), Mu'sasa al-'Arabiyya li al-dirasat wa al-nashar, Beirut, 2001, pp. 33–4.
4. Quoted in Adelson, p. 160.
5. Mahmoud Haddad, 'Iraq before World War 1: A Case of Anti-European Arab Ottomanism', in Rashid Khalidi et al. (eds), *The Origins of Arab Nationalism*, Columbia University Press, New York, 1991, p. 121.
6. 'Abd al-Razzaq al-Hasani, *Tarikh al-'Iraq al-haditha* (History of Modern Iraq), Matba' al-'Irfan, Sidon, 1957, p. 84.
7. Quoted in 'Abd al-Razzaq 'Abd al-Darraji, *Ja'far Abu al-Timman wa dawrahu fi al-harakat al-wataniyya fi al-'Iraq* (Ja'far Abu al-Timman and His Role in the Iraqi National Movement), 2nd edn, Ministry of Culture and Information, Baghdad, p. 39.
8. Abu Tabikh, p. 40.
9. Hasan al-Asadi, *Thawra al-Najaf 'ala al-Ingliz aw al shararat al-ula li*

thawra al-'ishrin (The Uprising against the British at Najaf or the First Sparks of the Revolution of 1920), Ministry of Information, Baghdad 1975, p. 90; see also Yitzhak Nakash, *The Shi'is of Iraq*, Princeton University Press, 1995, p. 61.

10. Abu Tabikh, p. 41.

11. IO/L/PS/20/235, The British Library, London, *Arab Tribes of the Baghdad* Vilayet, Government of India for Arab Bureau, July 1918, Calcutta 1919, p. 185.

12. Abu Tabikh, p. 42.

13. al-Darraji, p. 43.

14. Abid Khalid Muhsin, 'The Political Career of Muhammad Ja'far Abu al-Timman, 1908–1937: A Study in Modern Iraqi History', unpublished PhD thesis, School of Oriental and African Studies, London, 1983, p. 102.

15. 'Abd al-Halim al-Rahimi, *Al-haraka al-Islamiyya fi al-'Iraq: al-juthur al-fikriyya wa al-waqi' al-tarikhi (1900–24)* (The Islamic Movement in Iraq: Ideological Roots and Historical Situation, 1900–1924), Dar al-'alamiyya, Beirut 1985, appendix 6, pp. 297–8.

16. Ronald Storrs, *Orientations*, Nicolson & Watson, London, 1945, p. 122.

17. David Fromkin, *A Peace to End All Peace: Creating the Modern Middle East, 1914–1922*, André Deutsch, London, 1989, pp. 104–5.

18. Gerald de Gaury, *Rulers of Mecca*, Harrap, London, 1951, pp. 257–8.

Chapter 5: The Jihad Defeated

1. Abu Tabikh, p. 42.

2. 'Abd al-Razzaq al-Hasani, *Al-'Iraq fi dawra al-ihtilal wa al-intidab* (Iraq between the Occupation and the Mandate), vol. 1, Matba' al-'Irfan, Sidon, 1935, p. 16.

3. 'Abd 'Awn al-Rawdan, *Mausu'a 'Asha'ir al-'Iraq: Tarikh, Ansab, Rijalat, Ma'athir* (Encyclopaedia of the Tribes of Iraq: History, Genealogy, Leading Personalities, Achievements), Al-Ahliyya, Amman, 2003, vol. 2, p. 296.

4. The story is related by Wilson, *Loyalties*, p. 29.

5. Ibid., p. 38.

6. Philip Willard Ireland, *Iraq: A Study in Political Development*, Jonathan Cape, London, 1937, p. 63n.

7. Quoted in Ghassan R. Atiyyah, *Iraq: 1908–1921. A Socio-Political Study*, Arab Institute for Research and Publishing, Beirut, 1973, p. 131.

8. al-Hasani, *Al-'Iraq fi dawra al-ihtilal wa al-intidab*, p. 18.

9. The number and ethnic composition of the Ottoman combatants remain confused. The only contemporary Arab testimony – that of Sayyid Muhsin Abu Tabikh – puts the size of the total, combined force at 30,000 but does not give any further details (Abu Tabikh, p. 43). Gertrude Bell states, 'The Turkish (*sic*) Army consisted of between 6,000 and 7,000 regular troops, the Arab tribal levies from the Euphrates, some 9,000 tribesmen under 'Ajaimi (Sa'dun) and his cousin 'Abdallah al Falih, and over 1,000 Kurds. The tribesmen numbered in all over 18,000' ('Review of the Civil Administration of Mesopotamia', Cmd. 1061, 1920, p. 4); so summing 7,000 'regulars' (not necessarily ethnic Turks), 17,000 Arab 'tribesmen' and 1,000 Kurdish 'tribesmen', gives us a total of 25,000 troops. Carver (p. 105), probably following Bell, states that al-'Askari had 'some 6,000 soldiers and 10–20,000 armed Arabs'. Barker (p. 67) states that the Arab tribesmen numbered between 10,000 and 20,000 while the regular Ottoman troops were 'over 6,000 men in all – of whom nearly half were tough Anatolian Turks'.

10. Abu Tabikh, pp. 43–4.

11. According to Bell in her 'Review of the Civil Administration of Mesopotamia', not only did the Arab tribesmen take 'little or no part in the battle' (p. 4) but as the Ottoman regular troops (whom she refers to solely as 'Turkish') retreated they were attacked by the tribesmen who 'fell upon them, butchering and looting' (p. 5). This story of the attack on the 'Turks' by the 'treacherous Arabs' was later taken up by Barker in *The Neglected War*. However, A. T. Wilson, who might have been expected to relish reporting such an incident, makes absolutely no mention of it, neither does Lord Carver in *The Turkish Front*. Bell's exaggerated version of what appears to have been a number of isolated incidents, seems to have originally emanated from Turkish sources in Baghdad and should be treated with considerable scepticism. Firstly, it is not true that the tribesmen took 'little or no part in the battle'; they did, and they suffered so badly from it that they were forced to retreat. Secondly, as for 'treachery', Barker rather spoils his story by stating that it was the 'Turks' who first fired artillery at the Arabs as some kind of punishment for their retreating. Thirdly, after both Arab tribesmen and regular Ottoman troops had retreated to Nasiriyya, they continued to fight side by side against the advancing British; one cannot really believe that such relatively 'comradely' behaviour would have survived the treacherous 'butchery' described by Bell and Barker.

12. al-Hasani, *Al-'Iraq fi dawra al-ihtilal wa al-intidab*, p. 19.
13. According to Luizard, 'Des milliers de 'mujahidin' trouvèrent la mort au cours d'opérations quasi-suicidaires', Pierre-Jean Luizard, *La Formation de l'Irak Contemporain*, CNRS Editions, Paris, 1991, p. 328.

Chapter 6: Pacifying Arabistan

1. Wilson, *Loyalties*, p. 39.
2. Quoted in Marlowe, p. 65.
3. Quoted by Wilson, *Loyalties*, p. 44.
4. Ibid., p. 43.
5. Kent, pp. 202–3, assuming 8 barrels per long ton.
6. Quoted in Henry Longhurst, *Adventure in Oil: The Story of British Petroleum*, Sidgwick & Jackson, London, 1959, p. 54.

Chapter 7: Imperial Objectives in the East

1. Quoted in Salim Tamari, 'The Short Life of Private Ihsan', *Jerusalem Quarterly*, no. 30, Spring 2007, p. 40; available at www.jerusalemquarterly.org/ViewArticle.aspx?id=64
2. CAB/27/1, The National Archive, London, *British Desiderata in Turkey in Asia* (The De Bunsen Committee Report), 25 June 1915, p. 41. For a useful background to the De Bunsen Committee Report see Aron S. Klieman, 'Britain's War Aims in the Middle East in 1915', *Journal of Contemporary History*, vol. 3, no. 3, 1968, pp. 237–51.
3. CAB/27/1, *British Desiderata in Turkey in Asia*, p. 124.
4. Since a copy of these telegrams (see below) is included in the final report of the committee, it seems reasonable to assume that they were, in fact, placed before the committee at some stage. The second meeting seems the most likely occasion since this was the meeting which first discussed desirable spheres of control.
5. CAB/27/1, Note by Viceroy of India: Future Status and Administration of Basra, 24 February 1915.
6. Ibid., 15 March 1915.
7. CAB/27/1, *British Desiderata in Turkey in Asia*, p. 44.
8. See ibid., p. 46 (I have converted the original reportage in the minutes into direct speech here and in the text referenced by nn. 9 and 12 below). It is not at all clear what Jackson meant by 'draws through those regions'. Possibly he was referring to oil supplies from southern Persia which he

anticipated would be transported via Basra and Baghdad by a future pipeline to the Mediterranean.

9. Ibid., p. 47.
10. Kent, p. 48.
11. Ibid., p. 118.
12. CAB/27/1, *British Desiderata in Turkey in Asia*, p. 47.
13. Stephen Roskill, *Hankey, Man of Secrets*, 2 vols, Collins, London, 1972, vol. 1, p. 286.
14. CAB/27/1, *British Desiderata in Turkey in Asia*, p. 9.
15. Ibid., p. 25.
16. Sykes, pp. 107–8.
17. Quoted in Harvey Broadbent, *Gallipoli, the Fatal Shore*, Viking Penguin, Sydney 2005, p. 110.
18. Kemal's 19th Division contained the 72nd, 77th and Turkish 57th regiments; see E. J. Erickson, *Gallipoli: The Ottoman Campaign*, Pen and Sword Books, Barnsley, 2010, pp. 51–3. For questionable perceptions about the unreliability of the Arab troops at Gallipoli also see the criticism of this view by Erickson, ibid., pp. 56–7, 63–4.

Chapter 8: The Menace of Jihad and How to Deal with It

1. Quoted in Adelson, p. 190.
2. FO/882/13, The National Archive, London, Memorandum on Military, Political Situation in Mesopotamia (Section II), 28 October 1915.
3. Quoted in Adelson, p. 74.
4. Ibid., pp. 107–8.
5. Ibid., p. 242. Adelson actually describes the draft as 'Sykes's Formula'.

Chapter 9: The Lieutenant from Mosul

1. al-Hasani, *Al-'Iraq fi dawra al-ihtilal wa al-intidab*, p. 79.
2. Eliezer Tauber, 'The Role of Lieutenant Muhammad Sharif al-Faruqi – New Light on Anglo-Arab Relations during the First World War', *Asian and African Studies*, vol. 24, 1990, p. 22.
3. Ibid., p. 23.
4. Ibid.
5. FO/882/13, Sir John Maxwell (Cairo) to Lord Kitchener, War Office, 16 October 1915.

Chapter 10: The Peculiar Origins of an Infamous Agreement

1. FO/882/13, Sir Mark Sykes to Sir Percy Cox (Mesopotamia), Cairo 22 November 1915.
2. Ibid.
3. See Tauber, 'The Role of Lieutenant Muhammad Sharif al-Faruqi', pp. 26–9; for criticism of various authors' claims regarding the number of Ottoman officers who were members of al-'Ahd also see C. Ernest Dawn, 'The Origins of Arab Nationalism', in Khalidi et al., p. 13.
4. Vis-à-vis all of the concessions made by Faruqi, Tauber states that these 'were certainly not acceptable to Husayn', 'The Role of Lieutenant Muhammad Sharif al-Faruqi', p. 35.
5. The Sykes–Picot Agreement, reproduced in Antonius, Appendix B, pp. 428–30.
6. I base this interpretation of the events in question partly upon the evidence of Sykes's telegram to Cox, the substance of which is remarkably similar to the terms of the Sykes–Picot Agreement but also on the observation by Zeine that, 'It has been suggested that Sir Mark Sykes took into consideration the opinion and suggestions of Faruqi as a basis for the Sykes–Picot Agreement'; see Zeine N. Zeine, *The Struggle for Arab Independence*, Khayats, Beirut, 1960, p. 16n.

Chapter 11: Two British Defeats but a New Ally

1. Quoted in Roskill, vol. 1, p. 230.
2. Quoted in Wilson, *Loyalties*, p. 83.
3. Barker, p. 481.
4. Lawrence James, *The Golden Warrior: The Life and Legend of Lawrence of Arabia*, Abacus, London, 1990, p. 153.
5. Tauber, 'The Role of Lieutenant Muhammad Sharif al-Faruqi', p. 35.
6. Antonius, p. 427.
7. There is considerable confusion as to the precise day on which the Arab Revolt started. According to Joshua Teitelbaum (*The Rise and Fall of the Hashemite Kingdom of Arabia*, C. Hurst & Co., London, 2001, p. 78), it started on 9 June 1916. Other sources give the date as 6 June.

Chapter 12: Colonel Leachman and Captain Lawrence

1. Quoted in Tauber, 'The Role of Lieutenant Muhammad Sharif al-Faruqi', p. 39.

2. T. E. Lawrence, *The Seven Pillars of Wisdom*, Jonathan Cape, London, 1935, p. 47.

3. Robert Graves states categorically that 'Lawrence is not an Arabic scholar. He has never sat down to study it, *nor even learned its letters ...*' (Robert Graves, *Lawrence and the Arabs*, Jonathan Cape, London, 1927, p. 20).

4. N. N. E. Bray, *Shifting Sands: The True Story of the Arab Revolt*, Unicorn Press, London, 1934, p. 133.

5. Quoted in H. V. F. Winstone, *Leachman, O.C. Desert*, Quartet Books, London, 1982, p. 16. and photographs between pp. 118 and 119.

6. Quoted in N. N. E. Bray, *A Paladin of Arabia: The Biography of Brevet Lieut.-Colonel G. E. Leachman C.I.E., D.S.O.*, Unicorn Press, London, 1936, pp. 295–6.

7. Ibid., pp. 297–8.

8. Quoted in Winstone, *Leachman*, p. 182.

9. al-Rawdan, vol. 2, p. 299.

10. Briton Cooper Busch, *Britain, India and the Arabs, 1914–1921*, University of California Press, Berkeley, 1971, p. 140.

11. Quoted in Wilson, *Loyalties*, p. 238.

12. Ibid., p. 239.

13. al-Darraji, p. 51.

Chapter 13: Mosul and Oil

1. Malcolm Brown, *British Logistics on the Western Front, 1914–1919*, Praeger, Westport, 1998, p. 56.

2. R. W. Ferrier, *The History of the British Petroleum Company*, vol. 1, Cambridge University Press, 1982, p. 202.

3. This particular calculation was made by the Indian Army in 1919, see Brian Robson, *Crisis on the Frontier: The Third Afghan War and the Campaign in Waziristan, 1919–1920*, Spellmount, Staplehurst, 2004.

4. Barker, p. 496.

5. Quoted in Daniel Yergin, *The Prize: The Epic Quest for Oil, Money and Power*, Simon & Schuster, London, 1991, p. 177.

6. Kent, pp. 133, and 185–8.

7. Mejcher, *Imperial Quest for Oil*, p. 32.

8. Quoted ibid., p. 33.

9. FO/800/221, The National Archive, London, Memorandum, Sykes to Hirtzel, 16 January 1918.

10. Quoted in Mejcher, *Imperial Quest for Oil*, p. 34. (The quotation is originally from the minutes of the Middle East Committee. I have changed the tense of the verbs from past to present.)

11. IO/L/PS/10/815, The British Library, London, *Geological Reports, Mesopotamia and Kurdistan*, Preliminary Report on the Prospects of Petroleum in the Baghdad Wilaya, Government Press, Baghdad, March 1918, p. 1.

12. Ibid., Civil Commissioner Baghdad to Foreign Office, repeated to Secretary of State, India Office and Sir Percy Cox, Aden, 13 March 1918.

13. Ibid., Report on the Prospects of Petroleum in the Baghdad Wilaya, Ahwaz, 10 August 1918, p. 16.

14. CAB/21/119, The National Archive, London, Admiral Edmond Slade, 'Petroleum Situation in the British Empire', 29 July 1918.

15. Quoted in Mejcher, *Imperial Quest for Oil*, p. 39.

16. Quoted ibid., p. 40.

17. Quoted in Roskill, vol. 1, p. 586.

18. Quoted in Mejcher, *Imperial Quest for Oil*, p. 41.

19. Commenting on this issue, Roskill observes, 'Though Hankey's views on post-war oil policy were without doubt as overtly "imperialist" as Balfour had stated, the British Government aims after the war did in fact follow closely the lines proposed by Hankey'; and with reference to the views of Geddes and Slade, 'British policy did for many years take a shape which differed little from Geddes's proposals of 1918.' (vol. 1, p. 587).

20. Quoted in Mejcher, *Imperial Quest for Oil*, p. 41.

Chapter 14: 'Complete liberation'

1. Lady Florence Bell (ed.), *The Letters of Gertrude Bell*, Ernest Benn, London, 1927, vol. 2, pp. 410–11.

2. Gertrude Bell, *The Arab of Mesopotamia*, Government Press, Basra, 1917, p. 1.

3. Nakash, p. 35.

4. al-Rawdan, vol. 1, p. 214.

5. See IO/L/PS/20/235, pp. 147–51.

6. Bell, 'Review of the Civil Administration of Mesopotamia', p. 8.

7. Bell, *The Arab of Mesopotamia*, p. 5.

8. Nakash, p. 13.

9. There were two other, lesser important Shi'i shrines, one at Kadhimayn,

burial place of the seventh and ninth imams, and the other at Samarra, burial place of the tenth and eleventh imams.

10. Lady Anne Blunt, *The Bedouins of the Euphrates*, Harper & Bros, New York, 1879, p. 138n.

11. Kadhim, *Reclaiming Iraq*, pp. 120–21.

12. Bell, *The Arab of Mesopotamia*, p. 5.

13. See IO/L/PS/20/C151, The British Library, London, *Tribes of the Tigris*, Government of India for Arab Bureau, Calcutta, 1917; IO/L/PS/20/ C152, The British Library, London, *Tribes around the Junction of the Euphrates and Tigris*, Government of India for Arab Bureau, Calcutta, 1917; IO/L/PS/20/63, The British Library, London, *The Muntafiq. Al Sa'dun, Bani Malik, Ajwad, Bani Sa'id, Bani Huchaym*, Arab Bureau, Calcutta, 1917 and, for Bell, IO/L/PS/20/235.

14. Lady Bell, vol. 2, p. 447.

15. Abu Tabikh, p. 52.

16. Ibid., p. 56.

17. Quoted in Busch, p. 199, which contains the full text of the proclamation.

18. Wilson, *Mesopotamia, 1917–1920*, pp. 104–5.

19. Lady Bell, vol. 2, p. 421.

Chapter 15: Najaf 1918: First Uprising on the Euphrates

1. Bertram Thomas, *Alarms and Excursions in Arabia*, Bobbs-Merrill, Indianapolis, 1931, p. 78.

2. Luizard, p. 352.

3. Admiralty, *Iraq and the Persian Gulf*, B.R. 524 (restricted), Geographical Handbook Series, Naval Intelligence Division, London, 1944, p. 545.

4. Hanna Batatu, *The Old Social Classes and the Revolutionary Movements of Iraq*, Saqi Books, London, 2004, pp. 18–20.

5. Bray, *Shifting Sands*, pp. 187–8; Lady Bell, vol. 2, p. 477.

6. J. S. Mann, *The Making of an Administrator, 1893–1920*, Longmans, Green & Co., London, 1921, p. 149.

7. Ibid., p. 168. However, for a totally different and much more favourable impression of Najaf see Candler, *The Long Road to Baghdad*, vol. 2, Cassell, London, 1919, p. 219.

8. al-Asadi, p. 90.

9. Atiyyah, p. 220.

10. Ibid. On the burden of taxation in the period 1918–20 see also Abbas Muhammad Kadhim, *Al-haraka al-Islamiyya fi al-'Iraq (thaura al-'ishrin)* (The Islamic Movement in Iraq ([Revolution of 1920]), n.p., 1984, p. 166, and Ireland, pp. 118–19 and 143–4.

11. According to Marlowe, at this time the British political officers 'were largely engaged in the unpopular task of tax-collecting'. Marlowe, p. 128.

12. See Abu Tabikh, p. 61.

13. al-Asadi, p. 240. *Baqqal* is the Arabic word for 'greengrocer', or sometimes 'grocer'.

14. Ibid., pp. 246–7.

15. Ibid., p. 261.

16. Abu Tabikh, p. 63.

17. al-Asadi, p. 300.

18. Gertrude Bell Project, University of Newcastle, www.gerty.ncl.ac.uk, Gertrude Bell to Hugh Bell, 24 April 1918.

19. Wilson, *Mesopotamia, 1917–1920*, p. 76.

20. According to Atiyyah, p. 231, 'The punishment ... created deep resentment at British cruelty and a wide gulf between the populace and the British authorities.'

Chapter 16: Britain's New Colony

1. Mann, p. 182.

2. Ibid., p. 175.

3. Thomas Lyell, *The Ins and Outs of Mesopotamia*, A. M. Philpot, London, 1923, p. vii; second edition edited by Paul Rich and re-published as *Iraq and Imperialism: Thomas Lyell's The Ins and Outs of Mesopotamia*, Authors Choice Press, San Jose, 2001.

4. Wilson, *Mesopotamia, 1917–1920*, pp. 110.

5. Memorandum 27190, Acting Civil Commissioner to Political Officers, Baghdad, 30 November 1918, quoted in Ireland, p. 162.

6. Ireland, p. 253.

7. The date of this fatwa is something of a mystery. Both al-Rahimi (p. 204) and Luizard (p. 373) state that the date according to the Islamic calendar was 20 Rabi' al-Awal 1337, which Luizard's conversion to the Gregorian date is given as 23 January 1919. However, using the conversion algorithm in http://www.oriold.uzh.ch/static/hegira.html the correct Gregorian date would be 24 December 1918. That the December date seems correct is supported by Atiyyah, *Iraq:*

1908–1921, who states that the fatwa was issued in 'December 1918' (p. 330). However, it should be noted that unfortunately there are a number of different algorithms for converting the Islamic lunar system into the Gregorian calendar.

8. al-Rahimi, pp. 203–4.
9. Quoted in Ireland, p. 171.
10. Lady Bell, vol. 2, p. 464.
11. Wilson, *Mesopotamia, 1917–1920*, pp. 117–18.

Chapter 17: The Oil Agreements

1. Roskill, vol. 2, pp. 28–9.
2. William Stivers, *Supremacy and Oil: Iraq, Turkey and the Anglo-American World Order, 1918–30*, Cornell University Press, Ithaca and London, 1982, p. 26; see also Kent, p. 141, and David Gilmour, *Curzon*, John Murray, London, 1994, p. 519. However, it should be noted that according to Tardieu, the principal French source for this secret agreement (see H. W. V. Temperley, *History of the Peace Conference*, Oxford University Press, London, 1920–24, vol. 6, p. 182), what Lloyd George offered was the 'mandate' for Syria, if the mandate system were adopted. This is not the same thing as saying he offered to continue the Sykes–Picot Agreement with respect to Syria. Unfortunately, the whole incident is so obscure that it is impossible to know exactly what Lloyd George promised to Clemenceau. I have therefore adopted the most frequently repeated account.
3. Stivers, pp. 62–74.
4. See Salman Hadi Tu'ma, *Karbela' fi thawra al-'ishrin* (Karbela' in the Revolution of 1920), Beirut, 2000, Appendix p. 30.
5. Quoted in al-Rahimi, appendix 12, pp. 303–4.
6. Quoted in Kent, p. 143.
7. Busch, p. 308.
8. Benjamin Schwadran, *The Middle East, Oil and the Great Powers*, Atlantic Press, London, 1956, p. 204n.
9. Kent, pp. 172–3; Wilson, *Mesopotamia, 1917–1920*, p. 125.
10. For a good example of the kind of anti-British propaganda emanating from these sources see Dr George-Samne, *La Syrie*, Editions Bossard, Paris, 1920.
11. My explanation of this episode is based largely on Stivers, but it is fair to say that the event is still clouded in mystery. Most recently, Sluglett,

in the second edition of his classic *Britain in Iraq*, is himself reduced to stating, in relation to the oil agreements, that 'the causes of the seemingly interminable wranglings and procrastinations are still not entirely clear', asking (rhetorically), 'Exactly what was the nature of the Anglo-French dispute over Mosul that the Berenger–Long agreement of 1919 did not resolve?' See Sluglett, pp. 21–2.

12. IO/L/PS/10/815, Geological Report (Mesopotamia no. 1) District of Qaiyara, Government Press, Baghdad, 1919, p. 6.

13. Memorandum of Agreement between M. Philippe Berthelot ... and Professor Sir John Cadman, 24 April 1920, attached to CAB/24/108, The National Archive, London, CP 1524: Memorandum by the Minister in Charge of Petroleum Affairs, 21 June 1920.

Chapter 18: The Independence Movement in Baghdad

1. Philby Papers, Middle East Centre, St Antony's College, Oxford, PH VI/3/37, copy of memorandum no. 11947, Civil Commissioner Baghdad to Judicial Secretary Baghdad, 11 April 1920, and copy of memorandum G-101/2, Judicial Secretary Baghdad to Civil Commissioner Baghdad, 21 June 1920.

2. Zeine, p. 139. Ireland, p. 255, gives the date of the announcement as 8 March (not 6th) as does Marlowe, p. 180.

3. Tauber, 'The Role of Lieutenant Muhammad Sharif al-Faruqi', p. 49.

4. al-Rahimi, appendix 8, p. 299. However, according to Abbas Muhammad Kadhim, 'it is noted that since from beginning of the popular movement and then the Islamic uprising until the end of the revolution none of the leadership of the revolt or the *'ulama* or the masses called for an Emirate of the of one of the sons of the Sharif Husayn'. (Kadhim, *Al-haraka al-Islamiyya fi al-'Iraq*, p. 262). This view appears to reflect the author's strongly Shi'i Islamist perspective, although it seems inconsistent with the correspondence related above.

5. See al-Rahimi, appendix 9, p. 300.

6. Quoted in Nakash, p. 68.

7. Wilson, *Mesopotamia, 1917–1920*, pp. 248–9.

8. *Wisaya*, cognate with the verb *wasa*, meaning to entrust. See J. M. Cowan (ed.), *The Hans Wehr Dictionary of Modern Arabic*, Spoken Language Services, Inc., Ithaca, 1994, p. 1260, and Atiyyah, p. 315. However, it is also possible that the word 'mandate' was also being translated in the Arabic press as *amr*, equally offensive and meaning (among other things)

'supreme power', 'authority'. See Wilson, *Mesopotamia, 1917–1920*, p. 248n. Shirazi translated it as *himaya* (protectorate).

9. Philby Papers, PH VI/3/107–9, copy of letter from Gertrude Bell to Arnold Wilson, 3 June 1920.

10. *Intidab*, cognate with the verb *nadaba*, to appoint. See Cowan, p. 1116.

11. Luizard, p. 387, renders the Islamic date 15 Sha'ban 1338 as the Gregorian date 3 May 1919. Atiyyah dates the meeting as 'middle of Sha'ban' – 4/5 May. Unfortunately there are a number of different algorithms for converting the Islamic lunar system into the Gregorian. Throughout we have used the convertor available at www.oriold.uzh.ch/static/hegira.html, which gives a one-day difference from some of the conversions which appear to have been used by authors referred to in the text.

12. al-Hasani, *Al-'Iraq fi dawra al-ihtilal wa al-intidab*, p. 80. Al-Bazirgan gives the date of the establishment of the party as 'the end of 1917' (Hasan al-Bazirgan, *Min ahdath Baghdad wa al-Diyala ithna al-thawra al-'ishrin fi al-'Iraq* [Concerning the Events in Baghdad and the Diyala during the Revolution of 1920 in Iraq] new edn, Bayt al-Hikma, Baghdad, 2000, p. 27n,) but such a relatively early date seems unlikely.

13. Husayn Jamil, *Al-'Iraq: shahada siyasiyya, 1908–1930* (Iraq, Political Witness, 1908–1930), Dar al-Laam, London, 1987, p. 51.

14. al-Darraji, p. 76 and note; see also Batatu, p. 221.

15. Nakash, p. 52. See also Eric Davis, *Memories of State: Politics, History and Collective Identity in Modern Iraq*, University of California Press, Berkeley, 2005, pp. 35–6.

16. al-Darraji, p. 76.

17. Muhsin, pp. 112, 118.

18. al-Darraji, p. 82.

19. al-Bazirgan, p. 27n.

20. al-Darraji, p. 82.

21. Gertrude Bell Project, letter to Hugh Bell, 7 June 1920.

22. al-Darraji, p. 82.

23. They were recognised as such by Gertrude Bell. See Cmd. 1061, p. 140.

24. al-Bazirgan, p. 28.

25. Quoted in Atiyyah, p. 281.

26. Batatu, p. 1139.

27. Quoted ibid., pp. 1137–8.

28. FO/371, The National Archive, London, *Personalities, Mosul, Arbil and Frontier*, Government Press, Baghdad, 1921. Priya Satia, *Spies in Arabia:*

The Great War and the Cultural Foundations of Britain's Covert Empire in the Middle East, Oxford University Press, 2008, gives strong emphasis to this British fear of 'Bolshevism' in the Middle East.

29. Lyell, p. 177.

30. Cmd. 1061, p. 144.

31. al-Hasani, *Al-'Iraq fi dawra al-ihtilal wa al-intidab*, pp. 79–80; see also, Atiyyah, p. 275.

32. al-Hasani, *Al-'Iraq fi dawra al-ihtilal wa al-intidab*, p. 80.

33. al-Darraji, p. 78.

34. Abu Tabikh, p. 123.

35. al-Darraji, p. 84.

36. al-Hasani, *Al-thawra al-'Iraqiyya al-kubra, sana 1920*, pp. 98–100. See also Atiyyah, p. 334, and Luizard, p. 387.

37. Batatu, p. 1142.

38. Cmd. 1061, pp. 144–5.

39. al-Hasani, *Al-thawra al-'Iraqiyya al-kubra, sana 1920*, p. 99. Al-Hasani mentions by name only eight sheikhs, sada and clergy but the passage suggests these were only a few of those attending.

40. Ibid., p. 100.

41. Jamil, p. 51.

42. Sheikh Habib al-Khayizran, paramount sheikh of the 'Azza, quoted in Muhammad Husayn al-Zubaydi, *Al-siyasiyyun al-'Iraqiyyun al-munfiyyun ila jazira hinjam sana 1922*, (The Iraqi Politicians Exiled to Henjam Island, 1922), Al-Maktaba al-Wataniyya, Baghdad, 1989, p. 136.

43. The precise date of the first joint maulud is uncertain. Al-Darraji (p. 87), gives 'at the end of the month of *Sha'ban*' (19 May); however, Muhsin (pp. 125–6) puts it as early as 8 May.

44. Muhsin, p. 126.

45. Cmd. 1061, p. 140.

46. Philby Papers, PH VI/3/20, copy of Memorandum J.S. 420, Judicial Secretary Baghdad to Civil Commissioner Baghdad, 29 May 1920.

47. IO/MSS/EUR/F462, The British Library, London, Correspondence of Major General G. A. J. Leslie, Major General Leslie to his wife, Baghdad, 25 May 1920.

48. Atiyyah, p. 316; however, Sheikh Habib al-Khayizran, quoted in al-Zubaydi, p. 137, states that the poem was delivered on 25 May and the name of the young poet was 'Isa 'Afnadi while Muhsin (p. 126) gives the man's name as 'Isa Effendi al-Raizali'.

49. al-Zubaydi, p. 137.

50. IO/MSS/EUR/F462, Major General Leslie to his wife, Baghdad, 28 May 1920.

51. al-Zubaydi, p. 137.

52. al-Rahimi, appendix 15, p. 306.

53. Kadhim, *Al-haraka al-Islamiyya fi al-'Iraq*, p. 255.

54. With respect to the relationship between the British and one particular Jewish family, see the first two chapters of Marina Benjamin, *Last Days in Babylon: The Story of txhe Jews of Baghdad*, Bloomsbury, London, 2007.

55. al-Rahimi, p. 307. According to Muhsin (p. 128), the proclamation was issued on 1 June.

56. Quoted in Muhsin, p. 129.

57. Quoted in Wilson, *Mesopotamia, 1917–1920*, p. 339.

58. Philby Papers, 'Mesopotage' (unpublished manuscript, 1946?), ch. 11, p. 13.

59. Wilson, *Mesopotamia, 1917–1920*, p. 256.

60. al-Hasani, *Al-thawra al-'Iraqiyya al-kubra, sana 1920*, p. 71.

61. Philby Papers, 'Mesopotage', ch. 11, p. 16.

62. Philby Papers, PH VI/3/107–9.

63. Philby Papers, PH VI/3/56, copy of telegram 6791, Civil Commissioner Baghdad to Secretary of State India Office, London, 7 June 1920.

64. Gertrude Bell Project, Bell to her father, 7 June 1920.

Chapter 19: General Haldane's Difficult Posting

1. As described by Haldane, *The Insurrection in Mesopotamia*, p. 4.

2. Douglas S. Russell, *Winston Churchill, Soldier*, Brassey's, London, 2005, p. 260.

3. Sir Aylmer Haldane, *A Soldier's Saga*, William Blackwood & Sons, Edinburgh and London, 1948, p. 3.

4. Ibid., p. 391.

5. Martin Gilbert, *World in Torment: Winston Churchill 1917–1922*, Minerva, London, 1975, p. 370.

6. John Darwin, *Britain, Egypt and the Middle East*, Macmillan, London, 1981, p. 74.

7. CAB/24/106, The National Archive, London, CP 1320: Mesopotamian Expenditure. Memorandum by the Secretary of State for War, 20 May 1920.

8. Haldane, *The Insurrection in Mesopotamia*, p. 325. The book is an expanded version of Haldane's official report on the revolution published in War Office, *Supplement to the London Gazette*, HMSO, London, 5 July 1921.

9. In the British Army a brevet rank was a temporary and honorary promotion attached to some particular duty meriting it (in this case being acting civil commissioner).

10. Haldane, *A Soldier's Saga*, p. 372.

11. Colonel H. C. Wylly, *History of the Manchester Regiment*, vol. 2: *1883–1922*, Forster Groom & Co., London, 1925, p. 214.

12. Haldane, *The Insurrection in Mesopotamia*, p. 9.

13. Haldane, *A Soldier's Saga*, p. 371.

14. Cmd. 1061, p. 122. In 1920 one rupee was worth about ten pence at today's values. The calculation of current sterling value is based on the historical UK Retail Price Series: see www.measuringworth.com/ukcompare/

15. Philby Papers, 'Mesopotage', ch. 11, p. 7.

16. Ibid., p. 4.

17. Re. Leachman's cut-down polo stick see Bray, *A Paladin of Arabia*, p. 338.

18. Haldane, *The Insurrection in Mesopotamia*, p. 29.

19. Ireland, p. 126.

20. Ibid., p. 116.

21. Atiyyah, p. 234.

22. Ibid., p. 252.

23. Revd J. T. Parfit, *Marvellous Mesopotamia: The World's Wonderland*, S. W. Partridge & Co., London, 1920, p. 251.

24. Haldane, *The Insurrection in Mesopotamia*, p. 325.

25. Ibid., p. 12; Wilson, *Mesopotamia, 1917–1920*, p. 272.

26. Colonel E. B. Maunsell, *Prince of Wales's Own, The Scinde Horse*, Naval and Military Press, Uckfield, 2005, p. 256.

27. Ibid., p. 251.

28. Ibid., p. 253.

29. Haldane, *The Insurrection in Mesopotamia*, p. 92.

30. Wilson, *Mesopotamia, 1917–1920*, p. 273.

Chapter 20: Trouble on the Frontiers

1. David Garnett (ed.), *The Letters of T. E. Lawrence*, Jonathan Cape, London, 1938, pp. 280–82.

2. Ibid., p. 291.

3. Ibid., pp. 290–91.

4. Quoted in Marlowe, p. 183.

5. Quoted ibid., p. 177.

6. Quoted in Sluglett, p. 31.

7. The whole question of the relevance of Britain's continuing involvement
   in Iraq to what one historian has referred to as 'The Imperial Quest for
   Oil' has been much debated, with a number of historians minimising or
   actually denying any such relevance. I leave the final answer to this matter to Peter Sluglett: 'British concern for Iraqi oil was more profound
   in the early days of the mandate than has been thought and denials by
   statesmen that oil played any major part in British calculations [Sluglett
   is referring principally to a denial by Lord Curzon] seem to have been
   given exaggerated credence.' Sluglett, p. 75.

8. Eliezer Tauber, 'The Struggle for Dayr al-Zur: The Determination of
   Borders between Syria and Iraq', *International Journal of Middle East
   Studies*, vol. 23, no. 3, 1991, p. 366.

9. Ibid., p. 371.

10. Philby Papers, 'The Legend of Lijman' (unpublished manuscript, 1928),
    pp. 174–5.

11. Bray, *A Paladin of Arabia*, pp. 397–8.

12. Philby Papers, 'The Legend of Lijman', p. 177.

13. Ibid., p. 178.

14. CAB/24/111, The National Archive, London, CP 1801: Report on the
    Attack at Tel Afar, 25 June 1920.

15. It was customary for Ottoman officers of middle or lower class origin, like
    Jamil, to adopt a name signifying their military profession; thus Jamil
    al-Midfa'i's name refers to *midfa'* (Arabic for gun, or field gun). See
    Batatu, p. 320.

16. al-Hasani, *Al-thawra al-'Iraqiyya al-kubra, sana 1920*, p. 53.

17. FO/371.

18. Ibid. According to the anonymous *Personalities* document (the work of
    Gertrude Bell) it was Muslat Pasha 'who really made the Tal 'Afar coup
    possible. He led his tribesmen to Tal 'Afar.'

19. CAB/24/111, CP 1801.

20. F. F. Raskolnikov, *Tales of Sub-Lieutenant Ilyin: The Taking of Enzeli*,
    available at www.marxists.org. See also CAB/24/106, CP 1356: Bolshevik
    Aggression in Persia. Copy of correspondence between Persian Foreign
    Minister and Secretary General League of Nations, 19 May 1920.

21. Raskolnikov.

22. Gilmour, p. 516.

23. Gertrude Bell Project, letter to Hugh Bell, 1 June 1920.

24. Ibid., letter to Hugh Bell, 7 June 1920.

25. Atiyyah, p. 305. What precisely occurred at Tel 'Afar is unknown. The only witness was an Arab servant of one of the British officers killed. The description of the events which follows is based Haldane, *The Insurrection in Mesopotamia*, pp. 39–42 and Wilson, *Mesopotamia, 1917–1920*, pp. 273–4, supplemented by FO/371 and CAB/24/111, CP 1801.

26. FO/371.

27. CAB/24/111, CP 1801.

28. According to al-Hasani, *Al-thawra al-'Iraqiyya al-kubra, sana 1920*, p. 54, the armoured cars were put out of action by 'disabling their wheels' – presumably referring to their tyres.

29. Gertrude Bell Project, Gertrude Bell to Hugh Bell, 7 June 1920.

30. Wilson, *Mesopotamia, 1917–1920*, p. 274.

31. CAB/24/107, The National Archive, London, CP 1467: Appendix D. From Civil Commissioner, Baghdad, 15 May 1920.

32. Philby Papers, PH VI/3/20.

Chapter 21: The Drift to Violence

1. IO/L/PS/11/175, The British Library, London, Telegram 6948, Civil Commissioner Baghdad to India Office, 9 June 1920.

2. Ibid.

3. Ibid., War Office, London to India Office, London, 3 July 1920.

4. Ibid., Secretary of State India to Civil Commissioner Mesopotamia, 10 July 1920.

5. Ibid., Secret, Memorandum C/29/235, Office of the Military Governor and Political Officer, Baghdad to D.C. Police, 9 June 1929.

6. Ibid., Secret no. 4256, Political Serai, Samarra to Civil Commissioner, 11 June 1920.

7. Ibid., Confidential, No. 131-e, Military Governor & Political Officer, Basra to Civil Commissioner Baghdad, 12 June 1920.

8. Ibid., Judicial Secretary Baghdad to Civil Commissioner Baghdad, 16 June 1920.

9. CAB/24/107, CP 1475: Secretary of State (India) to Civil Commissioner Baghdad, 7 June 1920.

10. Philby Papers, PH VI/3/102, copy of telegram 3279, Political Officer Dulaym Division to Civil Commissioner Baghdad, 18 June 1920.

11. The numbers of fighting men attributed to each of these tribal confederations are taken from IO/L/PS/20/235. However, even this detailed source (presumably compiled by Gertrude Bell) is not always consistent as to the numbers of tribesmen, and in the case of the Khaza'il (2,500) is certainly too small since in a list of sixteen tribal sections giving the number of tribesmen in each section, there are three sections where the number is missing.

12. Atiyyah, p. 250.

13. Cmd. 1061, p. 145.

14. Ibid., pp. 145–6. Bell simply notes that there were '20 casualties in killed and wounded'. It was generally the practice in British reports on the bombing of Arab villages to either fail to mention the number of casualties at all or, where casualty numbers were stated, as in this case, to neglect to identify the sex or age of the victims. It is highly unlikely that women and children would somehow escape this manifestly indiscriminate bombing. See also Priya Satia, 'The Defence of Inhumanity: Air Control and the British Idea of Arabia', *American Historical Review*, February 2006, p. 39.

15. Kadhim, *Al-haraka al-Islamiyya fi al-'Iraq*, p. 266.

16. al-Hasani, *Al-thawra, al-'Iraqiyya al-kubra, sana 1920*, p. 106.

17. IO/L/PS/11/175, Telegram 8542, Civil Commissioner Baghdad to H.B.M. Minister Tehran, repeated to Bushire, Simla, Qasvin, India Office, Banda Abbas, 16 July 1920.

18. Ibid., Telegram 7825, Civil Commissioner Baghdad to India Office, 28 June 1920.

19. al-Rahimi, appendix 19, pp. 310–11. 'Nation' – '*Umma*' in the original.

20. Ibid., p. 219.

21. Ibid.

Chapter 22: The Revolution Begins

1. Failure to repay a loan is the reason given for the arrest in the British sources (cf. Wilson, *Mesopotamia, 1917–1920*, and Haldane, *The Insurrection in Mesopotamia*). However, Atiyyah, p. 340, states that the reason for the arrest was because 'the tribe was showing signs of resistance to the administration and the sheikh was accused of withholding taxes.' Luizard also appears to reject the 'loan argument', stating that the arrest

of Sha'lan was 'en represaille à la veritable fronde qu'il menait contre l'administration' (p. 399).

2. Philby Papers, PH VI/3/107–9.

3. Quoted in Atiyyah, p. 348.

4. Philby Papers, 'The Legend of Lijman', p. 179.

5. IO/L/PS/20/235, p. 100.

6. Haldane, *The Insurrection in Mesopotamia*, p. 73.

7. Hugh Hughes, *Middle East Railways*, The Continental Railway Circle, Harrow, 1981, p. 87.

8. Haldane, *The Insurrection in Mesopotamia*, p. 75. See also al-Hasani, *Al-thawra al-'Iraqiyya al-kubra, sana 1920*, p. 137, where the names of fourteen former Ottoman army officers are listed as helping the rebels with the digging of trenches, artillery etc.

9. IO/L/PS/20/C199, The British Library, London, *Personalities, Baghdad and Kadhimayn*, Baghdad, 1920.

Chapter 23: Discord and Disputation

1. Quoted in Marlowe, p. 205.

2. H. V. F. Winstone, *Gertrude Bell*, Jonathan Cape, London, 1978, p. 213.

3. Gertrude Bell Project, letter to Hugh Bell, 12 January 1920.

4. Quoted in Marlowe, p. 205.

5. IO/L/PS/11/175, Telegram 8312, Civil Commissioner Baghdad to India Office (Repeated to Viceroy), 10 July 1920.

6. Ibid.

Chapter 24: General Haldane's Indian Army

1. T. A. Heathcote, *The Indian Army: The Garrison of British Imperial India, 1822–1922*, David & Charles, Newton Abbot, 1974, p. 55. However, Charles Townshend (*When God Made Hell: The British Invasion of Mesopotamia and the Creation of Iraq*, Faber & Faber, London, 2010, p. 24) states that there were seventeen Indian officers to thirteen British.

2. Calculation based on Haldane, *The Insurrection in Mesopotamia*, pp. 315–17, 325.

3. Major G. F. MacMunn DSO and Major A. C. Lovett (illus.), *The Armies of India*, A. & C. Black, London, 1911.

4. Sir G. F. MacMunn, *The Martial Races of India*, Sampson Low, London, c.1930, p. 2.

5. Ibid., p. 130. On the 'rural' bias aspect of British Orientalism, see also Toby Dodge, *Inventing Iraq: The Failure of Nation Building and a History Denied*, Hurst & Co., London, 2003, ch. 4.

6. MacMunn, *The Martial Races of India*, p. 2.

7. Heathcote, p. 102.

8. Biographical data taken largely from now-deleted pages at www.king-emperor.com.

9. Ibid.

10. Heathcote, p. 141.

11. Ian F. W. Beckett, *Ypres, the First Battle, 1914*, Pearson, Harlow, 2004, pp. 44–5.

12. Wylly, vol. 2, p. 213.

13. Wylly states that the 2nd Manchesters 'formed part of the 55th Brigade of the 18th Division'. However, Wylly must be mistaken since Haldane (*The Insurrection in Mesopotamia*, p. 316) makes it clear that they belonged to the 53rd.

14. Darwent Collection (Manchester Regiment Archive), Ashton-under-Lyne Central Library, MR4/25/48/3, 2nd Battalion Digest of Services 1st April – 30 June 1920, p. 23.

15. Haldane, *The Insurrection in Mesopotamia*, p. 152.

16. Squadron Leader G. C. Piric, 'Some Experiences of No. 6 Squadron in the Iraq Insurrection 1920', *Air Publication*, no. 1152, June 1925, RAF Museum Archive, Hendon, p. 65. The number of aircraft in a flight at full strength would usually have been six, with two or three flights per squadron. However, in this particular environment the number of serviceable aircraft was much smaller.

17. Ibid., p. 70.

18. IO/L/PS/11/175, Telegram 8312, Civil Commissioner Baghdad to India Office (Repeated to Viceroy), 10 July 1920.

19. CAB/24/109, The National Archive, London, CP 1623: Strength of British Forces in the Middle East. War Office to GOC Mesopotamia, 14 July 1920.

Chapter 25: 'The situation has come to a head'

1. IO/MSS/EUR/F462, Major General Leslie to his wife, Baghdad, 13 June 1920.

2. Ibid., 15 June 1920.

3. Ibid., 3 July 1920.

4. Haldane, *The Insurrection in Mesopotamia*, p. 78.

5. Pirie, p. 74.

6. IO/MSS/EUR/F462, Major General Leslie to his wife, Baghdad, 10 July 1920.

7. Ibid., 15 July 1920.

8. Ibid., 11 July 1920.

9. Ibid., 15 July 1920.

10. Ibid.

11. CAB/24/109, CP 1646: Civil Commissioner Baghdad to Foreign Office, 8 July 1920.

12. Ibid., General Officer Commanding, Mesopotamia to War Office, 9 July 1920.

13. Ibid., 12 July 1920.

14. Ibid., 1515 hours.

15. IO/MSS/EUR/F462, Major General Leslie to his wife, Baghdad, 23 July 1920.

16. Haldane, *The Insurrection in Mesopotamia*, p. 81.

17. Colonel B. R. Mullaly, *Bugle and Kukri: The Story of the 10th Princess Mary's Own Gurkha Rifles*, William Blackwood & Sons, Edinburgh, 1957, p. 113.

18. IO/MSS/EUR/F462, Major General Leslie to his wife, Baghdad, 17 July 1920. However, Haldane states, *contra* Leslie, that in this matter APO Hyatt 'acted throughout with courage and good sense', Haldane, *The Insurrection in Mesopotamia*, p. 84.

19. IO/MSS/EUR/F462, Major General Leslie to his wife, Baghdad, 23 July 1920.

20. CAB/24/109, CP 1646: Situation in Mesopotamia. Memorandum by the Secretary of State for War, 17 July 1920.

21. Ibid.

22. Mullaly, p. 137.

23. Haldane, *The Insurrection in Mesopotamia*, pp. 87–8.

24. Lieutenant Colonel Sir Geoffrey Betham and Major H. V. R. Geary, *The Golden Galley: The Story of the Second Punjab Regiment, 1761–1947*, Oxford University Press, 1956, pp. 86–7.

25. Ibid., p. 87.

Chapter 26: The Destruction of the Manchester Column

1. Haldane, *The Insurrection in Mesopotamia*, p. 328.

2. Ibid., p. 187.
3. Wilson, *Mesopotamia, 1917–1920*, p. 297.
4. IO/MSS/EUR/F462, Major General Leslie to his wife, Baghdad, 23 July 1920; see also Darwent Collection, MR4/25/48/9: Letter marked 'strictly confidential' from Major General F. E. Coningham to Major General Sanders.
5. Ibid., Major General Leslie to his wife, Hilla, 27 July 1920. Leslie does not actually name this location. Of the four different accounts of the MANCOL advance, only one – that of Colonel H. C. Wylly – actually provides a name for the spot six miles south of Hilla where the column was supposed to remain and make camp. See Wylly, vol. 2, p. 218.
6. Unfortunately for our understanding of this episode, Leslie gives two slightly different accounts. In his letter of 23 July he describes Lukin's telegraph as *asking permission to march* to the position six miles south of Hilla. But in his next letter (27 July) he describes the march as *having already commenced*, with Lukin only asking him to authorise it. I have assumed that the first version is the more likely one. It is also the one which is consistent with the other sources.
7. Anon, 'Operations of the 2nd Battalion [Manchester Regiment] near Hillah, Mesopotamia, 1920', *Manchester Regiment Gazette*, vol. 2, no. 4, October 1921, p. 191.
8. See, e.g., Lieutenant Colonel Walter Hingston, *Never Give Up: Vol. V. of the History of the King's Own Yorkshire Light Infantry, 1919–1942*, Lund, Humphries & Co., London, 1950, p. 5.
9. These and other biographical data are taken from the 1881 and 1891 Census, the *London Gazette* (www.london-gazette.co.uk) and www.angloboerwar.com
10. Wilson, *Mesopotamia, 1917–1920*, p. 279.
11. Haldane, *The Insurrection in Mesopotamia*, p. 94. However, Maunsell (Colonel E. B. Maunsell, 'The Arab Rebellion: A Disaster and a Cavalry Rear-Guard Action', *Cavalry Journal*, vol. 14, 1924) p. 284, states that the water at Imam Bakr was in a railway tank, and while there was enough for the men there was insufficient water for the animals.
12. Wylly, probably following Haldane, simply states that 'the Commandant at Hilla ... ordered the force to advance ... to the Rustumiyya canal' (Wylly, vol. 2, p. 219), although Haldane adds that afterwards Colonel Lukin 'telegraphed at 12.15 a.m. on the 24th to the divisional general [i.e. Leslie] for approval of the action proposed' (Haldane, *The Insurrection*

in Mesopotamia, p. 95).

13. IO/MSS/EUR/F462, Major General Leslie to his wife, Hilla, 27 July 1920.

14. Maunsell, 'The Arab Rebellion', p. 286.

15. Ibid., p. 288.

16. Wylly, vol. 2, p. 220.

17. Ibid.

18. Darwent Collection, MR4/25/48/9, letter from A. Smith dated 2/11/28; 'court of inquiry', ibid., MR4/25/48/1: typed manuscript, 'Iraq 1920, the Missing Chapter'.

19. IO/MSS/EUR/F462, Major General Leslie to his wife, Hilla, 27 July 1920.

20. Ibid.

21. Ibid.

22. Haldane, *The Insurrection in Mesopotamia*, p. 102.

23. Ibid., p. 10.

24. Gertrude Bell Project, Bell to her father, Baghdad 26 July 1920.

25. CAB/24/110, The National Archive, London, CP 1710: Reinforcements for Mesopotamia, War Office, 30 July 1920.

26. Ibid.

27. Haldane, *The Insurrection in Mesopotamia*, p. 324.

28. CAB/24/111, CP 1715: Note on the Mesopotamia–Persia Situation by Sir Percy Cox, 30 July 1920.

Chapter 27: 'Further unfavourable developments'

1. Haldane, *The Insurrection in Mesopotamia*, p. 139.

2. Haldane, *A Soldier's Saga*, p. 378.

3. Wilfred Nunn, *Tigris Gunboats: The Forgotten War in Iraq, 1914–1917*, new edn, Chatham Publishing, London, 2007, p. 242.

4. Townshend, pp. 198, 286.

5. Nunn, p. 200.

6. The Royal Navy's Fly-class riverine vessels were transferred to the War Office in 1918 and reclassified with *F* numbers. *F10* was the renamed HMS *Blackfly* while *F11* in the next paragraph was once HMS *Gadfly*. See http://freepages.genealogy.rootsweb.ancestry.com/~pbtyc/Janes_1919/ Gun_Boats/Small_China_GunBoats.html. However, with a few exceptions, as late as 1920 most of the Fly-class gunboats were still being referred to by British forces in Iraq by their old names (see numerous

references in the accounts of both Haldane and Wilson).

7. Haldane, *The Insurrection in Mesopotamia*, p. 195.

8. al-Zubaydi, p. 139.

9. Quoted ibid., pp. 140–41.

10. Ibid., p. 141. The same incident is recorded in Fariq al-Mizhar al-Fira'un, *Al-haqa'iq al-nasi'a fi al-thawra al-'Iraqiyya, sana 1920* (The Clear Facts About the Iraqi Revolution of 1920), n.p. Baghdad, 1952, p. 322, as 'I did not intend to sell my country or my people for money'. It would be easy to dismiss this as some post-rebellion attempt to boost his 'nationalist' credentials, except that not only did Sheikh Habib go on to take part in the uprising but after the 1921 Amnesty, he continued to be a thorn in the side of the British authorities (when many other sheikhs had accommodated themselves to neo-colonial rule) and in 1922 was arrested and imprisoned in Henjam island along with Ja'far Abu al-Timman and five other nationalist politicians.

11. Quoted in al-Zubaydi, p. 142.

12. Admiralty, p. 292.

13. al-Zubaydi, p. 143.

14. al-Rawdan, vol. 2, p. 115.

15. al-Hasani, *Al-'Iraq fi dawra al-ihtilal wa al-intidab*, p. 95; see also CAB/24/110, CP 1796: Telegrams relating to the Mesopotamian Situation: Civil Commissioner Baghdad to India Office, n.d.

16. al-Zubaydi, p. 143.

17. Philby Papers, PH/VI/3/84, copy of telegram from Civil Commissioner Baghdad to India Office, 12 September 1920.

18. Atiyyah, p. 325.

19. CAB/24/110, CP 1796: Civil Commissioner Baghdad to India Office, 17 August 1920.

20. Ibid., 12 August 1920.

21. Zetton Buchanan, *In the Hands of the Arabs*, Hodder & Stoughton, London, c.1921, pp. 35–6.

22. Ibid., p. 51.

23. Haldane, *The Insurrection in Mesopotamia*, p. 165. However, Mrs Buchanan gives a different version in which two of the levies were sent out to parley with a white flag but were shot down by the rebels. I am more inclined to accept General Haldane's version.

24. Buchanan, pp. 57–8.

25. Wilson, *Mesopotamia, 1917–1920*, p. 284.

26. IO/MSS/EUR/F462, Major General Leslie to Acting Civil Commissioner Wilson, HQ 17th Division, Ba'quba, 17 September 1920. In the original Leslie refers to the abandonment to their fate of the officials at 'Ba'quba' but it is clear that this is simply a mistake and it is Shahraban to which he is meaning to refer.

27. Alois Musil, *The Middle Euphrates*, AMS Press Inc., New York, 1978 (reprint of original 1927 edn), p. 127.

28. Philby Papers, 'The Legend of Lijman', pp. 179–80.

29. Ibid., p. 181.

30. Winstone, *Leachman*, p. 219.

31. Wilson, *Mesopotamia, 1917–1920*, p. 292.

32. Winstone, *Leachman*, pp. 218–19.

33. Press cutting (no date) accompanying manuscript of Philby Papers, 'The Legend of Lijman'.

34. Even Bray's hagiographical *Paladin of Arabia* (p. 266) speaks of 'Leachman's methods ... his violent fits of berserk rage ... his beatings and abuse of wild Arabs'.

Chapter 28: The Structures of Insurgent Power

1. CAB/24/110, CP 1790: Note on the Causes on the Outbreak in Mesopotamia, n.d.

2. House of Commons Debates, 9 August 1920, vol. 133, cols 51–2.

3. CAB/24/110, CP 1790.

4. Kadhim, *Al-haraka al-Islamiyya fi al-'Iraq*, p. 297.

5. Tu'ma, p. 60.

6. al-Hasani, *Al-thawra al-'Iraqiyya al-kubra, sana 1920*, p. 210.

7. Ibid., p. 211.

8. Kadhim, *Al-haraka al-Islamiyya fi al-'Iraq*, p. 298. Also al-Hasani, *Al-thawra al-'Iraqiyya al-kubra, sana 1920*, p. 211.

9. al-Hasani, *Al-thawra al-'Iraqiyya al-kubra, sana 1920*, p. 211; Kotlov simply refers to it as the 'High Council', L. N. Kotlov, *Thawra al-'ishrin al-wataniyya al-taharuriyya fi al-'Iraq* (The Iraq National Liberation Revolution of 1920), translated from Russian into Arabic by Karam, 'Abd al-Wahid, Baghdad, 1985, p. 227. Other sources, e.g. Luizard (p. 404), refer to five senior clerical members.

10. The second committee was called by al-Hasani *'al-majlis al-milli'* (*Al-thawra al-'Iraqiyya al-kubra, sana 1920*, p. 211). However, the exact name remains something of a mystery. According to al-Rahimi

(p. 223), it was 'al-majlis al-'ilmi' (Committee of Scholars), while Kadhim (*Al-haraka al-Islamiyya fi al-'Iraq*, p. 298) also refers to '*al-majlis al-'ilmi*' but attributes this name to the first committee while the second committee is referred to as the 'local council' (*al-majlis al-mahalli*). A literal translation of al-Hasani's *al-majlis al-milli* would be 'the religious council' or 'denominational council' (hence Turkish *millet*, the denominational communities into which the Ottoman Empire divided its inhabitants). Presumably it is for this reason that Luizard (p. 404), himself citing al-Hasani, refers to this particular committee as the *Conseil Communautaire* and I have followed Luizard in this respect.

11. al-Hasani also refers to two other committees in Najaf, a Management Committee and a Committee of Executive Power, but their precise role and relationship to the City Council and Higher Religious Committee are unclear. See al-Hasani, *Al-thawra al-'Iraqiyya al-kubra, sana 1920*, pp. 209–10.

12. Luizard, p. 405.

13. Abu Tabikh, p. 157. The date on which the flag of independence was first raised is shrouded in mystery. Although Abu Tabikh mentions 18 Dhu al-Hijja (2 September 1920) (conversion to Gregorian using the algorithm in www.oriold.uzh.ch/static/hegira.html), it is unclear from this passage whether this was the actual date on which he was installed as governor and the flag was raised. According to Kadhim, *Reclaiming Iraq*, p. 93, the most likely date was 10 October 1920.

14. See Batatu, p. 174.

15. In this respect it is difficult to accept the general thesis of Kotlov that the uprising was a 'peasants' revolt'. It is true that in many cases that pressure to join the movement came from the peasantry and minor sheikhs but the role of some of the greater sheikhs and senior clergy was also a powerful factor in the mid-Euphrates.

16. al-Hasani, *Al-thawra al-'Iraqiyya al-kubra, sana 1920*, p. 212.

17. al-Darraji, p. 76; See also Luizard, pp. 182, 282, 321, 355, 390, 403.

18. Quoted in al-Hasani, *Al-thawra al-'Iraqiyya al-kubra, sana 1920*, pp. 215–16.

19. Ibid., p. 214. However, Kadhim, *Reclaiming Iraq*, p. 106, states that *Al-Furat* first appeared on 7 August 1920 and 15 September was its last edition. I think this is probably a mistake.

20. al-Hasani, *Al-'Iraq fi dawra al-ihtilal wa al-intidab*, pp. 117–18.

21. Kotlov, p. 218; see also al-Darraji, p. 119; Muhsin (p. 139) mentions only *Al-Furat* in connection with Abu Timman's journalism.
22. al-Hasani, *Al-thawra al-'Iraqiyya al-kubra, sana 1920*, p. 214.

Chapter 29: Trouble on the Home Front

1. *The Times*, 9 July 1920.
2. *The Times*, 12 July 1920.
3. House of Commons Debates, 13 July 1920, vol. 131, cols 2161–2.
4. See Satia, *Spies in Arabia*, p. 292.
5. House of Commons Debates, 23 June 1920, vol. 130, cols 2223–85.
6. Ibid.
7. For an exposition of the legal concept of 'eminent domain' and its history in relation to mineral and extractive industries see Bernard Mommer, *Global Oil and the Nation State*, Oxford Institute for Energy Studies & Oxford University Press, 2002.
8. Calculation made by the author based on Mikdashi, pp. 102, 106.
9. Quoted in John A. DeNovo, 'The Movement for an Aggressive American Oil Policy Abroad, 1918–1920', *American Historical Review*, vol. 61, no. 4, 1956, p. 860.
10. Darwent Collection, MR4/25/48/1.
11. Ibid., MR4/25/48/3.
12. Garnett, p. 313. It is unfortunate that some journalists have quoted this phrase about using poison gas without realising its deliberate irony. This can only be put down to laziness, since anyone reading the paragraph as a whole – in particular the reference to 'getting' the women and children – could not fail to understand that Lawrence was writing deliberately in the style of Jonathan Swift's 'A Modest Proposal'.
13. Ibid., p. 317.
14. Reproduced in CAB/24/111, CP 1871: Secretary of State for India to Cabinet. Copies of Indian newspaper articles, 16 September 1920.
15. Ibid.
16. Gilbert, p. 494.
17. Quoted ibid., pp. 495–6.
18. CAB/24/111, CP 1814: Secretary of State for War to GOC-in-Chief Mesopotamia, 26 August 1920.

Chapter 30: The Siege of Samawa

1. Hingston, pp. 3–4.
2. Ibid., p. 4.
3. Haldane, *The Insurrection in Mesopotamia*, p. 344.
4. Thomas, p. 96.
5. Anon, 'The Story of the Siege of Samawah', *Blackwoods Magazine*, January 1922, p. 103. For some reason Haldane refers to a 13-pounder gun.
6. Ibid., pp. 108, 111.
7. Quoted in Haldane, *The Insurrection in Mesopotamia*, pp. 326–7.
8. Anon, 'The Story of the Siege of Samawah', p. 115.
9. IO/MSS/EUR/F462, Major General Leslie to his wife, Hilla, 28 August 1920.
10. Ibid., Major General Leslie to Acting Civil Commissioner Wilson, Hilla, 17 September 1920.
11. Ibid.
12. Hingston, p. 5.
13. IO/MSS/EUR/F462, Major General Leslie to his wife, Hilla, 27 October 1920.
14. Ibid., 28 October 1920.

Chapter 31: Defeat

1. Haldane, *The Insurrection in Mesopotamia*, p. 328. According to Haldane, the cumulative total of enemy combatants by the end of August was 131,020 of whom 16,630 were armed with modern rifles and 43,175 with 'old but serviceable' rifles.
2. CAB/24/111, CP 1815: GOC-in-chief Mesopotamia to Secretary of State for War, 30 August 1920.
3. Maunsell, *Prince of Wales's Own*, p. 291.
4. Abu Tabikh, p. 161. For a discussion of the post-revolutionary accusations and antagonisms dividing the former leaders of the uprising see Kadhim, *Reclaiming Iraq*.
5. al-Darraji, p. 122.
6. Abu Tabikh, p. 162.
7. Maunsell, *Prince of Wales's Own*, pp. 291, 294.
8. Abu Tabikh, pp. 162–3.
9. Gertrude Bell Project, letter to her father, 7 November 1920.
10. al-Darraji, p. 122.

11. Quoted in al-Hasani, *Al-'Iraq fi dawra al-ihtilal wa al-intidab*, pp. 117–18.

12. See the testimony of a British private soldier in Anon, 'A Prisoner with the Arabs, from July–October 19, 1920', *Manchester Regiment Gazette*, vol. 2, no. 4, October 1921, pp. 185–8.

13. Haldane, *The Insurrection in Mesopotamia*, p. 312; Wilson, *Mesopotamia, 1917–1920*, p. 299.

14. Darwent Collection, MR4/25/48/1.

Chapter 32: A Death on the Baghdad Road

1. Not to be confused with the Al Bu Muhammad of the southern marshes.

2. FO/371.

3. Sir Percy Cox, *'Iraq, Report on Iraq Administration'*, October 1920–March 1922, HMSO, London, 1922, p. 3; see also Tauber, 'The Role of Lieutenant Muhammad Sharif al-Faruqi', p. 50.

4. Lady Bell, vol. 2, p. 568.

Chapter 33: The Punishment

1. al-Darraji, p. 123.

2. Abu Tabikh, p. 202.

3. For example, according to Charles Tripp (*A History of Iraq*, Cambridge University Press, 2000, p. 44), 'by the end of October, and, with the surrender of Najaf and Karbela', the rebellion was over'. See also Christopher Catherwood, *Winston's Folly: Imperialism and the Creation of Modern Iraq*, Constable, London, 2004, p. 89: 'by 12 October ... the rebellion had been totally crushed'. The error is probably partly accounted for by the fact that Haldane's statement of British and Indian casualties in the uprising only covers the period up to 17 October 1920 (Haldane, *The Insurrection in Mesopotamia*, p. 331). Jamil (p. 53), draws attention to officially recorded British and Indian casualties occurring *after* this date, although even he states that the insurrection 'lasted until the end of November'. Haldane himself states that combat operations did not cease until 3 February 1921 and that military operations against the insurgents 'had been in constant progress for seven months' (p. 297).

4. Gertrude Bell Project, Gertrude Bell to Hugh Bell, 17 October 1920.

5. Haldane, *The Insurrection in Mesopotamia*, p. 256.

6. Ibid., p. 261.

7. Ibid., p. 332.

8. Quoted in Townshend, p. 48.

9. Ibid., p. 49.

10. Haldane, *The Insurrection in Mesopotamia*, p. 342.

11. IO/MSS/EUR/F462, Major General Leslie to his wife, Hilla, 20 August and 10 and 19 October 1920.

12. Maunsell, *Prince of Wales's Own*, p. 287.

13. Philby Papers, 'The Legend of Lijman', p. 186.

14. See Kadhim, *Al-haraka al-Islamiyya fi al-'Iraq*, p. 341.

15. Pirie, p. 80.

16. Quoted in Andrew Boyle, *Trenchard, Man of Vision*, Collins, London, 1962, p. 89. It is not clear exactly when this attack took place; it could have been any time between February and May 1921. If towards the latter, this gives further indication of the continuity of the suppression campaign well into 1921.

17. Ibid.

18. Ibid.

Chapter 34: A 'friendly native state'

1. Disgusted with British policy in Iraq, Philby would soon resign his position.

2. Luizard, p. 417.

3. Quoted in Satia, *Spies in Arabia*, p. 253.

4. For a detailed analysis of the 1922 Treaty, see Ireland, pp. 341–52. A slightly modified version of the initially proposed treaty was not ratified until 1924, after the election of a Constituent Assembly by indirect voting with reserved seats for pro-British Christian and Jewish delegates and further packed by the automatic inclusion of forty largely pro-British sheikhs.

Afterword

1. See the works by Antonius and Zeine.

2. For critiques of the 'orthodox narrative' that both before and during the First World War the Arabs were 'anti-Ottoman' and saw the Turks as their enemy, see for example, the articles in Khalidi et al., *The Origins of Arab Nationalism*, by Dawn, op. cit.; Haddad, op. cit.; Lisa Anderson, 'The Development of Nationalist Sentiment in Libya, 1908–1922', pp. 225–42; and James Jankowski, 'Egypt and Early Arab Nationalism

1908–1922', pp. 243–70. See also Jonathan Gorvett, 'The Forgotten Arabs of Gallipoli', *Al Jazira Net*, 14, January 2004, available at www.aljazeera.com/archive/2004/01/200849135129326810.html

3. Private Ihsan, the Palestinian Arab whose diary is the principal material used in Tamari's biographical article, spent most of his time in uniform trying to avoid active service and was clearly opposed to the war. However, he was clearly a literate, if not intellectual, individual with very 'advanced' ideas, and it is difficult to know how typical he was since, to date, only one other such diary has been found and that belonged to a junior officer whose mother was actually Turkish and who wrote in Turkish – a junior officer named Muhammad al-Salih. In contrast to Private Ihsan, Second Lieutenant Al-Salih was strongly pro-Ottoman and a loyal and brave soldier. See Hasan Basri Danisman (ed.), *Gallipoli 1915. Bloody Ridge (Lone Pine). Diary of Lt. Mehmed Fasih*, Denizer Kitabevi, Istanbul 2001.

4. See E. J. Erickson, *Ottoman Army Effectiveness in WWI: A Comparative Study*, Routledge, Abingdon, 2007, pp. 120–21. The British Intelligence study of 7,233 Ottoman prisoners and deserters on the Palestine front, carried out over the period October–November 1917, showed that 64 per cent were ethnic Turks, 27 per cent Arabs and 9 per cent Greeks, Kurds, Jews and Armenians. These percentages were almost exactly the same as the British estimates for the actual composition of the Ottoman troops confronting them: 66 per cent Turks, 26 per cent Arabs and 8 per cent 'others'.

5. The notable exception being Ireland (1937).

6. Elie Kedourie, *England and the Middle East*, Bowes and Bowes, London, 1956, p. 205.

7. Marlowe, p. 212.

8. Bell, 'Review of the Civil Administration of Mesopotamia', p. 144.

9. Ibid., p. 147; Longrigg, *Iraq*, p. 122.

10. See e.g. Batatu, pp. 174, 220–21.

11. Amal Vinogradov, 'The 1920 Revolt in Iraq Reconsidered: The Role of the Tribes in National Politics', *International Journal of Middle East Studies*, vol. 3, no. 2, 1972, p. 125.

12. Jafna Cox, '"A splendid training ground": The Importance to the RAF of Its Role in Iraq, 1919–32', *Journal of Imperial and Commonwealth History*, vol. 13, no. 2, 1985, p. 175.

13. On the bombing of tribal villages in southern Yemen during the 1930s,

see H. St J. Philby, *Sheba's Daughters*, Methuen & Co., London, 1939, p. xiv.

14. 'Informal Empire' is the term used by Daniel Silverfarb, *Britain's Informal Empire in the Middle East: A Case Study of Iraq, 1929–41*, Oxford University Press, 1986; 'Covert Empire' is used by Satia, *Spies in Arabia*.

15. Ian Rutledge, *Addicted to Oil: America's Relentless Drive for Energy Security*, I. B. Tauris, London, 2005, p. 34.

16. Eugene Rogan, *The Arabs, A History*, Allen Lane, London, 2010, p. 173.

17. Ja'far al-Khaiyat, *Al-thawra al-'Iraqiyya* (The Iraqi Revolution), Dar al-Rafidayn, Beirut 2004, p. 5 (1st edn, 1971). The book is a selection of material from Sir Arnold Wilson's *Mesopotamia, 1917–1920: A Clash of Loyalties*, translated into Arabic with a prologue by the translator.

18. This was al-Hasani, *Al-'Iraq fi dawra al-ihtilal wa al-intidab*.

19. Vinogradov, p. 139.

20. See Kadhim, *Reclaiming Iraq*, pp. 31–2.

21. Kadhim states that while the uprising 'achieved its political goals ... the founding of the Iraqi state[,] [w]hat was not intended was the composition of the state that came into being.' Kadhim, *Reclaiming Iraq*, p. 164.

22. Tripp, p. 31, says it was 'less than 20 percent'.

23. See Jafna Cox, p. 174.

24. Dodge, p. 158. Essentially the same point is made by Davis.

25. For the sorry political history of Iraq since 1921 see, in particular, Batatu, Phebe Marr, *The Modern History of Iraq*, Westview, Colorado, 1985, Tripp, Dodge, Gema Martín Muñoz, *Iraq, un fracaso de Occidente, 1920–2003*, Tusqets Editores, Barcelona, 2003), Davis and Sluglett.

26. On the increasing involvement of Turkey in Kurdistan see 'Kurdistan Oil & Gas Report', *Financial Times*, 10 December 2012, pp. 3–4.

Appendix: Some Biographical Notes

1. On this and similar atrocities see Sluglett, pp. 188–91; Dodge, pp. 132–56; Satia, *Spies In Arabia*, pp. 239–62.

2. James, p. 327.

Bibliography

Archival Sources

OFFICIAL UK SOURCES

Published

Admiralty, *Iraq and the Persian Gulf*, B.R. 524 (restricted), Geographical Handbook Series, Naval Intelligence Division, London, 1944.

Bell, Gertrude, 'Review of the Civil Administration of Mesopotamia', Cmd. 1061, 1920, HMSO, London, 1920.

Cox, Sir Percy, *Iraq: Report on Iraq Administration, October 1920–March 1922*, HMSO, London, 1922.

House of Commons Debates [Hansard], at http://hansard.millbanksystems. com.

Pirie, G. C., 'Some Experiences of No. 6 Squadron in the Iraq Insurrection 1920', *Air Publication*, no. 1152, June 1925, RAF Museum Archive, Hendon.

War Office, *Supplement to the London Gazette*, HMSO, London, 5 July, 1921, *London Gazette*, www.london-gazette.co.uk.

Cabinet Papers (The National Archive, London)

CAB/21/119, Admiral Edmond Slade, 'Petroleum Situation in the British Empire', 29 July 1918.

CAB/24/106, CP 1320: Mesopotamian Expenditure. Memorandum by the Secretary of State for War, 20 May 1920; CP 1356: Bolshevik Aggression in Persia. Copy of correspondence between Persian Foreign Minister and Secretary General League of Nations, 19 May 1920.

CAB/24/107, CP 1467: Appendix D. From Civil Commissioner, Baghdad, 15 May 1920; CP 1475: Secretary of State (India) to Civil Commissioner Baghdad, 7 June 1920.

CAB/24/108, CP 1524: Memorandum by the Minister in Charge of Petroleum Affairs, 21 June 1920.

CAB/24/109, CP 1623: Strength of British Forces in the Middle East. Copy of telegram from the War Office to the General Officer Commanding, Mesopotamia, 14 July 1920; CP 1646: Civil Commissioner, Baghdad to Foreign Office, 8 July 1920; GOC, Mesopotamia to War Office, 9, 14, 15 July 1920; Situation in Mesopotamia: memorandum by the Secretary of State for War, 17 July 1920.

CAB/24/110, CP 1710: Reinforcements for Mesopotamia, War Office, 30 July 1920; CP 1796: Telegrams relating to the Mesopotamian Situation from Civil Commissioner, Baghdad; CP 1790: Note on the Causes on the Outbreak in Mesopotamia, n.d.

CAB/24/111, CP 1715: Note on the Mesopotamia–Persia Situation by Sir Percy Cox, 30 July 1920; CP 1801: Report on the Attack at Tel Afar, 25 June 1920; CP 1814, 1815: Copies of Telegram from Secretary of State for War to GOC-in-chief, Mesopotamia, 26 August 1920 and reply, 30 August 1920; CP 1871: Secretary of State for India to Cabinet. Copies of Indian newspaper articles, 16 September 1920.

CAB/27/1, *British Desiderata in Turkey in Asia* (The De Bunsen Committee Report), 25 June 1915.

Foreign Office Papers (The National Archive, London)

FO/371, *Personalities, Mosul, Arbil and Frontier*, Government Press, Baghdad, 1921.

FO/800/221, Memorandum, Sir Mark Sykes to Sir Arthur Hirtzel, 16 January 1918.

FO/882/13, Memorandum on Military, Political Situation in Mesopotamia (Section II), 28 October 1915; Copy of Telegram from Sir John Maxwell (Cairo) to Lord Kitchener, War Office, 16 October 1915; Copy of Telegram from Sir Mark Sykes to Sir Percy Cox (Mesopotamia), Cairo 22 November 1915.

India Office Papers (The British Library, London)

IO/L/PS/10/815, *Geological Reports, Mesopotamia and Kurdistan*, Preliminary Report on the Prospects of Petroleum in the Baghdad Wilaya, Government Press, Baghdad, March 1918; Geological Report (Mesopotamia no. 1) District of Qaiyara, Government Press, Baghdad 1919; Telegram, Civil Commissioner, Baghdad, to Foreign Office, 13 March 1918.

IO/L/PS/11/175, Telegram 6948, from Civil Commissioner Baghdad to India Office, 9 June 1920; Telegram 8312, from Civil Commissioner Baghdad to India Office, (Repeated to Viceroy) 10 July 1920; Telegram 8542, Civil Commissioner Baghdad to H.B.M. Minister Tehran, repeated to Bushire, Simla, Qasvin, India Office, Banda Abbas, 16 July 1920.

IO/L/PS/20/C151, *Tribes of the Tigris*, Government of India for Arab Bureau, Calcutta, 1917.

IO/L/PS/20/C199, *Personalities, Baghdad and Kadhimayn*, Baghdad 1920.

IO/L/PS/20/C152, *Tribes around the Junction of the Euphrates and Tigris*, Government of India for Arab Bureau, Calcutta, 1917.

IO/L/PS/20/63, *The Muntafiq. Al Sa'dun, Bani Malik, Ajwad, Bani Sa'id, Bani Huchaym*, Arab Bureau, Calcutta, 1917.

IO/L/PS/20/235, *Arab Tribes of the Baghdad* Vilayet, Government of India for Arab Bureau, July 1918, Calcutta 1919.

IO/MSS/EUR/F462, Correspondence of Major General G. A. J. Leslie. Letters copied and sent to Arnold T. Wilson, 24 August 1930, to assist Wilson in writing his own memoirs of these events.

OTHER ARCHIVAL SOURCES

Darwent Collection (Manchester Regiment Archive), Ashton-under-Lyne Central Library: MR4/25/48/1–10: *2nd Battalion Manchester Regiment in Mesopotamia 1920*.

Gertrude Bell Project, University of Newcastle, www.gerty.ncl.ac.uk.

Philby Papers, Middle East Centre, St Antony's College, Oxford: PH VI/3 (various correspondence); 'The Legend of Lijman' (unpublished manuscript, 1928); 'Mesopotage' (unpublished manuscript, 1946?).

RAF Museum Archives, Hendon.

Books in the Arabic Language

'Abd al-Darraji, 'Abd al-Razzaq, *Ja'far Abu al-Timman wa dawrahu fi al-haraka al-wataniyya fi al-'Iraq* (Ja'far Abu al-Timman and His Role in the Iraqi National Movement), 2nd edn, Ministry of Culture and Information, Baghdad, 1980.

Abu Tabikh, Jamil Muhsin (ed.), *Muthakarat al-Sayyid Muhsin Abu Tabikh, 1910–1960: khamsun 'aman min tarikh al-'Iraq al siyyasi al-hadith* (Memoirs of Sayyid Muhsin Abu Tabikh 1910–1960: Fifty Years of Iraq's Modern Political History), Mu'sasa al-'Arabiyya li al-dirasat wa al-nashar, Beirut, 2001.

al-Asadi, Hasan, *Thawra al-Najaf 'ala al-Ingliz aw al shararat al-ula li thawra al-'ishrin* (The Uprising against the British at Najaf or the First Sparks of the Revolution of 1920), Ministry of Information, Baghdad, 1975.

al-Bazirgan, Hasan 'Ali, *Min ahdath Baghdad wa al-Diyala ithna al-thawra al-'ishrin fi al-'Iraq* (Concerning the Events in Baghdad and the Diyala during the Revolution of 1920 in Iraq) new edn, Bayt al-Hikma, Baghdad, 2000.

al-Fira'un, Fariq al-Mizhar, *Al-haqa'iq al-nasi'a fi al-thawra al-'Iraqiyya, sana 1920* (The Clear Facts About the Iraqi Revolution of 1920), n.p., Baghdad, 1952.

al-Hasani, 'Abd al-Razzaq, *Al-'Iraq fi dawra al-ihtilal wa al-intidab* (Iraq between the Occupation and the Mandate), vol. 1, Matba' al-'Irfan, Sidon, 1935.

al-Hasani, 'Abd al-Razzaq, *Tarikh al-'Iraq al-haditha* (History of Modern Iraq), Matba' al-'Irfan, Sidon, 1957.

al-Hasani, 'Abd al-Razzaq, *Al-thawra al-'Iraqiyya al-kubra, sana 1920* (The Great Iraqi Revolution of 1920), 3rd edn, Matba' al-'Irfan, Sidon, 1972.

Jamil, Husayn, *Al-'Iraq: shahada siyasiyya, 1908–1930* (Iraq, Political Witness, 1908–1930), Dar al-Laam, London, 1987.

Kadhim, Abbas Muhammad, *Al-haraka al-Islamiyya fi al-'Iraq (thaura al-'ishrin)* (The Islamic Movement in Iraq ([Revolution of 1920]), n.p., 1984.

al-Khaiyat, Ja'far, *Al-thawra al-'Iraqiyya* (The Iraqi Revolution), Dar al-Rafidayn, Beirut, 2004.

Kotlov, L. N., *Thawra al-'ishrin al-wataniyya al-taharuriyya fi al-'Iraq* (The Iraq National Liberation Revolution of 1920), translated from Russian into Arabic by Karam, 'Abd al-Wahid, n.p., Baghdad, 1985.

al-Rahimi, 'Abd al-Halim, *Al-haraka al-Islamiyya fi al-'Iraq: al-juthur al-fikriyya wa al-waqi' al-tarikhi (1900–24)* (The Islamic Movement in Iraq: Ideological Roots and Historical Situation, 1900–1924), Dar al-'alamiyya, Beirut, 1985.

al-Rawdan, 'Abd 'Awn, *Mausu'a 'Asha'ir al-'Iraq: Tarikh, Ansab, Rijalat, Ma'athir* (Encyclopaedia of the Tribes of Iraq: History, Genealogy, Leading Personalities, Achievements), 2 vols., Al-Ahliyya, Amman, 2003.

Tu'ma, Salman Hadi, *Karbela' fi thawra al-'ishrin* (Karbela' in the Revolution of 1920), n.p., Beirut, 2000.

al-Zubaydi, Muhammad Husayn, *Al-siyasiyyun al-'Iraqiyyun al-munfiyyun ila jazira hinjam sana 1922* (The Iraqi Politicians Exiled to Henjam Island, 1922), Al-Maktaba al-Wataniyya, Baghdad, 1989.

Books and Theses in English and Other non-Arabic Languages

Adelson, Roger, *Mark Sykes: Portrait of an Amateur*, Jonathan Cape, London, 1975.

Anderson, J. R. L., *East of Suez*, Hodder and Stoughton, London, 1969.

Antonius, George, *The Arab Awakening*, Hamish Hamilton, London, 1945 (first published 1938).

Atiyyah, Ghassan R., *Iraq: 1908–1921. A Socio-Political Study*, Arab Institute for Research and Publishing, Beirut, 1973.

Barker, A. J., *The Neglected War: Mesopotamia, 1914–1918*, Faber & Faber, London, 1967.

Batatu, Hanna, *The Old Social Classes and the Revolutionary Movements of Iraq*, Saqi Books, London, 2004 (first published 1978).

Beckett, Ian F. W., *Ypres, the First Battle, 1914*, Pearson, Harlow, 2004.

Bell, Gertrude Lowthian (published anonymously), *The Arab of Mesopotamia*, Government Press, Basra, n.d. (probably 1917). Reprinted as *Arab War Lords and Iraqi Star Gazers* (ed. Paul Rich), Authors Choice Press, San Jose, 2001.

Bell, Lady Florence (ed.), *The Letters of Gertrude Bell*, Ernest Benn, London, 1927.

Benjamin, Marina, *Last Days in Babylon: The Story of the Jews of Baghdad*, Bloomsbury, London, 2007.

Betham, Lieutenant Colonel Sir Geoffrey, and Geary, Major H. V. R., *The Golden Galley: The Story of the Second Punjab Regiment, 1761–1947*, Oxford University Press, 1956.

Blunt, Lady Anne, *The Bedouins of the Euphrates*, Harper & Bros, New York, 1879.

Boyle, Andrew, *Trenchard, Man of Vision*, Collins, London, 1962.

Bray, N. N. E., *A Paladin of Arabia: The Biography of Brevet Lieut.-Colonel G. E. Leachman C.I.E., D.S.O.*, Unicorn Press, London, 1936.

Bray, N. N. E., *Shifting Sands: The True Story of the Arab Revolt*, Unicorn Press, London, 1934.

Broadbent, Harvey, *Gallipoli, the Fatal Shore*, Viking Penguin, Sydney, 2005.

Brown, Malcolm, *British Logistics on the Western Front, 1914–1919*, Praeger, Westport, 1998.

Buchan, John, *Greenmantle*, Kindle edn, Duke Classics, 2012.

Buchanan, Zetton, *In the Hands of the Arabs*, Hodder & Stoughton, London, c.1921.

Busch, Briton Cooper, *Britain, India and the Arabs, 1914–1921*, University of California Press, Berkeley, 1971.

Candler, Edmund, *The Long Road to Baghdad*, 2 vols, Cassell, London, 1919.

Carver, Field Marshal Lord, *The National Army Museum Book of the Turkish Front, 1914–1918*, Pan Books, London, 2000.

Catherwood, Christopher, *Winston's Folly: Imperialism and the Creation of Modern Iraq*, Constable, London, 2004.

Clark, Christopher, *The Sleepwalkers: How Europe Went to War in 1914*, Allen Lane, London, 2012.

Cowan, J. M. (ed.), *The Hans Wehr Dictionary of Modern Arabic*, Spoken Language Services, Inc., Ithaca, 1994.

Danisman, Hasan Basri (ed.), *Gallipoli 1915. Bloody Ridge (Lone Pine). Diary of Lt. Mehmed Fasih*, Denizer Kitabevi, Istanbul, 2001.

Darwin, John, *Britain, Egypt and the Middle East*, Macmillan, London, 1981.

Davis, Eric, *Memories of State: Politics, History and Collective Identity in Modern Iraq*, University of California Press, Berkeley, 2005.

de Gaury, Gerald, *Rulers of Mecca*, Harrap, London, 1951.

Delve, K., *Source Book of the RAF*, Airlife Publishing, Shrewsbury, 1994.

Dodge, Toby, *Inventing Iraq: The Failure of Nation Building and a History Denied*, Hurst & Co., London, 2003.

Erickson, E. J., *Ottoman Army Effectiveness in WW1: A Comparative Study*, Routledge, Abingdon, 2007.

Erickson, E. J., *Gallipoli: The Ottoman Campaign*, Pen and Sword Books, Barnsley, 2010.

Ferrier, R. W., *The History of the British Petroleum Company*, vol. 1, Cambridge University Press, 1982.

Fromkin, David, *A Peace to End All Peace: Creating the Modern Middle East, 1914–1922*, André Deutsch, London, 1989.

Garnett, David (ed.), *The Letters of T. E. Lawrence*, Jonathan Cape, London, 1938.

George-Samne, Dr, *La Syrie*, Editions Bossard, Paris, 1920.

Gilbert, Martin, *World in Torment: Winston Churchill 1917–1922*, Minerva, London, 1975.

Gilmour, David, *Curzon*, John Murray, London, 1994.

Graves, Robert, *Lawrence and the Arabs*, Jonathan Cape, London, 1927.

Haldane, Lieutenant General Sir Aylmer, *The Insurrection in Mesopotamia, 1920*, William Blackwood & Sons, Edinburgh and London, 1922.

Haldane, Lieutenant General Sir Aylmer, *A Soldier's Saga*, William Blackwood & Sons, Edinburgh and London, 1948.

Hamilton, Charles W., *Americans and Oil in the Middle East*, Gulf Publishing Company, Houston, 1962.

Heathcote, T. A., *The Indian Army: The Garrison of British Imperial India, 1822–1922*, David & Charles, Newton Abbot, 1974.

Hingston, Lieutenant Colonel Walter, *Never Give Up: Vol. V of The History of the Kings Own Yorkshire Light Infantry, 1919–42*, Lund, Humphries & Co. London, 1950.

Hughes, Hugh, *Middle East Railways*, The Continental Railway Circle, Harrow, 1981.

Ireland, Philip Willard, *Iraq: A Study in Political Development*, Jonathan Cape, London, 1937.

James, Lawrence, *The Golden Warrior: The Life and Legend of Lawrence of Arabia*, Abacus, London, 1990.

Jones, Stephanie, *Trade and Shipping: Lord Inchcape, 1852–1932*, Manchester University Press, 1989.

Kadhim, Abbas, *Reclaiming Iraq: The 1920 Revolution and the Founding of the Modern State*, University of Texas Press, Austin, 2012.

Keay, John, *Sowing the Wind: The Seeds of Conflict in the Middle East*, John Murray, London, 2003.

Kedourie, Elie, *England and the Middle East*, Bowes and Bowes, London, 1956.

Kent, Marian, *Oil and Empire*, Macmillan, London, 1976.

Khalidi, Rashid, Anderson, Lisa, Muslih, Muhammad and Simon, Reeva S. (eds.), *The Origins of Arab Nationalism*, Columbia University Press, New York, 1991.

Lawrence, T. E., *The Seven Pillars of Wisdom*, Jonathan Cape, London, 1935.

Longhurst, Henry, *Adventure in Oil: The Story of British Petroleum*, Sidgwick & Jackson, London, 1959.

Longrigg, Stephen H., *Oil in the Middle East: Its Discovery and Development*, Oxford University Press, London, 1954.

Longrigg, Stephen H., *Iraq, 1900–1950*, Oxford University Press, London, 1953.

Luizard, Pierre-Jean, *La Formation de l'Irak Contemporain*, CNRS Editions, Paris, 1991.

Lyell, Thomas, *The Ins and Outs of Mesopotamia*, A. M. Philpot, London, 1923.

MacMunn, Sir G. F., *The Martial Races of India*, Sampson Low, London, c.1930.

MacMunn, Major G. F. DSO and Lovett, Major A. C. (illus.), *The Armies of India*, A. & C. Black, London, 1911.

Mann, J. S., *The Making of an Administrator, 1893–1920*, Longmans, Green & Co., London, 1921.

Marlowe, John, *Late Victorian: The Life of Sir Arnold Wilson*, The Cresset Press, London, 1967.

Marr, Phebe, *The Modern History of Iraq*, Westview, Colorado, 1985.

Maunsell, Colonel E. B., *Prince of Wales's Own, The Scinde Horse*, Naval and Military Press, Uckfield, 2005.

Mejcher, Helmut, *Imperial Quest for Oil: Iraq 1910–1928*, Ithaca Press, London, 1976.

Mikdashi, Zuhair, *A Financial Analysis of Middle Eastern Oil Concessions: 1901–1965*, Praeger, New York, 1966.

Mommer, Bernard, *Global Oil and the Nation State*, Oxford Institute for Energy Studies & Oxford University Press, 2002.

Mullaly, Colonel B. R., *Bugle and Kukri: The Story of the 10th Princess Mary's Own Gurkha Rifles*, William Blackwood & Sons, Edinburgh, 1957.

Muñoz, Gema Martín, *Iraq, un fracaso de Occidente, 1920–2003*, Tusqets Editores, Barcelona, 2003.

Musil, Alois, *The Middle Euphrates*, AMS Press Inc., New York, 1978 (reprint of original 1927 edn).

Nakash, Yitzhak, *The Shi'is of Iraq*, Princeton University Press, Princeton, 1995.

Nunn, Wilfred, *Tigris Gunboats: The Forgotten War in Iraq, 1914–1917*, new edn, Chatham Publishing, London, 2007.

Parfit, J. T., *Marvellous Mesopotamia: The World's Wonderland*, S. W. Partridge & Co., London, 1920.

Philby, H. St J., *Sheba's Daughters*, Methuen & Co., London, 1939.

Rich, Paul (ed.), *Iraq and Imperialism: Thomas Lyell's The Ins and Outs of Mesopotamia*, Authors Choice Press, San Jose, 2001.

Robson, Brian, *Crisis on the Frontier: The Third Afghan War and the Campaign in Waziristan, 1919–1920*, Spellmount, Staplehurst, 2004.

Rogan, Eugene, *The Arabs: A History*, Allen Lane, London, 2010.

Roskill, Stephen, *Hankey, Man of Secrets*, 2 vols, Collins, London, 1972.

Russell, Douglas S., *Winston Churchill, Soldier*, Brassey's, London, 2005.

Rutledge, Ian, *Addicted to Oil: America's Relentless Drive for Energy Security*, I. B. Tauris, London, 2005.

Satia, Priya, *Spies in Arabia: The Great War and the Cultural Foundations of Britain's Covert Empire in the Middle East*, Oxford University Press, 2008.

Schwadran, Benjamin, *The Middle East, Oil and the Great Powers*, Atlantic Press, London, 1956.

Silverfarb, Daniel, *Britain's Informal Empire in the Middle East: A Case Study of Iraq, 1929–41*, Oxford University Press, 1986.

Sluglett, Peter, *Britain in Iraq*, 2nd edn, I. B. Tauris, London, 2007.

Stivers, William, *Supremacy and Oil: Iraq, Turkey and the Anglo-American World Order, 1918–30*, Cornell University Press, Ithaca and London, 1982.

Storrs, Ronald, *Orientations*, Nicolson & Watson, London, 1945.

Sykes, Mark, *Dar-ul-Islam: A Record of a Journey through Ten of the Asiatic Provinces of Turkey*, Bickers & Son, London, 1904, repr. Darf Publishers, London, 1988.

Sykes, Mark, *Through Five Turkish Provinces*, Bickers & Son, London, 1900.

Tauber, Eliezer, *The Arab Movements in World War One*, Frank Cass, London, 1993.

Teitelbaum, Joshua, *The Rise and Fall of the Hashemite Kingdom of Arabia*, C. Hurst & Co., London, 2001.

Temperley, H. W. V., *History of the Peace Conference*, 6 vols., Oxford University Press, London, 1920–24.

Thomas, Bertram, *Alarms and Excursions in Arabia*, Bobbs-Merrill, Indianapolis, 1931.

Townshend, Charles, *When God Made Hell: The British Invasion of Mesopotamia and the Creation of Iraq*, Faber & Faber, London, 2010.

Tripp, Charles, *A History of Iraq*, Cambridge University Press, 2000.

Wilson, Arnold T., *Loyalties: Mesopotamia, 1914–1917*, Oxford University Press, London, 1930.

Wilson, Arnold T., *Mesopotamia, 1917–1920: A Clash of Loyalties*, Oxford University Press, London, 1931.

Wilson, Arnold T., *S.W. Persia. Letters and Diary of a Young Political Officer 1907–1914*, Readers Union, London, 1942.

Winstone, H. V. F., *Gertrude Bell*, Jonathan Cape, London, 1978.

Winstone, H. V. F., *Leachman, O.C. Desert*, Quartet Books, London, 1982.

Wylly, Colonel H. C., *History of the Manchester Regiment*, vol. 2: 1883–1922, Forster Groom & Co., London, 1925.

Wynn, Antony, *Persia in the Great Game: Sir Percy Sykes, Explorer, Consul, Soldier, Spy*, John Murray, London, 2003.

Yergin, Daniel, *The Prize: The Epic Quest for Oil, Money and Power*, Simon & Schuster, London, 1991.

Zeine, Zeine N., *The Struggle for Arab Independence*, Khayats, Beirut, 1960.

Articles/Chapters in Scholarly Journals, Books, Conferences

Air Publication no. 1152, June 1925, RAF Museum Archive, Hendon.

Anderson, Lisa, 'The Development of Nationalist Sentiment in Libya, 1908–1922', in Khalidi et al., pp. 225-42.

Boyce, Gordon, 'Reviews', *Business History Review*, vol. 63, no. 3, 1989.

Cox, Jafna, '"A splendid training ground": The Importance to the RAF of Its Role in Iraq, 1919–32', *Journal of Imperial and Commonwealth History*, vol. 13, no. 2, 1985, pp. 157–84.

Dann, Uriel, 'Report on the Petroliferous Districts of Mesopotamia (1905) – an Annotated Document', *Asian and African Studies*, vol. 24, no. 3, 1990, pp. 283–92.

Dawn, C. Ernest, 'The Origins of Arab Nationalism', in Khalidi et al., pp. 3–30.

DeNovo, John A., 'The Movement for an Aggressive American Oil Policy Abroad, 1918–1920', *American Historical Review*, vol. 61, no. 4, 1956, pp. 854–76.

Haddad, Mahmoud, 'Iraq before World War 1: A Case of Anti-European Arab Ottomanism', in Khalidi et al., pp. 120–50.

Jack, Marian, 'The Purchase of the British Government's Shares in the British Petroleum Company, 1912–1914', *Past and Present*, no. 39, 1968, pp. 139–68.

Jacobsen, Mark, '"Only by the Sword": British Counter-insurgency in Iraq, 1920', *Small Wars and Insurgencies*, vol. 2, no. 2, 1991, pp. 323–63.

Jankowski, James, 'Egypt and Early Arab Nationalism, 1908–1922', in Khalidi et al., pp. 243–70.

Klieman, Aron, S., 'Britain's War Aims in the Middle East in 1915', *Journal of Contemporary History*, vol. 3, no. 3, 1968, pp. 237–51.

Mejcher, Helmut, 'Oil and British Policy Towards Mesopotamia', *Middle Eastern Studies*, vol. 8, no. 3, 1972, pp. 377–91.

Muhsin, Abid Khalid, 'The Political Career of Muhammad Ja'far Abu al-Timman, 1908–1937: A Study in Modern Iraqi History', unpublished PhD thesis, School of Oriental and African Studies, London, 1983.

Satia, Priya, 'The Defence of Inhumanity: Air Control and the British Idea of Arabia', *American Historical Review*, February 2006, pp. 16–51.

Tamari, Salim, 'The Short Life of Private Ihsan', *Jerusalem Quarterly*, no. 30,

Spring 2007, available at http://www.jerusalemquarterly.org/ViewArticle.aspx?id=64

Tauber, Eliezer, 'The Role of Lieutenant Muhammad Sharif al-Faruqi – New Light on Anglo-Arab Relations during the First World War', *Asian and African Studies*, vol. 24, 1990, pp. 17–50.

Tauber, Eliezer, 'The Struggle for Dayr al-Zur: The Determination of Borders between Syria and Iraq', *International Journal of Middle East Studies*, vol. 23, no. 3, 1991, pp. 361–85.

Vinogradov, Amal, 'The 1920 Revolt in Iraq Reconsidered: The Role of the Tribes in National Politics', *International Journal of Middle East Studies*, vol. 3, no. 2, 1972, pp. 123–39.

Articles in Other Journals, Newspapers and the Internet

Anon., 'Operations of 2nd Battalion [Manchester Regiment] near Hillah, Mesopotamia, 1920', *Manchester Regiment Gazette*, vol. 2, no. 4, October 1921, pp. 189–94.

Anon., 'A Prisoner with the Arabs, from July-October 19, 1920', *Manchester Regiment Gazette*, vol. 2, no. 4, October 1921, pp. 185–8.

Anon., 'The Story of the Siege of Samawah', *Blackwood's Magazine*, January 1922.

Ferguson, Niall, 'This Vietnam Generation of Americans Has not Learnt the Lessons of History', *Daily Telegraph*, 10 April 2004.

Financial Times, 'Kurdistan Oil & Gas Report', 10 December 2012.

Fisk, Robert, 'Iraq 1917', *Independent*, 17 June 2004.

Gorvett, Jonathan, 'The Forgotten Arabs of Gallipoli', *Al Jazeera Net*, 14 January 2004, available at www.aljazeera.com/archive/2004/01/200849135129326810.html

Indian Army Officers and Men, www.king-emperor.com

Maunsell, Colonel E. B., 'The Arab Rebellion: A Disaster and a Cavalry Rear-Guard Action', *Cavalry Journal*, vol. 14, 1924.

Raskolnikov, F. F., *Tales of Sub-Lieutenant Ilyin: The Taking of Enzeli*, available at www.marxists.org

The Times (Archive), http://archive.timesonline.co.uk/tto/archive

Image Credits

With the exception of those images specifically mentioned below, the photographs used in the text are taken from Wikimedia Commons and are in the public domain. The photograph of Captain Arnold Wilson (p. 50) is taken from John Marlowe, *Late Victorian*, published by the Cresset Press, 1967, an imprint of the Penguin Random House Group; the photographs of Gertrude Bell (p. 124) and Sheikh ʿAbd al-Wahid al-Sikar (p. 179) are courtesy of the Gertrude Bell Archive, University of Newcastle; and the photograph of Jaʿfar Abu al-Timman (p. 176) is taken from Pierre-Jean Luizard, *La formation de l'Irak contemporain*, CNRS Editions, Paris 1991.

Index